PIVOTAL RESEARCH IN EARLY LITERACY

Pivotal Research in Early Literacy

Foundational Studies and Current Practices

edited by
Christina M. Cassano
Susan M. Dougherty

Foreword by Joanne Knapp-Philo
Afterword by Heidi Anne E. Mesmer
and M. M. Rose-McCully

THE GUILFORD PRESS
New York   London

Copyright © 2018 The Guilford Press
A Division of Guilford Publications, Inc.
370 Seventh Avenue, Suite 1200, New York, NY 10001
www.guilford.com

Printed in the United States of America

This book is printed on acid-free paper.

Last digit is print number: 9   8   7   6   5   4   3   2   1

Library of Congress Cataloging-in-Publication Data is available from the publisher.

ISBN 978-1-4625-3617-7 (paperback)
ISBN 978-1-4625-3618-4 (hardcover)

About the Editors

Christina M. Cassano, EdD, is Associate Professor of Childhood Education and Care at Salem State University in Massachusetts, where she teaches graduate and undergraduate courses in early literacy and language development, reading foundations, and child development, and provides professional development on language and literacy for preschool teachers. A former kindergarten teacher and literacy specialist, she is the current president of the Literacy Development in Young Children special interest group of the International Literacy Association. Dr. Cassano's research interests include the study and support of vocabulary and concept knowledge in preschoolers, using science–literacy interventions in Head Start, and examining the relationship between vocabulary and phonological awareness. She has coauthored several publications on early literacy development and research.

Susan M. Dougherty, EdD, is Associate Professor of Literacy Education in the College of Education and Human Services at Rider University in Lawrenceville, New Jersey. She teaches undergraduate and graduate courses in literacy and has a particular interest in preparing preservice and future literacy specialists to support children who find literacy learning difficult. Dr. Dougherty began her career in education as an elementary teacher in New Jersey and is currently on the board of the New Jersey Literacy Association. Her research interests include parent–preschooler talk, family literacy, and early literacy and science learning. She has published articles and book chapters in these areas and has coauthored the book *Engaging Readers: Supporting All Students in Knowledge-Driven Instruction, 4–8.*

Contributors

Jordan Buckrop, PhD, Curry School of Education, University of Virginia, Charlottesville, Virginia

Christina M. Cassano, EdD, Department of Childhood Education and Care, Salem State University, Salem, Massachusetts

Donna Celano, PhD, School of Arts and Sciences, LaSalle University, Philadelphia, Pennsylvania

Molly F. Collins, EdD, Peabody College, Vanderbilt University, Nashville, Tennessee

Rebecca Dore, PhD, School of Education, University of Delaware, Newark, Delaware

Susan M. Dougherty, EdD, College of Education and Human Services, Rider University, Lawrenceville, New Jersey

Roberta Michnick Golinkoff, PhD, School of Education, University of Delaware, Newark, Delaware

Alisa Hindin, EdD, Department of Educational Studies, Seton Hall University, South Orange, New Jersey

Kathy Hirsh-Pasek, PhD, Department of Psychology, Temple University, Philadelphia, Pennsylvania, and Brookings Institution, Washington, DC

Emily Brown Hoffman, PhD, Department of Elementary Education, Ball State University, Muncie, Indiana

Marcia Invernizzi, PhD, Curry School of Education, University of Virginia, Charlottesville, Virginia

Rufan Luo, PhD, Department of Psychology, Rutgers, The State University of New Jersey, Camden, New Jersey

Lillian R. Masek, MAT, Infant and Child Laboratory, Temple University, Ambler, Pennsylvania

Heidi Anne E. Mesmer, PhD, School of Education, Virginia Tech, Blacksburg, Virginia

Lesley Mandel Morrow, PhD, Graduate School of Education, Rutgers,
The State University of New Jersey, New Brunswick, New Jersey

Susan B. Neuman, EdD, Steinhardt School of Culture, Education, and Human
Development, New York University, New York, New York

Kathleen A. Paciga, PhD, School of Liberal Arts and Sciences, Columbia College
Chicago, Chicago, Illinois

Jeanne R. Paratore, EdD, School of Education, Boston University,
Boston, Massachusetts

Muriel K. Rand, EdD, Department of Early Childhood Education,
New Jersey City University, Jersey City, New Jersey

Theresa A. Roberts, PhD, Oregon Research Institute, Eugene, Oregon

M. M. Rose-McCully, PhD, School of Education, Virginia Tech,
Blacksburg, Virginia

Judith A. Schickedanz, PhD (Emerita), School of Education, Boston University,
Boston, Massachusetts

Molly E. Scott, BA, Infant and Child Laboratory, Temple University,
Ambler, Pennsylvania

William H. Teale, EdD (deceased), College of Education, University of Illinois
at Chicago, Chicago, Illinois

Ruth M. Wharton-McDonald, PhD, Department of Education,
University of New Hampshire, Durham, New Hampshire

Colleen E. Whittingham, PhD, Cato College of Education,
University of North Carolina Charlotte, Charlotte, North Carolina

Foreword

If only teaching young children to read was as simple as it seemed when I took the class Teaching Reading as a college senior. I had no idea—even at the end of the semester—that it was a complicated process that is ideally nurtured prenatally and throughout early childhood. I did not realize then that it includes a rich variety of verbal and text-related experiences provided by each child's family, teachers and caregivers, and community.

Over the past 48 years of my career as a teacher, researcher, and codirector of the National Center on Cultural and Linguistic Responsiveness and the National Head Start Family Literacy Center, our knowledge of early literacy and our teaching practices have moved forward—albeit in a zigzag fashion. This effort was abetted by scholars, teachers, and families who have never wavered in their goal to ensure that every child achieves his or her personal best literacy skills.

Reflecting on my own journey, the book I coedited with Sharon Rosenkoetter, *Learning to Read the World: Language and Literacy in the First Three Years* (2004), was the first to make the case for strong, planned early literacy experiences for young children, from birth to age 3. This book argued that language experiences should be optimal for all children, including those with disabilities and those who are learning multiple languages. Currently there are a plethora of appropriate books for teachers of our youngest children who are committed to assuring developmentally appropriate early literacy experiences for infants, toddlers, and preschoolers.

However, we are not there yet!

Today *hundreds of thousands* of the youngest, and often poorest, children do not have strong enough language and literacy experiences to be "ready to read" when they begin school. In response to this early literacy crisis, the Head

Start National Center for Family Literacy (2005–2010) developed a number of free materials to serve our neediest children and families (*https://eclkc.ohs.acf. hhs.gov/*).

Today, children who are *dual language learners*, and their parents and care-givers, are a rapidly growing population that requires our strong support in the ongoing development of their home languages. Our nation is still not unified behind the scientific understanding that young children can and should learn multiple languages in order to thrive in an increasingly multiethnic society.

In *Pivotal Research in Early Literacy: Foundational Studies and Current Practices*, editors Christina M. Cassano and Susan M. Dougherty and the contrib-uting authors have given each of us who care about nurturing young children's emerging literacy skills a unique opportunity to apply our current knowledge about early language and literacy, as well as the strategies known to stimulate children's growth in the complicated process called "literacy development."

This book has the potential to move the field in a positive direction by encouraging readers to

- examine key research in a historical context,
- reflect on what has changed over time in our understanding of the various aspects of literacy, as well the methods of literacy teaching and learning,
- realize that the latest studies may not necessarily contradict earlier work but often contribute to a larger story, and
- consider new information in the context of what is already known, rather than embracing one new study after another.

Readers have the opportunity to ponder the interplay between early piv-otal research, well-established practices, and new information. Thus, readers can determine which approaches they will continue to use and identify new teaching strategies to add to their repertoires.

Each chapter author examines how our understanding of the reading process has developed historically. They bring together a complicated body of knowledge that has often seemed overwhelming—and sometimes disjointed. *Pivotal Research in Early Literacy* enables us to consider and reflect on a holistic and grounded view of many aspects of early literacy development, including

- approaches that have stood the test of time,
- strategies that were not as successful as hoped for—and why they did not work, and
- how families, teachers, and educational leaders can join together to ensure that *every* young child receives regular, ongoing language and literacy experiences that will enable him or her to be ready to thrive in school and beyond.

Finally, a book that examines a body of literature written over time helps educators embrace the reality that advances in early language and literacy require continual searching, learning, adapting, and reevaluating.

It is fitting that this book takes the longitudinal view of what we know—and that I have been given the opportunity to reflect on it—as I end my 48-year commitment to early childhood education. My parting advice for the readers of this text: *Never* forget the wonder and access that come from the ability to read and write well! Young children and those who educate and support them deserve our best efforts to ensure that they achieve this goal.

JOANNE KNAPP-PHILO, PHD
Former Director, National Head Start Family Literacy Center
and National Center on Cultural and Linguistic Responsiveness

REFERENCE

Rosenkoetter, S. E., & Knapp-Philo, J. (Eds.). (2004). *Learning to read the world: Language and literacy in the first three years.* Washington, DC: Zero to Three.

Preface

A Letter from Jumpstart

Dear Reader,

As an organization that uses storybooks to open the world of learning to children, Jumpstart is honored to be recognized in a book that underscores the importance of early literacy. At Jumpstart, learning is one of our core values, and we welcome this opportunity to learn from the experts and researchers, whose efforts in this field have shaped our program design since our founding in 1993. Pivotal research, and its contribution to our collective understanding of children's literacy development, help us to get closer to Jumpstart's vision of kindergarten readiness for all children.

Jumpstart is a national early education organization that is fueled by the core belief that providing high-quality educational opportunities to all young children contributes to breaking the cycle of poverty. With more than 6 million children across the country living in poverty, the need for Jumpstart's program is at an all-time high. Jumpstart recruits and trains adult volunteers, college students, and community members who implement the Jumpstart program in preschools across the country where the need is highest. Our volunteers, known as Corps members, help prepare children for kindergarten, and set them on a path for lifelong success.

Teams of Jumpstart Corps members volunteer in a variety of preschool settings in low-income communities, such as Head Start programs, community-based classrooms, and public school PreK. Corps members typically commit to serving 200 or more hours over the course of the school year or during the summer and engage children each week in intentional programming. Corps members engage small groups of children in reading a high-quality storybook, participating in language-rich interactions, and developing conceptual knowledge and vocabulary through play-based activities. We also document children's progress toward kindergarten readiness throughout their participation in Jumpstart, and use these data to continuously improve our program and ensure a high-quality experience.

At Jumpstart, we believe in the importance of an evidence-based approach to early childhood education. The Jumpstart program features a curriculum that focuses specifically on building skills that research has shown to be critical in supporting children's language, literacy, and social–emotional development. Our curriculum design and instructional practices are drawn directly from educational research, and indeed from the work of many of the authors featured in this book, including Judith A. Schickedanz, Kathy Hirsh-Pasek, Roberta Michnick Golinkoff, and Molly F. Collins. To maximize our impact on outcomes for children, we regularly review and make adjustments to our curriculum to reflect the latest findings and best practices. In a recent revision to the curriculum, Jumpstart deepened its concentration on the skills of vocabulary and comprehension, while also incorporating a more deliberate focus on social–emotional development. This curriculum change enriches children's oral language experiences and provides a basis for future social–emotional competence and literacy success.

Zora Neale Hurston has written that "research is formalized curiosity. It is poking and prying for a purpose." Jumpstart wholeheartedly supports the use of relevant, well-designed research to better understand young children's development and learning. With this book, Christina M. Cassano and Susan M. Dougherty have compiled an informative analysis of how research and practice in the field have evolved over time. We are grateful to be included as a collaborator in the endeavor to understand and promote early literacy, ensuring that all children have an equal chance to succeed. Thank you to the editors and authors for recognizing Jumpstart in such a generous and insightful way.

Sincerely,

NAILA BOLUS
Jumpstart President and CEO

Contents

Introduction   1

Christina M. Cassano and Susan M. Dougherty

PART I. EARLY LANGUAGE DEVELOPMENT

1.   Now You're Talking: Vocabulary Development in the Home Context   9

Lillian R. Masek, Molly E. Scott, Rebecca Dore, Rufan Luo,
Kathy Hirsh-Pasek, and Roberta Michnick Golinkoff

Pivotal studies discussed:
- Hart and Risley (1995). *Meaningful Differences in the Everyday Experience of Young American Children*
- Pan, Rowe, Singer, and Snow (2005). *Maternal Correlates of Growth in Toddler Vocabulary Production in Low-Income Families*
- Tomasello and Farrar (1986). *Joint Attention and Early Language*

2.   Pivotal Theory and Research Affecting Emergent Bilingual Children's Language and Literacy Achievement   29

Theresa A. Roberts

Pivotal studies discussed:
- Cummins (1979). *Linguistic Interdependence and the Educational Development of Bilingual Children*
- Cummins (1981). *The Role of Primary Language Development in Promoting Educational Success for Language Minority Students*
- Dulay and Burt (1974). *Errors and Strategies in Child Second Language Acquisition*
- Hoover and Gough (1990). *The Simple View of Reading*
- Krashen (1982). *Principles and Practice in Second Language Acquisition*
- Willig (1985). *A Meta-Analysis of Selected Studies on the Effectiveness of Bilingual Education*

PART II. LITERACY DEVELOPMENT IN THE EARLY YEARS

3.   Writing in the Early Years: Understanding the Past,   55
     Confronting the Present, Imagining the Future
     Judith A. Schickedanz

     Pivotal studies discussed:
     • Durkin (1966). *Children Who Read Early: Two Longitudinal Studies*
     • Hildreth (1936). *Developmental Sequences in Name Writing*
     • Read (1975). *Children's Categorization of Speech Sounds in English*

4.   Reconceptualizing Alphabet Learning and Instruction   85
     Marcia Invernizzi and Jordan Buckrop

     Pivotal studies discussed:
     • Mason (1980). *When Do Children Begin to Read?: An Exploration
       of Four-Year-Old Children's Letter and Word Reading Competencies*
     • Treiman and Broderick (1998). *What's in a Name: Children's Knowledge
       about the Letters in Their Own Names*
     • Treiman, Tincoff, Rodriguez, Mouzaki, and Francis (1998).
       The Foundations of Literacy: Learning the Sounds of Letters

5.   A Close and Careful Look at Phonological Awareness   111
     Christina M. Cassano

     Pivotal studies discussed:
     • Juel (1988). *Learning to Read and Write: A Longitudinal Study of 54
       Children from First through Fourth Grades*
     • Liberman, Shankweiler, Fischer, and Carter (1974). *Explicit Syllable
       and Phoneme Segmentation in the Young Child*
     • Lundberg, Frost, and Petersen (1988). *Effects of an Extensive Program
       for Stimulating Phonological Awareness in Preschool Children*

6.   The Role of Word Recognition in Beginning Reading: 142
     Getting the Words off the Page
     Ruth M. Wharton-McDonald

     Pivotal studies discussed:
     • Adams (1990). *Beginning to Read: Learning and Thinking about Print*
     • Share (1995). *Phonological Recoding and Self-Teaching: Sine Qua Non
       of Reading Acquisition*
     • Stanovich (1980). *Toward an Interactive–Compensatory Model
       of Individual Differences in the Development of Reading Fluency*

7. Engagement, Motivation, Self-Regulation, and Literacy Development 160
in Early Childhood
Alisa Hindin

Pivotal studies discussed:
- Blair (2002). *School Readiness: Integrating Cognition and Emotion in a Neurobiological Conceptualization of Children's Functioning at School Entry*
- Guthrie and Wigfield (2000). *Engagement and Motivation in Reading*
- Spira, Bracken, and Fischel (2005). *Predicting Improvement after First-Grade Reading Difficulties: The Effects of Oral Language, Emergent Literacy, and Behavior Skills*

PART III. HOME AND COMMUNITY LITERACY EXPERIENCES OF CHILDREN

8. Starting Them Young: How the Shift from Reading Readiness 181
to Emergent Literacy Has Influenced Preschool Literacy Education
William H. Teale, Emily Brown Hoffman, Colleen E. Whittingham,
and Kathleen A. Paciga

Pivotal studies discussed:
- Almy (1949). *Children's Experiences Prior to First Grade and Success in Beginning Reading*
- Teale and Sulzby (1986). *Emergent Literacy: Writing and Reading*

9. Storybook Reading: Insights from Hindsight 201
Molly F. Collins

Pivotal studies discussed:
- Cochran-Smith (1984). *The Making of a Reader*
- Dickinson and Smith (1994). *Long-Term Effects of Preschool Teachers' Book Readings on Low-Income Children's Vocabulary and Story Comprehension*
- Whitehurst, Falco, Lonigan, Fischel, DeBaryshe, Valdez-Menchaca, and Caulfield (1988). *Accelerating Language Development through Picture Book Reading*

10. The Impact of Pivotal Research on the Role of Play 238
in Early Literacy Development
Muriel K. Rand and Lesley Mandel Morrow

Pivotal studies discussed:
- Morrow and Rand (1991). *Promoting Literacy during Play by Designing Early Childhood Classroom Environments*
- Neuman and Roskos (1990). *Play, Print, and Purpose: Enriching Play Environments for Literacy Development*
- Pellegrini (1985). *The Relations Between Symbolic Play and Literate Behavior: A Review and Critique of the Empirical Literature*

11.   Family Literacy: Is It Really All About Storybook Reading?   257
       Susan M. Dougherty and Jeanne R. Paratore

       Pivotal studies discussed:
       • Bus, van IJzendoorn, and Pellegrini (1995). *Joint Book Reading Makes
         for Success in Learning to Read: A Meta-Analysis on Intergenerational
         Transmission of Literacy*
       • Heath (1983). *Ways with Words: Language, Life and Work in Communities
         and Classrooms*
       • Purcell-Gates (1996). *Stories, Coupons, and the "TV Guide": Relationships
         between Home Literacy Experiences and Emergent Literacy Knowledge*
       • Scarborough and Dobrich (1994). *On the Efficacy of Reading
         to Preschoolers*
       • Sénéchal, Lefevre, Thomas, and Daley (1998). *Differential Effects of Home
         Literacy Experiences on the Development of Oral and Written Language*

12.   Enhancing Children's Access to Print   279
       Susan B. Neuman and Donna Celano

       Pivotal study discussed:
       • Neuman and Celano (2001). *Access to Print in Low-Income
         and Middle-Income Communities: An Ecological Study of Four
         Neighborhoods*

AFTERWORD
       Pivotal Research in Early Literacy: Lessons Learned   297
       and a Call to Action
       Heidi Anne E. Mesmer and M. M. Rose-McCully

       Index   315

Introduction

Christina M. Cassano and Susan M. Dougherty

If I have seen further, it is by standing on the shoulders of giants.
—Isaac Newton

If ever a book was created on the shoulders of giants, then this is it. Each chapter includes thoughtful analyses of the work of "giants" in early literacy research—that is, scholars whose research and writing ultimately led to a shift—or pivot—in the field. Once we selected these influential works, which we call *pivotal studies,* we invited current "giants" and up-and-coming scholars in the field to write chapters that enable us to "see further." Each of these authors assumes a historical stance as they describe the impact of the pivotal studies and trace that influence to the current day. Our authors then help us to envision the path forward for early childhood practitioners, researchers, administrators, and policymakers who are committed to the very best early literacy instruction for all children.

PURPOSE

It is a challenging time for early childhood educators. In our work in early childhood classrooms and as we interact with inservice teachers, parents, and administrators, we hear the following concerns:

- There has been a "pushing down" of the academic curriculum, so that PreK and kindergarten children are expected to master skills once expected of older children.

- Recess and play-based learning opportunities have been reduced to make more room for academics, particularly in schools with large numbers of children living in poverty.
- Families are feeling burdened by news that their young child is "falling behind" or that they are not doing enough at home to support skill acquisition.
- Opportunities to learn about science, art, history, and other content areas are being diminished, as children spend their time practicing discrete reading- and writing-related skills.

In some respects, as our chapter authors explain, these concerns are not new. In fact, many of the pivotal studies were conducted in response to these same questions and offered solid advice on which educators might act. What troubles us, then, is that in some cases these answers have been muted or forgotten. It is our hope that this book will prompt us to remember what previous research has already revealed about best practices and will inform us about the subsequent research that offers further guidance.

This book is not a series of literature reviews or "all about" chapters. The chapters do not include lamentations about the "good ole days," while calling for a return to simpler times. Instead, this book is about examining the roots of our understandings in order to consolidate our knowledge and move the field forward. We truly believe that it is only by knowing the history of our field that we will arrive at the very best future for all children.

ORIGIN OF THE IDEA

The idea for an edited volume on pivotal research came from our early literacy doctoral seminar with Judith Schickedanz at Boston University. In this seminar, we read Gesell, Hunt, Hildreth, Read, Durkin, Mason, Teale, Morrow, Dickinson, and Neuman—and other scholars whose research and writing had a profound and lasting impact on approaches to early literacy research and practice. As we read the work of these scholars, we discussed how they were related to current early literacy practices, assuming the historical stance used throughout this text. As new (and naïve) doctoral students, we questioned why practices with a strong research base were notably absent from some of the early childhood classrooms we frequented and why, as former practitioners, we were unaware of some of the foundational research that should have guided our own practice. This experience inspired our commitment to connect research to practice that continues to guide our work with preservice and inservice teachers.

Studying the history of early literacy soon became our passion. We celebrated when we found unmarked copies of seminal works (our collections now overtaking our shelves after editing this book). We cherished our interactions with Lee

Indrisano and Jeanne Paratore, who encouraged our interest in the "long view" of early literacy and directed us to "dig deeper" into topics of interest—particularly family literacy, vocabulary development, and reading acquisition.

After completing our doctorates, we continued to discuss our mutual interest in the history of our field. At conferences, we listened attentively as current "giants" reflected on the works that had influenced their academic journeys. We took copious notes, attempting to write the names of all the studies that had shaped the thinking of those authors who had influenced our own thoughts about early literacy. Finally, in 2016, the idea for this book was solidified after hearing Bill Teale's keynote address "Be Careful What You Wish For: Emerging Literacy in the Classroom and Emerging Policy Priority on Early Childhood Education," at the International Literacy Association's Early Literacy Preconference Institute. That was the moment when we knew that this book had to be written!

PIVOTAL STUDIES

The pivotal research studies highlighted in this book are seminal works that are cited often and, in most cases, known well. They are studies that *we* identified as having a profound impact on *our* own thinking, research, and writing. We then shared our list with the chapter authors, inviting them to make revisions based on their own work. Although many of our pivotal studies are expected, a few may surprise our readers. They are the work of visionaries. That is, scholars, whose findings warranted attention that may not have been received. In other cases, we believe that the pivotal works had unintended effects—leading to ineffective classroom practices or to erroneous, yet appealing messages about early literacy development.

A bibliography of the pivotal works and links to their locations can be found at *www.facebook.com/earlyliteracyresearch*. We invite our readers to read them in their entirety and to share the pivotal works that shaped their own journeys on our Facebook page or on Twitter using #earlyliteracyresearch. We also encourage publishers to make these studies available to a broader audience by reducing, and perhaps eliminating, the cost of access.

SCOPE

This book is organized topically into three parts: "Early Language Development," "Literacy Development in the Early Years," and "Home and Community Literacy Experiences of Children." In each chapter, our authors contextualize and describe from one to six pivotal studies explaining how they helped shape our current understanding. This approach typically includes a description of research that is connected to or derived from the pivotal works—including the work of the chapter author(s)—and/or a discussion of current teaching practices and how they either conform to or deviate from the focal studies. We also encouraged our authors to comment on the current status of early literacy education and to suggest best practices and future directions for policy, research, and practice. Thus, each chapter includes:

- *Background*—The pivotal studies are situated within a historical or developmental context.
- *Description*—Each of the pivotal studies is described, and the relationships between the studies are explored.
- *Impact*—The authors provide an overview of the research's impact on the field. Relationships to subsequent theory, research, and teaching practice are described. In some cases, the authors trace a historical path from the pivotal works to the current time; in others, they compare the context at the time the pivotal studies were published to the current day.
- *Take-aways*—The authors synthesize the most important ideas revealed by the pivotal studies and offer specific advice or "action steps" for teachers, administrators, and policymakers.

The Afterword, "Pivotal Research in Early Literacy: Lessons Learned and a Call to Action," includes a synthesis of important ideas gleaned from the pivotal research, as well as specific research- and practice-based steps required to propel the field of early literacy forward.

AUDIENCE

This book is designed to be used as a resource for graduate and doctoral students and their professors, as well as practicing teachers, coaches, administrators, and specialists who want to understand the foundational research that has helped to shape current practices. Our topical approach enables readers to explore specific aspects of early literacy development and instruction. We encourage our readers to consider the relationships among the chapters, noting the particular time period in which pivotal research occurred and to think about the historical and developmental contexts their findings reflect.

ACKNOWLEDGMENTS

We are grateful that so many scholars, whose work we admire and rely upon, agreed to contribute to this book. We thought that the best way to thank these individuals, who we know share a commitment to supporting the literacy development of *all* children, was to find a way to pay it forward. For this reason, we are donating 20% of our royalties to Jumpstart, an organization that partners with colleges and community organizations to promote young children's literacy, language, and social–emotional development. More information about Jumpstart's mission can be found in the Preface or by visiting *www.jstart.org*.

In addition to the many chapter authors and the original "giants" in early literacy, there are several others who were pivotal to this project. We thank Craig Thomas, Senior Editor at The Guilford Press, for his ongoing encouragement and support. We appreciated his skilled problem solving and his sense of humor as deadlines loomed. Thank you, Craig, for believing in our "little idea." There would be no book without you!

We also want to express our gratitude to Judith Schickedanz, who inspired us to write this book and who was instrumental in its development. Thank you for thoughtfully responding to our (many) questions and for sharing your knowledge of and passion for early literacy history with us.

After this book was firmly in production at Guilford, the early literacy field lost one of its most pivotal—and well-loved—scholars, William H. Teale. From the start we knew that this book needed a chapter written by Bill. We held our breath as we opened his e-mail response to our invitation, which we share with you below:

> "Hello, Christina and Susan. Thank you very much for the invitation to contribute a chapter to this book. I think that it is very interesting conceptually and promises to contribute an important perspective on early literacy learning and teaching. That said, I also vowed three years ago that I wouldn't be writing any more chapters for any edited books (despite your kind words and high praise). And yet, for some inexplicable reason I forwarded your e-mail to two of my current doctoral students, saying 'What do you think?' all the while indicating that I was disinclined to do this. They are smart, savvy, convincing individuals. So, I have a proposition for you: If you want a chapter not authored by me, but authored by the three of us, you have a deal. What think ye?"
> —Bill

What did we think? We thought we were so immensely lucky. And now that feeling is only amplified. Thank you, Bill Teale, for all of your incredible work in our field. We are so grateful to be able to include your reflections on your own pivotal work in this book.

Finally, Christina would also like to thank her husband, Brian, for his gentle encouragement to turn off the computer when the writing was hard and for assuming extra child-juggling duties when the ideas flowed; her children, Olivia, Alexander, and Lily, whose passion and enthusiasm for reading and writing serve as a constant reminder of the "end goal;" her family and friends, who offered ongoing support and encouragement; and Lynne Walker and Sarah Oppenheimer, who were "giants" in the lives of her children, fostering a love of literacy and learning the way only gifted teachers can.

Susan expresses her thanks to Kyle Johnson, her loving husband, who offered encouragement and helped her carve out time to work on the book; her children, Marshall and Darcy, who delightfully bring early literacy learning to life every day; her siblings, parents, in-laws, extended family, friends, and colleagues who have always been unwavering supporters; and the childcare providers at Kangaroo Kids, who foster language and literacy as they help children plant the garden, wade in the stream, build block towers, and paint masterpieces.

We would also like to thank "whine and cheese" (pun intended). Our ability to laugh at ourselves was also essential to the writing process.

CHRISTINA M. CASSANO
SUSAN M. DOUGHERTY

PART I

EARLY LANGUAGE DEVELOPMENT

Now You're Talking

Vocabulary Development in the Home Context

Lillian R. Masek, Molly E. Scott,
Rebecca Dore, Rufan Luo, Kathy Hirsh-Pasek,
and Roberta Michnick Golinkoff

> Words are, in my not-so-humble opinion, our most
> inexhaustible source of magic.
> —ALBUS DUMBLEDORE (in J. K. Rowling's
> *Harry Potter and the Deathly Hollows*)

A strong vocabulary is vital to literacy development (Cunningham & Stanovich, 1997; Dickinson, Golinkoff, & Hirsh-Pasek, 2010; National Early Literacy Panel, 2008; Ouellette, 2006; Storch & Whitehurst, 2002). Vocabulary knowledge helps children decode text through phonological awareness and print knowledge (Storch & Whitehurst, 2002), but being a good reader involves more than decoding. Without a strong vocabulary knowledge to back it up, decoding leaves a child with strings of meaningless sounds. Anderson and Freebody's (1981) knowledge hypothesis posits that a broad network of conceptual knowledge is needed to understand text. A child who knows a lot of words and the associations between those words will sail through a text more smoothly than a child who does not have a strong vocabulary. For example, if a child knows many words associated with trains (e.g., uncoupling, caboose) they will have an easier time reading about the transcontinental railroad than a child who does not know those words. Extracting meaning from a variety of texts demands a diverse vocabulary, which starts developing long before children learn to read and has a lasting effect. Preschool vocabulary predicts reading comprehension all the way to fourth grade (Dickinson & Porche, 2011) and gains in literacy from first to third and from third to fifth grade (Burchinal, Pace, Alper, Hirsh-Pasek, & Golinkoff, 2016). Yet, vocabulary development begins before children enter early schooling (Fernald, Marchman, & Weisleder, 2013; Hirsh-Pasek et al., 2015; Kuhl, 2010), meaning that much of children's early exposure to language occurs at home.

Here, we focus on the home context of children's vocabulary development, highlighting three pivotal studies that shaped the way we look at language input and its effect on vocabulary. Each study spawned new research, as well as early language interventions. Three main lessons flow from these classic studies: (1) Early-language input matters; and, in particular, (2) the quality of language input matters and (3) conversational context matters.

THREE PIVOTAL PIECES ON VOCABULARY LEARNING

The first piece, Hart and Risley's (1995) now-classic work, highlights the gap between families of lower and higher socioeconomic status (SES) in children's home-language experiences and reminds us that both quantity and quality are key to successful language and vocabulary development. The second piece by Pan, Rowe, Singer, and Snow (2005) illuminated the substantial individual variation in parental language input, even *within* a low-SES sample. They stressed the importance of the *quality* of talk for children's later language amid discussions tilted toward quantity. The last piece by Tomasello and Farrar (1986) demonstrates that quality and quantity occur in a rich, coconstructed context. Without joint or shared attention between the child and a sensitive, responsive caregiver, what could be language learning moments fail to be realized. Winnowing down the research showing a link between language input and vocabulary to a mere three studies is, of course, a somewhat artificial exercise given the mountain of data speaking to these issues. The three pieces selected have deeply influenced not only early language research, but also interventions designed to support children in getting off to a strong start.

Hart and Risley (1995): *Input Matters and Matters Early*

In the 1960s, poverty had become the enemy of the common good, and politicians rallied behind the so-called "War on Poverty." Programs such as Head Start, a government initiative started in 1965 to support children of families living in poverty (National Head Start Association, 2017), were initiated as part of an effort to disrupt the cycle. The rationale was that if children in poverty were given a "booster" shot of early stimulation, they would be better prepared for formal schooling. Although at the time, the data were mixed (Cicirelli, 1969; Lazar, Darlington, Murray, Royce, Snipper, & Ramey, 1982), these initiatives became the impetus for research on socioeconomic status (SES) differences in social, cognitive, and health outcomes, as well as the experiences that might foster positive outcomes. Given that language is a strong predictor of improved reading, mathematics and social skills (Burchinal et al., 2016; Hoff, 2013), it became an area of increased concentration. It is in this context, centered on the expectation for and creation of high-quality preschools, that Hart and Risley's novel work sent a chill through research and policy circles. Their relatively limited but now classic study influenced those who want to heighten opportunity for low-income children and their families.

In 1968, Hart and Risley began work at the Turner House Preschool in an impoverished area of Kansas City. Although when observed independently, the 4- and 5-year-olds at Turner House were competent language users, Hart and Risley noticed that their language skills paled compared to preschoolers at the university laboratory school, despite their similar ages and programs. To bridge this gap, they attempted a series of interventions to teach children at Turner House new words. Much to their dismay, these programs had little effect (Hart & Risley, 1980). Faced with a mystery, they decided to find out what was going on at home, very early in children's lives, that might be contributing to the observed differences between the Turner House children and the professors' children once they got to preschool.

Hart and Risley set out to document the home language environments of young children, as well those children's language development. They recruited local families representing three SES groups that they dubbed "professional" (n = 13), "working-class" (n = 23), and "welfare" (n = 6). Notably, this differentiation has been criticized for both terminology and grouping ("working-class" represented both low- and mid-SES families), and subsequent research has shifted to labels that more accurately reflect families' economic situations.

Starting before the child could talk (7–12 months), researchers recorded each child's home language environment for 1 hour, once a month through the third year of the child's life. This resulted in 1,318 hours of transcripts documenting the language children heard during these early years. In addition, a variety of outcome measures were assessed, including the child's vocabulary and IQ at age 3 and literacy in third grade. The findings were profound. On average, children in professional families heard 2,153 words addressed to them every hour, whereas children in working-class families heard 1,251 words, and children in welfare families heard a mere 616 words. From these numbers, Hart and Risley projected that by age 4, children in poverty would hear 30 million fewer words than children in the highest SES strata. The researchers examined the quality of language as well and found that, beyond hearing more words, children in high-SES homes heard more responses, declarative sentences, auxiliary-fronted yes/no questions (e.g., "Can you clean up?" vs. "Clean up."), affirmative feedback (e.g., "That's right!"), and richer language (nouns, modifiers, and past tense verbs) than children in lower-SES homes.

Furthermore, these gaps in exposure appeared to have implications for children's later language and school achievement. Children who heard more words learned more words. By age 3, a full year or two *before* most of the remedial preschool programs such as Head Start began, there were already large differences in the number of words children knew. Whereas the average 3-year-old vocabulary size for the children in professional families was 1,116 words, for children in working-class families it was 749 words and for children in welfare families it was 525 words. Hart and Risley found that parental talk related not only to the child's vocabulary and IQ at age 3, but to the child's language and reading skills in third grade as well, showing a persistent effect of children's early language environment. These findings highlighted two important lessons: that the language children heard mattered to their later school achievement, and that the "booster shot" remedial preschool programs were starting too late. To be effective, interventions had to start early. This finding on quantity struck a nerve with the public. Hart and Risley coined the term, the 30-million word gap, which became a rallying cry inspiring considerable research in the field (Hoff, 2003; Pan, Rowe, Singer, & Snow, 2005) and new intervention efforts (Providence Talks, 2017; Suskind, Suskind, & Lewinter-Suskind, 2015; Talking is Teaching, 2017).

Although Hart and Risley's research (1995) was pivotal, it has also been widely criticized for its methodology, including, but not limited to, its small sample size, especially the "welfare" sample of six children (Pan et al., 2005), the homogeneity of its welfare sample (Dudley-Marling & Lucas, 2009), only evaluating mother's talk (Sperry, Miller, & Sperry, 2015), and using cumulative word types as a measure of children's vocabulary (Huttenlocher, Waterfall, Vasilyeva, Vevea, & Hedges, 2010). It has further been criticized for ignoring cultural differences in talk (Dudley-Marling & Lucas, 2009; Michaels, 2013; Sperry et al., 2015) and perpetuating a deficit model of poverty (Dudley-Marling & Lucas, 2009; Michaels, 2013). As discussed later, within SES strata, there is enormous variability in the quantity and quality of language input children receive and the developmental trajectories of early language skills. Furthermore, while Hart and Risley did examine aspects of language quality, the headlines that emerged too often emphasized quantity, giving rise to a misconception that the number of words a child heard was the most important feature of the early language environment. Despite these substantial limitations, the work of Hart and Risley has been widely replicated (e.g., Hoff, 2003; Huttenlocher et al., 2010) and continues to influence research, policy, and practice.

Beyond Hart and Risley: The Push for Quantity

At the same time that Hart and Risley's book was published, other researchers began to examine the relationship between language input, language development, and factors that relate to the amount of speech children heard. Some reported that older mothers spoke more to their children than adolescent mothers (Culp, Osofsky, & O'Brien, 1996). Compared to mothers from middle- or high-SES backgrounds, low-SES mothers were more likely to suffer from depression and stress, which was further associated with less talk to children (Lovejoy, Graczyk, O'Hare, & Neuman, 2000). Research showed that first-born children heard more language addressed to them than later-born children (Hoff-Ginsberg, 1998), and that the child's participation in a conversation influenced the amount of parental talk (Hoff-Ginsberg, 1994). The setting influenced speech as well, such that all mothers, regardless of SES, talked most during book reading and least during mealtimes, although SES differences in talk were most apparent during dressing and mealtime and least apparent during book reading and toy play (Hoff-Ginsberg, 1991). Overall, this research expanded the field by asking what factors, beyond SES, related to differences in talk while replicating Hart and Risley's critical finding: that children in poverty hear fewer words.

This research on language input and language gaps continued to flourish in the decade after Hart and Risley published their book, as it continued to focus on the relationship between language input and children's output. While this approach had deep roots (e.g., Furrow, Nelson, & Benedict, 1979; Nelson, Carskaddon, & Bonvillian, 1973; Snow, 1972), this incarnation seemed to have narrowed its focus to the amount of language rather than to the equipotent findings on the quality of the interactions. Indeed, some argue that, in the right context, a word need only to be heard once to be acquired. For example, the human simulation model studies suggest a "sweet spot" for language learning that has little to do with quantity, but a lot to do with the quality of the interaction (Gillette, Gleitman, Gleitman, & Lederer, 1999; Trueswell, Lin, Armstrong, Cartmill, Goldin-Meadow, & Gleitman, 2016). The almost exclusive emphasis on quantity also gave the impression that the SES levels of participants were the primary predictor of later language abilities, without regard to variation *within* SES level (Cartmill, Armstrong, Gleitman, Goldin-Meadow, Medina, & Trueswell, 2013; Hirsh-Pasek et al., 2015; Pan et al., 2005). That is, the Hart and Risley study was and often still is erroneously interpreted to suggest that poor children inevitably have weak language skills and limited vocabularies. Surely there is variation of both quantity and quality within SES levels that could account even more for the children's language outcomes. Although headlines citing the 30-million word gap persist, another wave of research went beyond the deficit model to examine this variability in both language input and outcomes within a low-SES sample.

Pan, Rowe, Singer, and Snow (2005): *Quality of Language Input within a Low-SES Sample*

The work of Barbara Pan and colleagues was among the first to suggest heterogeneity in both the quantity and quality of language input within low-income families. Furthermore, the findings from Hart and Risley (1995), along with subsequent research (e.g., DeTemple & Snow, 1996), needed to be shown in a larger sample more likely to demonstrate this heterogeneity. Given that much of the research documented the SES-based language gap, Pan and colleagues wanted to change the perspective to focus instead on the variability within SES and how that variability might relate to children's later vocabulary. They performed the first large-scale longitudinal study examining language growth in an entirely low-income sample.

Pan and colleagues (2005) examined 108 mother–child dyads who were eligible for government assistance. Mothers were videotaped playing with their child at home at 14, 24, and 36 months. Mothers were instructed to play for 10 minutes with their children using the standardized, age-appropriate materials provided (a book and toys, such as a kitchen set).

During this interaction, researchers looked at the behaviors and language of the mother and child, including the number of words (as in Hart & Risley, 1995), the diversity of words, and the number of pointing gestures. They also examined the number of different words children used at each age. Contrary to what many people deduced from Hart and Risley's work, Pan and colleagues found a large variability in both mothers' and children's talk. While the least talkative mothers spoke fewer than 200 words per observation, the most talkative spoke over 1,200. Looking at children's talk at 14 months, the beginning of expressive language, the range was 0–22 words, with the least-verbal children saying no words at all. By age 3, the gap between the most- and least-verbal children had grown to 122 words, suggesting not only a range in vocabulary size at the onset of language development, but also a diverse rate of growth over the first few years.

Pan and colleagues reported no effect of quantity of speech on children's language growth between age 1 and 3: Simply hearing more language did not influence children's later abilities. Number of different words and pointing gestures, however, did predict children's language growth, but since the overlap between the two measures was high, it was difficult to determine whether both were independently important in predicting language outcomes. Mother's education and literacy levels were also predictors of children's language growth as was maternal depression. The latter was negatively related to children's language growth.

Pan and colleagues' work changed the conversation about early vocabulary learning in two major ways. First, it shifted the focus from differences *between* SES strata to the variability *within* SES strata. They demonstrated that among children growing up in socially and economically disadvantaged backgrounds, there were some who excelled in language and others who struggled, as well as parents who provided different levels of input. However, when averaged together, their low-SES sample did, in fact, have lower language abilities than middle- and high-SES children in earlier studies. This replication of the previous finding reiterated the criticism of earlier work that by averaging across a very heterogeneous group, researchers miss large individual differences. Caregivers even under the stress of poverty can help build children's vocabularies. Instead of looking for a deficit, subsequent research began to examine aspects of talk that did *not* differ across SES. For example, one study asked how well adult viewers could guess a target word (represented by a beep) in an otherwise silent clip of a mother–child interaction. That is, how well nonverbal cues such as eye gaze and gesture conveyed the meaning of a word. This measure of language quality, called *referential transparency*, is unrelated to a family's SES and still a robust predictor of vocabulary (Cartmill et al., 2013). Pan and colleagues brought a new perspective to research and interventions on the language gap: Rather than focusing on coaching low-SES parents to talk like high-SES parents, which is both unrealistic and patronizing, researchers began to focus on the types of high-quality language that occur in low-income homes and think about how to encourage an increase in the quality of language interactions more broadly (Cartmill et al., 2013; Hirsh-Pasek et al., 2015).

The second way this pivotal work influenced the field was in its de-emphasis of word quantity in favor of quality. Up until this point, as noted, most of the research on SES differences in language environments had focused on quantity, following from the popular focus on Hart and Risley's 30-million word gap. By showing that the quality of language, and not the number of words children heard, was a consistent predictor of children's language growth, Pan and colleagues highlighted an important point: Hearing more *unique* words allows a child to learn more words. For example, saying "come sit" four times does not help a child learn as many new words as "Come sit on the floor next to Mommy," even though in both cases, the child hears eight words. Furthermore, gestures are beneficial. If "next to Mommy" is accompanied by a pat on the carpet, it clarifies the meaning of the words "next to." It is the way in which meaning is communicated, and not the number of words, that helps children build their vocabularies.

Beyond Pan and Colleagues: A Shift toward Quality and the Recognition of Heterogeneity

These findings launched a series of new research efforts aimed at the quality of language children hear, including more research on unique words (Huttenlocher et al., 2010; Rowe, 2012), different types of sentence structures (e.g., "*When you leave*, close the door." vs. "Close the door *when you leave*."; Huttenlocher et al., 2010), and utterance complexity defined as the average length in words (Hoff, 2003). These aspects of language quality have been found to account for SES differences in language outcomes (Hoff, 2003; Huttenlocher et al., 2010). Research also looked more broadly at the type of language children hear and found that certain types of talk are more predictive of language outcomes than others. Among the most predictive are wh-questions (e.g., "Where is the doggy?"; Rowe, Leech, & Cabrera, 2017; Rowland, Pine, Lieven, & Theakston, 2003; Valian & Casey, 2003), referential language (e.g., "That's a red truck"; Tamis-LeMonda, Song, Leavell, Kahana-Kalman, & Yoshikawa, 2012), explanations (e.g., "We eat vegetables so we'll be healthy"; Rowe, 2012), pretend utterances (e.g., "It's time for the baby doll to go to bed"; Rowe, 2012), and narrative (e.g., "We saw chickens at the farm, remember?"; Rowe, 2012). These types of language are infused with high-quality elements, such as building on children's interests, asking them to respond to queries, and offering a variety of words and sentences types. Research has also highlighted the importance of nonverbal communication. Parental gesture use, which varies as a function of SES, predicts a child's early gesture use, and in turn, a child's vocabulary (Rowe & Goldin-Meadow, 2009), suggesting another pathway through which SES influences language input and, in turn, a child's language skills (Goldin-Meadow, Levine, Hedges, Huttenlocher, Raudenbush, & Small, 2014).

Tomasello and Farrar (1986): *The Dyadic Context of Language Interaction*

Many studies that followed Hart and Risley's research focused on the words children heard. However, one aspect that fell out of the spotlight is now making a comeback: the dyadic context of the interaction. In 1986, long before Hart and Risley's seminal work was published, Tomasello and Farrar studied not only parental talk, but the context in which the talk was embedded. Tomasello and Farrar argued that shared attention through routines established between the child and caregiver, such as feeding, provide a referent for communication, supporting the child's communicative skills and adding meaning to the language they hear. Although previous research had identified joint attention as important for vocabulary development (Adamson & Bakeman, 1984; Tomasello & Todd, 1983), Tomasello and Farrar were the first to examine language input in the context of joint attention.

"Joint attention" occurs when a caregiver and child are both focusing on the same object or event at the same time. It can be examined on the macrolevel, in episodes in which both the caregiver and child are engaged in the same activity, or at the microlevel, in specific attention-related behaviors such as following another's eye gaze. Tomasello and Farrar examined both, through observation of 24 children interacting with their mothers in the home at ages 15 and 21 months. The mother and child were given a set of props (e.g., a toy cup and spoon) and instructed to play as they normally would for 15 minutes. From this session, Tomasello and Farrar examined the mother's references to objects (e.g., "look at the spoon"), specifically the types of references (i.e., comments, questions, directives) that occurred within and outside of joint attention and how they related to the child's vocabulary size.

The researchers identified three major findings. First, within episodes of joint attention at the macrolevel, mothers and children engaged in longer con-versations, and mothers used shorter utterances and made more comments to children, compared to interactions outside of joint attention. This suggests that during these episodes of joint attention, mothers are more likely to adjust their speech to the child's level of understanding. Thus, joint attention itself may support the ongoing language interaction by allowing a child who has limited language skills to understand the mother's communicative intent and partici-pate. For example, during a feeding session, in which the child and the mother are looking at a spoon, the phrase "It's a spoon!" conveys meaning through the shared context, while also providing simple enough input for the child to match the word "spoon" to the appropriate referent. The relationship between interaction, joint attention, and language was further studied by Adamson and Bakeman (1984), who investigated not only the discrete behaviors of parents and children but how the dyad together establishes *joint engagement,* a state of shared attention in which both parent and child are active participants in the interaction. This macrolevel, high-quality interaction has been shown to relate to children's vocabulary throughout toddlerhood (Adamson, Bakeman, & Deckner, 2004) and into the preschool years (Adamson, Bakeman, Deck-ner, & Nelson, 2014).

The second finding from Tomasello and Farrar (1986) was that object references *within* macrolevel joint attention (e.g., "Look at the spoon" when the child holds it up), were related to the child's vocabulary, whereas references made *outside* of macrolevel joint attention (e.g., "Look at the spoon" when the child is trying to open a door) were not. In both cases the child is hearing lan-guage, but in the first case the language is relevant to what the child is doing, making it easier for the child to link the sounds she hears to objects around her, whereas in the second case the language is background chatter, unrelated to the child's focus. This finding held, even though there were no differences in the frequency of microlevel joint attention (i.e., shared looking time) within and outside of macrolevel joint attentional episodes (see also Dunham, Dun-ham, & Curwin, 1993).

The third finding was that within macrolevel episodes of joint engage-ment, object references that positively predicted children's vocabulary were those that either followed the child's attentional focus (e.g., "It's a puppy," when the child looked at a dog) or were accompanied by a gesture (e.g., "It's a puppy," and pointing to a dog). Other types of references (e.g., "It's a puppy," without pointing to the animal while the child played with a truck) were negatively associated with the child's vocabulary.

The importance of this last finding was further demonstrated in an experimental manipulation published in the same article (Tomasello & Far-rar, 1986). An experimenter taught children the names of four objects (e.g., gauge, clip), either through following the child's focus or directing the child's focus. Consistent with the observational data, children learned better when the experimenter followed the child's focus despite hearing the name equally across conditions. A more tightly controlled experimental manipulation by Dunham, Dunham, and Curwin (1993) showed the same phenomenon. These findings suggest that hearing a word in the right context is more important than hearing a word more often. This conclusion is supported by the work on the human simulation model (Gillette et al., 1999; Trueswell et al., 2016), which showed that word learning occurs in mainly the right context. Although more exposures to a word likely increases the opportunity for it to be introduced in an ideal context, the number of exposures in and of itself is less relevant. The situation in which a child hears a new word is important, regardless of the amount or type of language input. Parents who follow their children's lead and create episodes of joint attention are invoking an important mechanism for word learning above and beyond the amount and type of language that children hear.

Beyond Tomasello and Farrar: A Shift Back to the Role of Context

Following Tomasello and Farrar's findings, the literature on parent–child interaction and language continued to grow. Subsequent research found that parental sensitivity and cognitive stimulation predict children's later language abilities (Leigh, Nievar, & Nathans, 2011), suggesting that parent interaction style accounts for SES differences in vocabulary (Mistry, Biesanz, Chien, Howes, & Benner, 2008; Raviv, Kessenich, & Morrison, 2004).

Additional studies on joint attention showed that sustained states infused with language and gestures predicted language skills across toddlerhood (Adamson et al., 2004; Hirsh-Pasek et al., 2015). Indeed, children learn a novel name when they visually attend to the object, but the number of times they hear the name does not predict better learning (Yu & Smith, 2012). Other aspects of parent–child interaction are also important. For example, how a caregiver responds to a child and how appropriate those responses are both temporally and thematically are important predictors of language development (Tamis-LeMonda, Kuchirko, & Song, 2014). Responsiveness predicts the onset of early language milestones (Tamis-LeMonda, Bornstein, & Baumwell, 2001), overall vocabulary size (Tamis-LeMonda, Bornstein, Kahana-Kalman, Baumwell, & Cyphers, 1998), and growth in vocabulary (Baumwell, Tamis-LeMonda, & Bornstein, 1997; Bornstein, Tamis-LeMonda, & Haynes, 1999).

One study examining variability within a low-income sample found that high-quality parent–child interaction predicted children's vocabulary a year later, and was a *better* predictor than the number of words mothers addressed to children (Hirsh-Pasek et al., 2015). High-quality interactions were characterized by shared attention infused with words and symbols, patterns of behaviors like routines, and balanced interaction in which the child and mother took turns initiating and continuing the conversation either through language or gesture.

These high-quality dyadic interactions are characterized by "adaptive contingency," which involves prompt and meaningful responses to children's bids (Reed, Hirsh-Pasek, & Golinkoff, 2016). By engaging in adaptive contingency, caregivers establish learning moments appropriate to the child's interest that increase the communication abilities they already have. When this contingency is interrupted, by a phone call for instance, children's word learning suffers. In one experiment by Reed, Hirsh-Pasek, and Golinkoff (2017), parents were asked to teach their children two novel words. While the parent was teaching one of the words, the researcher called the parent's cell phone, disrupting the interaction. The other word was taught without interruption. Results showed that children learned the word taught without interruption, but when the teaching was interrupted by a cell phone call, children did not learn the novel word, even though there were no differences in the amount of time spent teaching or the number of times the novel word was said. This finding suggests that disrupting adaptive contingency can have important implications for children's word learning. These findings highlight the issue of today's "distracted parent." Now that smartphones and screens are ubiquitous, it is easier than ever to disrupt the delicate interaction that promotes word learning. Adaptive contingency must become even more intentional than ever.

IMPACT OF PIVOTAL RESEARCH ON PRACTICE

Interventions Targeting Quantity

Beyond their effect on the field of language development, these pivotal studies have prompted a series of interventions to promote more talk and higher-quality interactions at home. Driven by the findings of Hart and Risley (1995), many interventions have focused on increasing the number of words children hear. The Thirty Million Words Initiative, for example, is a large-scale intervention in Chicago that encourages caregiver–child talk through the Three T's: Parents are encouraged to "Tune In," or pay attention to what the child is communicating; "Talk More," using rich and descriptive words; and "Take Turns," or encourage the child to respond, verbally or nonverbally (Suskind et al., 2015). Through the Language Environment Analysis (LENA; Gilkerson & Richards, 2008) program, the initiative collects data on children's language exposure and uses these data to coach caregivers to increase their talk to their child, and so far, the intervention has shown some success (Suskind, Leffel, Hernandez, Sapolich, Suskind, Kirkham, & Meehan, 2013).

Interventions Targeting Quantity and Quality

Whereas the Thirty Million Words Initiative focuses on making gains in the amount of caregiver talk, other intervention programs also highlight educational opportunities that promote higher-quality language. Providence Talks is an initiative undertaken by the city of Providence, Rhode Island, similar to the Thirty Million Words Initiative, in that caregivers are given feedback on their language use and are coached on ways to improve it. Beyond coaching and feedback, Providence Talks connects families to larger educational experiences, such as libraries and museum events, which are sources of rich language (Providence Talks, 2017). Research shows that the majority of families who participate show improvements in the amount of talk and engagement, especially families that start out below the national average, and the increase persists even after the end of the program (Molina, 2017). To our knowledge, existing evaluations have not assessed changes in language quality.

Taking a different approach, Talking is Teaching, part of the Clinton Foundation's Too Small to Fail Initiative, uses a multimedia public awareness and action campaign designed to encourage caregiver–child talk in everyday situations, such as riding the bus or shopping for groceries. Beyond increasing the amount of language children hear, Talking is Teaching promotes the use of diverse language to promote outcomes such as early math learning, through talk about number and sizes (Talking is Teaching, 2017). In an evaluation, participants reported that they learned from the program; used the books, CDs, and other materials; and planned to read, talk, and sing more with their child (Philip R. Lee Institute for Health Studies, 2016).

Interventions Targeting the Learning Context

Last, other intervention programs have targeted caregiver–child interactions rather than the quantity of words. For example, the Video Interaction Project (VIP) focuses on improving caregiver–child interaction during regularly scheduled well-child visits. Families meet with an interventionist to discuss goals for the child, as well as record and review a video of the caregiver interacting with the child. The caregiver then receives a developmentally appropriate book or toy and a pamphlet reinforcing the session (Video Interaction Project, 2017). VIP has been rigorously evaluated and shown to affect both parent (Cates, Weisleder, Dreyer, Johnson, Vlahovicova, Ledesma, & Mendelsohn, 2016; Mendelsohn, Huberman, Berkule, Brockmeyer, Morrow, & Dryer, 2011) and child (Mendelsohn et al., 2007; Weisleder et al., 2016) outcomes.

A newer program, Vroom, is an app-based service that sends parents prompts for high-quality, language-rich interactions. The prompts are customized based on the child's name and birth date and include a topic to talk about and a suitable response to the child's actions, along with an explanation of how the interaction helps development. Each prompt is research based and includes a blurb explaining the science at an accessible level (Vroom, 2017). A large-scale, randomized control trial of the program is currently underway, but a smaller-scale study found increases in children's cognitive skills over just 6 weeks (Galinsky, Bezos, McClelland, Carlson, & Zelazo, 2017).

Finally, Duet is a community-based participatory research study designed to improve the quality of the caregiver–child interaction and, in turn, child vocabulary. Home visitors use multimedia modules that include an informational cartoon and video examples of the interaction. Caregivers are also recorded interacting with their child and given an opportunity to reflect on the interaction with the home visitor (Luo et al., 2017). Although it is too early to determine the effectiveness of this intervention, preliminary results are promising.

Although many of these interventions were designed with low-income families in mind (all are free to participate in and easy to access), all have the goal of population-wide implementation. Just as there is large heterogeneity within low-SES families, there is heterogeneity among higher-SES families, meaning that parents from all backgrounds can benefit from support in providing a high-quality language environment for young children.

LESSONS LEARNED FROM THREE PIVOTAL PIECES IN THE FIELD

From these three pivotal pieces and the subsequent developments, we reiterate the important lesson that we highlighted at the outset: the need for early-language input that focuses in particular on the quality of language and the conversational context.

Early-Language Input Matters

Children's early-language environments substantially influence later language development. Although this was not news in the research community, Hart and Risley made this point visible in a powerful way when they introduced the 30-million word gap. Their striking findings with respect to the talk children hear and its later impact on language and academic skills sparked a wave of research and policy. Although narrow interpretations of Hart and Risley's findings have led to an overemphasis on the amount of talk and a view of low-income households as linguistically deficient, the most important lesson to be gained from Hart and Risley is that what caregivers say has a big impact on their children's language beginning very early.

The lesson of the 30-million word gap has become a national call to action and has penetrated popular culture, challenging the commonly held belief that language development begins when children start to talk. The increased recognition of the importance of the early language environment is seen in the push for age 0–3 interventions to improve outcomes even prior to preschool, the effects of which may already be emerging. After decades of stagnancy, the academic gap between low- and high-SES children at kindergarten entry is beginning to narrow (Reardon & Portilla, 2016). Furthermore, there have been improvements in children's exposure to learning experiences, including books, educational games, and caregiver engagement both in the home (e.g., arts and crafts) and outside of the home (e.g., trips to the library), especially among low-income families (Bassok, Finch, Lee, Reardon, & Waldfogel, 2016), indicating that the narrowing achievement gap may be at least in part a result of what parents are doing to support their children's development.

The importance of early language input extends into the classroom. Teachers' language use in the classroom relates to preschoolers' growth of vocabulary knowledge over the course of the year (Barnes & Dickinson, 2017), as well as literacy in elementary school (Dickinson & Porsche, 2011). Unfortunately, we also know that in economically disadvantaged early childhood classrooms, teachers explain words less often and are less likely to use sophisticated vocabulary when compared to more advantaged schools (Wright & Neuman, 2014). Unless teachers increase the amount of language and, in particular, high-quality language and one-on-one conversations, a golden opportunity for building language will be lost.

Quality of Language Input Matters

The quality of the language to which children are exposed is crucial for promoting their development. This is seen in the research by Pan and colleagues (2005) as well as in the many studies that followed (e.g., Cartmill et al., 2013; Hirsh-Pasek et al., 2015; Rowe, 2012). Children need to hear high-quality language, even before they speak, that includes a variety of different words, sentence structures, and age-appropriate questions, and is accompanied by related nonverbal communication including gesture (e.g., Rowe & Goldin-Meadow, 2009). This wave of research challenged the overemphasis on quantity that arose out of the work of Hart and Risley (1995). The new message was that talking to children a lot is not enough to create a high-quality language environment if that speech is not also high quality.

These findings have crucial educational implications. Teachers and caregivers should not teach words in isolation, but in an integrated way that connects words to various related concepts. Through teaching words in this deep manner, children can form a strong conceptual network that they can use to build their vocabularies (Coyne, McCoach, & Kapp, 2007; Neuman, Newman, & Dwyer, 2011).

Conversational Context Matters

It is essential to recognize the context in which talk occurs and to encourage learning moments. Tomasello and Farrar's results showed that maternal talk relates to children's vocabulary only when embedded in joint attention. This means that teaching vocabulary is not limited to a specific time or activity, such as circle time or book sharing; any moment can be a learning moment. When children are playing in puddles outside, it is a great time to teach relevant words such as *droplet* and *soaked*. When adults capitalize on what children are focused on, the interaction can help strengthen the vocabularies they will need to be strong readers, regardless of the activity. Furthermore, a back-and-forth conversation between caregivers and children is fundamental for early language learning. Caregivers and educators can "coconstruct" a language interaction with children, by responding to children's communicative cues in a timely manner and encouraging children to make verbal or nonverbal contributions. As David Dickinson (2003) suggests, we must encourage caregivers and children to "strive for five"—five back and forth turns in a conversation. Only when we engage children in conversations will their language grow.

CONCLUSION

We have highlighted three pivotal pieces of research that show the importance of the early language environment, the impact of high-quality talk, and the value of a responsive context. Each piece inspired not only subsequent research on the importance of the home context, but also efforts to improve the language environments of young children to build a robust vocabulary and establish a foundation for literacy. Empowered with this knowledge, we are in a better position to intervene with a stronger understanding of what matters for improving children's vocabulary and, in turn, their early literacy skills.

ACKNOWLEDGMENTS

This research is funded by Institute of Education Sciences (IES) Grant Nos. R305A150435 and R324A160241, and by IES Training Grant No. R305B130012 (to Rebecca Dore).

REFERENCES

Adamson, L. B., & Bakeman, R. (1984). Mothers' communicative acts: Changes during infancy. *Infant Behavior and Development, 7*(4), 467–478.

Adamson, L. B., Bakeman, R., & Deckner, D. F. (2004). The development of symbol-infused joint engagement. *Child Development, 75,* 1171–1187.

Adamson, L. B., Bakeman, R., Deckner, D. F., & Nelson, P. B. (2014). From interactions to conversations: The development of joint engagement during early childhood. *Child Development, 85,* 941–955.

Anderson, R. C., & Freebody, P. (1981). Vocabulary knowledge. In J. T. Guthrie (Ed.), *Comprehension and teaching: Research reviews* (pp. 77–117). Newark, DE: International Reading Association.

Barnes, E. M., & Dickinson, D. K. (2017). The impact of teachers' commenting strategies on children's vocabulary growth. *Exceptionality, 25*(3), 186–206.

Bassok, D., Finch, J. E., Lee, R., Reardon, S. F., & Waldfogel, J. (2016). Socioeconomic gaps in early childhood experiences: 1998 to 2010. *AERA Open, 2*(3), 1–22.

Baumwell, L., Tamis-LeMonda, C. S., & Bornstein, M. H. (1997). Maternal verbal sensitivity and child language comprehension. *Infant Behavior and Development, 20,* 247–258.

Bornstein, M. H., Tamis-LeMonda, C. S., & Haynes, M. (1999). First words in the second year: Continuity, stability, and models of concurrent and lagged correspondence in vocabulary and verbal responsiveness across age and context. *Infant Behavior and Development, 22,* 67–87.

Burchinal, M. R., Pace, A., Alper, R., Hirsh-Pasek, K., & Golinkoff, R. M. (2016, July). *Early language outshines other predictors of academic and social trajectories in elementary school.* Paper presented at the Association for Children and Families Conference (ACF), Washington, DC.

Cartmill, E. A., Armstrong, B. F., Gleitman, L. R., Goldin-Meadow, S., Medina, T. N., & Trueswell, J. C. (2013). Quality of early parent input predicts child vocabulary 3 years later. *Proceedings of the National Academy of Sciences of the USA, 110*(28), 11278–11283.

Cates, C. B., Weisleder, A., Dreyer, B. P., Johnson, S. B., Vlahovicova, K., Ledesma, J., & Mendelsohn, A. L. (2016). Leveraging healthcare to promote responsive parenting: Impacts of the video interaction project on parenting stress. *Journal of Child and Family Studies, 25*(3), 827–835.

Cicirelli, V. G. (1969). *The impact of Head Start.* Athens, OH: Westinghouse Learning Corporation & Ohio University.

Coyne, M. D., McCoach, D. B., & Kapp, S. (2007). Vocabulary intervention for kindergarten students: Comparing extended instruction to embedded instruction and incidental exposure. *Learning Disability Quarterly, 30*(2), 74–88.

Culp, A., Osofsky, J. D., & O'Brien, M. (1996). Language patterns of adolescent and older mothers and their one-year-old children: A comparison study. *First Language, 16*(46), 61–75.

Cunningham, A. E., & Stanovich, K. E. (1997). Early reading acquisition and its relation to reading experience and ability 10 years later. *Developmental Psychology, 33*(6), 934–945.

DeTemple, J. M., & Snow, C. E. (1996). Styles of parent–child book-reading as related to mothers' views of literacy and children's literacy outcomes. In J. Shimron (Ed.), *Literacy and education: Essays in honor of Dina Feitelson* (pp. 49–68). Cresskill, NJ: Hampton.

Dickinson, D. K. (2003). Why we must improve teacher–child conversations in preschools and the promise of professional development. In L. Girolametto & E. Weitzman (Eds.), *Enhancing caregiver language facilitation in childcare settings* (pp. 41–48). Toronto, ON, Canada: Hanen Institute.

Dickinson, D. K., Golinkoff, R. M., & Hirsh-Pasek, K. (2010). Speaking out for language:

Why language is central to reading development. *Educational Researcher, 39*(4), 305–310.

Dickinson, D. K., & Porche, M. V. (2011). Relation between language experiences in preschool classrooms and children's kindergarten and fourth-grade language and reading abilities. *Child Development, 82*(3), 870–886.

Dudley-Marling, C., & Lucas, K. (2009). Pathologizing the language and culture of poor children. *Language Arts, 86*(5), 362–370.

Dunham, P. J., Dunham, F., & Curwin, A. (1993). Joint-attentional states and lexical acquisition at 18 months. *Developmental Psychology, 29*(5), 827–831.

Fernald, A., Marchman, V. A., & Weisleder, A. (2013). SES differences in language processing skill and vocabulary are evident at 18 months. *Developmental Science, 16*(2), 234–248.

Furrow, D., Nelson, K., & Benedict, H. (1979). Mothers' speech to children and syntactic development: Some simple relationships. *Journal of Child Language, 6*(3), 423–442.

Galinsky, E., Bezos, J., McClelland, M., Carlson, S. M., & Zelazo, P. D. (2017). Civic science for public use: Mind in the Making and Vroom. *Child Development, 88*(5), 1–10.

Gilkerson, J., & Richards, J. A. (2008). *The LENA natural language study*. Boulder, CO: LENA Foundation.

Gillette, J., Gleitman, H., Gleitman, L., & Lederer, A. (1999). Human simulations of vocabulary learning. *Cognition, 73*(2), 135–176.

Goldin-Meadow, S., Levine, S. C., Hedges, L. V., Huttenlocher, J., Raudenbush, S. W., & Small, S. L. (2014). New evidence about language and cognitive development based on a longitudinal study: Hypotheses for intervention. *American Psychologist, 69*, 588–599.

Hart, B., & Risley, T. R. (1980). In vivo language intervention: Unanticipated general effects. *Journal of Applied Behavior Analysis, 13*(3), 407–432.

Hart, B., & Risley, T. R. (1995). *Meaningful differences in the everyday experience of young American children*. Baltimore: Brookes.

Hirsh-Pasek, K., Adamson, L. B., Bakeman, R., Owen, M. T., Golinkoff, R. M., Pace, A., . . . Suma, K. (2015). The contribution of early communication quality to low-income children's language success. *Psychological Science, 26*(7), 1071–1083.

Hoff, E. (2003). The specificity of environmental influence: Socioeconomic status affects early vocabulary development via maternal speech. *Child Development, 74*(5), 1368–1378.

Hoff, E. (2013). Interpreting the early language trajectories of children from low-SES and language minority homes: Implications for closing achievement gaps. *Developmental Psychology, 49*(1), 4–14.

Hoff-Ginsberg, E. (1991). Mother–child conversation in different social classes and communicative settings. *Child Development, 62*(4), 782–796.

Hoff-Ginsberg, E. (1994). Influences of mother and child on maternal talkativeness. *Discourse Processes, 18*(1), 105–117.

Hoff-Ginsberg, E. (1998). The relation of birth order and socioeconomic status to children's language experience and language development. *Applied Psycholinguistics, 19*(4), 603–629.

Huttenlocher, J., Waterfall, H., Vasilyeva, M., Vevea, J., & Hedges, L. V. (2010). Sources of variability in children's language growth. *Cognitive Psychology, 61*(4), 343–365.

Kuhl, P. K. (2010). Brain mechanisms in early language acquisition. *Neuron, 67*(5), 713–727.

Lazar, I., Darlington, R., Murray, H., Royce, J., Snipper, A., & Ramey, C. (1982). Lasting effects of early education: A report from the Consortium for Longitudinal Studies. *Monographs of the Society for Research in Child Development, 47*(2, Suppl. 3), 1–151.

Leigh, P., Nievar, M. A., & Nathans, L. (2011). Maternal sensitivity and language in early childhood: A test of the transactional model. *Perceptual and Motor Skills, 113*, 281–299.

Lovejoy, M. C., Graczyk, P. A., O'Hare, E., & Neuman, G. (2000). Maternal depression and parenting behavior: A meta-analytic review. *Clinical Psychology Review, 20*(5), 561–592.

Luo, R., Alper, R., Pace, A., Mogul, M., Hirsh-Pasek, K., Adamson, L., . . . Masek, L. (2017, April). Developing an early language intervention for children from at-risk families: Benefits of community-based participatory research. In A. Pace (Chair) *Innovative models for language and literacy intervention with at-risk children: From conception to implementation.* Poster symposium conducted at the Society for Research in Child Development, Austin, TX.

Mendelsohn, A. L., Huberman, H. S., Berkule, S. B., Brockmeyer, C. A., Morrow, L. M., & Dreyer, B. P. (2011). Primary care strategies for promoting parent–child interactions and school readiness in at-risk families: The Bellevue Project for Early Language, Literacy, and Education Success. *Archives of Pediatrics and Adolescent Medicine, 165*(1), 33–41.

Mendelsohn, A. L., Valdez, P. T., Flynn, V., Foley, G. M., Berkule, S. B., Tomopoulos, S., . . . Dreyer, B. P. (2007). Use of videotaped interactions during pediatric well-child care: Impact at 33 months on parenting and on child development. *Journal of Developmental and Behavioral Pediatrics, 28*(3), 206–212.

Michaels, S. (2013). Commentary: Déjà vu all over again: What's wrong with Hart & Risley and a "linguistic deficit" framework in early childhood education? *Learning Landscapes, 7*(1), 23–41.

Mistry, R. S., Biesanz, J. C., Chien, N., Howes, C., & Benner, A. D. (2008). Socioeconomic status, parental investments, and the cognitive and behavioral outcomes of low-income children from immigrant and native households. *Early Childhood Research Quarterly, 23*(2), 193–212.

Molina, C. (2017, February). *Providence talks: How to close a "word gap" at a city-wide scale.* Paper presented at the AAAS annual meeting, Boston, MA.

National Early Literacy Panel. (2008). *Developing early literacy: Report of the National Early Literacy Panel.* Washington, DC: National Institute for Literacy.

National Head Start Association. (2017). About us: Mission, vision, history. Retrieved from *www.nhsa.org/about-us/mission-vision-history.*

Nelson, K., Carskaddon, G., & Bonvillian, J. (1973). Syntax acquisition: Impact of experimental variation in adult verbal interaction with the child. *Child Development, 44*(3), 497–504.

Neuman, S. B., Newman, E. H., & Dwyer, J. (2011). Educational effects of a vocabulary intervention on preschoolers' word knowledge and conceptual development: A cluster-randomized trial. *Reading Research Quarterly, 46*(3), 249–272.

Ouellette, G. P. (2006). What's meaning got to do with it: The role of vocabulary in word reading and reading comprehension. *Journal of Educational Psychology, 98*(3), 554–566.

Pan, B. A., Rowe, M. L., Singer, J. D., & Snow, C. E. (2005). Maternal correlates of growth in toddler vocabulary production in low-income families. *Child Development, 76*(4), 763–782.

Philip R. Lee Institute for Health Studies. (2016). Talk, Read and Sing Intervention at University of California San Francisco Benioff Children's Hospital Oakland. Retrieved from *https://healthpolicy.ucsf.edu/sites/healthpolicy.ucsf.edu/files/wysiwyg/ Documents/ucsf-bcho-evaluation.pdf*.

Providence Talks. (2017). Retrieved from *www.providencetalks.org/about/*.

Raviv, T., Kessenich, M., & Morrison, F. J. (2004). A mediational model of the association between socioeconomic status and three-year-old language abilities: The role of parenting factors. *Early Childhood Research Quarterly, 19*(4), 528–547.

Reardon, S. F., & Portilla, X. A. (2016). Recent trends in income, racial, and ethnic school readiness gaps at kindergarten entry. *AERA Open, 2*(3), 1–18.

Reed, J., Hirsh-Pasek, K., & Golinkoff, R. M. (2016). Meeting children where they are: Adaptive contingency builds early communication skills. In P. Witt (Ed.), *Communication and learning* (Vol. 16, pp. 601–627). Berlin: deGruyter Mouton.

Reed, J., Hirsh-Pasek, K., & Golinkoff, R. M. (2017). Learning on hold: Cell phones sidetrack parent–child interactions. *Developmental Psychology, 53*(8), 1428–1436.

Rowe, M. L. (2012). A longitudinal investigation of the role of quantity and quality of child-directed speech in vocabulary development. *Child Development, 83*(5), 1762–1774.

Rowe, M. L., & Goldin-Meadow, S. (2009). Early gesture selectively predicts later language learning. *Developmental Science, 12*(1), 182–187.

Rowe, M. L., Leech, K. A., & Cabrera, N. (2017). Going beyond input quantity: Wh-questions matter for toddlers' language and cognitive development. *Cognitive Science, 41*(S1), 162–179.

Rowland, C., Pine, J., Lieven, E., & Theakston, A. (2003). Determinants of acquisition order in wh- questions: Re-evaluating the role of caregiver speech. *Journal of Child Language, 30*(3), 609–635.

Snow, C. (1972). Mothers' speech to children learning language. *Child Development, 43*(2), 549–565.

Sperry, D. E., Miller, P. J., & Sperry, L. (2015, November). *Is there really a word gap?* Paper presented at the annual meeting of the American Anthropological Association, Denver, CO.

Storch, S. A., & Whitehurst, G. J. (2002). Oral language and code-related precursors to reading: Evidence from a longitudinal structural model. *Developmental Psychology, 38*(6), 934–947.

Suskind, D., Leffel, K. R., Hernandez, M. W., Sapolich, S. G., Suskind, E., Kirkham, E., & Meehan, P. (2013). An exploratory study of "quantitative linguistic feedback": Effect of LENA feedback on adult language production. *Communication Disorders Quarterly, 34*(4), 199–209.

Suskind, D., Suskind, B., & Lewinter-Suskind, L. (2015). *30 million words: Building a child's brain*. New York: Dutton.

Talking is Teaching. (2017). Retrieved June 6, 2017, from *http://talkingisteaching.org.*

Tamis-LeMonda, C. S., Bornstein, M. H., & Baumwell, L. (2001). Maternal responsiveness and children's achievement of language milestones. *Child Development, 72*(3), 748–767.

Tamis-LeMonda, C. S., Bornstein, M. H., Kahana-Kalman, R., Baumwell, L., & Cyphers, L. (1998). Predicting variation in the timing of linguistic milestones in the second year: An events-history approach. *Journal of Child Language, 25*(3), 675–700.

Tamis-LeMonda, C. S., Kuchirko, Y., & Song, L. (2014). Why is infant language learning facilitated by parental responsiveness? *Current Directions in Psychological Science, 23*(2), 121–126.

Tamis-LeMonda, C. S., Song, L., Leavell, A. S., Kahana-Kalman, R., & Yoshikawa, H. (2012). Ethnic differences in mother–infant language and gestural communications are associated with specific skills in infants. *Developmental Science, 15*(3), 384–397.

Tomasello, M., & Farrar, M. J. (1986). Joint attention and early language. *Child Development, 57*(6), 1454–1463.

Tomasello, M., & Todd, J. (1983). Joint attention and lexical acquisition style. *First Language, 4*(12), 197–211.

Trueswell, J. C., Lin, Y., Armstrong, B., Cartmill, E. A., Goldin-Meadow, S., & Gleitman, L. R. (2016). Perceiving referential intent: Dynamics of reference in natural parent–child interactions. *Cognition, 148*, 117–135.

Valian, V., & Casey, L. (2003). Young children's acquisition of wh- questions: The role of structured input. *Journal of Child Language, 30*(1), 117–143.

Video Interaction Project. (2017). Retrieved June 6, 2017, from *www.videointeraction-project.org/about-vip.html.*

Vroom. (2017). Retrieved June 6, 2017, from *www.joinvroom.org.*

Weisleder, A., Cates, C. B., Dreyer, B. P., Johnson, S. B., Huberman, H. S., Seery, A. M., . . . Mendelsohn, A. L. (2016). Promotion of positive parenting and prevention of socioemotional disparities. *Pediatrics, 137*(2), 1–9.

Wright, T. S., & Neuman, S. B. (2014). Paucity and disparity in kindergarten oral vocabulary instruction. *Journal of Literacy Research, 46*(3), 330–357.

Yu, C., & Smith, L. B. (2012). Embodied attention and word learning by toddlers. *Cognition, 125*(2), 244–262.

CHAPTER 2

Pivotal Theory and Research Affecting Emergent Bilingual Children's Language and Literacy Achievement

Theresa A. Roberts

Take from the altars of the past the fire—not the ashes.
—Jean Jaurès

Five "big ideas" and influential articles related to the language and literacy success of emergent bilingual (EB) students are presented and analyzed in this chapter. These five concepts are natural sequences in language acquisition, comprehensible input, the threshold and developmental interdependence hypotheses, bilingual education, and the simple view of reading. The potential positive effects of these pivotal theory and research articles on the language and literacy achievement of young children who have the capacity to become bilingual and to reap its benefits for academic and broader success have not been fully capitalized on in educational settings. In some cases the selected pivotal articles have led and continue to lead educators astray, typically through the implementation of language and literacy programs in which powerful and important concepts have dominated too strongly. This dominance has been associated with conceptually and instructionally narrow and rigid language and literacy programs that current evidence indicates lack the full range of instruction necessary for EBs to achieve high levels of English oral proficiency and English reading comprehension. Not all these seminal papers are based on research; in some cases they are conceptual or theoretical treatises with more or less research support.

Our walk down memory lane will identify that many of the waymarkers first posted some 30 to 50 years ago continue to point the way. In some instances we will see that the wrong or less-direct paths were followed, in spite of research that indicated another direction. Subsequent research in some cases has produced additional or clearer waymarkers. Better guidance and direction are sorely needed and more wayfarers on the path requested, as much of the journey remains.

I begin this chapter by briefly describing key features of the societal context in which the education of emergent bilingual students in the United States has taken place for the last 50 years. Many of the social and political issues present some 25 to 40 years ago that influenced the pivotal research related to these students, the educational philosophy on which this research was based and that was influenced by it, the interpretations and educational applications of this research, and legislation and public sentiment related to it remain influential today. In this chapter, I refer to children who first learned a language other than English and are acquiring English as a second language as *emergent bilinguals* (EBs). The terms *English language learners* (ELLs) or more recently *dual language learners* (DLLs) have typically been used. I have selected the term *emergent bilingual* because it clearly positions the possibility for bilingualism as a key language potential of these children.

Many EB children historically and currently share socioeconomic, educational, and political circumstances influencing language and literacy achievement (National Center for Education Statistics, 2015). The families of EBs are more likely to have lower incomes and consequently limited resources for the kind of cognitive stimulation valued in mainstream American classrooms, compared with children from more privileged homes whose first language (L1) is English. Currently, more than 66% of EB children reside in households with incomes below 200% of the federal poverty level (EPE Research Center, 2009). The majority of EB children have been taught and continue to be taught by teachers that do not share their ethnic, cultural, and linguistic foundations. White females retain an overwhelming presence in the early education force; white females are 82% of the teaching force, with the remaining 8% Hispanic and 2% Asian (Lucas, 2011). Teachers continue to feel underprepared to effectively teach EB children (Karabenick & Noda, 2004). EB children have been educated during this time period overwhelmingly in English-only school settings with English development supports that are often lacking in coherence, consistency, and quality. EB children continue to experience significant disparity in language and literacy achievement compared to non-EB children (National Center for Education Statistics, 2015).

Civil rights actions, both at the grassroots level and in the form of organized protest, swept communities across the nation during the 1960s and 1970s, when a number of the selected pivotal papers were published. Newspapers, speeches, treatises, and legislative bodies regularly reported, commented on, debated, and responded to these societal currents. The passage of the Civil Rights Act of 1964 greatly expanded the Civil Rights Act of 1957 to include a prohibition on discrimination on the basis of race, color, religion, sex, or national origin. Language was soon thereafter identified as a proxy for national origin. In the landmark *Lau v. Nicholls* decision (1974), the Supreme Court unanimously affirmed the right of EBs to receive supplemental English language education and mandated schools to provide the instruction in order to ensure equal access to educational opportunity. This time period was marked by an invigorated humanism in which the universal equality of all humans was emphasized. Change, flux, and passion in many areas that connected directly to cultural and language variation permeated popular, political, and academic life.

Similar major developments within the research community occurred in the same period with respect to learning, development, language, and literacy. The paradigm shift from behaviorism to cognitive psychology was igniting. Methodology shifted from observations of external behavior to efforts to reveal, using scientific methodology, the internal workings of the mental black box of thoughts, strategies, learning, feelings, dispositions, and values. The departure from behaviorist-dominated views of language acquisition was signaled by the 1965 publication of Chomsky's seminal book *Aspects of the Theory of Syntax*, in which the idea of an innate Language Acquisition Device and a distinction between language performance and underlying language competence were put forth. At this time the field of child language study was emerging. Piaget's (1972, 1977) genetic epistemology captured the minds and hearts of those interested in children's cognitive development. Vygotsky's Soviet-born ideas of constructivist learning, mediated by social interaction, took their first popular hold in the western world in 1978 with the publication of *Mind in Society*. Educators were beginning to extract from Piaget's and Vygotsky's work simplified generalizations about children as 'little scientists" capable of significantly generating their own development and were developing versions of the principles of both giants for classroom application (e.g., Furth & Wachs, 1975). It was within this admittedly simplified societal, political, educational, and academic context dating from 1964 to 1990 that the pivotal theory and research selected for this chapter was produced.

Although *Lau v. Nicholls* still stands today, in the last two decades the federal courts have decided cases on equal educational opportunity less favorably to EBs than those decided in the heyday of Civil Rights activity and in the decade or two after. The demise of bilingual education and the increase of English-only legislative initiatives fueled by political and populist forces have created a more restrictive societal and educational milieu in which to make language support services available to EBs. Anti-immigrant sentiment, an increasingly strong assertion of English language privilege, and intensification of ethnic and socioeconomic stratification are resurgent societal forces pointing to the continuing difficulties under which EBs must learn.

NATURAL SEQUENCES IN LANGUAGE ACQUISITION

> A number of researchers have suggested that the general process of second language acquisition may be similar to that of first language acquisition . . . a creative construction process. This account of language acquisition attributes to the child specific innate mechanisms which guide his discovery of the rules of the language to which he is exposed.
>
> —DULAY AND BURT (1974, p. 129)

Dulay and Burt (1974): *Errors and Strategies in Child Second Language Acquisition*

The quotation above comes from a study conducted by Dulay and Burt (1974) in which similar development sequences were observed in first (L1) and second language (L2) acquisition. The results were widely interpreted to suggest that acquisition of a second language follows an innately motivated and "natural" progression. This idea was overextended to incorporate the belief that explicit instruction is not necessary or helpful for second language learning.

Dulay and Burt (1974) analyzed 513 spoken errors produced by 179 5- to 6-year-old Spanish speakers. The errors were elicited by a set of pictures and questions related to them designed to tap into a variety of grammatical structures. The theoretical framing of the research was drawn from Brown's (1973) earlier characterization of L1 acquisition as a "creative construction process" sparked by an innate language learning mechanism that led to a child discovering the features and rules of the adult grammar. Dulay and Burt reasoned that the occurrence of errors similar to those documented in English acquisition for native-speaking children would constitute evidence for this creative construction process in L2 acquisition. On the other hand, errors reflecting the structure of L1, such as a child whose first language is Chinese consistently omitting plural forms, as indicated by utterances such as "three dog" or "two shoe," would suggest that SLA was a function of a more mechanistic, habit-formation (behaviorist) process. Errors based on the structure of L1 are called "negative transfer." The authors coded errors as similar to L1 acquisition, as reflecting Spanish language structure, or as unique. They found that only 4.7% of the errors reflected Spanish influence. In contrast, 87.1% of the errors reflected the developmental structures used by children in learning English as their L1.

Dulay and Burt concluded that children do not simply transfer their L1 "habits" to SLA and that errors are a necessary part of L2 learning that self-correct. Remarkably they generalized well beyond their data and made the following suggestion for second language teaching: "The mismatch between the child's developing forms and the developed forms of adult grammar will also diminish and disappear without the help of explicit instruction, positive reinforcement of correct structures or correction of incorrect structures" (p. 135).

In other words, L2 learning followed a child's proclivity for an innately guided natural sequence by which they would increasingly construct (match) the adult grammar.

Over the next 50 years research continued to identify L1 and L2 similarity in a number of language processes. The Dulay and Bart quotation in the preceding paragraph is an early reference to what would become the overarching concept of L2 and reading pedagogy under the umbrella concepts of comprehensible input and the whole language philosophy of reading, respectively. This concept was that language and reading were natural processes driven by an innate Language Acquisition Device that responded to the fuel of language exposure, spoken or written.

The idea that language was a natural, universal, and largely child-driven process became a foundational view of whole language reading instruction, in which reading was characterized as a "psycholinguistic guessing game" (Goodman & Goodman, 1977, 1979; Goodman, 1986). The term "whole" was applied to both the teaching of word reading and to a general instructional orientation to reading, in which "meaning," "purpose," "authentic," "integrated," "context," and "constructed" became key terms. Along with this almost exclusively top-down view of reading and the related instruction to enact it, the importance of teaching or even attending to lower-level processes, such as decoding, was pushed aside because it was seen as interfering with the reading process. This view of reading was widely influential, passionately implemented in classrooms, and enthusiastically endorsed by professional organizations.

One reason the whole language philosophy of reading was so appealing to researchers, teachers, and advocates for EBs was because of the dignity, autonomy, and respect it afforded English learners and their experiences, dispositions historically in short supply for many emergent bilinguals. Well-conducted research on the importance of background knowledge that emerged at the same time aligned readily with this philosophy. This research revealed that cultural experiences, information related to text content and text structures, and reader perspectives influence comprehension (Carrell, 1983; Mandler & Johnson, 1977; Steffensen, Joag-Dev, & Anderson, 1979). Practices that increase or activate prior knowledge became and remain centerpieces of comprehension instruction. The recent emphasis on acquiring the meaning within the text suggests the increased importance of *text-relevant* background knowledge. Thus the development of children's broad and rich knowledge of the physical, social, aesthetic and ideational world is important for becoming proficient at reading.

Reviews of whole language reading outcomes and of the role of decoding in skilled reading in the 1990s through early 2000s revealed that (1) whole language was not as effective as methods that included code instruction, particularly for children at risk for reading difficulties, such as EBs and (2) that word reading difficulty was one of the major sources of poor reading comprehension

(Foorman, 1995; Jeynes & Littell, 2000; National Reading Panel, 2000). The recent call for "balanced" literacy instruction, an approach that few would disagree with, suggests the importance of both meaning-focused and code-focused instruction. However, concern has been expressed that balanced literacy is largely a return to whole language because it does not deeply embrace teaching decoding and precursor alphabetic and phonemic awareness skills, nor the necessary linguistic sophistication required of teachers to teach it well (Moats, 2000). We turn now to the concept of comprehensible input and the pivotal work of Krashen (1982) in which the idea of natural and learner-constructed language learning is also embedded.

COMPREHENSIBLE INPUT

Real language acquisition develops slowly, and speaking skills emerge significantly later than listening skills, even when conditions are perfect. The best methods are therefore those that supply "comprehensible input" in low anxiety situations, containing messages that students really want to hear. These methods do not force early production in the second language, but allow students to produce when they are "ready," recognizing that improvement comes from supplying communicative and comprehensible input, and not from forcing and correcting production.

—KRASHEN (1982, p. 11)

Krashen (1982): *Principles and Practice in Second Language Acquisition*

Krashen (1982) introduced the concept of *comprehensible input* in what was mainly a conceptual paper. Comprehensible input is language heard by a second language acquirer that is understandable to them and communicates meaningful information. Krashen proposed that language growth occurs by receiving comprehensible input that is slightly above the learner's current level of second language competence ($L + 1$). The concept of comprehensible input was enormously important because it shifted the focus of language instruction away from repetitive and formulaic practice to a focus on meaning and communication. This previous method of language teaching, called the audiolingual, or linguistic method, was associated with low levels of language competence and poor learner motivation (Nord, 1980). On the other hand, Krashen's writings and subsequent applications of the comprehensible input hypothesis led to a narrow and dogmatic SLA pedagogy in which only communication about topics interesting to children was accepted.

Krashen (1982) used the principle of caretaker speech to describe how teacher models providing the input should modulate their talk to ensure that it was comprehensible. With young children, shortening sentences, using more common vocabulary, accompanying language with gestures and demonstrations, and slowing the rate of language delivery are methods that can be used to make language more comprehensible. The research base discussed within the article supporting the comprehensible input hypothesis consisted of seven studies that compared an informal, comprehensible input type of acquisition to alternatives that included instruction. Only two of the studies involved children. Only three of the seven studies supported the view that providing meaningful language input on topics of interest to learners was associated with better language acquisition. Significant methodological limitations of these studies were later noted.

The concept of comprehensible input was easily understood by teachers, philosophically appealing, and compatible with contemporaneous societal and research dynamics that were described at the beginning of the chapter. It incorporated instructional practices that could be put into play quickly to meet the mandated need for English language support. However, this approach was not without its critics. Critics argued that the evidence was thin, and that language instruction and language output—language production—were important (e.g., Long, 1983). But these voices remained peripheral. A sharp turn in the road was taken with a dogged certainty that the route was correct. Comprehensible input rapidly became the dominant principle in L2acquisition for the last three decades and continues to have strong advocates. A 2017 check on Google Scholar found that Krashen's work has been cited over 14,000 times—a huge citation level.

Three instructional implications of the comprehensible input hypothesis have led to practices that current evidence shows are inaccurate or incomplete.

- Children will learn second language structure implicitly, language instruction is not needed and will interfere with the natural learning process, and error correction is ineffective and damaging.
- Language is acquired through listening, and language production is not needed and should be delayed until learners begin to speak spontaneously.
- Communication of meaning should be the preeminent and exclusive focus of SLA pedagogy.

One particular consequence of downplaying the value of language production was the widespread promotion of the idea that a silent period or stage in SLA was to be expected, accepted, and viewed as beneficial because it provided a child the opportunity to begin L2 learning through observation without negative emotional circumstances. In a recent review, I reported that there was very little evidence for a silent stage in L2 acquisition. None of the studies meeting inclusion criteria for the Roberts (2014) review provided data permitting the assertion that silence or less talking led to second language growth. I also suggested that belief in the silent stage has contributed to a laissez-faire approach to educational support for L2, because it leads to a reliance on informal language exposure and children's natural language learning ability as sufficient (Roberts, 2014). Yet the inaccurate notions that there is a silent stage in L2 acquisition, and that during this time children are actively involved in learning a language, continues to be widely held and expressed in current scholarly writing, by professional organizations, and within teacher preparation programs (e.g., National Association for the Education of Young children, 1995; Tabors, 1997; Tabors & Snow, 2001; U.S. Department of Health and Human Services, Administration on Children, Youth, and Families, 2005).

The importance of meaning and language input is recognized in almost all current theories of language development. However, the three instructional implications just stated have been called into question in the face of research that has been published since 1982 indicating that instruction, early language production, and formal attention to language structure helps EBs gain English proficiency (Ellis, 2005). A course correction is needed with three additional waymarkers added for the value of language instruction, early language production, and teaching language structure.

THE THRESHOLD HYPOTHESIS AND THE DEVELOPMENTAL INTERDEPENDENCE HYPOTHESIS

The level of competence bilingual children achieve in their two languages acts as an intervening variable in mediating the effects of their bilingual learning experiences on cognition. Specifically, there may be threshold levels of linguistic competence which bilingual children must attain both in order to avoid cognitive deficits and to allow the potentially beneficial aspects of becoming bilingual to influence their cognitive growth.
—CUMMINS (1979, p. 229)

To the extent that instruction in a certain language is effective in promoting proficiency in that language, transfer of this proficiency to another language will occur, provided there is adequate exposure to that other language (either in the school or environment) and adequate motivation to learn that language.
—CUMMINS (1981, p. 233)

Cummins (1979): *Linguistic Interdependence and the Educational Development of Bilingual Children*

Cummins (1981): *The Role of Primary Language Development in Promoting Educational Success for Language Minority Students*

In his 1979 work, Cummins presented two new appealing theoretical ideas that indicate the reciprocal relationship between L1 and L2 and school experience. These theoretical constructs were the *threshold hypothesis* (TH) and the *developmental interdependence hypothesis* (DIH). These ideas were seminal in that they singled out bilingualism and the development of children's first language as major wayposts in achieving high levels of second language competence.

The threshold hypothesis, represented in the first quotation, stipulates that the potential benefits of bilingualism are dependent on the level of proficiency in each language. Bilingualism was argued to have the potential of leading to better academic and cognitive functioning and a more analytic orientation to linguistic structures, with the greatest benefit occurring when high proficiency in both languages is achieved. Cummins identifies three possible effects resulting from different levels of proficiency in L1 and L2.

- Additive bilingualism, in which there is a high level of proficiency in both languages—positive cognitive effects
- Dominant bilingualism, in which there is a nativelike level of proficiency in one language but not in the other—neither negative or positive cognitive effects
- Semilingualism, in which there is a low level of proficiency in both languages—negative cognitive effects

The second pivotal concept introduced by Cummins, the *developmental interdependence hypothesis* (DIH), posits that L1 and L2 are interdependent, and consequently that cognitive and linguistic skills acquired in one language can be transferred to another language. The likelihood of transfer will depend on the extent to which cognitive development and instruction result in high levels of conceptual knowledge embedded in each language. Cummins (1979) initially proposed that the underlying proficiency is grounded in the child's first language. He proposed that both L1 to L2 *and* L2 to L1 transfer, as reflected in the second quotation, were possible (Cummins, 1981). An important point in Cummins conceptual framework is that interdependence between the two languages is more active in context-reduced and cognitively demanding tasks common to school and literacy learning. However, the cognitive mechanisms and processes by which this transfer occurs was not detailed and remains underspecified, although recent research is beginning to examine the details of transfer.

The TH and DIH concepts provide a provocative understanding for the long-term achievement gap in early language and literacy, present in 1979 and present today, between EBs and other children. The achievement gap can be seen, in part, as a consequence of the underdevelopment of both L1 and L2. L1 is underdeveloped because it is not used in most schooling for EBs, is not encouraged in out-of-school contexts, or has limited use within cognitively demanding, academic-like pursuits. L2 is underdeveloped because EBs continue to have persistent low levels of English proficiency even when they have been educated for many years in American schools. In fact, in the state of

California, the California English Language Development Standards (2014) formally identifies those students who have attended U.S. schools for more than 6 years without having achieved levels of English proficiency to support academic learning as "long term English learners" (California Department of Education, 2014). Of course, language is but one factor leading to the achievement gap.

Subsequent research on the TH and DIH and its corollary of a *common underlying proficiency* (CUP), empirically corroborate the concepts. These newer studies reflect both broad and detailed levels of inquiry and include the study of words that are similar in L1 and L2, the relationship between L1 and L2 and language and literacy, the cognitive correlates of CUP related to early literacy, and the effects of bilingual education. For example, neurobiological studies made possible by sophisticated brain-imaging technology that became available after Cummins published his pivotal research provide strong evidence supporting the idea of developmental interdependence between L1 and L2. Fluent bilinguals' L1 and L2 systems overlap in the brain, and there is greater L1 and L2 integration in individuals with higher levels of L2 oral proficiency (Mechelli, Crinion, Noppeney, Doherty, Ashburner, Frackowiak, & Price, 2004).

Research showing that language and literacy skills can be transferred across languages has been viewed as validating the DIH and the CUP hypotheses. Studies indicate a transferability of phonemic awareness, word reading, and fluency between languages, although the findings are also inconsistent (e.g., Durgunoğlu, Nagy, & Hancin-Bhatt, 1993; Geva & Ryan, 1993; Gottardo & Mueller, 2009). L1 and L2 vocabulary are more independent in school-age (Gottardo & Mueller, 2009) and preschool children (Goodrich & Lonigan, 2017; Goodrich, Lonigan, Kleuver, & Farver, 2016) compared to older children. Transfer occurs more readily when there is a greater similarity between L1 and L2 orthography and phonology (Bialystok, MacBride-Chang, & Luk, 2005). For example, the orthography of Chinese is based more on morphemes than phonemes; therefore transfer from Chinese to English decoding is limited. Ironically, it is the topic of negative transfer between L1 and L2, meaning that L1 will impede L2 acquisition, that has historically caught the attention of researchers and the public. The erroneous popular belief that learning and using two languages will lead to cognitive confusion and stunt the growth of English proficiency is part of the rationale for English-only education for EBs held by many.

However, studies supporting L1 to L2 beneficial transfer mostly indicate a correlational relationship between L1 and L2, which does not constitute strong evidence of transfer because of the well-known problem of intervening variables, such as verbal intelligence or perhaps even instruction. Clever micro-level experiments, initially small scale, in which concepts or information are induced in one language, followed by various instructional methods designed to facilitate transfer, wherein the effectiveness of the methods is gauged by measuring the learning of the induced information in the L2, are needed. Such studies could result in schools' having the capacity to provide effective instruction for promoting transfer.

Another topic of research connected to the idea of the DIH is the potential benefit of transferring L1 vocabulary to learning similar L2 vocabulary. Words that are similar in both languages are called *cognates*. There is some preliminary evidence that points to the benefits of using cognates. However, there are issues related to the availability of cognates for young children. First, about 70% of the words known by EBs are known in one language only (Pena, Bedore, & Zlatic-Giunta, 2002). In addition, the availability of true cognates is limited by the similarity between L1 and L2 (Bialystok, Luk, & Kwan, 2005). Transfer between languages does not occur automatically, may be more challenging for young children, and has less research support for learning vocabulary than for learning reading foundations such as word decoding and phonemic awareness (Goodrich & Lonigan, 2017; Kelley & Kohnert, 2012). More research is needed before the potential benefits of using cognates within an instructional context for young EBs can be confidently recommended.

Two challenges for future investigation based on the Cummins framework are to uncover (1) how L1 and L2 interact and how to facilitate a beneficial transfer from one language to the other and (2) the unique cognitive requirements involved in coordinating two language systems and how and if this coordination can be advanced by classroom instruction. Progress in these two areas holds promise for EBs' language and literacy achievement. This research may lead to opportunity to provide EBs with metacognitive tools for language and literacy achievement that will allow them to capitalize most fully on their dual proficiency and the metacognitive strengths gifted by it. This investigation is particularly important for early language and literacy, because young children are limited in their conscious, strategic, and automatic transfer capabilities, and may therefore be more dependent on instruction to actualize possible transfer and achieve the benefits from coordinating language interdependence.

BILINGUAL EDUCATION META-ANALYSIS

A major result of the current synthesis has been the revelation that bilingual education has been badly served by a predominance of research that is inadequate in design and that makes inappropriate comparisons of children in bilingual programs to children who are dissimilar in many crucial respects. In every instance where there did not appear to be crucial inequalities between experimental and comparison groups, children in the bilingual programs averaged higher than the comparison children on criterion instruments.

—WILLIG (1985, p. 312)

Willig (1985): *A Meta-Analysis of Selected Studies on the Effectiveness of Bilingual Education*

Willig (1985) reviewed the available studies on bilingual education and analyzed them with the relatively new methodological approach of meta-analysis (Glass, 1976). Her findings and those of several similar subsequent reviews revealed that bilingual education is better for English language and literacy outcomes than education that is not bilingual. And yet the clearly marked path forward of providing high-quality and comprehensive bilingual education for EBs revealed by the research from 1985 onward has been missed or barely traveled.

In meta-analysis, statistical outcomes can be synthesized and compared across studies to indicate the *effect* of one type of educational practice compared to another. Willig calculated effect sizes for bilingual compared to nonbilingual education by dividing the difference in the means of the bilingual and nonbilingual groups by the standard deviation of the comparison group. Hedge's correction for bias due to sample size was applied, and effect sizes were weighted based on the number of effect sizes calculated in each sample. This methodology allowed for combining results across studies and for adjusting results for any problems encountered in conducting the research. It is largely consistent with current approaches to meta-analysis. Willig reported that participation in bilingual education consistently produced small-to-moderate differences in favor of bilingual education for tests in English reading, language skills, and mathematics. Not surprisingly, tests in L1 showed broader benefits, including advantages for reading, language, mathematics, writing, social studies, listening comprehension, and attitudes about school or themselves. In addition, studies with random assignment, indicating a stronger research design, produced larger effects than other studies. A result that is particularly significant in the context of current English-only education for EBs is that the largest effect size in favor of bilingual education was found in the comparison between bilingual and submersion programs ($ES = 0.63$). Submersion programs are essentially English-only programs.

Willig also drew attention to problems in the way that studies evaluating bilingual education had been conducted prior to 1985. These inadequacies are reflected in the quotation that begins this section and include

- making sure that the bilingual and nonbilingual program groups were equivalent in language factors, such as the amount of language exposure, the relative strengths of the two languages, whether language production or language comprehension were measured, and whether language measures were reliable and measured what they were supposed to,
- documenting that descriptions of the features of programs being compared were accurate, and

- conducting the correct statistical analyses, and ensuring that the method for comparing the two groups would actually contrast bilingual and nonbilingual programs.

These limitations were so pervasive in studies and evaluations of bilingual education prior to 1985 that only 5–10% of the studies had met criteria for inclusion in previous narrative reviews. These methodological limitations draw attention to the way in which flawed science contributes to the controversies and differences in conclusions about bilingual education.

The results of three subsequent meta-analyses mirror what was reported some 30 years ago (Cheung & Slavin, 2005; Rolstad, Mahoney, & Glass, 2005, 2008). Nuances of the original findings were revealed as well. Rolstad et al. (2005, 2008) conducted a meta-analysis of bilingual education studies that appeared after Willig's seminal review. Seventeen studies were chosen, and no methodological selection criteria were applied. Rolstad et al. (2008) compared transitional bilingual education, in which English is the goal with, for the first time, developmental bilingual programs, in which English *and* maintenance of L1 are the selected goals. They found an overall mean $ES = 0.23$ in favor of developmental bilingual programs for English outcomes and a mean ES of 0.86 for outcomes in other languages. Cheung and Slavin (2005) performed a meta-analytic and narrative review of studies on reading outcomes. They reported an overall mean $ES = 0.52$ in favor of bilingual programs. Interestingly Slavin & Cheung (2005) found that programs including both L1 and L2 in the same year benefited reading achievement the most. Implementation of this effective model of bilingual education that uses L1 and L2 in instruction during the same year may be implemented and justified in current English-only settings because English instruction would not be delayed in favor of L1 instruction and L1 instruction could be reasonably defended as English language support (see Roberts, 2013, 2017, for elaboration).

These reviews of bilingual education did not include preschool-age children. It has been thought that English-only instruction may be especially pernicious for very young EB children because of the potential for L1 loss or reduction in L1 proficiency (Portes & Hao, 1998). Research on the age of acquisition and its relationship to eventual levels of L2 proficiency has intrigued SLA scholars for decades and has engendered significant debate. Some studies have suggested that children learn an L2 better when they are older and more cognitively mature. Other studies have indicated that children learn an L2 better when they are younger because they have an innate and powerful language learning proclivity when they are young. The current evidence reveals a tipping of the scale toward a younger age of acquisition leading to higher levels of second language proficiency (MacSwan & Pray, 2005). Neurobiological research documents this claim with results showing that brain structure, not only brain function, is reorganized with bilingualism. Gray matter in areas of the brain associated with language increases as a function of age of acquisition (the earlier, the better) and attained proficiency. In short, acquiring a second language earlier, particularly when that acquisition is greater, increases the size of areas in the brain that process language (Mechelli et al., 2004). Capitalizing on the potential advantages for L2 acquisition in young children, while at the same time ensuring continued development in the L1, will require very thoughtful and delicately balanced educational programs. In light of this evidence, preschool programs, which are usually positively disposed toward children's L1, are a particularly important target for increasing the availability of bilingual programs and very strong English language development programs.

Individual studies published after Willig's (1985) pivotal research have demonstrated the benefits of using both L1 and L2 in instruction to teach cognitively demanding academic content and metacognition and to promote language and literacy achievement (e.g., August, Artzi, & Barr, 2016; for a preschool review, see Buysse, Peisner-Feinberg, Paez, Hammer, & Knowles, 2014). A successful approach for preschoolers combined at-home experiences in L1 with linked school experiences in L2 (Roberts, 2008). Results from this study mirrored those for bilingual education with older children. Preschool children made as much gain in story-specific English vocabulary and important gains in *general* English vocabulary when they read storybooks at home in L1 as when they read storybooks at home in English. Dual or two-way immersion programs in which EBs and non-EBs attend programs in two languages with the goal of establishing additive bilingualism are becoming more prevalent. Emerging evidence reveals these programs can be very effective (Kim, Hutchison, & Winsler, 2015). Issues related to status and socioeconomic differences between EBs and non-EBs in these programs have been noted. Dual immersion programs may be particularly beneficial for young emergent bilinguals whose command of L1 is incomplete and may therefore be at risk of loss or limited proficiency.

A recent evaluation of transitional bilingual education compared with structured immersion included more recent and longer-term studies and found equivalent English reading and language outcomes several years after implementation (Cheung & Slavin, 2012). The authors concluded that the quality of instruction is an important feature of the several studies showing positive results for EBs' English achievement. Noted indicators of quality include professional development, supporting curricular materials, and the use of collaborative learning activities.

This evidence taken together indicates that those involved in language and literacy education of EBs should feel encouraged and indeed pressed to advocate for and implement high-quality bilingual education programs to increase the odds that EBs will fulfill their promise for English language and literacy achievement. Social–emotional outcomes are also better in bilingual programs. The real challenges of providing high-quality, multiyear bilingual programs must be acknowledged. One favorable circumstance for successfully implementing bilingual programs in the United States is that more than 80% of emergent bilinguals are Spanish speaking. There is wide availability of literacy curricula in Spanish for early elementary and preschool children and a growing number of Spanish–English bilingual teachers. When bilingual education is not available, educators can still utilize and improve EBs L1 with special attention to using L1 for academic learning, not just routine classroom functions like class management and informal conversation. Roberts (2017) presents practical suggestions for how children's L1 can be activated in classrooms comprising many languages, in those where materials in children's L1 are not available, or in classrooms where teachers do not have linguistic competence in the first language of their students.

There are advantages to being bilingual beyond the benefits of linguistic and literacy achievement documented for bilingual education. Peal and Lambert's (1962) seminal study found verbal and nonverbal intelligence advantages for bilinguals. Their results contradicted prevailing views that bilingualism caused linguistic and cognitive deficits, a viewpoint that is still retained by some members of the public and even educators. The research of Bialystok and others have carried Pearl and Lambert's work forward. Advantages for bilinguals compared to monolinguals are found on measures of problem solving, attentional control, linguistic awareness, cross-cultural skills, executive function, and even in later life reduced risk and reduction in severity of Alzheimer's and dementia (for a review, see Barac, Bialystok, Castro, & Sanchez, 2014; Bialystok, Craik, & Freedman, 2007). Indeed the reasons for striving for the continued development of L1 and L2 are broad and significant.

THE SIMPLE VIEW OF READING MODEL

> Moreover, the simple view holds that these two parts [decoding and listening comprehension] are of equal importance. The simple view does not reduce reading to decoding, but asserts that reading necessarily involves the full set of linguistic skills, such as parsing, bridging, and discourse building; decoding in the absence of these skills is not reading. At the same time, the simple view holds that decoding is also of central importance in reading, for without it, linguistic comprehension is of no use. Thus, a second central claim of the simple view is that both decoding and linguistic comprehension are necessary for reading success, neither being sufficient by itself.
> —HOOVER AND GOUGH (1990, p. 128)

Hoover and Gough (1990): *The Simple View of Reading*

Hoover and Gough's (1990) article is unique in that a theoretical model of reading was presented and then tested initially with a bilingual sample. The results of their study of 256 English–Spanish bilingual children drawn from 25 classrooms provided strong support for their simple view that reading comprehension could be parsimoniously explained as the interaction between decoding skills and listening comprehension. The sample was followed from kindergarten through grade 4.

Many subsequent studies have replicated the findings that corroborated the two-component model across languages and age groups. Recent theory and research have challenged the view asserting that the model is too simple. For example, it has been argued that vocabulary knowledge, oral language more generally, or executive processes are necessary to take into account, over and beyond decoding and listening comprehension. A recent study offers strong evidence that the simple view parsimoniously represents reading (Kim, 2017). Kim presented results from four models in which direct and indirect effects on reading comprehension were estimated in a sample of English-fluent second graders showing that decoding and listening comprehension mediated 100% of the variance in reading comprehension. Decoding and listening comprehension are upper-level skills influenced by related subskills, such as vocabulary, grammar, working memory, and theory of mind.

Another reason for selecting Hoover and Gough (1990) as pivotal research in early literacy is that it highlights the importance of word reading efficiency (decoding) in L2 reading (Nassaji, 2014). Historically, models of L2 reading and L2 acquisition (as reviewed in the sections on natural sequences in L2 comprehensible input) have emphasized top-down processes (Barnitz, 1985). The prominence of word decoding within the simple view is a reminder that it is invaluable in L2 reading. A key understanding for why this is so is that the human mind has a limited processing capacity. When slow and inaccurate word decoding demands too much cognitive energy, there is less capacity available for top-down processes involved in reading comprehension. No matter how good comprehension strategies, vocabulary knowledge, the construction of text-situation models, and motivation are, if children have inefficient decoding abilities the print will be impenetrable for them. Capacity limitations are likely to be even more acute when EBs are learning under the high-processing load required when reading in their L2.

The work of Esther Geva and colleagues over some 30 years has been particularly important in detailing the relationships among linguistic, conceptual, bottom-up, and top-down processes in L2 reading (e.g., Geva & Ryan, 1993; Geva, Yaghoub-Zadeh, & Schuster, 2000). Their work has demonstrated with scientific rigor, as noted by scholars in linguistics, SLA, and reading in the pivotal papers reviewed in this chapter, that there is a significant similarity in L1 and L2 reading, including an interaction between top-down (cognitive control, verbal ability) and bottom-up language processes (skill in language analysis and decoding). The framing of decoding as a constrained skill (Paris, 2005) has been interpreted as affirming anew that word decoding is less important, easier to learn, or of more limited utility in reading than comprehension. This point of view is unhelpful to EBs. A dual lane down the path must be maintained.

The simple view of reading research may also be considered pivotal, because it draws attention to the fact that effective listening comprehension activities for prereaders, and listening to a teacher's reading of text scaffolded with teacher explanation and other supports, may help young EBs to extract meaning from texts that are too challenging to read or beyond their English proficiency to understand.

The simple view has been indirectly extended to preschool with studies distinguishing between code-related, print-related, and outside-in competencies on the one hand, and oral language, meaning-focused, and language proficiency competencies on the other. The studies with preschoolers are at least consistent with the simple view in showing that competencies from these two domains are associated with later acquisition of both decoding skills and reading comprehension (e.g., Lonigan, Farver, Nakamoto, & Eppe, 2013; Quirk, Grimm, Furlong, Nylund-Gibson, & Swami, 2016).

CONCLUSION: WAYMARKERS
FROM PIVOTAL THEORIES AND RESEARCH

The clearest and most significant finding from the pivotal theories and research discussed in this chapter is that utilization and strengthening of children's L1, with high levels of bilingualism as the gold standard outcome, will contribute to English language proficiency and English literacy achievement. It will also gift other cognitive strengths to emergent bilinguals for school accomplishment and life success. Thus, the strong claim that one of the most important educational advancements for ensuring higher levels of language acquisition and literacy achievement for emergent bilinguals is for educators to advocate for, value, utilize, and activate EBs' L1 in educational settings is justified.

A second reoccurring idea is the similarity and interdependence between L1 and L2 in language acquisition and literacy learning. The second pattern was theoretically articulated in the pivotal work by Cummins (1979, 1981) and confirmed in later research, although many uncertainties remain. Dulay and Burt's (1974) work was critical in exhibiting early evidence of the similarity in L1 and L2 language acquisition. These researchers also drew attention to the potential active role of children in constructing the adult language grammar. In describing this language process, they used the term *natural*, which was embedded in subsequent L2 acquisition and reading theory that had enormous influence on L2 acquisition and reading pedagogy, namely comprehensible input and whole language.

The concept of comprehensible input proposed by Krashen (1982) swept across the L2 field and became *the* dominant pedagogical approach for developing L2 proficiency. The importance of rich and comprehensible input and the attendant focus on meaning and communication in both L1 and

L2 acquisition and learning are indisputable. However, we now know that they are insufficient and incomplete recipes for high levels of SLA (Tomasello, 2003; Swain, 2005). It also influenced the field to adopt a set of beliefs that mischaracterized L2 learning as almost exclusively a child-driven process, in which language production and instruction were unnecessary and potentially an interference. Emergent bilingual children's natural learning capabilities can be speeded along by instruction, language production, and attention to language structure. Similarly we now know that whole language, which downplays and disparages the importance and instruction of bottom-up skills such as decoding, is insufficient for skilled reading acquisition. This insufficiency is particularly acute for socioeconomically at-risk children, a group to which many EBs belong. Hoover and Gough (1990), in a unique model of reading that was initially validated by emergent bilinguals, capture the dual importance of bottom-up and top-down processes for reading comprehension. As such, their research was pivotal in providing a needed course correction for the overly narrow emphasis on meaning and comprehension in both L2 learning and L2 reading. We now know that effective literacy programs for EBs, like those for their L1 counterparts, will position decoding (or precursor phonological awareness and alphabetic skills) as equally important and provide the robust and carefully planned instruction required. A strength of the comprehensible input concept and of whole language is that they contributed to researchers and practitioners validating EBs cognitive and linguistic strengths and deeply rooted capacity to learn. Embedding these positive dispositions and high expectations within comprehensive and scientifically indicated practices to strengthen bottom-up and top-down language and literacy competencies will benefit the language and literacy development of EBs.

The challenge for educators dedicated to ensuring high levels of language proficiency and literacy competence is to incorporate the full range of validated findings revealed in these pivotal studies and research from 25 to 40 years ago and to step forward to proactively correct the missteps, some of which remain strongly embedded in educational programs. This seminal work calls for additional research, some of which was suggested within this chapter, to enrich the science and classroom applications pertaining to young EBs language and literacy competence.

The pivotal theory and research reviewed in this chapter creates a vision of PreK through grade 3 classrooms in which (1) various models of developmental bilingual education are implemented or children's L1s are regularly activated for academic learning accompanied by high-quality instructional practices; (2) extensive high-quality and meaning-focused input, output, and language instruction are provided; (3) practices to facilitate positive transfer from L1 to L2 are enacted; and (4) high-quality learning activity and instruction in decoding (or its precursors), language structure, and listening and reading comprehension are regularly taught in an explicit and coherent manner by a teacher skilled in making learning accessible for EB children.

REFERENCES

August, D., Artzi, L., & Barr, C. (2016). Helping ELLs meet standards in English language arts and science: An intervention focused on academic vocabulary. *Reading and Writing Quarterly, 32,* 373–396.

Barac, R., Bialystok, E., Castro, D. C., & Sanchez, M. (2014). The cognitive development of young dual language learners: A critical review. *Early Childhood Research Quarterly, 29,* 699–714.

Barnitz, John G. (1985). *Reading development of nonnative speakers of English: Research and instruction. Language in education: Theory and practice, No. 63.* Orlando, FL: Harcourt Brace Jovanovich.

Bialystok, E., Craik, F. I., & Freedman, M. (2007). Bilingualism as a protection against the onset of symptoms of dementia. *Neuropsychologia, 45*(2), 459–464.

Bialystok, E., Luk, G., & Kwan, E. (2005). Bilingualism, biliteracy, and learning to read: Interactions among languages and writing systems. *Scientific Studies of Reading, 9*(1), 43–61.

Bialystok, E., McBride-Chang, C., & Luk, G. (2005). Bilingualism, language proficiency, and learning to read in two writing systems. *Journal of Educational Psychology, 97,* 580–590.

Brown, R. (1973). *A first language: The early stages.* Cambridge, MA: Harvard University Press.

Buysse, V., Peisner-Feinberg, E., Páez, M., Hammer, C. S., & Knowles, M. (2014). Effects of early education programs and practices on the development and learning of dual language learners: A review of the literature. *Early Childhood Research Quarterly, 29,* 765–785.

California Department of Education. (2014). *California English Language Development Standards: Kindergarten through Grade 12.* Sacramento, CA: CDE Press, Department of Education.

Carrell, P. L. (1983). Three components of background knowledge in reading comprehension. *Language Learning, 33,* 183–203.

Cheung, A. C., & Slavin, R. E. (2005). A synthesis of research on language of reading instruction for English language learners. *Review of Educational Research, 75,* 247–284.

Cheung, A. C., & Slavin, R. E. (2012). Effective reading programs for Spanish-dominant English language learners (ELLs) in the elementary grades: A synthesis of research. *Review of Educational Research, 82,* 351–395.

Chomsky, N. (1965). *Aspects of the theory of syntax.* Cambridge, MA: MIT Press.

Civil Rights Act of 1964 (Pub. L. 88–352, 78 Stat. 241, enacted July 2, 1964).

Cummins, J. (1979). Linguistic interdependence and the educational development of bilingual children. (1979). *Review of Educational Research, 49,* 222–251.

Cummins, J. (1981). The role of primary language development in promoting educational success for language minority students. In *Schooling and language minority students: A theoretical framework* (pp. 3–49). Sacramento: California State Department of Education.

Dulay, H. C., & Burt, M. K. (1974). Errors and strategies in child second language acquisition. *TESOL Quarterly, 8,* 129–136.

Durgunoğlu, A. Y., Nagy, W. E., & Hancin-Bhatt, B. J. (1993). Cross-language transfer of phonological awareness. *Journal of Educational Psychology, 85,* 453–465.

Ellis, R. (2005). Principles of instructed language learning. *System, 33,* 209–224.

EPE Research Center. (2009). Analysis of the U.S. Census Bureau's American Community Survey (2005–2007). Retrieved from *www.edweek.org.*

Foorman, B. R. (1995). Research on "The great debate": Code-oriented versus whole language approaches to reading instruction. *School Psychology Review, 24,* 376–92.

Furth, H. G., & Wachs, H. (1975). *Thinking goes to school: Piaget's theory in practice.* New York: Oxford University Press.

Geva, E., & Ryan, E. B. (1993). Linguistic and cognitive correlates of academic skills in first and second languages. *Language Learning, 43,* 5–42.

Geva, E., Yaghoub-Zadeh, Z., & Schuster, B. (2000). Understanding individual differences in word recognition skills of ESL children. *Annals of Dyslexia, 50,* 121–154.

Glass, G. V. (1976). Primary, secondary, and meta-analysis of research. *Educational Researcher, 5,* 3–8.

Goodman, K. S. (1986). *What's whole in whole language?* Portsmouth, NH: Heinemann.

Goodman, K. S., & Goodman, Y. M. (1977). Learning about psycholinguistic processes by analyzing oral reading. *Harvard Educational Review, 40*(3), 317–333.

Goodman, K. S., & Goodman, Y. M. (1979). Learning to read is natural. *Theory and Practice of Early Reading, 1,* 137–154.

Goodrich, J. M., & Lonigan, C. J. (2017). Language-independent and language-specific aspects of early literacy: An evaluation of the common underlying proficiency model. *Journal of Educational Psychology, 109,* 782–793.

Goodrich, J. M., Lonigan, C. J., Kleuver, C. G., & Farver, J. M. (2016). Development and transfer of vocabulary knowledge in Spanish-speaking language minority preschool children. *Journal of Child Language, 43*(5), 969–992.

Gottardo, A., & Mueller, J. (2009). Are first-and second-language factors related in predicting second-language reading comprehension?: A study of Spanish-speaking children acquiring English as a second language from first to second grade. *Journal of Educational Psychology, 101,* 330–334.

Hoover, W. A., & Gough, P. B. (1990). The simple view of reading. *Reading and Writing, 2,* 127–160.

Jeynes, W. H., & Littell, H. W. (2000). A Meta-analysis of studies examining the effect of whole language instruction on the literacy of low-SES students. *The Elementary School Journal, 101,* 21–33.

Karabenick, S. A., & Noda, P. A. (2004). Professional development implications of teachers' beliefs and attitudes toward English language learners. *Bilingual Research Journal, 28,* 55–75.

Kelley, A., & Kohnert, K. (2012). Is there a cognate advantage for typically developing Spanish-speaking English-language learners? *Language, Speech and Hearing Services in Schools, 43,* 191–204.

Kim, Y. K., Hutchison, Y. A., & Winsler, A. (2015). Bilingual education in the United States: An historical overview and examination of two-way immersion. *Educational Review, 67,* 236–252.

Kim, Y. S. G. (2017). Why the simple view of reading is not simplistic: Unpacking component skills of reading using a direct and indirect effect model of reading (DIER). *Scientific Studies of Reading, 21,* 310–333.

Krashen, S. (1982). *Principles and practice in second language acquisition.* New York: Pergamon Press.

Lau v. Nichols, 414 US 563 (1974).

Long, M. H. (1983). Does second language instruction make a difference?: A review of research. *TESOL Quarterly, 17,* 359–382.

Lonigan, C. J., Farver, J. M., Nakamoto, J., & Eppe, S. (2013). Developmental trajectories of preschool early literacy skills: A comparison of language-minority and monolingual-English children. *Developmental Psychology, 49,* 1943–1957.

Lucas T. (2011). Language, schooling, and the preparation of teachers for linguistic diversity. In T. Lucas (Ed.), *Teacher preparation for linguistically diverse classrooms: A resource for teacher educators* (pp. 3–17). New York: Routledge.

MacSwan, J., & Pray, L. (2005). Learning English bilingually: Age of onset of exposure, and rate of acquisition among English language learners in a bilingual education program. *Bilingual Research Journal, 29,* 653–678.

Mandler, J. M., & Johnson, N. S. (1977). Remembrance of things parsed: Story structure and recall. *Cognitive Psychology, 9,* 111–151.

Mechelli, A., Crinion, J. T., Noppeney, U., Doherty, J., Ashburner, J., Frackowiak, R. S., & Price, C. J. (2004). Neurolinguistics: Structural plasticity in the bilingual brain. *Nature, 431,* 757–757.

Moats, L. C. (2000). *Whole language lives on: The illusion of "balanced" reading instruction.* Philadelphia: DIANE Publishing.

Nassaji, H. (2014). The role and importance of lower-level processes in second language reading. *Language Teaching, 47,* 1–37.

National Association for the Education of Young Children. (1995). *Responding to linguistic and cultural diversity: Recommendations for effective early childhood education* (position statement of the National Association for the Education of Young Children). Washington, DC: Author.

National Center for Education Statistics. (2015). *The Nation's report card: A first look: 2013 mathematics and reading* (NCES 2014-451). Washington, DC: Institute of Education Sciences, U.S. Department of Education.

National Reading Panel. (2000). *Report of the National Reading Panel. Teaching children to read: An evidence-based assessment of the scientific research literature on reading and its implications for reading instruction.* Washington, DC: National Institute of Child Health and Human Development.

Nord, J. R. (1980). Developing listening fluency before speaking: An alternative paradigm. *System, 8,* 1–22.

Paris, S. G. (2005). Reinterpreting the development of reading skills. *Reading Research Quarterly, 40,* 184–202.

Peal, E., & Lambert, W. E. (1962). The relation of bilingualism to intelligence. *Psychological Monographs, 76,* 1–23.

Pena, E. D., Bedore, L. M., & Zlatic-Giunta, R. (2002). Category generation performance of bilingual children: The influence of condition, category, and language. *Journal of Speech, Language and Hearing Research, 45*, 938–947.

Piaget, J. (1972). *The principles of genetic epistemology.* New York: Basic Books.

Piaget, J. (1977). *The development of thought: Equilibration of cognitive structures.* New York: Viking Press.

Portes, A., & Hao, L. (1998). E pluribus unum: Bilingualism and loss of language in the second generation. *Sociology of Education, 71,* 269–294.

Quirk, M., Grimm, R., Furlong, M. J., Nylund-Gibson, K., & Swami, S. (2016). The association of Latino children's kindergarten school readiness profiles with grade 2–5 literacy achievement trajectories. *Journal of Educational Psychology, 108,* 814–829.

Portes, A., & Hao, L. (1998). E Pluribus Unum: Bilingualism and loss of language in the second generation. *Sociology of Education, 71,* 269–294.

Roberts, T. A. (2008). Home storybook reading in primary or second language with preschool children: Evidence of equal effectiveness for second-language vocabulary acquisition. *Reading Research Quarterly, 43,* 103–130.

Roberts, T. A. (2013). Opportunities and oversights within the Common Core State Standards for English learners' language and literacy achievement. In S. B. Neuman & L. B. Gambrell (Eds.), *Quality reading instruction in the age of common core standards* (pp. 90–106). Newark, DE: International Reading Association.

Roberts, T. A. (2014). Not so silent after all: Examination and analysis of the silent stage in childhood second language acquisition. *Early Childhood Research Quarterly, 29,* 22–40.

Roberts, T. A. (2017). *Literacy success for emergent bilinguals: Getting it right in the preK–2 classroom.* New York: Teachers College Press.

Rolstad, K., Mahoney, K., & Glass, G. V. (2005). The big picture: A meta-analysis of program effectiveness research on English language learners. *Educational Policy, 19*(4), 572–594.

Rolstad, K., Mahoney, K., & Glass, G. V. (2008). The big picture in bilingual education: A meta-analysis corrected for Gersten's coding error. *Journal of Educational Research and Policy Studies, 8,* 1–15.

Steffensen, M. S., Joag-Dev, C., & Anderson, R. C. (1979). A cross-cultural perspective on reading comprehension. *Reading Research Quarterly, 15,* 10–29.

Swain, M. (2005). The output hypothesis: Theory and research. In E. Hinkel (Ed.), *Handbook of research in second language teaching and learning* (pp. 471–483). Mahwah, NJ: Erlbaum.

Tabors, P. O. (1997). *One child, two languages: A guide for preschool educators of children learning English as a second language.* Baltimore: Brookes.

Tabors, P. O., & Snow, C. E. (2001). Young bilingual children and early literacy development. In D. Dickinson & S. Neuman (Eds.), *Handbook of early literacy research* (Vol. 1, pp. 159–178). New York: Guilford Press.

Tomasello, M. (2003). *Constructing a language: A usage-based theory of language acquisition.* Cambridge, MA: Harvard University Press.

U.S. Department of Health and Human Services, Administration on Children, Youth, and Families (ACYF). (2005). *Head Start Bulletin #78. English Language Learners.* Washington, DC: Head Start Bureau.

Vygotsky, L. S. (1978). *Mind in society: The development of higher psychological processes.* Cambridge, MA: Harvard University Press.

Willig, A. C. (1985). A meta-analysis of selected studies on the effectiveness of bilingual education. *Review of Educational Research, 55,* 269–317.

PART II

LITERACY DEVELOPMENT
IN THE EARLY YEARS

Writing in the Early Years

Understanding the Past, Confronting the Present, Imagining the Future

Judith A. Schickedanz

Begin with a teacher who not only answers questions about written language, but who also plans ways to increase the questioning.

—DOLORES DURKIN

The three pivotal studies considered in this chapter are "Developmental Sequences in Name Writing" (Hildreth, 1936); *Children Who Read Early* (Durkin, 1966); and *Children's Categorization of Speech Sounds in English* (Read, 1975). I start with information about the context of each pivotal work and its key findings, and then trace each researcher's influence on subsequent research and writing practices at the preschool level. At the end, I draw upon several key ideas from the pivotal studies to compare early writing practices in preschool classrooms during the period from the late 1980s to the late 1990s with practices found in many preschools today.

GERTRUDE HILDRETH

After completing a doctorate in psychology at Columbia University in New York, Gertrude Hildreth served as a psychologist in the Lincoln School at

55

Teachers College. The Lincoln included an elementary school with first through fifth grades and a junior and senior high school. Testing was common at this time (Anderson, 1956), and Lincoln personnel conducted yearly assessments of students' mental abilities and school achievement (Lincoln School, 1922). Hildreth was responsible for assessing first graders and younger children with applications on file. *The Draw-A-Man Test* (Goodenough, 1926) was among the assessments Hildreth used, and she always asked children to write their names on their papers. After noticing that name writing improved gradually between 3 and 6 years of age, she had the idea that establishing norms for name-writing development could provide a nonverbal means of identifying children who lacked readiness for penmanship instruction in first grade after they had learned to read. She thought that giving these children an extended period of exploration until readiness emerged would decrease their frustration with penmanship and increase the efficiency of a teacher's instructional effort.

Hildreth divided the children she recruited for a study of name-writing development into eight half-year age groups. The youngest children were between 3 years and 3 years, 5 months; the oldest were between 6 years, 6 months, and 6 years, 11 months. Hildreth arranged samples obtained for each age group from the least to the most mature and selected a median sample as representative. Data showed that with increasing age there were fewer circular scribbles and more linear, wavy line scribbles; more characters separated from wavy lines; more instances of the correct number of characters for a child's name; and more letters without errors.

Hildreth (1936) also asked parents about the origin of their children's name-writing interest and summarized what they reported.

> Apparently these children acquired their writing accomplishment by begging to know how to write when seeing others writing, and in response to the parent's suggestions as to how to form letters and to spell their names. . . . Name writing results from the child's interest in practicing, not solely from the child's being told how to do it. Parents reported that the children spent hours writing, but results were often unintelligible. . . . (p. 301)

Parents also told Hildreth that they had not set out to teach their children to read or write; some said they had tried to discourage writing, given the time their children spent on it. Based on her study's data and parents' reports, Hildreth concluded that name-writing progress varied from fast to slow, depending on the child's basic "learning ability" (i.e., IQ), "stage of maturation" when the child became interested, the intensity of a child's interest, and parental help (p. 301). She noted, as well, that children had ABC blocks and books at home, ample opportunities to observe their parents writing, and parents who responded "intelligently" to their questions (p. 301).

DOLORES DURKIN

In 1957, while conducting case study research in an Oakland, California, first grade, Dolores Durkin (1966) noticed that a child was able to read headings in a reading readiness workbook. Testing showed that the child, Midge, read at the fourth-grade level. Durkin wondered how many children could read at first-grade entry, how home experiences supported early reading, and what effect an early start with reading had on later reading. Because many school personnel at this time believed that children could not benefit from instruction until they had attained a mental age of 6 years, 6 months, children used readiness workbooks for the first months of first grade. Durkin knew that this norm was based on just one study (Morphett & Washburne, 1931), and that other researchers had found a range of mental ages associated with success in learning to read (e.g., Gates, 1937). Durkin included IQ testing in her early reader studies to learn more about the mental-age and learning-to-read relationship, thinking that a teacher's instructional approach and a child's readiness might interact.

Durkin's first study included 49 early readers found from among 5,103 first graders tested in the Oakland, California, public schools. The study started in 1958 and lasted until children had finished sixth grade. After moving from the University of California to Teachers College, Columbia, Durkin started a second study in 1961. From the 156 early readers found among 4,465 first graders that were tested in the city's public schools, Durkin randomly selected 30 early readers to match with 30 nonearly readers on IQ and gender to create experimental and control groups. This study lasted 3 years. In both Oakland and New York City, Durkin interviewed parents about their children's personalities and their own behavior in relation to their child's reading development. In the New York City study, Durkin compared the parental behavior of the early and nonearly readers.

Parent interviews indicated that early readers had access to blackboards, paper, and pencils, and had scribbled first and then drew, before asking about printing letters and writing words, including their name and the names of family members. According to parents, the children had become interested in the letters they saw on blackboard frames and siblings' school papers and in the words on street signs, storefronts, food containers, and TV commercials. Early readers also asked about words in books that both parents and older siblings read to them. Their parents also reported discussing letter sounds when answering spelling questions. Durkin described early readers as "paper and pencil" kids and early reading as almost a "by-product" of printing and spelling (p. 137). Far fewer parents of nonearly readers had responded to their children's interest in print. Durkin concluded that early reading was a consequence of parental support, as well as encouragement from older siblings, who read to and played school with many early readers, especially in the Oakland study.

CHARLES READ

Charles Read became interested in invented spellings when friends called his attention to two children who had produced them. He found other children through teachers and parents (Read, 1975, p. 31). As a student of linguistics, Read was familiar with speech sound perception and realized that these children had the capacity to both judge phonetic similarities and use this skill. Although a few 3-year-olds were among the children that Read had observed, he used only samples from 4- and 5-year-olds, because, at these ages, there were more invented spelling samples per child.

Read learned from parents that many children had first used wooden alphabet blocks, then switched to pencil or crayon on paper when fine-motor skills allowed. Parents also told Read that their children had usually learned to name some alphabet letters between the ages of 2 and 3, and then noticed that a sound in the name of the first letter of a familiar word (e.g., the child's name or a word in the environment) matched the word's first sound. After making this observation, a child then began "to apply this insight as a principle, using letters to spell new words" (Read, 1975, p. 29). Read observed that the children wrote for a variety of purposes, but thought that they wrote primarily for enjoyment (Read, 1975, p. 8). Read also realized that only a few children created spellings, but thought all children could do this if parents gave "greater importance to the creative and independent nature of the child's spelling than to its correctness" (Read, 1975, p. 31).

Carol Chomsky, a colleague of Read's, said that inventive spellers in kindergarten and first grade could write their names and recognize words that rhyme or begin with the same sound (Chomsky, 1971, pp. 501–502). She also wrote that "It is surprising how much phonetic information is available to introspection at this age and how readily this knowledge can be raised to the level of awareness through word play, questioning, and talk about sounds," and claimed that "only the simplest phonetic awareness" (i.e., first sound detection) was necessary for getting started, and that inventing spelling was "spontaneous" or nearly so (1971, pp. 502–503). As far as I could determine, however, neither Chomsky nor Read conducted extensive interviews with parents, as Durkin had, to learn more about specific interactions between parent and child around early literacy skills and invented spellings. Read was working retrospectively (i.e., he asked parents to recall behavior from earlier years), which is likely to limit the inclusion of at least some details, and Chomsky's extensive knowledge of the foundational skills for invented spelling came from her classroom-based work with kindergarten children and first graders.

THE IMPACT OF THE PIVOTAL STUDIES

Hildreth (1936): *Developmental Sequences in Name Writing*

By the time Hildreth finished her study, Arnold Gesell had been conducting studies for more than 10 years in his Yale Child Development Clinic to establish norms for many aspects of children's behavior (Anderson, 1956, p. 184). Because the prevailing child development theory viewed changes in physical development as indicators of mental development, and maturation, not experience, as the sole cause of these changes (Anderson, 1956; Hunt, 1961), attempts at writing during the preschool years were not thought to benefit its development. Moreover, given that large muscles mature before the smaller muscles of the hands, experts thought preschoolers should engage primarily in large motor activities. (See Huey, 1908, pp. 307–308.) Thus, although Hildreth's data indicated that 3-year-olds were interested in writing their names, she did not conduct further studies about how parents helped their children to form letters and spell their names, nor did other researchers.

After leaving Teachers College for Brooklyn College, Hildreth wrote an article she hoped would persuade first-grade teachers to teach writing along *with* beginning reading, not after, and included information about writing done by 4-year-olds in the Early Childhood Center at Brooklyn College (Hildreth, 1963). Hildreth explained that, in the context of making Valentines, the children " . . . wrote messages and their names with colored marking pens" and that some made "individual letters of their names" and "simple words" with teacher assistance (1963, p. 16). Hildreth also stated her observation that writing is "too often identified with penmanship drills . . . " and she recommended that teachers consider even beginning writing as "serving the child's real purposes of communication" (p. 19). As was true of Hildreth's 1936 study, this 1963 study had no effect on preschool practices. In fact, Hildreth's 1936 study of preschoolers' writing stood alone for 40 years (Rowe, 2009) and had no effect on preschool practices for 50.

In the early 1970s, however, Hildreth's 1936 study had caught the attention of a Cornell graduate student, Linda Lavine, who saw in Hildreth's name-writing samples the young child's capacity to abstract global features of writing from the print observed in the environment. Her 1977 study confirmed the hypothesis that young children acquire knowledge of writings' global features (i.e., linear, horizontal array; variations in the height of wavy lines to indicate variation in symbols used) before acquiring knowledge about letters' distinctive features. In 1975, Gibson and Levin included Hildreth's name-writing samples, along with similar ones from Legrun (1932) and Lavine's (1977) graphic displays, in their book *The Psychology of Reading*. Mason (1981) cited Hildreth's connection to Lavine's work in a report to the Center for the Study of Reading at the University of Illinois and in the *Handbook of Reading Research* (Mason,

1984). Others cited Gibson and Levin's book or Lavine's (1977) study without noting Hildreth's inspiration (e.g., Ferreiro & Teberosky, 1979; Pick, Unze, Brownell, Drozdal, & Hopmann, 1978). In the mid-1970s, the work of both Hildreth and Durkin influenced me to join Jim Flood in obtaining a PreK, Right-to-Read grant from the U.S. Department of Education because both had stressed children's interest in writing and considered scribbling a legitimate start. The writing centers in the Boston Right-to-Read classrooms gave me a first glimpse of preschoolers' writing. As a consequence, early writing became an abiding interest and a major impetus for writing *More than the ABCs* (Schickedanz, 1986).

The first hint that mainstream preschool educators accepted writing centers came in 1987 when the National Association for the Education of Young Children (NAEYC) included "experimenting with writing by drawing, copying, and inventing spelling" as a developmentally appropriate practice (DAP) for 4- and 5-year-olds (Bredekamp, 1987, p. 55). Just 4 years earlier, NAEYC's editorial board had rejected a manuscript with samples of preschoolers' writing and had stated their reason clearly: "As you know, only oral language experiences are appropriate until children are 6.5 years old" (i.e., the norm from Morphett and Washburne's 1931 study). It had been 22 years since Hunt (1961) had dealt a blow to maturation as the primary cause of developmental change in his book *Intelligence and Experience* and 17 since Durkin had reported that some early readers' mental ages were less than 6.5 years. NAEYC board members were soon concerned that the International Reading Association (IRA) might publish an early literacy book, because the IRA had included PreK Right-to-Read presentations in annual conferences. The board now thought NAEYC should ensure that practices were developmentally appropriate and decided to publish *More than the ABCs* (Schickedanz, 1986) 1 year before NAEYC's DAP document. Writing centers in preschools began to appear gradually after 1987.

Hildreth's work was recognized by authors of early literacy case studies (e.g., Baghban, 1984) and by researchers who expanded her name-writing rubric (e.g., Lieberman, 1985) or explored preschoolers' broad understanding of their names (e.g., Villaume & Wilson, 1989). Other researchers who cited Hildreth's work explored relationships between name writing and emergent literacy skills or sought to obtain a broader picture of writing behavior and development throughout the preschool years (e.g., Bloodgood, 1999; Cabell, Justice, Zucker, & McGinty, 2009; Drouin & Harmon, 2009; Puranik & Lonigan, 2011, 2012; Puranik, Lonigan, & Kim, 2011; Rowe & Wilson, 2015; Treiman & Broderick, 1998; Welsch, Sullivan, & Justice, 2003). Despite the narrow focus and purpose of her 1936 study, Hildreth's influence has now spanned more than 80 years. Hildreth also made other contributions. For example, between 1965 and 1968, she wrote about learning to read and write in languages other than English, including Greek, Armenian, Arabic, and Russian. (See Gibson & Levin, 1975, p. 524, for a discussion.)

Durkin (1966): *Children Who Read Early*

Given the launch of Sputnik in 1957 and Hunt's 1961 book *Intelligence and Experience*, Durkin's data about the critical role of experience in early reading received considerable attention and gained acceptance. Three Right-to-Read projects that included writing opportunities for preschoolers were under way within 10 years of Durkin's study. Her work affected the decision to create writing centers in the Boston project's classrooms, and also the decisions to add writing tools and print-related materials to dramatic play (e.g., doctor's office, post office) and to use names on helpers and attendance charts. In 1967, Durkin used the lessons learned from the early reader studies to design a 2-year language arts intervention starting when children were 4 years old, the age that early readers had first showed interest in writing letters and words.

In a second study, Durkin followed the children who had participated in the 2-year, language arts intervention (i.e., experimental children) until they had finished fourth grade in public school (Durkin, 1970a; Durkin, 1974–1975). Durkin found that the experimental children performed significantly better on reading measures through second grade and also performed better than control children (i.e., classmates who had not participated in the 2-year intervention) in both third and fourth grades, though not significantly. Based on extensive observations in the first- through fourth-grade classrooms, Durkin found that (1) teachers did not change to accommodate learners with different levels of reading-related achievement; (2) basal programs dominated, preventing teachers from individualizing instruction; (3) instructional time was allocated primarily to children who experienced difficulty with reading, because teachers viewed higher achieving children as capable of faring well no matter the instructional content; and (4) learning-related behavior (e.g., attention, persistence on tasks) strongly affected achievement from preschool through the elementary grades. Of interest, too, was the finding that the children's performance in one first-grade classroom was far better than the performance of children in the other first grades. The teacher in this one first grade had moved from the 2-year experimental classroom at the end of the intervention to a first-grade position. Unlike other first-grade teachers, this teacher individualized instruction, supplemented the basal program, and was more responsive to higher achievers' need for challenging materials. After first grade, when all teachers' experience was acquired in elementary school grades, no teacher effects were found.

Little attention was paid to Durkin's preschool intervention, perhaps because two new initiatives, one using model preschool programs to test the new idea that IQ and school achievement were malleable (Day & Parker, 1972), the other, Head Start, diverted attention from Durkin's study. This was unfortunate because Durkin highlighted the connection between learning-related social behavior and academic learning, a topic of current interest (Duncan et al., 2007; Raver, Jones, Li-Grining, Zhai, Bub, & Pressler, 2011), and also took a very strong stance against claiming effectiveness for preschool interventions without long-term follow-up data that support it (Durkin, 1974).

Durkin's 1966 study on early readers was cited by researchers who implemented classroom practices based on its results (Klein & Schickedanz, 1980; Schickedanz, 1978) and by authors of case studies (e.g., Baghban, 1984; Bissex, 1980; Plessas & Oakes, 1964; Schickedanz, 1990) or studies of preschoolers' current home experiences with reading and writing (e.g., Schickedanz & Sullivan, 1984). Durkin's 1966 study also prompted some researchers to identify specific skills in early versus nonearly readers (e.g., Crain-Thoreson & Dale, 1992; Huba & Ramisetty-Mikler, 1995; Jackson, Donaldson, & Cleland, 1988), while others focused on features of home environments, including opportunities to explore writing (e.g., Adams, 1990; Gibson & Levin, 1975; Mason, 1981, 1984; Teale, 1978).

Because Durkin communicated the new views that *experience* matters for achievement and waiting for maturation to produce readiness is not useful, her influence affected not only kindergarten-level programming, but also paved the way for writing in preschool, starting in 1987, and for both Head Start in 1964 and *Sesame Street* in 1969. Durkin's influence waned, however, because her "paper and pencil kids" had not experienced, or she had not described, the rich range of writing purposes that other researchers began to document, starting in the early 1980s (e.g., Dyson, 1981; Harste, Woodward, & Burke, 1984; Teale & Sulzby, 1986). Durkin continued to have a major effect on reading in kindergarten and the primary grades through a textbook (*Teaching Them to Read,* 1970b) and through research on reading comprehension (e.g., Durkin, 1979).

Read (1975): *Children's Categorization of Speech Sounds in English*

Read's work had an immediate effect on kindergarten and the early primary grades, in part because of Chomsky's publications (e.g., Chomsky, 1971, 1979). It had much less effect on preschool practices because writing was not yet considered developmentally appropriate in 1975 when Read's book about his research was published, and because even after 1987, when NAEYC had deemed that exploring writing was developmentally appropriate for 4- and 5-year-olds, prerequisite skills put invented spelling out of reach for many preschoolers. For example, children in Read's study had learned letter names when they were between 2 and a little over 3 years of age. Yet, intentional efforts to teach letter names in preschools were not common until state standards became available between 2000 and 2004. Moreover, many parents continued to think that teaching letter names was inappropriate until late in the preschool period (see Burgess, 2006, p. 97).

Parents reported to Read that, after learning some letter names, invented spellers then noticed that a sound in the name of the first letter in their name or another familiar word matched its first sound. Following this observation, children began "to apply this insight to spell sounds in other words" (1975, p. 29). Chomsky (1971) added a few more prerequisites, such as phonological awareness (pp. 502–503), and also stressed that the start of invented spelling in any child depends on the child's "own timing" (p. 504). Piaget's theory that children develop true understanding by constructing their own knowledge and that verbal explanation (i.e., instruction/teaching) interferes with this process was widely accepted at this time, and Chomsky agreed with Piaget's claims (Chomsky, 1979, p. 49). Once, after helping a nursery school child segment /t/ in the word *karate*, Chomsky described her behavior as "questionable," saying that the child "should have done it himself" (Chomsky, 1971, p. 504). When writing centers first appeared in mainstream preschools in the late 1980s, many teachers seemed to follow Chomsky's advice to wait for invented spelling, even when children knew letter names and could detect words beginning with the same sound. Perhaps Chomsky's stance was compatible with preschool educators' own long-held beliefs that readiness unfolds with maturation.

Read (1986) later acknowledged that older preschoolers were just beginning to develop phonological awareness (PA) (Read, 1986), basing this view on a 1974 study by Liberman, Shankweiler, Fischer, and Carter, in which no preschoolers and only 17% of the kindergartners could tap out phonemes in words that researchers presented. He also became aware that many literacy experts thought explicit training was required to develop PA. This view was also adopted in most early learning standards that states developed between 2000 and 2004. That is, many PreK teachers used PA tasks that asked preschoolers to blend, segment, and delete speech units, starting with words and syllables, moving next to onsets and rimes, and, finally, to phonemes. Teachers used other tasks to teach letter names, and they often taught letter sounds in rote fashion as part of letter–name instruction (e.g., "B makes the /b/ sound, T makes the /t/ sound"). Although learning rote associations can increase scores on assessments that ask children about each letter's sound, it does not inform preschoolers that the "sound" their teacher says a letter "makes" is found in spoken words. Additional experiences are needed to help children link letters to sounds in word contexts (Ball & Blachman, 1991). Once children have the idea that letters represent sounds in spoken words (i.e., understand the *alphabetic principle*), phonics (i.e., rote letter–sound instruction) will transfer to the end games of spelling and reading.

The California Preschool Curriculum Framework for literacy states that some older preschoolers might "have figured out that letters selected to make words relate to the sounds in spoken words, and invent spellings (e.g., *KK* for *cake* or *CD* for *candy*)" (Child Development Division, California Department of Education, 2010, p. 160). This statement suggests an assumption that some preschoolers will automatically link sounds in words they learn to segment in

PA tasks to sounds in letters whose names they learn, or will use their experience in listening to alphabet books "to get the idea of what letters 'do' in written words" (p. 144). While reading alphabet books *can* include adult mediation that supports phonological awareness (e.g., Bradley & Jones, 2007; Murray, Stahl, & Ivey, 1966), the occasional reading of alphabet books in which the adult reader links first sounds in the names of items pictured to featured letters on pages probably won't provide enough support for inventing spelling. (See Appendix, C, pp., 313–318, in the California Preschool Curriculum Framework for more discussion.)

A position statement on DAP practices in learning to read and write, developed jointly by the IRA and the NAEYC after the IRA's president expressed concern that NAEYC's DAP documents were not "explicit enough" about teaching literacy skills, recommends that teachers say a word slowly to emphasize each of its sounds when children ask for spelling help (Neuman, Copple, & Bredekamp, 2000, p. 83), and also "talk about letters and sounds" when writing messages with children (Neuman et al., p. 90). As of 2017, however, research indicated that even beginning levels of phonetically based spelling are still rare in PreK classrooms (e.g., Treiman, Kessler, Boland, Clocksin, & Chen, 2018).

Research that followed from Read's study has focused on stages of invented spelling development (e.g., Gentry, 1982) and on children's identification of sounds in letters' names in both English (e.g., Treiman, Weatherspoon, & Berch, 1994) and other languages (e.g., Pollo, Treiman, & Kessler, 2008). Other studies have focused on the relationship between invented spelling and PA and conventional spelling and learning to read (e.g., Mann, Tobin, & Wilson, 1987), and these areas have been the most frequent and enduring (e.g., Adams, 1990; Clarke, 1988; Groff, 1986; Ouellette & Senechal, 2008, 2017; Richgels, 2001). Some recent research has concentrated on visual knowledge of letter patterns in words during the prephonological phase (e.g., Treiman, et al., 2018). Practitioners have long observed that preschoolers do not select letters at "random" when creating letter-string words, as has been claimed (e.g., Gentry, 1982, p. 193), but, instead, use visual rules based on information they abstract from words in the environment. For example, BANODM, BODNAM, and BOLLND are six letters long, about average for words in the environment, and have vowels. Moreover, in the third word, a letter is doubled, as is permitted in standard spelling, not tripled. Two of these strings also contain an identical set of letters ordered differently. Multiplicity and variability are two features that Lavine (1977) found among preschoolers' rules for "wordness," and Marie Clay (1975) noted others. (See more examples in Schickedanz & Collins, 2013, pp. 158–164.) More recent interest in this area stems from research findings indicating that early visual knowledge is related to later spelling (Levy, Gong, Hessels, Evans, & Jared, 2006; Kessler, Pollo, Treiman, & Cardoso-Martins, 2012).

Future research in this area will likely include a thorough look at the preschool print environment and children's engagement with it, and at teachers' decisions about spelling words when sounding out and modeling for children. This current research suggests that practitioners should use conventional spelling when helping young children write words, not just letters for sounds that children are able to detect (e.g., *Turn off the lights* not *Trn off the lits*), as Richgels (2008, p. 41) suggested.

PRESCHOOLERS' INTERESTS AND QUESTIONS IN TODAY'S WRITING CENTERS

This part focuses on the role that interest plays in preschoolers' writing and on the conditions in preschools today that affect whether children can pursue their interests in a writing center and also in dramatic play, block, and art centers. I start by reviewing the role of children's interests and curiosity in the three pivotal studies and the importance of responsiveness to the questions that stem from children's curiosity and interest. I then describe a classroom environment that was designed to spark preschoolers' engagement with writing and provide a portrait of writing behavior in this environment, including at the writing center. This portrait is based on my experiences from the mid-1980s through the late 1990s in two contexts, one a university-based preschool serving a linguistically and culturally diverse population of both local and international families, all of higher SES; the other, a public school in a city near Boston serving children from lower-SES families, many of whom were recent immigrants. The teachers' goals for children and their instructional strategies were very similar in both contexts, as was the children's writing behavior. After this look back, I discuss writing centers in today's preschools and also consider whole-group, teacher-directed literacy skills instruction, which influences the knowledge, skills, and attitudes about writing that preschoolers take to the writing center; the time teachers allocate to a daily center time; and how teachers use the writing center during this portion of the PreK day.

The Roles of Interest and Curiosity in the Pivotal Studies

Hildreth learned that children in her study begged to write their names after seeing others write, and also had ABC blocks and books, which no doubt added to their interest in print and writing. Some parents also reported that their children had spent hours creating marks that seemed unintelligible. Yet, despite misgivings, parents responded. Hildreth linked children's interest in writing to their willingness to practice writing and their interest in practicing to improvements in name-writing skills, within limits allowed by maturation.

Read noted the enjoyment that children derived from inventing spellings, and also commented about the child's name or another familiar word having provided the context in which children linked a word's first letter to its first sound. This observation then led to the insight that a letter's name often contains the sound it spells (e.g., C contains /s/ and P contains /p/, which yields CP for *soup*). Although the parents of the children that Read studied did not say they had focused on the first sounds and first letters in words, it's difficult to imagine that young preschoolers would link a first letter to its first sound without having observed someone doing it. Some of the children in Read's study had attended a Montessori school, where alphabet materials are typically available and letter sounds are stressed. These experiences might also have increased children's awareness of the sounds in letters' names.

Chomsky described what kindergartners and first graders brought to invented spelling (e.g., an ability to detect rhyme and alliteration), but provided few details about the origin of these invented spelling foundations, apart from indicating that word play, questioning, and talking about sounds were involved. At the same time, she was adamant that children should figure out for themselves how to invent spellings, and claimed they would, without providing data showing that parents hadn't helped children get started. Chomsky thought that inventing spellings was self-motivating, fueled by an ability to spell words that adults could read and the satisfaction children can often derive from the process of solving cognitive challenges.

Durkin discussed early readers' interest in letters and words, the questions these interests spawned, and how parental instruction in the absence of interest could backfire. Most early readers in Oakland were from "blue collar" families, 25% of whom were African American and 12% Chinese, not higher-income homes, as were the children in Read's study. Parents said that their child's first questions about print occurred at about 3 years of age, with printing emerging at about age 4. Durkin also reported that some parents of nonearly readers tried to teach their children to read, but not in response to the child's curiosity or interest. Durkin said this approach "strained the parent–child relationship" and didn't accomplish the parent's goal. She stressed "the very important role of the child's interest" and said her studies "clearly demonstrate that the everyday world of a preschool child is replete with opportunities to begin to learn to read" (Durkin, 1966, pp. 135–136). Durkin also wrote that, if her studies' findings were put to use in kindergarten classrooms, she would "begin with a teacher who not only answers questions about written language, but who also plans ways to increase the questioning" (Durkin 1964, p. 6).

Of the three researchers discussed in this chapter, Durkin was the only one who interviewed parents in depth to learn about experiences that led to the children's interest in writing, although all three researchers made it clear that the children's own interest, curiosity, and motivation contributed significantly to their writing. With these researchers in mind, and especially Durkin's research about what constitutes a good "everyday environment" for learning to read and write, I worked with teachers to create similar environments in preschool classrooms.

An Everyday World in Preschool Classrooms that Prompted an Interest in Print

In these classrooms, children's names were used to label children's cubbies and the pockets of the classroom attendance chart, and were also posted daily beside jobs on a helper chart (e.g., FEED FISH, GATHER PAINTBRUSHES). When children's paintings and drawings were displayed on bulletin boards, each was labeled with its creator's name, and names also identified individual mailboxes, which were used first in February for Valentine's Day, and remained for the rest of the year. Teachers also had mailboxes, and they often wrote notes to children and answered notes they received from them.

Children also wrote their names on index cards when checking out books from the class lending library, on lists of names in centers with limits on the number of children allowed at one time, and on strips of paper attached to tongue depressors that were inserted in the children's bean seedling pots. Children also signed their names on thank-you messages that teachers occasionally wrote on a large piece of chart paper to a janitor who had repaired a classroom item or to a visitor who had shared an interest, and on easel paintings, finger paintings, and collages. In addition to writing their names, children wrote grocery lists and took phone messages in dramatic play and sometimes created recipes before pretending to cook. A post office or doctor's office provided other opportunities for writing in dramatic play, and children used clipboards, paper, and markers placed in the block area to make signs for their buildings.

Children also saw print in the block area on small vehicles (e.g., a taxi, police car, ambulance, and garbage truck) and on signs (e.g., STOP, ONE-WAY, SLOW), and on recipe charts used for cooking and other projects (e.g., planting seeds). Empty food cartons in the playhouse were covered with print, and we posted several signs in the classroom: WASH HANDS, in the bathroom; QUIET PLEASE, in the book nook; WALK PLEASE, in the hallway leading to the playground. Teachers also labeled items that children contributed to a small science table (e.g., acorns, seashells), and placed related informational books beside them. Puzzles with print were included in classroom materials, and books were placed face out on display-style shelves to expose their titles. Teachers usually put an alphabet chart on the wall in the whole-group meeting area for occasional use as a reference, along with a daily schedule that used both pictures and words to indicate the experiences children enjoyed each day (e.g., stories, activity time, playground time, circle time).

Preschoolers at the Writing Center: Mid-1980s through the Late 1990s

In this part, I explain the rationale for decisions that classroom teachers and I made about interacting with children at the writing center during center time, and then describe the range of child behavior we observed in this context. Enrollment per class ranged from 15 to 18 with both 3- and 4-year-olds in some groups. A few children in every class had special needs, and some were dual language learners.

Rationales for Responding to Requests for Spellings

We sounded out words when children requested spellings rather than insist, as Chomsky had advised, that children do this on their own from the beginning. We were mindful of not only Piaget's stage theory of development and the associated processes of assimilation and accommodation, but also of several excellent critiques of Piaget's theory and research methodology (e.g., Donaldson, 1978; Richards & Siegler, 1981). I paid more attention to the critiques, than to Chomsky's advice, and also attended to what Donaldson said about not oversimplifying complex situations. A few years into our work, I also became aware of the work of Collins, Brown, and Newman (1987) on "cognitive apprenticeships," which are demonstrations that make mental processes visible to children. Sounding out words and linking letters to the segmented sounds provided such apprenticeships. As in working with any apprentice, we upped the ante as individual children gained skill, by pausing after isolating a word's first sound, to ask, "What letter do we need?" Later, we asked a child to say the requested word and then its first sound and to think about a letter to spell it. At some point, we suggested that a child say the whole word slowly and match the letters to the sounds detected. By using a cognitive apprenticeship approach, we simplified the learning *situation* by demonstrating and scaffolding, while maintaining a considerable amount of content complexity, as appropriate for each individual child.

When engaging children in a cognitive apprenticeship, Donaldson's work also influenced our decision to tell them that some situations are complex. For example, children saw that letters in some words did not match a sound in their spoken counterparts; that some sounds are spelled by different letters, depending on the word; and that others are spelled with two letters working together, not one letter. We also told a child the letter or letters that were missing in an invented spelling when the child asked, "Is this right?" or "Is something missing in this word?" after having invented a spelling (e.g., *STR, PPL, LV*). Here is Donaldson's thinking about such matters:

> It seems to be widely believed that children must not be told the truth about the system to begin with because they could not cope with . . . complexities

. . . what underlies this mistake is . . . a failure . . . to see the difference between understanding the nature of the system and mastering all the individual patterns of relationship. It will inevitably take a child some time to learn all the . . . correspondences. The question is . . . whether he will do this better if he is correctly informed about the kind of thing to expect. (1978, pp. 108–109)

Of course, adults cannot just tell young children what to expect. Kathrine Nelson (2007) also described the importance of "externalizing mental processes" for learners, and contrasted this process with school-based teaching that tries to "impart large organized domains of knowledge for which there is no prior basis in the student's meaning memory" (p. 266). She knew that this process required many interactions between adult and child, which we also discovered. This is a larger problem in classrooms than in the home, because teacher–child ratios in preschool classrooms are often 1:10 or, at best, 1:8.

Preschoolers at the Writing Center (Mid-1980s through the 1990s)

In the mid- to late 1980s, when writing centers first appeared in mainstream preschools, and most teachers were uneasy about dealing with print, children could explore their interests freely at the writing center and teachers responded to children's questions. As was true of children in the three pivotal studies, preschoolers in these classrooms were interested in their names. The name cards teachers made for writing centers were two-sided, were all uppercase on one side, and upper- and lowercase on the other. Six-to-eight names were secured in a set with metal ring binders. As children used these cards, a teacher named the letters and also demonstrated how to form letters, if children asked. Teachers wrote the whole letter first, then segment-by-segment, pausing to allow the child to complete each part.

Children sometimes decorated their names or wrote letters in different colors (see Figures 8–20a and 8–20b in Schickedanz & Collins, 2013, p. 164). Some children wrote their names several times, varying the forms (e.g., all uppercase or a combination of upper- and lowercase), or writing individual letters again, separately from the full name, tucking a few into the corners of their paper and scattering others about in empty spaces. Children sometimes also drew several long, meandering lines around and through the whole page, creating a picture–name essay of sorts. Some children also wrote classmates' names, filling several single pieces of paper or multiple pages of a blank book.

Children had access to unlined paper in various sizes and forms (e.g., single sheets, folded sheets for cards, sheets assembled into blank books), and created letters or more rudimentary forms (e.g., linear, wavy lines; mock letters). Teachers provided a few small alphabet charts with all 26 English letter pairs, without arrows and numerals to indicate the order and direction in which to add segments, because those details made charts too "busy" for preschoolers. We also thought that live demonstrations were more useful, even though children's renderings often strayed far from what we modeled. Writing does not differ from other areas of development in this regard. For example, an adult says, "That's the dog's tail." A toddler says, "Dog tail?" The adult says, "Yes, that is the dog's tail. It's a long tail, isn't it?" Children absorb what they can and understand more the next time, and the dozens of times that follow.

Sometimes, children just wrote letters and experimented, as if trying to find out how a letter would look if lines were moved slightly or more were added. Children also made clusters of letters that shared features (e.g., Ps, Rs, and Bs), as if sorting out in their minds exactly how they differed. A few children even created letter like forms, using their knowledge of letters' distinctive features, apparently thinking that more letters existed. For example, after finishing an alphabet puzzle, one child asked if these were all the letters in the "whole wide world." His teacher confirmed that these were all the English letters, then asked why he had wondered. "Well," he said, "everywhere I look, I see the same old ones!" He seemed disappointed, as if he had been hoping to see more letters, especially some that resembled his own creations.

At some point, virtually all children created letter strings, using visual knowledge of letter patterns they had abstracted from names and other words in the environment (e.g., EXIT, WASH HANDS, FEED FISH). When showing letter strings to a teacher, a child often asked, "What words are these?" At first, teachers said, "You tell me; you wrote them." But children's glum facial expressions prompted a rethinking of this response. After concluding that this question stems from a child's interest in finding out how print works, we started answering by sounding the words out. In contrast, when children created letter strings in dramatic play (e.g., a grocery list) or at the writing table to accompany a drawing, we asked, "Oh, what's on your grocery list?" or "What does this writing under your drawing say?" In these situations, children responded happily (e.g., "My dad and me was trick-and-treating and got candy").

After exploring letter strings for weeks or months and observing teachers sound out many of these, most preschoolers seemed to conclude that letter strings were rarely real words (i.e., did not sound like a known word when a teacher read it), and started asking for spellings. These requests raised new questions: (1) How thoroughly should we segment words? (2) What should we say about letters in words that don't represent a sound (e.g., *river*, *bird*, **kneecap**) or when children name a letter for a sound we have segmented and it is not the word's conventional spelling? (3) What should we do in response to the questions "Is that right?" or "Does something else go in?" which children sometimes asked after inventing a spelling?

In general, the degree of segmenting depended on the child and a word's length—the younger the child, the more often we isolated only the word's first sound and just dictated remaining letters. For more experienced children, we segmented words more thoroughly, but only the most salient sounds in long words, and dictated letters for the others. When a letter did not represent a sound in the spoken word, we said something like this: "*Cake* has an *e* at the end, but we don't hear that sound when we say the word." When the letter a child linked to a sound we had segmented was not the conventional spelling, we said: "*K* is used for /k/ in many words, such as *kitten* and your friend *Kendra*'s name, but, in *candy*, /k/ is spelled with *c*," sometimes adding, "You may use *k* if you'd like, because everyone could read your word."

We answered honestly when children asked if an invented spelling was correct or if something was missing. For example, after writing *STR* for *STAR*, when making a sign for a block building of a STAR MARKET (i.e., a popular supermarket), the child asked, "Does something else go in there?" (The child was familiar with the name on the store's front and its grocery bags.) The teacher told the child that there is an *a* before *r*, in *star*, but that the spoken word doesn't contain a sound to go with this letter. The child added it, then wrote M and stopped to ask the same question. "Yes," the teacher said, "there is a letter before *r*—*a*, like in *star*.

Children spent a great deal of time at the writing center engaged in drawing pictures, adding writing of some kind, and then talking with a teacher or classmates about the meaning of the finished product. When writing long messages, children often continued to string letters together, even after they had started asking for spellings, and often combined these with wavy-line scribbles and drawing. Older preschoolers sometimes started with a couple of invented spellings, then used some letter strings before switching to linear wavy lines. Children's messages were about trips to playgrounds and to relatives' homes, slights from siblings, and fears (e.g., shadows at night, loud noises, getting lost in a store). Children also wrote about losing a favorite stuffed animal, grandparents who lived far away, parents' scolding them, and up-coming events (e.g., birthday parties, leaving America to go back home, a trip to the zoo or the beach).

To sum up, children engaged in a wide variety of writing behaviors at the writing center and in different behaviors at different times, depending on their specific goals for each occasion. Even among the five or six children working at the writing table at the same time, considerable variation was on display. This was due, in part, to the mixed-age groups, but probably was also related to the freedom children had to do what they wanted here. Teachers were incredibly busy, because amid responding to requests at the writing center to help form letters and spell words, and listening to what a child wanted to tell them about their messages, children summoned teachers from other centers to assist with a puzzle, a sign for a block building, or a doll in need of dressing. Teachers sometimes asked children in the writing center to come to them for help in a nearby center. The 4-year-olds could also help the 3-year-olds, and some older fours, who had missed the kindergarten cutoff by a few days or months, often had quite a lot to offer.

We also organized classrooms to decrease moment-by-moment management demands. For example, we (1) put easel paper within the children's reach and replaced small tight clips with larger clips that preschoolers could open and close; (2) sawed off an inch or two from the legs of easels to put paper clips within reach; (3) put drying racks within reach; and (4) replaced the commercially purchased smocks that had holes for both arms and head, and also numerous straps, with simple, teacher-made smocks with only a head hole, using lined vinyl intended for tablecloths purchased at a hardware store. Children learned to remove their own paintings, hang them to dry, replace the easel paper, and put on and remove their smocks. With a stool at the sink, they were also able to turn the faucet on and off. We were determined to make interaction with children a priority, and also thought that children could take some responsibility for the classroom. They loved the autonomy, and the older children also liked coaching the younger ones.

TODAY'S DEMANDS, TEACHER–CHILD RATIOS, AND WHOLE-GROUP INSTRUCTION

Given teacher–child ratios in most preschool classrooms, it is impossible for teachers to interact enough with individual children during center time to support language and literacy development at the levels expected today, especially if they are working with lower-SES children. Therefore, it is necessary to use some whole-group, teacher-directed instruction to develop early literacy and math skills. In some PreK classrooms today, however, early literacy and math skills instruction has almost taken over the PreK day (Bouffard, 2017; Valentino, 2018). For example, some teachers pull children into a small group for 10–15 minutes during center time, leaving a second teacher to supervise the remaining 15 to 20 students. Quality interactions are difficult, if not impossible, under such circumstances. Scheduling small groups during center time also decreases children's ability to implement their own ideas for writing, block building, or dramatic play because each child is interrupted to take his or her turn in a small group, and play partners also come and go. Teachers sometimes allocate little time for centers because so much time is devoted to whole-group, teacher-directed instruction, or they require children to complete work before playing in a center.

These are worrisome trends, especially in light of the negative, long-term results found in the statewide PreK program in Tennessee. In a nutshell, children enrolled in the program outperformed control children at the end of PreK on all literacy and math achievement measures. Control children caught up by the end of kindergarten, and the two groups' achievement levels remained the same at the end of first grade, although first-grade teachers rated program children's attitudes toward school, as well as attention and persistence in teacher-led instruction, lower than the control children's. The control group's achievement had surpassed the control children's by the end of the second grade, and the control group maintained its lead through third grade (Lipsey, Farran, & Hofer, 2015). Farran (2016) provided this description of the PreK intervention classrooms:

> What we have observed in the classrooms suggests a particular vision . . . The vision seems to consist of a dominating focus on teacher-directed instruction, with little time for children to construct learning themselves from independent activities, and no time at all to play. Education appears to be serious business, better started young, especially for children from low-income families. (Farran, 2016, p. 4)

Farran and Lipsey (2015, p. 6) also warned that if personnel don't "protect the instructional environment for 4-year-olds," preschoolers might later show evidence of "burning out in the early grades from too much repetition of the same content and instructional format."

What to Protect in the Preschool Instructional Environment

Center time, with its traditional array of centers (e.g., writing, dramatic play, blocks, water table, art area, and book nook), is high on my list of segments in the PreK day that are worth protecting. There is too little space here to discuss fully the benefits of a child-initiated and teacher-supported center time each day, but there is reason to believe that several social skills related to academic achievement, including self-regulation (i.e., the ability to control behavior and thoughts to accomplish the goal at-hand), benefit when children set some of their own goals, are motivated to carry them out, and are supported by teachers who scaffold their efforts (e.g., Chang & Burns, 2005; Dweck & Leggett, 1988; Stipek, Feiler, Daniels, & Milburn, 1995). It is also likely that the development of self-regulation requires an environment in which children are not required to sit and listen far beyond their capacity (Hamre, Hatfield, Pianta, & Jamil, 2014; Rimm-Kaufman, La Paro, Downer, & Pianta, 2005; Skibbe, Conner, Morrison, & Jewkes, 2011). Moreover, sharing messages with teachers and other children at the writing center encourages deep engagement, builds relationships, and contributes to warm and emotionally supportive classroom climates that are associated with better emotional control and self-regulation (e.g., Blankson, O'Brien, Leerkes, Marcovitch, Calkins, & Weaver, 2013; Valiente, Swanson, & Eisenberg; Willford, Maier, Downer, Pianta, & Howes, 2013). And, of course, there is considerable value in the thinking and problem solving that occur at the writing center, as illustrated in the portrait that was provided.

Dramatic play provides a context in which children can use budding writing and other literacy skills in ways that grown-ups use writing and reading. Neuman and Roskos (1997) suggested that participating in such settings gives children the "opportunity to use knowledge and strategies . . . and represents critical cognitive work," while noting that preschoolers do not learn new literacy or math skills in this context (p. 30). Engaging in literacy-related behavior in dramatic play settings also enables children to practice and internalize classroom rules and expectations, such as requiring their pretend "children" (i.e., dolls, classmates) to abide by the same rules and expectations that their own teachers stipulate. Berk (1994, p. 32) summarizes the value of representational play as envisioned by Vygotsky: "Play supports two complementary capacities: (1) the ability to separate thought from actions and objects, and (2) the capacity to renounce impulsive action in favor of deliberate, self-regulatory activity." I can't see the wisdom of removing these opportunities for children to imagine themselves filling adults' shoes in their play, while tutoring themselves in classroom routines, rules, and expectations.

Improving Whole-Group, Teacher-Directed Instruction

To protect center time, teachers must use better instruction in whole-group, teacher-directed contexts, and change their expectation that writing center activities, such as name writing, should contribute extensively to children's acquisition of emergent literacy skills. These expectations increased substantially in many preschools in 2008 after the National Early Literacy Panel's analyses found that name-writing skill predicted later decoding skill. Although writing *can* support literacy skills when adults engage with children in ways that support phonological awareness and the acquisition of knowledge about grapheme–phoneme relationships (Aram & Biron, 2004; Aram & Leving, 2011), interactions with individual children as they write are very labor intensive. PreK teachers should provide some support for higher-level skills development when they are in the writing center working with individual children, but there is no good reason to make the writing center and preschoolers' rudimentary fine-motor skills carry most of the literacy-skills weight. Instruction in other contexts can also support children in acquiring alphabetic skills (see Schickedanz & Collins, 2013, Chapters 5 and 8; Schickedanz & Marchant, 2018, pp. 91–100).

The burden on the writing center is also reduced when PreK teachers understand that writing letters is not the most effective way for preschoolers to learn to distinguish among letters and name them. While some researchers (Skibbe, Bindman, Hindman, Aram, & Morrison, 2013) have noted that writing letters is better for learning letters than is typing or tracing them, they have not pointed out that engaging children in visually comparing letters is better than writing letters (Gibson, 1975; Schickedanz & Marchant, 2018, pp. 145–153). J. McVicker Hunt (1961) was fond of saying in his infant cognition class that "infants' heads are always ahead of their hands." Because this truth also holds for many preschoolers, we should protect them from the tyranny involved when rudimentary fine-motor skills are forced to do what they cannot. It is one thing for preschoolers to experiment with and explore writing letters or their names, and quite another to expect preschoolers to practice and practice until they can form letters well. Nothing dampens interest in writing more than using such approaches.

There is not space here to discuss fully the kinds of literacy skills activities that might interest and engage preschoolers in a whole-group, teacher-directed context, but the reader can find a few examples in Table 3.1 and more in Schickedanz and Marchant (2018). The first items in Table 3.1 introduce children to their names and their uses on classroom attendance and helper charts and on name cards at the writing table. In some activities (e.g., "the letter clue game" and "What letter did I write with my finger?"), the teacher writes letters using the standard letter formation procedure. Seeing an adult form a letter does not provide enough support for a child to know how, but, in Durkin's words, these demonstrations prompt questions. For example, at the writing table, children sometimes ask, "What part comes next in (letter's name)?" PreK teachers who are interested in developing children's writing fluency should focus on exposing preschoolers to standard approaches letter formation, because knowledge of order and direction of adding segments affect fluency in letter writing skill. Fine-motor skill also affects fluency, but without efficient letter formation, it does not contribute very much. Of course, teachers should allow preschoolers to write freely when at the writing center during center time, while also modeling standard procedure when taking dictation or writing messages in a group setting and use descriptive verbal language as they form letters.

If one easel in the art area has whiteboard faces and dry-erase markers, children sometimes write big letters there, inspired by the teacher's finger writing of letters in the air, followed by writing each letter with a marker on the whiteboard or chart paper, as children observe. When writing at an easel, children use the large muscles in their upper arms and talk themselves through the process, mimicking the teacher's language: a long vertical line and then a horizontal line this way, and then curve it to hit the vertical line in the middle." This verbal guidance is similar to the talk a parent used when writing for her young son (Neumann, Hood, & Neumann, 2009). She used the terms "up, down, around, and across," which her son used later to guide his independent writing. Although I prefer technical terminology—*vertical, horizontal, diagonal, curved, short, top, bottom*—the point is that adult verbalization while writing letters is used later by children to guide their own writing.

Other tasks listed in Table 3.1 focus on first letters and first sounds in children's names and in the names of items pictured in alphabet books. These

TABLE 3.1. Using Names to Support Literacy Skills in a Whole-Group Context

Literacy skills tasks	Materials	Procedure
Introducing name cards	Name cards (all uppercase on one side; first letter only uppercase on the other)	Show each child's name card, uppercase side facing out, when introducing to children on the first days of school. Point to each name's first letter each day.
Introducing one name card use	Name cards; pocket attendance chart	On the second day, point out name labels on attendance chart pockets. Show each name card, read it to the group, and then match it to a name on a pocket, naming the first letter and next one or two, then put it in the pocket. Tell children that in a few days they will put name cards in their pocket on the attendance chart each morning.
Reviewing attendance chart name card use and introducing second use	Name cards; pocket attendance chart; helper chart; additional name cards to post beside helper chart jobs (hook and loop to attach)	On the third day, show name card, name first letter, and ask children whose it is. Read answer to confirm correct identification. Match names to name labels on the attendance chart pockets, and put all name cards in. Show helper chart. Read each job title and name beside it. Explain that children should check the chart the next day to see if their name is beside a job and a teacher will help.
Introducing name card sets for writing center	Writing center name card sets—6–7 name cards, secured with a ring binder	Show a set, reading names on the individual cards. Tell children that these sets will be in the writing center from now on.
Find this letter in your name	*Children:* Own name card *Teacher:* 7–8 uppercase letters each on a card large enough for group use; alter collection somewhat for each of 3–5 days for use over following 2 weeks; list of children's names (all uppercase) on chart stand	Give children their own name card, and pair children to work together. Hold up one letter card at a time, name it, and ask children to check their names to see if the letter is in it. Paired children help one another search. Repeat with somewhat different letter sets 3–5 times over the next 2 weeks.
The letter clue game	Chart paper or white erase board; regular or dry-erase marker, depending on writing surface the teacher uses	Explain that you have a letter in your mind and will make just one part at a time as a clue to help them guess it. Write all guesses that are not the letter below where the mystery letter is taking form. Use one letter each time you play, once a week for several months, starting in the second month (see Schickendanz & Marchant, 2018, pp. 145–153, for more game details.)

(continued)

TABLE 3.1. *(continued)*

Literacy skills tasks	Materials	Procedure
First letter/first sounds in name	*Children:* No materials *Teacher:* Uppercase letter tiles—all that are first letters in the children's names; name cards as backup if needed	Hold up and name one letter tile at a time; children raise their hands if it is the first letter in their name. Show name card and point to the first letter if a child does not raise her hand. Repeat task for 3–4 days. After these days, present the first sounds in children's names, one at a time, and ask children to raise their hands for their name. Segment the first sound and say the rest of a child's name if she needs help. Use for another 3–4 days, then use the first letter *or* first sound task 1 day a week for 6–8 weeks.
Alphabet books	Alphabet book that pictures and names items that begin with a sound the feature letter on the page spells (e.g., *Dr. Seuss's ABC*)	Read occasionally. Review a few pages after reading the whole book and ask children whether items you name could go on each page or not (e.g., /b/ . . . ook on B page; /m/ . . . arker on M page).
What letter did I write with my finger?	Chart paper on stand and marker or white dry-erase board, dry-erase markers, and eraser	Stand to side of the chart paper or white-board and write a letter in the air, segment by segment, with index finger, using standard letter formation procedure. Describe actions: "A long vertical line goes down like this; then a horizontal line goes to the right at the very top; then another horizontal line goes to the right from the middle of the vertical line." After writing the letter in the air, write it with a marker on paper or whiteboard using the same descriptive language. Do a second letter. Use weekly, asking children to guess the "invisible" letter before you write it with a marker.
Introducing attendance chart pocket labels with only the first letter in uppercase (*Note:* Do this task about 4 months into the year)	Name cards; attendance chart pockets	Explain that attendance chart pockets will have new name labels the next day that match the name on the other side of the name cards. Show and read each name card.
Mystery classroom items	Examples: PAINTBRUSH & PENCIL; FORK & FUNNEL; items' names are on chart paper or whiteboard, on display, but not read until later (see "Procedure")	Tell where items are used in the classroom, and what each does. Point out and name *P* in both names, and isolate the /p/ sound. Have children guess. Read words, underlining slowly, to confirm or to provide answers that children don't guess.

activities engage children actively in comparing letters to distinguish among them and learn their names. As the year proceeds, teachers add PA segmentation tasks (e.g., "Say the first sound you hear in *book*; say the last sound you hear in *book*") and letter-naming tasks that include lowercase letters. For example, a teacher might use the title of a favorite book in the following way: "Here's a title of a favorite book on this card (e.g., *The Very NOISY Night*, Hendry, 1999). Look at your name card on the side with some small letters to see if it has a lowercase *h* or *e*," and so on. I advise against asking children to look for letters in book titles when introducing a book for read-aloud, because, in that context, children's minds should be focused, instead, on a title's meaning (see Schickendanz & Marchant, 2018, pp. 13–18; van Kleeck, 2009, pp. 121–134).

If literacy skills tasks are tucked in between songs, poems, and other activities in a whole-group, teacher-directed setting, children remain interested and engaged. Over a year, they acquire many literacy skills and use them at the writing table and other centers, where they are strengthened and expanded through productive teacher mediation. At first, the goal is to teach literacy skills in ways that help children learn about their names and their uses in classroom routines. Over time, goals include helping children link some sounds to letters, based on pairings they see and hear in their own names, in other children's names, and in other familiar words.

CONCLUSION: FINAL THOUGHTS INSPIRED BY J. McVICKER HUNT (1961)

At the end of the book in which Hunt laid out the case for the important role of experience in cognitive development, he made the following observation.

> It is no longer unreasonable to consider that it might be feasible to discover ways to govern the encounters that children have with their environments . . . to achieve . . . a substantially higher adult level of intellectual capacity. Moreover, inasmuch as the optimum rate of intellectual development would mean also self-directing interest and curiosity and genuine pleasure in intellectual activity, promoting intellectual development properly need imply nothing like the grim urgency of pushing children. (p. 363)

Challenging children, even tugging steadily in the direction they must go, is not a problem when whole-group, teacher-directed instruction is interesting and engaging. Having said that, the PreK day needs the counterweight of child-initiated and -directed activity, if children are to make what they learn in a whole-group context their own. Teachers will also want to exercise judgment in using commercial materials in whole-group, teacher-directed instruction, picking and choosing wisely, to supplement teacher-devised materials. Interestingly,

Durkin worried in 1966 about the commercial materials that were aimed at getting parents to teach their children to read. She advised instead that parents and kindergarten teachers use the everyday environment to prompt children's curiosity, and then answer children's questions. PreK teachers today should ask whether commercial materials and strategies they consider are good enough to fulfill the claim that PreK education will "level the playing field" at school entry for children from lower-SES families. It's difficult to see how this can happen when programming provided to many lower-SES preschoolers differs from the playing fields on which higher-SES preschoolers learn (Putnam, 2015, pp. 248–254). Despite good intentions, I fear that we have in current approaches to literacy skills instruction in many preschools what Bruner referred to as "an excess of virtue" to the point that it has become a vice (1971, p. 115).

REFERENCES

Adams, M. J. (1990). *Beginning to read*. Cambridge, MA: MIT Press.

Anderson, J. E. (1956). Child development: An historical perspective. *Child Development, 27*, 181–196.

Aram, D., & Biron, S. (2004). Joint storybook reading and joint writing interventions among low SES preschoolers: differential contributions to early literacy. *Early Childhood Research Quarterly, 19*, 588–610.

Aram, D., & Levin, I. (2011). Home support of children in the writing process: Contributions to early literacy. In S. B. Neuman & D. K. Dickinson (Eds.), *Handbook of early literacy research* (Vol. 3, pp. 189–199). New York: Guilford Press.

Baghban, M. (1984). *Our daughter learns to read and write*. Newark, DE: International Reading Association.

Ball, I. W., & Blachman, B. A. (1991). Does phoneme awareness training in kindergarten make a difference in early word recognition and developmental spelling? *Reading Research Quarterly, 26*, 49–66.

Berk, L. E. (1994). Vygotsky's theory: The importance of make-believe play. *Young Children, 50*, 30–38.

Bissex, G. L. (1980). *GNYS AT WRK: A child learns to read and write*. Cambridge, MA: Harvard University Press.

Blankson, A. N., O'Brien, M., Leerkes, E. M., Marcovitch, S., Calkins, S. D., & Weaver, J. M. (2013). Developmental dynamics of emotions and cognitive processes in preschoolers. *Child Development, 84*, 346–360.

Bloodgood, J. W. (1999). What's in a name?: Children's name writing and literacy acquisition. *Reading Research Quarterly, 34*, 342–367.

Bouffard, S. (2017). *The most important year: Pre-Kindergarten and the future of our children*. New York: Avery.

Bradley, B. A., & Jones, J. (2007). Sharing alphabet books in early childhood classrooms. *The Reading Teacher, 60*, 452–463.

Bredekamp, S. (Ed.). (1987). *Developmentally appropriate practice in early childhood programs serving children from birth through age 8*. Washington, DC: National Association for the Education of Young Children.

Bruner, J. S. (1971). *On knowing: Essays for the left hand*. New York: Atheneum Press.

Bruner, J. S. (1977). *The process of education*. Cambridge, MA: Harvard University Press.

Burgess, S. R. (2006). The development of phonological awareness. In D. K. Dickinson & S. B. Neuman (Eds.), *Handbook of early literacy research* (Vol. 2, pp. 90–100). New York: Guilford Press.

Cabell, S. Q., Justice, L. M., Zucker, T. A., & McGinty, A. S. (2009). Emergent name-writing abilities of preschool-age children with language impairment. *Language, Speech, and Hearing Service in Schools, 40*, 53–66.

Chang, F., & Burns, B. M. (2005). Attention in preschoolers: Associations with effortful control and motivation. *Child Development, 76*, 247–263.

Child Development Division, California Department of Education. (2010). *The California preschool curriculum framework* (Vol. 1). Sacramento, CA: Author.

Chomsky, C. (1979). Approaching reading through invented spelling. In L. B. Resnick & P. A. Weaver (Eds.), *Theory and practice of early reading* (Vol. 2, pp. 43–65). Hillsdale, NJ: Erlbaum.

Chomsky, C. (1971). Invented spelling in the open classroom. *Word, 27*, 499–518.

Clarke, L. K. (1988). Invented versus traditional spelling in first graders' writings: Effects on learning to spell and read. *Research in the Teaching of English, 22*, 281–309.

Clay, M. M. (1975). *What did I write?* Auckland, New Zealand: Heinemann.

Collins, A., Brown, J. S., & Newman, S. E. (1987). *Cognitive apprenticeship: Teaching the craft of reading, writing, and mathematics* (Technical Report No. 403). Urbana–Champaign: University of Illinois Center for the Study of Reading.

Copple, C., & Bredekamp, S. (Eds.). (2009). *Developmentally appropriate practice in early childhood* (3rd ed.). Washington, DC: National Association for the Education of Young Children.

Crain-Thoreson, C., & Dale, P. S. (1992). Do early talkers become early readers?: Linguistic precocity, preschool language, and emergent literacy. *Developmental Psychology, 28*, 421–429.

Day, M. C., & Parker, R. K. (1972). *The preschool in action: Exploring early childhood programs*. Boston: Allyn & Bacon.

Donaldson, M. (1978). *Children's minds*. New York: Norton.

Drouin, M., & Harmon, J. (2009). Name writing and letter knowledge in preschoolers: Incongruities in skills and the usefulness of name writing as a developmental indicator. *Early Childhood Research Quarterly, 24*, 263–270.

Duncan, G. J., Dowsett, C. J., Claessens, A., Magnuson, K., Huston, A. C., Klebanov, P., . . . Duckworth, K. (2007). School readiness and later achievement. *Developmental Psychology, 45*, 1428–1446.

Durkin, D. (1964). Early readers: Reflections after six years of research. *The Reading Teacher, 18*, 3–7.

Durkin, D. (1966). *Children who read early: Two longitudinal studies*. New York: Teachers College Press.

Durkin, D. (1970a). A language arts program for pre-first-grade children: Two-year achievement report. *Reading Research Quarterly, 5*, 534–565.

Durkin, D. (1970b). *Teaching them to read*. Boston: Allyn & Bacon.

Durkin, D. (1974–1975). A six-year study of children who learned to read in school at the age of four. *Reading Research Quarterly, 10,* 9–61.

Durkin, D. (1979). What classroom observations reveal about reading comprehension instruction. *Reading Research Quarterly, 14,* 481–533.

Dweck, C. S., & Leggett, E. (1988). A social-cognitive approach to motivation and personality. *Psychological Review, 95,* 256–273.

Dyson, A. H. (1981). Oral language: The rooting system for learning to write. *Language Arts, 58,* 776–784.

Farran, D. C. (2016). Federal preschool development grants: Evaluation needed. *Evidence Speaks Reports, BROOKINGS, 1*(22), 1–6.

Farran, D. C., & Lipsey, M. W. (2015). Expectations of sustained effects from scaled up preK: Challenges from the Tennessee study. *Evidence Speaks Reports, BROOKINGS, 1*(3), 1–7.

Ferreiro, E., & Teberosky, A. (1979). *Literacy before schooling.* Exeter, NH: Heinemann Educational Books.

Gates, A. J. (1937). The necessary mental age for beginning reading. *Elementary School Journal, 37,* 497–508.

Gentry, J. R. (1982). An analysis of developmental spelling in "GNYS AT WRK." *The Reading Teacher, 36,* 192–200.

Gibson, E. J. (1975). Theory-based research on reading and its implications for instruction. In J. B. Carroll & J. S. Chall (Eds.), *Toward a literate society* (pp. 288–321). New York: McGraw-Hill.

Gibson, E., & Levin, H. (1975). *The psychology of reading.* Cambridge, MA: MIT Press.

Goodenough, F. (1926). *Measurement of intelligence by drawings.* New York: World Book.

Groff, P. (1986). The implications of developmental spelling research: A dissenting view. *The Elementary School Journal, 86,* 317–322.

Hamre, B., Hatfield, B., Pianta, R., & Jamil, F. (2014). Evidence for general and domain-specific elements of teacher–child interactions: Associations with preschool children's development. *Child Development, 85,* 1257–1274.

Harste, J. E., Woodward, V. A., & Burke, C. L. (1984). *Language stories and literacy lessons.* Portsmouth, NH: Heinemann.

Hendry, D. (1999). *The very NOISY night.* New York: Puffin Books.

Hildreth, G. (1936). Developmental sequences in name writing. *Child Development, 7,* 291–303.

Hildreth, G. (1963). Early writing as an aid to reading. *Elementary English, 40,* 15–20.

Huba, M. E., & Ramisetty-Mikler, S. (1995). The language skills and concepts of early and nonearly readers. *Journal of Genetic Psychology, 156,* 313–331.

Huey, E. B. (1908). *The psychology and pedagogy of reading.* Cambridge, MA: MIT Press.

Hunt, J. M. (1961). *Intelligence and experience.* New York: Ronald Press.

Jackson, N. E., Donaldson, G. W., & Cleland, L. N. (1988). The structure of precocious reading ability. *Journal of Educational Psychology, 80,* 234–243.

Kessler, B., Pollo, T. C., Treiman, R., & Cardoso-Martins, C. (2012). Frequency analyses of prephonological spellings as predictors of success in conventional spelling. *Journal of Learning Disabilities, 46,* 252–259.

Klein, A., & Schickedanz, J. (1980). Preschoolers write messages and receive their favorite books. *Language Arts, 57,* 742–749.

Lavine, L. O. (1977). Differentiation of letterlike forms in prereading children. *Developmental Psychology, 14,* 89–94.

Legrun, A. (1932). Wie und was "schreiben" Kindergarten-zoglinge? *Zeitschreift fur Padagogische Psychologie und Jugendkunde, 33,* 323–324.

Levy, B. A., Gong, Z., Hessels, S., Evans, M. A., & Jared, D. (2006). Understanding print: Early reading development and the contributions of home literacy. *Journal or Experimental Child Psychology, 93,* 63–93.

Liberman, I. Y., Shankweiler, D., Fischer, F. W., & Carter, B. (1974). Explicit syllable and phoneme segmentation in the young child. *Journal of Experimental Child Psychology, 18,* 201–212.

Lieberman, E. (1985). *Name writing and the preschool child.* Unpublished doctoral dissertation, University of Arizona, Tucson, AZ.

Lincoln School. (1922). *The Lincoln School booklet.* New York: Author.

Lipsey, M. W., Farran, D. C., & Hofer, K. B. (2015). *A randomized control trial of the effects of a statewide voluntary prekindergarten program on children's skills and behaviors through third grade.* Nashville, TN: Vanderbilt University, Peabody Research Institute.

Mann, V. A., Tobin, P., & Wilson, R. (1987). Measuring phonological awareness through the invented spellings of kindergarten children. *Merrill–Palmer Quarterly, 33,* 366–391.

Mason, J. M. (1981). *Prereading: A developmental perspective* (Technical Report No. 198). Urbana-Champaign: University of Illinois Center for the Study of Reading.

Mason, J. M. (1984). Early reading from a developmental perspective. In P. D. Pearson, R. Barr, M. L. Kamil, & P. Mosenthal (Eds.), *Handbook of reading research* (pp. 505–543). New York: Longman.

Morphett, M. V., & Washburne, C. (1931). When should children begin to read? *The Elementary School Journal, 31,* 496–503.

Murray, B. A., Stahl, S. A., & Ivey, M. G. (1996). Developing phoneme awareness through alphabet books. *Reading and Writing: An Interdisciplinary Journal, 8,* 307–322.

National Early Literacy Panel (NELP). (2008). *Developing early literacy: Report of the National Early Literacy Panel.* Washington, DC: National Institute for Literacy.

Nelson, K. (2007). *Young minds in social worlds: Experience, meaning, and memory.* Cambridge, MA: Harvard University Press.

Neuman, S. B., Copple, C., & Bredekamp, S. (Eds.). (2000). *Learning to read and write: Developmentally appropriate practices for young children.* Washington, DC: National Association for the Education of Young Children.

Neuman, S. B., & Roskos, K. (1997). Literacy knowledge in practice: Contexts of participation for young writers and readers. *Reading Research Quarterly, 32,* 10–32.

Neumann, M. N., Hood, M., & Neumann, D. L. (2009). The scaffolding of emergent literacy skills in the home environment. *Early Childhood Research Quarterly, 36,* 313–319.

Ouellette, G., & Senechal, M. (2008). Pathways to literacy: A study of invented spelling and its role in learning to read. *Child Development, 79,* 899–913.

Ouellette, G., & Senechal, M. (2017). Invented spelling in kindergarten as a predictor of reading and spelling in grade 1: A new pathway to literacy, or just the same road, less known? *Developmental Psychology, 54,* 77–88.

Pick, A. D., Unze, M. G., Brownell, C. A., Brozdal, J. G., & Hopmann, M. R. (1978). Young children's knowledge of word structure. *Child Development, 49,* 669–680.

Plessas, G. P., & Oakes, C. R. (1964). Prereading experiences of selected early readers. *The Reading Teacher, 17,* 241–245.

Pollo, T. C., Treiman, R., & Kessler, B. (2008). Preschoolers use partial letter names to select spellings: Evidence from Portuguese. *Applied Psycholinguistics, 29,* 195–212.

Puranik, C. S., & Lonigan, C. J. (2011). From scribble to scrabble: Preschool children's developing knowledge of written language. *Reading and Writing, 24,* 567–589.

Puranik, C. S., & Lonigan, C. J. (2012). Name-writing proficiency, not length of name, is associated with preschool children's emergent literacy skills. *Early Childhood Research Quarterly, 27,* 284–294.

Puranik, C. S., Lonigan, C. J., & Kim, Y. (2011). Contributions of emergent literacy skills to name writing, letter writing, and spelling in preschool children. *Early Childhood Research Quarterly, 26,* 465–474.

Putnam, R. D. (2015). *Our kids: The American dream in crisis.* New York: Simon & Schuster.

Raver, C. C., Jones, S. M., Li-Grining, C., Zhai, F., Bub, K., & Pressler, E. (2011). CSRP's impact on low-income preschoolers' preacademic skills: Self-regulation as a mediating mechanism. *Child Development, 82,* 362–378.

Read, C. (1975). *Children's categorization of speech sounds in English.* Urbana, IL: National Council of Teachers of English.

Read, C. (1986). *Children's creative spelling.* Boston: Routledge & Kegan Paul.

Richards, D. D., & Siegler, R. S. (1981). Very young children's acquisition of systematic problem-solving strategies. *Child Development, 52,* 1318–1321.

Richgels, D. J. (2001). Invented spellings, phonemic awareness, and reading and writing instruction. In S. B. Neuman & D. K. Dickinson (Eds.), *Handbook of early literacy research* (pp. 142–155). New York: Guilford Press.

Richgels, D. J. (2008). Practice to theory: Invented spelling. In A. DeBruin-Parecki (Ed.), *Effective early literacy practice* (pp. 39–51). Baltimore: Brookes.

Rimm-Kaufman, S. E., La Paro, K. M., Downer, J. T., & Pianta, R. C. (2005). The contributions of classroom setting and quality of instruction to children's behavior in kindergarten classrooms. *The Elementary School Journal, 105,* 377–394.

Rowe, D. W. (2009). Early written communication. In R. Beard, D. Myhill, & J. Riley (Eds.), *SAGE handbook of writing development* (pp. 213–231). Los Angeles: SAGE.

Rowe, D. W., & Wilson, S. J. (2015). The development of a descriptive measure of early childhood writing: Results from the Write Start! writing assessment. *Journal of Literacy Research, 47,* 245–292.

Schickedanz, J. (1978). "You be the doctor and I'll be sick": Preschoolers learn the language arts through play. *Language Arts, 56,* 713–718.

Schickedanz, J. A. (1986). *More than the ABCs: The early stages of reading and writing.* Washington, DC: National Association for the Education of Young Children.

Schickedanz, J. A. (1990). *Adam's righting revolutions: One child's literacy development from infancy through grade one.* Portsmouth, NH: Heinemann.

Schickedanz, J. A., & Collins, M. F. (2013). *So much more than the ABCs.* Washington, DC: National Association for the Education of Young Children.

Schickedanz, J. A., & Marchant, C. (2018). *Inside the preK classroom: A school leader's guide to effective instruction*. Cambridge, MA: Harvard Education Publishing Group.

Schickedanz, J. A., & Sullivan, M. (1984). Mom. What does U-F-F- spell? *Language Arts, 61,* 1–17.

Skibbe, L. E., Bindman, S. W., Hindman, A. H., Aram, D., & Morrison, F. J. (2013). Longitudinal relations between parental writing support and preschoolers' language and literacy skills. *Reading Research Quarterly, 48,* 387–401.

Skibbe, L. E., Connor, C. M., Morrison, F. J., & Jewkes, A. M. (2011). Schooling effects on preschoolers' self-regulation, early literacy, and language growth. *Early Childhood Research Quarterly, 26,* 43–49.

Stipek, D., Feiler, R., Daniels, D., & Milburn, S. (1995). Effects of different instructional approaches on young children's achievement and motivation. *Child Development, 66,* 209–223.

Teale, W. (1978). Positive environments for learning to read. *Language Arts, 5,* 922–932.

Teale, W., & Sulzby, E. (Eds.). (1986). *Emergent literacy: Writing and reading* (pp. vi–xv). Norwood, NJ: Ablex.

Treiman, R., & Broderick, V. (1998). What's in a name: Children's knowledge about letters in their own names. *Journal of Experimental Psychology, 70,* 97–116.

Treiman, R., Kessler, B., Boland, K., Clocksin, H., & Chen, Z. (2018). Statistical learning and spelling: Older prephonological spellers produce more wordlike spellings than younger prephonological spellers. *Child Development.*

Treiman, R., Weatherspoon, S., & Berch, D. (1994). The role of letter names in children's learning of phoneme-grapheme relations. *Applied Psycholinguistics, 15,* 97–122.

Valentino, R. (2018). Will public pre-K really close achievement gaps?: Gaps in prekindergarten quality between students and across states. *American Educational Research Journal, 55,* 79–116.

Valiente, C., Swanson, J., & Eisenberg, N. (2012). Linking students' emotions and academic achievement: When and why emotions matter. *Child Development Perspectives, 2,* 129–135.

Villaume, S. K., & Wilson, L. C. (1989). Preschool children's explorations of letters in their own names. *Applied Psycholinguistics, 10,* 283–300.

Welsch, J. G., Sullivan, A., & Justice, L. M. (2003). That's my letter!: What preschoolers' name writing representations tell us about emergent literacy knowledge. *Journal of Literacy Research, 35,* 757–776.

Williford, A. P., Maier, M. F., Downer, J. T., Pianta, R. C., & Howes, C. (2013). Understanding how children's engagement and teachers' interactions combine to predict school readiness. *Journal of Applied Developmental Psychology, 34,* 299–309.

CHAPTER 4

Reconceptualizing Alphabet Learning and Instruction

Marcia Invernizzi and Jordan Buckrop

A few centuries ago, mothers baked gingerbread in the shape
of letters, and the child might eat all he could name. Perhaps
even now pedagogy would not suffer so much as stomachs
from this practice.

—EDMUND BURKE HUEY

We've come a long way since Anne McGill-Franzen's discovery that many
of the publically funded preschools in her study were actually withholding
direct alphabet instruction until the children were developmentally "ready"—
never mind the fact that their more affluent peers in private preschools were
getting direct instruction in alphabet recognition and letter sounds for years
(McGill-Franzen, 2002). Nowadays, national standards for preschool and kindergarten position alphabet instruction as a nonnegotiable component in early
childhood classrooms (National Governors Association Center for Best Practices and Council of Chief State School Officers [NGA & CCSSO], 2010;
Office of Head Start, 2015). Still, teachers continue to have questions, some of
which have answers, and some of which we are still exploring. These include
questions like when to start alphabet instruction and which to teach first—
letter names or letter sounds. Or perhaps both simultaneously? What order
should the letters be taught in? And how? What should high-quality alphabet instruction look like? And even though most preschool classrooms now
include an alphabet curriculum, the issue of readiness keeps turning up like
a bad penny. Decades earlier the question may have been when are children

ready for reading instruction. Now the question has morphed into how many letters should a child know at the beginning of kindergarten to ensure success.

This chapter discusses alphabet knowledge. *Alphabet knowledge* has traditionally been defined as the recognition and naming of uppercase and lowercase letters and the paired associations between letter names and letter sounds. More recently scholars have expanded that definition to also include the formation of upper- and lowercase letters and their use or application for reading, spelling, and writing words. We organize this chapter according to the questions teachers have about alphabet instruction and the research that has been done to address these inquiries. We focus on three pivotal studies that have changed the course of our exploration and understanding about these inquiries significantly. The first study changed our thinking about when and how children are ready to learn to read and write (Mason, 1980). The second and third studies opened the door to a consideration of children's personal experiences with letters of the alphabet and characteristics of the letters themselves (Treiman & Broderick, 1998; Treiman, Tincoff, Rodriguez, Mouzaki, & Francis, 1998). These three pivotal studies subsequently spawned new research, using more sophisticated analytic methods, that also addresses critical questions teachers have about alphabet instruction, and this research will be discussed in turn.

WHEN SHOULD ALPHABET INSTRUCTION BEGIN?

Ms. Meyer was assessing her kindergartners' knowledge of letter sounds. She presented a sheet of randomized uppercase alphabet letters to Alfred, who had just turned 5. "Put your finger on the first letter. Tell me what sound this letter makes," she asked. Alfred dutifully placed his finger on the first letter and replied, "It makes the sound of a dog barking!" When Ms. Meyer moved on to the next letter, Alfred said, "It makes the sound of coffee brewing!" And on the third, "The sound of car horns honking!"

Alfred's response to Ms. Meyer's simple alphabet assessment reveals important insights into his understanding of written language. While Alfred was able to name some letters, he has yet to grasp that letters not only have names, but also represent speech sounds. Although he can write his own name, his other writing shows no connection to sound. He does not yet understand the *alphabetic principle,* or the understanding that speech can be divided into individual units of sound and matched to letters in a systematic way (Liberman, Shankweiler, & Liberman, 1989). For Ms. Meyer, the question becomes:

What do I do now? Is it too soon to start letter–sound instruction? After all, Alfred is on the young side for kindergarten!

If Ms. Meyer had been teaching Alfred in the early to mid-1900s when maturation theory dominated reading education, she would have checked Alfred's birth date. According to this theory, determining when to start instruction depended on children reaching a specific chronological age. If Alfred had been a kindergartner in the 1930s, formal literacy instruction would have started when he reached a mental age of 6 years, 6 months (Morphett & Washburne, 1931). His parents would have been discouraged from teaching him themselves because their misguided attempts might have damaged his literacy learning later on. If Alfred had lived in the early 1900s, Ms. Meyer wouldn't worry about him until he reached the requisite age.

If Ms. Meyer had been teaching Alfred in the 1960s or 1970s, she would have had a different response: She would have encouraged him to pretend to "read" and "write" words, using what he knew, as best he could. Marie Clay had just written a groundbreaking dissertation in which she described children's behaviors as they interacted with books and writing well before they could actually read or write conventionally (Clay, 1966). Based largely on her work, young children began to be viewed as *emergent readers,* who were constantly progressing along a continuum of literacy development that begins at birth (Clay, 1977). Instead of viewing children as "mature" or "not mature" enough to begin formal instruction, researchers began to explore the similarities between children's early language development and their emerging concepts about print. Prior to this groundbreaking research, it was believed that children could not, and indeed should not, write before they could read and spell conventionally, a view that was challenged by researchers such as Chomsky (1971) and Clay (1977). Their work sparked an interest in exploring the relationship between children's early writing attempts and their evolving capabilities to notice letters and read words.

Still, even with this explosion of interest in emergent literacy in the 1970s, the degree to which these emergent readers could actually "read" signs or labels or how they learned to do so before formal schooling was unknown. Although studies examined what preschoolers knew about reading (Downing, 1970; Ehri, 1975; Read, 1971), few researchers had actually followed the *development* of prereaders' knowledge or their changing competencies in letter naming, letter writing, using letter sounds, or their early "reading" of signs and labels. At that time, no one knew whether children's understanding about how to print and recognize letters and words on signs and labels in their environment was even related to their recognition of words in books later on. If such was the case, then teachers like Ms. Meyer would have had more confidence about how to leverage emergent literacy behaviors, such as noticing letters and signs, toward the next level of understanding: the alphabetic principle.

Mason (1980): *When Do Children Begin to Read?*

This charge was taken up by Mason in a landmark study exploring 4-year-old children's changing letter and word reading expertise (1980). In her study, Mason followed two classrooms of preschool children for 9 months. One classroom exposed children to letters (e.g., alphabet strips, beginning-letter picture cards, and spelling) but not to words, while the other class was exposed to printed words (e.g., color and number words, word–picture cards) but not to letters. Both classrooms listened to stories, looked at books, wrote their names, labeled pictures, and did cooking activities using recipes. Parents in both classrooms were surveyed about their child' s curiosity, awareness, and knowledge of letters and words, and they were asked to describe what they did to help their child learn their letters and figure out words in reading and writing. In addition to observing the children's evolving literacy behaviors in the classrooms across the 9-month period, Mason assessed them at regular intervals to measure their alphabet knowledge and their ability to read words and to document their changing approaches to learning and remembering words and how to spell them.

Children from both classrooms "underwent striking changes" in their letter and word knowledge during the 9 months, even though half of them did not receive classroom instruction in either letters or words (p. 215). Further, children in both classrooms learned similar numbers of letters and words, suggesting that their gains were attributable, at least in part, to their home environments. Parents from both classrooms reported that most children learned to write (using uppercase letters before lowercase letters) during this year and that almost all could recognize and name the letters of the alphabet. Most parents reported that their children first learned to recognize letter forms, then learned to connect letters to the act of reading and writing, and finally, learned to associate speech sounds with letters. Mason concluded that emergent readers attain important literacy skills, including alphabet knowledge and awareness of speech sounds (phonological awareness), well before formal instruction, and that these skills evolve into conventional reading with considerable parental support.

Mason's study was pivotal in our understanding of emergent readers not only because it contributed to the reconceptualization and solidification of emergent literacy theory, but also because the number and sophistication of words and labels that parents reported that their children had learned to read by the end of the study could be predicted by the measures of alphabet knowledge that Mason had collected earlier in the preschool classroom. For example, children who attended to contextual cues surrounding words, as opposed to the specific letters within them, had difficulty learning and remembering any of the words they were taught. On the other hand, children who had mastered letter names and how to print them and who showed some interest in using letters to "spell" words began to notice specific letters in signs and labels and were able to remember a few of the words Mason attempted to teach them. Mason's longitudinal data suggested a "natural hierarchy of knowledge development in learning to read words" (p. 203), starting with the alphabet. Had Ms. Meyer understood this hierarchy, she would have known exactly how to instruct Alfred to help him move forward.

Mason described this developmental hierarchy as divided into three levels based on the kinds of words children recognized and the strategies they appeared to use to do so. Children in the *context-dependent* level didn't appear to recognize printed words "differently from pictures" (p. 217). That is, the words were recognized only in a particular context, such as the MacDonald's sign cued by the golden arches. While these children were able to recognize a few signs or labels this way, they couldn't recognize these words if they appeared in a different context. They couldn't even recognize words they had been taught when they were presented in a different case, even though most children had been able to identify both upper- and lowercase letters in isolation. As they became increasingly interested in letters though, Mason described how children seemed to gain a more *visual recognition* of the words themselves, noticing specific letters within them. Children at this second level in Mason's study had learned the names of letters and could recognize a few familiar words. More important, they started to recognize those words in different contexts because, Mason believed, they were noticing specific letters in the words, and this visual analysis of letters within words aided their recognition of them in different contexts. This conjecture was supported by the kinds of mistakes the children made when they miscalled a word—mistakes that seemed to reflect their reliance on letter names. They often miscalled a word that began with same consonant, saying *bat* for *bin*, for example. Mason's parental data also supported this speculation. Parents reported that as their children learned to print letters on their own, they showed a greater interest in using letters to spell and puzzle out words in reading and writing. Mason's level-two children (visual recognition) were better than her level-one children (context dependent) in learning and remembering words in different contexts, even when they were presented in different cases.

As children's letter–sound knowledge solidified, they increasingly drew on this knowledge to sound out unfamiliar words. Mason classified such children at level three, or the *letter–sound analysis* level. These children could spell three-letter words, could read most of Mason's three-to-five letter words, and "had no problem learning or remembering new words" (p. 217). The parents of such children reported that they were learning to read words so quickly that they could no longer guess how many words they actually knew. Some were already reading storybooks independently.

Mason's study was remarkable for several reasons. First, it was the first study to follow children's literacy development longitudinally and to document their changing competencies in alphabet knowledge in tandem with other early literacy behaviors, such as the reading and writing of signs, labels and words. Second, Mason's study was the first to link emergent reader skills and behaviors, such as letter naming, sign reading, and letter writing attempts to later word reading and spelling skills, a linkage that strengthened and expanded the emergent literacy theories advanced earlier by Clay (1977). Mason's study provided evidence that the emergent reading and writing behaviors previously described were linked to children's depth of alphabetic understanding and were actually precursors to and predictive of later reading success. Third, Mason documented children's early literacy development from preliterate, context-dependent strategies to increasingly literate graphophonic tactics that pressed the analysis of letter sounds into the service of word reading and spelling. Incremental growth in alphabet knowledge was at the core of this developmental continuum. Had Ms. Meyer recognized that Alfred's level of literacy development was context dependent, she might have considered bringing him to the next level of emergent literacy development by drawing his attention to the letters within personally important printed words, like his own name, and by leveraging his growing knowledge of letter names to learn and remember letter sounds.

Thanks to Mason's seminal study, alphabet knowledge started to be regarded as a catalyst that moved children along a developmental trajectory toward conventional literacy even before formal schooling. Her work suggested that the main contribution of letter knowledge to emergent literacy was to advance the onset of visual word recognition. Ehri and Wilce (1985) claimed that her label, *visual recognition,* was misleading, and that a better label for word learning at Mason's second level would have been "visual-phonetic recognition learning" (p. 174). Later research would confirm that letter–name knowledge plays an important role in the early phases of literacy development by stimulating more phonologically based strategies in early reading and writing (Foulin, 2005). In fact, the sizable correlations between knowledge of letter names in kindergarten and reading achievement in first grade have led some researchers to argue that a simple assessment of letter names "appears to be nearly as successful at predicting future reading as is giving a more comprehensive readiness battery" (Scarborough, 1998, p. 83).

Alphabet knowledge is now the Ouija board of literacy success across the United States, where kindergarten children are routinely administered tests of letter naming and letter sounds at entry to school to determine their degree of risk for developing reading difficulties. Now, instead of determining maturity or "readiness," we determine whether children meet a benchmark or an ideal number of letter names and letter sounds that research has shown that children should already know at kindergarten entry to ensure later literacy success. Piasta, Petscher, and Justice (2012a) found that the optimal number of upper- and lowercase letters that end-of-preschool children should be able to name is

18 and 15, respectively. Invernizzi, Juel, Swank, and Meier (2015), set the bar at 12 lowercase letters and 5 letter sounds for kindergarten entry. In either case, Alfred is performing well below either of these benchmarks, and Ms. Meyer must get to work on implementing classroom instruction and additional literacy interventions that will help him make progress. But where exactly does Ms. Meyer start? Should she start with letter names or letter sounds?

SHOULD WE TEACH LETTER NAMES OR LETTER SOUNDS?

A Montessori preschool teacher was explaining to a child's parent how, in Montessori schools, they teach letter sounds, not letter names. The parent asked if they encouraged children to write phonetically using their own invented spelling. To assure the parent that they did, the teacher showed her a letter that her child, Parmis, had written earlier that day: YN R U K M? It said, When are you coming?; and the message was written using letter names.

The relationship between knowledge of letter names and knowledge of letter sounds is complex, and whether to teach letter names or letter sounds first is often debated. Parents in the United States tend to emphasize letter names as opposed to letter sounds by spelling out their children's names by while pointing to or printing the letters (e.g., Sam—S, A, M!), and by exposing their children to alphabet toys, books, and educational television shows, such as *Sesame Street,* that privilege letter names—all well before sending their children to school (Ellefson, Treiman, & Kessler, 2009). Most early childhood curricula in the United States also emphasize letter names first, with some exceptions, such as the Montessori curriculum and the approach advocated in the Core Knowledge Sequence: Content and Skill Guidelines for Preschool (Core Knowledge Foundation, 2013; Montessori & Gutek, 2004). This fact alone may well explain why Parmis wrote her message using letter names to represent the sounds instead of using letter sounds. The *when* in *When are you coming?* starts with a /w/ sound, and so does the letter name Y (*why*). The /k/ sound at the beginning of *coming* is also heard when pronouncing the letter name K (kay). So, in spite of Montessori's practice of teaching letter sounds instead of letter names, Parmis most likely used what she already knew, letter names from her home environment.

In England, however, letter sounds are privileged. Parents *sound out,* rather than *spell out* the children's names while pointing to printed letters (e.g., SAM—/s/, /ae/, /m/), and the government mandates a national curriculum requiring first instruction in letter sounds, not letter names. In England, letter names are not even introduced until *after* the first year of school. Like Parmis's teacher at the Montessori school, British teachers instruct their students to label letters with the phonemes they represent. But unlike Parmis, most English children don't already know the letter names.

So, which is best to teach first: letter names or letter sounds? And does it matter in the end? Evidence to date suggests that it does not (Ellefson et al., 2009). At the outset, early in development, children in the United States do better than children in England on tests of letter naming, whereas children in England do better than children in the United States on tests of letter sounds. These differences diminish over time. In either case, children work with what they know about the labels they use to refer to letters as they write words they don't already know how to spell. While Parmis might use letter name Q to represent the first sound in the word *cute*, spelling *cute QT*, her counterpart in England might use the letter sound of Q (e.g., /kwu/) to represent the initial sound in Kwanza, spelling *Kwanza* QONZO. In either case children use what they know to invent a spelling for a word they don't know how to spell conventionally. In Ellefson et al.'s words, " . . . children learn what they are taught. There are no intrinsic differences in the ease of learning between conventional letter names and sounds that are strong enough to overcome the effects of experience" (p. 338).

Treiman and Broderick (1998): *What's in a Name*

The effects of experience are personal and profound. Thanks to the seminal research of Treiman and Broderick (1998) we've moved beyond the either–or thinking of letter names versus letter sounds to consider the effects of children's earliest experiences with letters, specifically the letters in their own names. Treiman and Broderick demonstrated that the identity and characteristics of the first letter of a child's first name (or nickname) has a significant effect on the child's knowledge of letter names, such that children named Sam or Sarah are more likely to know the name of the letter S than are children named Alfred or Parmis. While they did not find similar effects of children's first name on their knowledge of letter sounds, subsequent studies, using larger samples and more sophisticated analytic strategies, have demonstrated an "own-name advantage" for letter sounds as well (Huang, Tortorelli, & Invernizzi, 2014, p. 190). When children are exposed to the spellings of their own names, they have many opportunities to associate the first letter with the first-letter name and the first sound of their name. The own-name advantage discovered initially by Treiman and Broderick (1998) has important implications for personalizing and differentiating instruction.

Treiman and Broderick also broadened our thinking about children's alphabet knowledge. Prior to their 1998 study, "What's in a Name: Children's Knowledge about the Letters in Their Own Names," the term *alphabet knowledge* was used rather vaguely. Researchers rarely disambiguated letter names from letter sounds and almost never considered children's ability to either print letters or to make decisions about which letters or sounds to use in writing words. Treiman and Broderick, however, found that the own-name advantage made a significant difference in the ability to print letters in addition to naming them. Although their study did not yield similar results for tasks that required the use of letter sounds, children's performance on the letter–sound tasks was affected by the position of the letter's associated sound within the letter name. Specifically, children in the Treiman and Broderick study performed better on letter–sound tasks when the sound that the letter represents was present at the beginning of the letter name. For example, the /b/ sound is positioned at the beginning of the letter name *B* (bee). Researchers refer to such letter names as *acrophonic* CV (consonant–vowel) names because the sound that the letter represents in spoken words is in the beginning position or *onset* of the letter's name. The letters *B* (bee), *D* (dee), *J* (jay), *K* (kay), *P* (pee), *T* (tee), *V* (vee), and *Z* (zee) are all acrophonic CV letter names. On the other hand, letters, such as *F* (eff), *L* (el), *M* (em), *N* (en), *R* (ar), and *S* (es), share a VC *acrophonic* (vowel–consonant) structure, because the sound that the letter represents is at the end of the letter's name. Other researchers have since corroborated the finding that children learn the sounds of CV letters, such as *B*, *D*, and *J*, more easily than the sounds of VC letters, such as *F*, *L*, or *N* (McBride-Chang, 1999; Huang et al., 2014), and both types of acrophonic letter names are superior to nonacrophonic letters, such as *W* (double you) or *Y* (why), that don't contain the sound in their name at all. So, while Treiman and Broderick did not find an own-name advantage for letter–sound tasks or tasks that required children to make decisions about the beginning sounds or initial letters of words, performance on these tasks was improved by the presence of the sound the letter represents in the letter name. This finding was important because it suggested that "children use the names of letters to learn and remember their sounds" (Treiman & Broderick, p. 112). Further, this approach appears to be prompted when the speech sound that a letter represents is positioned at the beginning or onset of the letter's name.

While subsequent research has contributed further nuances about these findings, Treiman and Broderick's seminal study "What's in a Name" (1998) opened the door to unpacking what Rieben and Perfetti (2013) called the *cryptanalytic intent*, which is necessary to acquire the alphabetic principle, something Alfred, Ms. Meyer's student, sorely needed. To acquire the alphabetic principle children must first become aware that there is a "system of correspondences" that exist and must intentionally begin to analyze those correspondences (p. 34). Children's strong attraction to their own names may help them develop the cryptanalytic intent necessary to start to analyze the letters, first within their own names, and later, perhaps in other words. This may help explain the progression from level one to level two in Mason's "natural hierarchy" in the development of learning to read words, when children appear to be analyzing letters within words. "Just as personal names appear to play a special role in the development of spoken language, so names may be important in the development of literacy" (Treiman & Broderick, p. 114).

WHICH ONES FIRST?

Lee was at her orientation for the daycare/preschool class she would start attending in the fall. As part of that orientation she was shown the "cubby" area where she would have her very own space to store her backpack and clothes. Each cubby was labeled with a child's name. To Lee's dismay, other children's cubby labels also included an L, a letter she considered hers and only hers. A temper tantrum ensued.

Given Treiman and Broderick's (1998) findings about the own-name advantage for learning letter names, it stands to reason that Lee would have an intense cryptanalytic intent to decipher all the *els* in the world. Mason (1980) would have applauded her progress along the natural hierarchy of emergent literacy! But does it stand to reason that letter–sound instruction should always begin with the grapheme–phoneme correspondences associated with children's names, or are there other factors to consider? Given the wide range of names within a classroom, does it make sense to start with Alfred and continue in alphabetic order (e.g., Bianca, Cailin, Deja, then Fern)? Should some names be "put off" until later because of ambiguities in the pronunciation of their letter sound? How would we explain the grapheme–phoneme correspondence for the first letter in José's name, for example? And what about names that start with difficult to elongate first sounds, like the first phoneme in the name *Deja*, in which the /d/ sound cannot be held and stretched out without distortion, as opposed to the first phoneme in the name Zavon, in which the /z/ sound can be held indefinitely?

Treiman, Tincoff, Rodriguez, Mouzaki, and Francis (1998): *The Foundations of Literacy: Learning the Sounds of Letters*

In a second landmark study, Treiman, Tincoff, Rodriguez, Mouzaki, and Francis (1998) tried to untangle important questions such as these by exploring more deeply the linguistic characteristics of letter names that facilitate or hinder children's learning of letter sounds. Specifically, they explored (1) the relative effects of letter–name structures on learning letter sounds, (2) the ambiguity of the associated letter sound, and (3) linguistic properties of the phoneme associated with the letter sound. *Letter–name structure* refers to the acrophonic existence or nonexistence of the associated letter sound embedded within the letter name (e.g., the letter *B* has the phoneme /b/ in the name, while the letter *W* does not have the /w/ sound in its name). Letter–name structure also refers to the position of the sound within an acrophonic letter name (e.g., the letter name *B* [bee] has a CV structure, whereas the letter *F* [eff] has a VC structure). The *ambiguity of the letter sound* refers to alternative pronunciations (e.g., the letter sound for *G* can be pronounced two ways: /gee/ or /guh/. The *linguistic properties of the phoneme* associated with the letter sound refer to how the associated phoneme is produced. The letter sounds for *obstruent* consonants obstruct or restrict air (e.g., stop consonants such as *B*, *P*, and *T* obstruct, then release, air; fricatives such as *S*, *Z*, and *V* restrict air). *Sonorants* include the vowels and certain consonants that are produced with continuous air flow that is not obstructed or restricted (e.g., /r/). Many educators believe that letter–sound instruction should begin with grapheme–phoneme correspondences that are obstruent, particularly fricatives (e.g., *F*, *S*, *V*), because the fricative sound (e.g., /zzzzzzz/ can be "held" and emphasized without distortion. In the latter case, the first sound in Zavon's name, a fricative, would be taught earlier in the lineup of grapheme–phoneme correspondences than Parmis's name, despite the fact that the letter *Z* appears last in the alphabet.

Treiman and colleagues (1998) were the first to explore these issues. In a series of related studies, they found once again that children performed better on letter sounds when the sound was in the letter name than when it was not. In other words, children learned more letter sounds when the letters were acrophonic than when they were not. Children did especially well when the associated letter sound was positioned at the beginning of the letter name (e.g., a CV structure, such as in *B* [bee]). Conversely, children performed more poorly on ambiguous sounds or on letters that had more than one associated letter sound (e.g., *C*, *G*, and all the vowels). They did not find consistent evidence for the type of phoneme associated with the letter sound (e.g., obstruent versus sonorant). Nevertheless, Treiman et al. (1998) demonstrated that the linguistic characteristics of a letter's name influence children's ability to learn its letter sound, even when other factors were statistically controlled. Specifically, they demonstrated positive effects for acrophonic letter–name structures, deleterious effects for letter–sound ambiguity, and no effects for the linguistic properties of the phoneme associated with the letter sound itself. Future researchers, extrapolating from this work, would corroborate these findings using stricter controls and more sophisticated analytic strategies. Share (2004), for example, demonstrated the letter–name advantage in learning letter sounds in Hebrew, entitling his study *Knowing Letter Names and Learning Letter Sounds: A Causal Connection.*

How can these two pivotal studies inform the questions teachers have about teaching letter recognition and letter sounds? First, their work suggests that one of the most important influences on learning letter names has to do with children's experiences with their own names. As Lee demonstrated, children have an emotional attachment to the letters in their name, particularly the initial letter, and they will likely learn those letters first. Second, at least in the United States, knowing letter names actually helps children learn letter sounds because most letter names contain the sound within them (*bee* has /b/ in the name). Those that don't are harder to learn. Instead of memorizing letter–sound links as rote-paired associates, children "try to make sense of their relations based on what they know about letter names and the sounds the name contains" (Treiman et al., 1998, p. 1537). Third, their work demonstrated that linguistic differences embedded in letter names demand different amounts of instructional time. Nonacrophonic letters, or those that do not contain the associated letter sound in the name itself, will take more instructional time than acrophonic letters, and letters that have more than one associated sound (C, G, and J in *José*) will need more time still. Fourth, their work suggests that the linguistic properties related to the way a phoneme is produced (e.g., obstruent or sonorant), has less bearing on children's uptake of the associated letter sound. The first sound in Zavon's name, which can easily be elongated, should be no less difficult than the first sound in Deja's, which can't. Finally, when considered alongside the work of Mason (1980), the research of Treiman and Broderick (1998) and Treiman et al. (1998) suggests that letter–name knowledge can bridge the gap between visual-cue strategies of the prereader to phonetic-cue strategies of early literacy. Letter–name knowledge can facilitate early printed word recognition even before children have achieved an awareness of letter sounds or the alphabetic principle (Foulin, 2005)

IN WHAT ORDER SHOULD LETTERS BE TAUGHT?

Ms. Taylor is a first-year kindergarten teacher. She learned some instructional activities for teaching the alphabet in her teacher education program, such as name of the day (Cunningham, 2016), letter and picture sorts (Bear, Invernizzi, Templeton, & Johnston, 2016), and using student-made alphabet books (Murry, Stahl, & Ivy, 1996). But Ms. Taylor is still uncertain about the exact sequence of instruction. Should she teach a letter a week, starting with A and continuing to Z? Should she teach uppercase or lowercase letters first—or maybe both simultaneously? Should she teach the consonants in the order in which children learn to produce them in speech development—bilabials like B and M first, and so on? What about starting with the most frequently occurring letters—the letters that children will see most often in early picture books and on word walls?

Even though we know that U.S. children typically learn letter names before learning letter sounds and that they learn the letters in their own names first, many teachers struggle with decisions about letter order or the optimal sequence for instruction. A quick internet search for an answer to the question "In what order do I teach the alphabet?" yields a long list of suggestions, ranging from working through the alphabet systematically, starting with A and proceeding to Z (e.g., letter-of-the-week method) to specific letter sequences that will allow children to form words right way (e.g., Jolly Phonics). Some advocate teaching the letters *s, a, t, i, p,* and *n* first because children can then "build" many words using combinations of those letters right away (e.g., *sit, sat, tap, tip, pit, pat, pan, tan*). Others insist on starting letter–sound instruction with continuants, which are consonants that are pronounced with the vocal tract partially open, allowing the air to pass through and the sound to be prolonged (e.g., *f, l, m, n, r, s, v*). This belief prevails despite Treiman et al.'s earlier finding that the linguistic properties of the phoneme itself (e.g., obstruent vs. sonorant) did not make an appreciable difference (1998, p. 1535).

Advancing the work of Mason (1980), Treiman and Broderick (1998), and Treiman et al. (1998), later researchers sought to tease out other questions related to the association of letter names and letter sounds and to explore additional issues that might inform Ms. Taylor's instructional planning. The research of McBride-Chang (1999), for example, corroborated Mason and Treiman et al.'s findings but also demonstrated developmental changes that occurred from the beginning of kindergarten to the middle of first grade. McBride-Chang concluded that letter names and letter sounds are "differentially associated" with literacy development (p. 302). She particularly noted the strengthening associations between letter–sound knowledge, phonological awareness, and invented spelling as children get closer to actually reading. Germane to Ms. Taylor's dilemma, McBride-Chang's research demonstrated that both letter–name and letter–sound knowledge were indeed correlated with alphabetic letter order, with higher correlations favoring the beginning of the alphabet (p. 304), perhaps because of the cultural emphasis on the beginning of the alphabet song and the primacy effects of reciting the alphabet in order The pervasive use of the letter-of-the-week approach to alphabet instruction, starting with A and moving forward, could also result in dissymmetric advantages for letters appearing earlier in the lineup. Of note too is the fact that more non-acrophonic letters appear in the latter half of the alphabet, a fact that would argue for more instructional time to be allotted to those letters (e.g., *w, x, y*).

Justice, Pence, Bowles, and Wiggins (2006) explored the letter-order issue further using a more sophisticated analytic strategy that yielded odds ratios expressed as probabilities for knowing letter names. They investigated four hypotheses concerning the order in which 4-year-olds learn uppercase letters of the alphabet: (1) Treiman and Broderick's (1998) own-name advantage; (2) Treiman et al.'s (1998) letter–name structures; (3) McBride-Chang's (1999) letter order; and (4) the importance of Ms. Taylor's concern about the order of consonant production in speech production. They reaffirmed Treiman and Broderick's (1998) and Treiman et al.'s (1998) findings in spades: Children are 1.5 times more likely to know the letters in their first name, 7.5 times more likely to know the letter of their first initial, and 1.8 times more likely to know acrophonic letter names than nonacrophonic letter names, such as *w* or *y*. They also reaffirmed McBride-Chang's findings: children were 1.02 times more likely to know letter names positioned earlier in the alphabetic lineup. However, they found only a modest advantage for the order of consonant production in speech development.

But what about the order in which uppercase and lowercase letters should be taught and letter frequency in print, other concerns of Ms. Taylor? Turnbull, Bowles, Skibbe, Justice, and Wiggins (2010) investigated this issue too, along with, once again, Treiman and Broderick's own-name advantage. They found that children's familiarity with uppercase letters was the strongest predictor of children's lowercase letter knowledge. In fact, children were 16 times more likely to know a lowercase letter if they already knew the corresponding upper-case one. This is not surprising, given that uppercase letters are more visually distinctive than many lowercase letters that present mirror images such as *b*, *d*, *p*, and *q* (Clay, 1975). The degree of visual similarity between the upper- and lowercase letters also predicted children's lowercase letter knowledge. Letters like *C*, *K*, *O*, *S*, *V*, *W*, *X*, and *Z* are visually identical in the upper- and lower-case forms and differ only in size, whereas letters like *B* or *G* have completely different shapes in the upper- and lowercases. Lowercase letters that had dis-similar shapes compared with their lowercase forms were much less likely to be known. The frequency with which lowercase letters occur in printed English also predicted children's lowercase letter knowledge. The letter *e* (the most frequently occurring lowercase letter in printed English) was 3.8 times more likely to be correctly identified than the letter *q* (the least frequent lowercase letter), while controlling for the familiarity of the corresponding uppercase letter, for upper- and lowercase similarities, and for whether the letter was the first one in the child's name. But unlike the previous research, Turnbull et al. (2010) also demonstrated interactions among the variables, meaning that the effects of one variable on a second variable depended to some extent on the involvement of a third variable. Specifically, they demonstrated a connec-tion between uppercase familiarity and the own-name advantage and between uppercase familiarity and upper- and lowercase similarities. Overall, Turnbull et al.'s (2010) results suggest that knowledge of uppercase letters generalizes to the learning of lowercase letters, the acquisition of which is multiply deter-mined by other factors, such as whether the letter is the first initial of the child's name and the degree of visual similarity between corresponding upper- and lowercase letters.

Huang and Invernizzi (2012) extended this line of research by investigating five hypotheses about knowledge of lowercase letter names simultaneously—many of the same ones previously discussed and some new ones, such as visual and phonological confusability. *Visual confusability* was based on a letter's visual similarity to other letters (e.g., *b/d*; *p/q*), whereas *phonological confusability* was based on shared phonemes within the letter name (e.g., *bee* and *pee* share the phoneme *ee*). All of the hypotheses were tested simultaneously within a single multilevel model in which the variables included also acted as controls for all the other hypotheses tested. For example, a child named *Oscar* may know the lowercase letter *o* because this letter is the first initial of his name, because the upper- and lowercase similarity of the letter is high, and/or because *o* is a frequently occurring letter. Like Turnbull et al. (2010), their results showed that lowercase letter knowledge is determined by multiple factors that are intrinsic to the child (i.e., knowing the letters their own name), based on the letter itself (i.e., letter name structure, similarity to other letters, uppercase similarity, and letter order), or influenced by the environment (i.e., letter frequency). All five hypotheses contributed to a child's lowercase letter knowledge, although odds ratios and effect sizes indicated that the own-name advantage, upper-and lowercase similarities, and visual confusability had the greatest association with lowercase letter–name knowledge. Letter order, phonological confusability, and letter frequency, which also yielded statistically significant results, had effect sizes that were much smaller in comparison. Altogether, Huang and Invernizzi's (2012) findings indicate that the own-name advantage and upper- and lowercase similarities help children learn lowercase letter names, while visual confusability among lowercase letters (e.g., *b/d*) make it more difficult.

In a follow-up study, Huang et al. (2014) used a similar methodology to explore children's knowledge of letter sounds. Six hypotheses were tested simultaneously, many of which were derived from the original work of Treiman and Broderick (1998) and Treiman et al. (1998) (1) the own-name advantage, (2) letter–name knowledge, (3) letter–name structure effects, (4) letter–sound ambiguities, (5) the facilitative effects of children's phonological awareness, and (6) interactions between phonological awareness and letter–name structure. Their results, using three-level multilevel modeling, indicated that like letter names, letter sounds have varying levels of difficulty, and several child- and letter-related factors were associated with children's knowledge of letter sounds. Child-level factors included Treiman and Broderick's (1998) and Treiman et al.'s (1998) own-name advantage, letter–name knowledge, and phonological awareness. Children were more likely to know a letter sound if it was the first letter of their own name and if they also knew the letter name. Medium effects were noted for children's degree of phonological awareness. Letter-related factors included letter–name structures (e.g., CV or VC letter–name structures versus nonacrophonic letter names) and letter–sound ambiguity (e.g., letters that are associated with more than one sound or that share a sound with another letter). There was a significant association between children's phonological awareness and letter–name structures. The probability of knowing a letter sound increased with greater levels of phonological awareness, when the letter name was known, and when a letter name was acrophonic. Thus, coming full circle back to the 1998 pioneering studies of Treiman and colleagues, Huang and colleagues (2014) extended findings that were previously demonstrated only for letter names to letter sounds as well.

Several of the researchers discussed in this chapter have concluded that "all letters are not equal" and have questioned the wisdom of teaching a letter a week, a long-standing instructional method for teaching the alphabet in American kindergarten classrooms. Constructing a curriculum around letter order (e.g., starting at the beginning of the alphabet and continuing from there, one letter at a time), does not acknowledge the differential difficulty of certain letter names and sounds or the variety in children's personal experiences with letters and print in their home, daycare, or preschool environments. Rather than teaching one letter a day or one letter a week, Ms. Taylor should consider how she might organize multifaceted teaching approaches that take into account the child, letter, and environmental characteristics that the research of Mason (1980), the 1998 studies of Treiman and colleagues, and others have shown to be important.

WHAT SHOULD INSTRUCTION LOOK LIKE?

Henry sprawls out on the carpet to practice his writing. After a couple minutes, he proudly shows his teacher his whiteboard. He's filled up the entire board with five neat rows of random letters. "What does this say?" he asks. Clearly Henry understands that print conveys meaning, but has yet to recognize the connection between letters and sounds. The teacher pauses. There's no way to make sense of his random string of letters. "What were you trying to say?" she asks. "Katie came to play," he replies. "Hmm. Henry, what letters would you need to spell Ka-tie? she says, emphasizing each syllable. He looks at her and hesitates. Then suddenly, like a light switch has been flipped, he says, "Oh. K T!" He furiously erases his whiteboard and then deliberately writes K T as he pronounces each syllable.

Henry illustrates an *ah ha* moment in early literacy development—a tentative first step toward the alphabetic principle, the understanding that speech can be divided into smaller bits of sound and matched to alphabetic letters that represent them. Becoming aware of the alphabetic principle marks a developmental shift from context-dependent pretend reading and writing to print-reliant real reading and writing.

While Henry's decision to use letter names to represent the sound of each syllable in *Katie* may seem sudden, his insight is probably the culmination of intentional instruction over time. Research that explores how to teach alphabet knowledge suggests there are two key aspects of intentional alphabet instruction: (1) direct instruction of letter names and sounds and (2) contextualized instruction for *applying* such knowledge to read words in connected text and to write them on paper or whiteboards.

Experimental research exploring the effects of alphabet instruction suggest that explicit instruction in letter names and sounds is necessary but insufficient for transferring this knowledge to other areas of literacy. Piasta, Purpura, and Wagner (2010), for example, demonstrated that children who received both letter–name and letter–sound instruction group learned significantly more letter names and sounds than children in the letter–sounds-only group, but they found little evidence that alphabet instruction transferred to other early literacy skills. Piasta et al. (2010) conjectured that this lack of transfer may have occurred because the sole focus of the experimental instruction was on letter names and letter sounds and excluded the application of that knowledge to contextual reading and writing.

Other studies have specifically explored the transfer of alphabet knowledge to other early literacy skills such as word reading. In a series of word learning experiments, for example, Ehri and Wilce (1985) organized kindergartners into three groups based on their initial ability to read words, roughly equivalent to Mason's (1980) previous three levels. *Prereaders* recognized no words, *novices* recognized some words, and *veterans* recognized several words. All children were taught to recognize simplified phonetic spellings (e.g., *JRF* for *giraffe*) and visually distinct nonphonetic spellings (e.g., *uHe* for *mask*). Prereaders had more success reading the visually distinct spellings, while novice and veteran readers learned the phonetic spellings. Ehri and Wilce concluded that alphabet knowledge enables children to use phonetic cues instead of visual cues, which in turn allows them to retain words in memory (1985, p. 74). Roberts (2003) applied these findings to an instructional setting by examining the effects of alphabet–letter instruction on young children's word recognition. Thirty-three preschoolers received instruction in either alphabet letter names or comprehension. After the lessons, Roberts compared their recognition of phonetically spelled words that included letters they had been taught (e.g., *BL* for *ball*), with phonetically spelled words that included letters they had *not* been taught (e.g., *ZR* for *zipper*), and with visually distinct spellings that were *not* phonetic (e.g., *cN* for *ball*). The preschoolers who received alphabet instruction in letter names were able to recognize and remember simplified phonetic spellings better than the nonphonetic spellings; the opposite was true for the preschoolers who received the comprehension-only instruction. Moreover, the preschoolers receiving the alphabet letter–name instruction recognized more phonetically spelled words when they contained the letters that had been previously taught. Roberts concluded that these results showed that "phonetic spellings were only advantageous when the prereaders had received extensive prior instruction on the letter names included in the spellings" (2003, p. 49). Taken together, these researchers demonstrated that alphabet instruction can be applied to early word learning with instructional support that intentionally links letter names to phonemes in print. Henry's teacher was right on target to encourage his phonetic spelling of Katie using the names K and T.

Treiman and colleagues' 1998 work implied that letter–sound knowledge and phonological awareness, rather than being two distinct underpinnings of emergent literacy, were closely intertwined. Boyer and Ehri (2011) leveraged that idea to explore whether deliberate efforts to link phonological aspects of letter sounds to letter forms would further support children's word learning. This intentional linking involved pairing the letter with a picture of how to form the letter's associated speech sound in the mouth—the articulatory gesture of the letter sound. Sixty nonreading preschoolers were taught to divide words into individual phonemes using either letters only or the letters paired with a picture of its corresponding articulatory gesture. The preschoolers who were instructed to divide words with both letters and pictures of their corresponding articulatory gestures learned to read more words than the children in the letter only group. In this study, Boyer and Ehri (2011) showed that deliberately supporting the linkages between letters and the phonemes of their associated letter sounds facilitates the application of the alphabetic principle to word learning.

How can we contextualize all that we've learned about alphabet instruction and its connection to other important early literacy skills to the classroom? One approach to alphabet instruction is known as enhanced alphabet knowledge (EAK; Jones & Reutzel, 2012; Jones, Clark, & Reutzel, 2013). Drawing on key studies related to alphabet knowledge (e.g., Mason, 1980; Piasta & Wagner, 2010a; Treiman et al., 1998), EAK represents a shift from the traditional letter-of-the week, one-size-fits-all approach to a more comprehensive, inclusive approach that incorporates opportunities for application and transfer to reading and writing. All EAK lessons include teacher modeling and student-guided practice. Three components of EAK lessons incorporate the existing evidence base related to (1) naming the letter and producing the corresponding speech sound, (2) identifying the letter in text, and (3) writing the letter. During lessons, students work with both the uppercase and lowercase letter forms, and teachers provide explicit directions for how to produce the speech sound (e.g., "When I say the sound /__/, I place my tongue and mouth like this __"; Jones, Clark, & Reutzel, 2013, p. 83) and how to form the letter (e.g., "Here's where I begin on the paper lines to write the letter __"; Jones, Clark, & Reutzel, 2013, p. 83). These daily lessons are brief—lasting 10–12 minutes—and build on each other through distributed cycles of review.

Unlike traditional lessons, which devote equal amounts of time to each letter and slowly move through the alphabet at a letter-a-week pace, EAK lessons move at a quicker pace and allow students to spend additional time with more difficult letters (e.g., visually similar letters, letters with multiple sounds, nonacrophonic letters, and letters in the middle of the alphabet). EAK lessons are organized into six instructional cycles that capitalize on the research about which letters children tend to learn more easily and which letters they tend to find more challenging. These six cycles employ the results from studies engendered by Mason (1980) and Treiman and colleagues (1998): (1) own-name advantage—select letters based on frequency of initial letter in children's names; (2) alphabetical-order advantage—teach all 26 letters in 26 days, starting with *a* and ending with *z*; (3) letter–name and letter–sound relationship advantage—begin with acrophonic consonants with the associated letter sound embedded at the beginning of the name (CV), then at end of the name (VC), and finally letters with more than one sound and nonacrophonic letters; (4) letter-frequency advantage—focus on letters occurring less frequently in text; (5) consonant–phoneme acquisition-order advantage—focus on letters with sounds that are potentially more difficult to produce (e.g., *l, r, v, z, sh, ch, j, zh, th*); (6) distinctive-visual-features-letter-writing advantage—emphasize critical differences between similar letters (e.g., "first we have an O, add a tail, and it becomes a *Q*"; Jones, Clark, & Reutzel, 2013, p. 87). Jones et al. (2013) point out that multiple instructional cycles provide formative information about children's differential alphabet knowledge, which makes it possible for teachers to differentiate instruction through subsequent adjustments to pacing and exposure (p. 84).

A multitude of studies (e.g., Jones & Reutzel, 2012; Roberts, 2003; Piasta et al., 2010b; Piasta & Wagner, 2010a; Piasta & Wagner, 2010c) have demonstrated the importance of direct instruction for alphabet learning. They underscore the value of learning letter names and sounds but also the value of leveraging that learning through the recognition of the letters in text, forming letters in writing, and applying alphabetic knowledge to reading simplified, phonetically spelled words (e.g., *GRF* for *giraffe*) and other printed words in books and in the environment. But how else can teachers support the transfer of alphabet knowledge to other important early literacy behaviors, such as attending to and analyzing print? After all, a major difference between Mason's level-one and level-two students pertained to their treatment of printed words as different from pictures. Horner (2001) and Wasik (2001) both explored this issue by developing the insights provided by Mason (1980).

Mason (1980) offered a picture of what our earliest instruction might look like by describing what and how children learned prior to formal schooling. As she explained, "with substantial help from parents and teachers who answer their questions about Sesame Street and point out and quiz them about signs, who reread alphabet books and stories until children have them memorized, who help them spell and print words, and who coach them to try to identify letters and words, children begin to extrapolate some of the critical relationships between sounds of words and sounds of letters" (p. 221). In Mason's study, children developed a solid foundation for alphabet knowledge and early reading through everyday interactions that capitalized on their natural curiosity about *the print* they encountered in their environments.

To learn to read, children must first become "conscious of print"—both of its function and its form (Clay, 1991), and this consciousness can be facilitated though intentionally prompted interactions with print. Horner (2001) explored such interactions in an experimental study in which preschool children were randomly assigned to one of three video conditions that prompted their attention to either the pictures in the book, the print in the book, or neither. In the first condition, children observed other children on videotape asking questions about the *pictures*. In the second condition, children observed other children on videotape asking questions about the *print*. In the third condition children observed other children who were not asking any questions about either the pictures or the print. Horner (2001) found that children who watched others ask questions about the print subsequently made more print-related comments than the children who observed others asking picture-related questions or no questions at all. Although no differences in children's alphabet knowledge were revealed after the children observed any of the videotaped models, Horner (2001) demonstrated that children can be taught to attend to print by observing models of other children focusing on and asking questions about the printed word.

Motivating children to shift their attention from pictures to the printed word is an essential early literacy behavior if we want them to make connections between alphabet instruction and reading and writing. When teachers draw children's attention to print in explicit ways and "think aloud" about the many ways they use print, they are practicing what Justice and Ezell (2004) call *print referencing*. When teachers use print referencing during read-alouds by naming or pointing out letters, by asking questions about print, and by pointing to words as they read, children show growth on measures of print concepts, letter recognition, and name writing (Justice, Kaderavek, Fan, Sofka, & Hunt, 2009), with lasting effects on reading, spelling, and comprehension 2 years beyond preschool (Piasta, Justice, McGinty, & Kaderavek, 2012). Print referencing is another way to foster connections between alphabet instruction and reading.

Wasik (2001) argued that while young children may be able to memorize the letters of the alphabet through rote drill and practice, such practices "may not have meaning to the children and may not facilitate the longer-term goal of reading" (p. 35). Wasik (2001) and Bredekamp and Copple (1997) advocated contextualizing alphabet instruction in meaningful and "developmentally appropriate" ways that connect to reading and writing. For Wasik, "developmentally appropriate practices" meant beginning with the familiar (e.g., children's own names) and creating instructional contexts, such as print referencing, that make it possible to link alphabet knowledge to books and print. Like Chomsky (1971) and Clay (1975) before her, Wasik recommended that in addition to using direct instruction for letter names and sounds, early childhood teachers should provide opportunities for writing as frequently as possible. To successfully engage children in writing, Gerde, Bingham, and Wasik (2012) offered a set of recommendations for weaving writing into the daily schedule of early childhood classrooms. Early childhood teachers can even encourage independent writing, which will vary depending on an individual child's literacy development. Some children will scribble; others will use letterlike shapes and then random letters. With practice, they will use increasingly phonetic invented spelling in which they represent the sounds they hear in words (Johnston, Invernizzi, Helman, Bear, & Templeton, 2014).

Wasik's focus on the application of alphabet knowledge to reading and writing highlights earlier conclusions drawn by Mason (1980), Treiman and Broderick (1998), Treiman et al. (1998), and later researchers on instruction. Teachers can follow an intentional sequence (e.g., Jones & Reutzel, 2012). Also, teachers can make letter–name knowledge meaningful and exciting by capitalizing on children's interest in and motivation to learn the letters in their own names (e.g., Mason, 1980; Treiman & Broderick, 1998; Treiman et al., 1998). Finally, letter–name knowledge and letter–sound learning can be connected to print and writing (Justice & Ezell, 2004; Justice et al., 2009; Wasik, 2001). Alternatives to the pervasive letter-of-the-week approach capitalize on these basic tenets and include differentiated alphabet instruction; letter and picture sorting; and lessons integrating alphabet knowledge with phonological awareness, print awareness, and writing. As shown in Table 4.1, there are many resources available for teachers who are interested in making alphabetic

TABLE 4.1. Instructional Approaches and Resources for Alphabetic Instruction

Differentiated Alphabet Instruction (Piasta, 2014)

A framework for assessment-guided alphabet instruction to meet a range of student needs in a classroom. Features a set of guidelines for teachers to consider when choosing which letters to teach.

No More Teaching a Letter a Week (McKay & Teale, 2015)

A description of intentional and systematic alphabet instruction situated within meaningful practice. Features a set of recommended practices.

Emergent Literacy: Lessons for Success
(Cabell, Justice, Kaderavek, Pence, & Breit-Smith, 2009)

Features a set of code-related lesson plans designed for early readers and writers. Integrates early literacy skills including alphabet knowledge, print awareness, phonological awareness, and writing.

Words Their Way Letter and Picture Sorts for Emergent Spellers
(Bear, Invernizzi, Johnston, & Templeton, 2018)

Provides materials to plan for letter–sound contrasts. Compares and contrasts features of letters and connects alphabet learning with print concepts, phonological awareness, and writing.

Writing in Early Childhood Classrooms: Guidance for Best Practices
(Gerde, Bingham, & Wasik, 2012)

Features a set of recommendations for incorporating writing into the daily classroom schedule. Encourages children to apply their growing alphabet knowledge.

TABLE 4.2. Evidence-Based Principles and Practices for Alphabet Learning and Instruction

- Children are more likely to learn the letters in their own name first (especially the first initial), so being systematic with activities such as "name of the day" is likely to be effective.

- Learning letter names helps children learn letter sounds because most letter names contain the sound in them (B [bee] has /b/ in the name). Letters that don't have the associated sound in their name (and letters than have more than one sound associated with their name) are harder to learn and will require more instructional time.

- Lowercase letters that resemble their uppercase partners are easier to learn than lowercase letters that don't resemble their uppercase partners.

- Certain letters occur in print, in names, and in the environment more frequently than others. Frequently occurring letters will be easier to learn than those that appear less frequently.

- Letter–shape confusability (*b–d; p–q; u–n*) makes those letters harder to learn and will require more instructional time. It might be best to avoid teaching these letters back to back at first.

- It may be helpful to compare and contrast the shapes, names, and sounds of letters at least two letters (if not three or four) at a time, so children can observe and discuss the differences among them.

- Alphabet instruction is enhanced when it is also linked to print—in the environment, in writing, and in the books children are read.

---

instruction meaningful, purposeful, and motivating, even as early as the preschool years.

CONCLUSION

There is no one "right" way to teach children about the alphabet. Rather, there are evidence-based principles and practices derived from pivotal research pertaining to factors about the child, the letters themselves, and the context that influence alphabet learning and instruction. These principles are summarized in Table 4.2.

Teachers who understand the many child, letter, and contextual factors reviewed here can ask themselves a series of questions that will help them make intentional decisions in addressing the differential needs of each student. First and foremost among those questions is asking what each child already knows about alphabet letters—what they look like, how they are formed, what they are used for, their equivalents in upper- and lowercases, and their associated letter sounds. Finding out what each child knows about the alphabet requires an assessment of a range of skills, in isolation, and in literate contexts, that will lead to the acquisition the alphabetic principle: phonological awareness, letter names, letter sounds, and the application of these skills in writing and in puzzling out words in print (Invernizzi & Tortorelli, 2013). Alfred and Lee knew the letters in their own names. Henry had just taken his first tentative steps toward applying his letter–name knowledge in writing. Parmis was already using letter names and some letter sounds to represent phonemes in words and in constructing sentences. Armed with the evidence base discussed here, Ms. Meyer and Ms. Taylor can differentiate their alphabet instruction to move each of these children forward in Mason's (1980) "natural hierarchy" of alphabet knowledge toward literacy.

REFERENCES

Bear, D., Invernizzi, M., Johnston, F., & Templeton, S. (2018). *Words their way letter and picture sorts for emergent spellers* (3rd ed.). Boston: Pearson.

Bear, D., Invernizzi, M., Templeton, S., & Johnston, F. (2016). *Words their way: Word study for phonics spelling, and vocabulary instruction* (6th ed.). Boston: Pearson.

Boyer, N., & Ehri, L. C. (2011). Contribution of phonemic segmentation instruction with letters and articulation pictures to word reading and spelling in beginners. *Scientific Studies of Reading, 15,* 440–470.

Bredekamp, S., & Copple, C. (1997). *Developmentally appropriate practice in early childhood programs.* Washington, DC: National Association for the Education of Young Children.

Cabell, S. Q., Justice, L. M., Kaderavek, J., Pence, K. L., & Breit-Smith, A. (2008). *Emergent literacy: Lessons for success.* San Diego, CA: Plural Publishing.

Chomsky, C. (1971). Write first, read later. *Childhood Education, 47,* 296–299.

Clay, M. M. (1966). *Emergent reading behavior.* Unpublished doctoral dissertation. University of Auckland, New Zealand.

Clay, M. M. (1975). *What did I write?: Beginning writing behavior.* Portsmouth, NH: Heinemann Educational Books.

Clay, M. M. (1977). *Reading: The patterning of complex behavior.* Portsmouth, NH: Heinemann Educational Books.

Clay, M. M. (1991). *Becoming literate: The construction of inner control.* Portsmouth, NH: Heinemann Educational Books.

Core Knowledge Foundation. (2013). *Core knowledge sequence: Content and skill guidelines for preschool.* Charlottesville, VA: Author.

Cunningham, P. (2016). *Phonics they use: Words for reading and writing* (7th ed.). Boston: Pearson.

Downing, J. (1970). Relevance versus ritual in reading. *Literacy, 4*(2), 4–12.

Ehri, L. C. (1975). Word consciousness in readers and prereaders. *Journal of Educational Psychology, 67*(2), 204–212.

Ehri, L. C., & Wilce, L. S. (1985). Movement into reading: Is the first stage of printed word learning visual or phonetic? *Reading Research Quarterly, 20,* 163–179.

Ellefson, M., Treiman, R., & Kessler, B. (2009). Learning to label letters by sounds or names: A comparison of England and the United States. *Journal of Experimental Child Psychology, 102,* 323–341.

Foulin, J. N. (2005). Why is letter–name knowledge such a good predictor of learning to read? *Reading and Writing, 18*, 129–155.

Gerde, H. K., Bingham, G. E., & Wasik, B. A. (2012). Writing in early childhood classrooms: Guidance for best practices. *Early Childhood Education Journal, 40*, 351–359.

Horner, S. L. (2001). The effects of observational learning on preschoolers' book-related behaviors and alphabet knowledge. *Child Study Journal, 31*, 1–11.

Huang, F., & Invernizzi, M. (2012). The case for confusability and other factors associated with lowercase alphabet naming in kindergartners. *Applied Psycholinguistics, 35*, 943–968.

Huang, F. L., Tortorelli, L. S., & Invernizzi, M. A. (2014). An investigation of factors associated with letter-sound knowledge at kindergarten entry. *Early Childhood Research Quarterly, 29*, 182–192.

Invernizzi, M., Juel, C., Swank, L., & Meier, J. (2015). *Phonological awareness literacy screening—kindergarten.* Charlottesville: University of Virginia Printing Services.

Invernizzi, M., & Tortorelli, L. (2013). Phonological awareness and alphabet knowledge: The foundations of early reading. In D. Barone & M. H. Mallette (Eds.), *Best practices in early literacy instruction* (pp. 155–174). New York: Guilford Press.

Johnston, F., Invernizzi, M., Helman, L., Bear, D., & Templeton, S. (2014). *Words their way for PreK–K.* Boston: Pearson.

Jones, C. D., Clark, S., & Reutzel, D. R. (2013). Enhancing alphabet knowledge instruction: Research implications and practical strategies for early childhood educators. *Early Childhood Education Journal, 41*(2), 81–89.

Jones, C. D., & Reutzel, D. R. (2012). Enhanced alphabet knowledge instruction: Exploring a change of frequency, focus, and distributed cycles of review. *Reading Psychology, 33*, 448–464.

Justice, L. M., & Ezell, H. K. (2004). Print referencing: An emergent literacy enhancement strategy and its clinical applications. *Language, Speech, and Hearing Services in Schools, 35*(2), 185–193.

Justice, L. M., Kaderavek, J. N., Fan, X., Sofka, A., & Hunt, A. (2009). Accelerating preschoolers' early literacy development through classroom-based teacher–child storybook reading and explicit print referencing. *Language, Speech, and Hearing Services in Schools, 40*, 67–85.

Justice, L. M., Pence, K., Bowles, R. B., & Wiggins, A. (2006). An investigation of four hypotheses concerning the order by which 4-year-old children learn the alphabet letters. *Early Childhood Research Quarterly, 21*, 374–389.

Liberman, I. Y., Shankweiler, D., & Liberman, A. M. (1989). *The alphabetic principle and learning to read.* Bethesda, MD: National Institute of Child Health and Human Development.

Mason, J. M. (1980). When do children begin to read: An exploration of four-year-old children's letter and word reading competencies. *Reading Research Quarterly, 15*, 203–227.

McBride-Chang, C. (1999). The ABCs of the ABCs: The development of letter-name and letter-sound knowledge. *Merrill–Palmer Quarterly, 45*, 285–308.

McGill-Franzen, A., Lanford, C., & Adams, E. (2002). Learning to be literate: A comparison of five urban preschools. *Journal of Educational Psychology, 94*(3), 443–464.

McKay, R., & Teale, W. H. (2015). *No more teaching a letter a week*. Portsmouth, NH: Heinemann.

Montessori, M., & Gutek, G. L. (2004). *The Montessori method: The origins of an educational innovation*. Lanham, MD: Rowman & Littlefield.

Morphett, M. V., & Washburn, C. (1931). When should children begin to read? *Elementary School Journal, 31*, 496–503.

Murray, B. A., Stahl, S. A., & Ivey, M. G. (1996). Developing phoneme awareness through alphabet books. *Reading and Writing, 8*, 307–322.

National Governors Association Center for Best Practices and Council of Chief State School Officers. (2010). *Common core standards for English language arts and literacy in history/social studies, science, and technical subjects*. Washington DC: Author.

Office of Head Start. (2015). *Head Start early learning outcomes framework: Ages birth to 5*. Washington, DC: Office of Head Start, Administration for Children and Families, U.S. Department of Health and Human Services.

Piasta, S. B. (2014). Moving to assessment-guided differentiated instruction to support young children's alphabet knowledge. *The Reading Teacher, 68*, 202–211.

Piasta, S. B., Justice, L. M., McGinty, A. S., & Kaderavek, J. N. (2012a). Increasing young children's contact with print during shared reading: Longitudinal effects on literacy achievement. *Child Development, 83*(3), 810–820.

Piasta, S. B., Petcher, Y., & Justice, L. M. (2012b). How many letters should preschoolers in public programs know?: The diagnostic efficiency of various preschool letter-naming benchmarks for predicting first-grade literacy achievement. *Journal of Educational Psychology, 104*, 945–958.

Piasta, S. B., Purpura, D. J., & Wagner, R. K. (2010b). Fostering alphabet knowledge development: A comparison of two instructional approaches. *Reading and Writing, 23*, 607–626.

Piasta, S. B., & Wagner, R. K. (2010a). Developing emergent literacy skills: A meta-analysis of alphabet learning and instruction. *Reading Research Quarterly, 45*, 8–38.

Piasta, S. B., & Wagner, R. K. (2010c). Learning letter names and sounds: Effects of instruction, letter type, and phonological processing skill. *Journal of Experimental Child Psychology, 105*, 324–344.

Read, C. (1971). Pre-school children's knowledge of English phonology. *Harvard Educational Review, 41*, 1–34.

Rieban, L., & Perfetti, C. A. (2013). *Learning to read: Basic research and its implications*. Mahwah, NJ: Erlbaum.

Roberts, T. A. (2003). Effects of alphabet-letter instruction on young children's word recognition. *Journal of Educational Psychology, 95*, 41–51.

Scarborough, H. S. (1998). Early identification of children at risk for reading disabilities: Phonological awareness and some other promising predictors. In B. K. Shapiro, P. J. Accardo, & A. J. Capute (Eds.), *Specific reading disability: A view of the spectrum* (pp. 75–119). Timonium, MD: York Press.

Share, D. L. (2004). Knowing letter names and learning letter sounds: A causal connection. *Journal of Experimental Child Psychology, 88*, 213–233.

Treiman, R., & Broderick, V. (1998). What's in a name: Children's knowledge about the letters in their own names. *Journal of Experimental Child Psychology, 70*, 97–116.

Treiman, R., Tincoff, R., Rodriguez, K., Mouzaki, A., & Francis, D. J. (1998). The foundations of literacy: Learning the sounds of letters. *Child Development, 69,* 1524–1540.

Turnbull, K. L. P., Bowles, R. P., Skibbe, L. E., Justice, L. M., & Wiggins, A. K. (2010). Theoretical explanations for preschoolers' lowercase alphabet knowledge. *Journal of Speech, Language, and Hearing Research, 53,* 1757–1768.

Wasik, B. A. (2001). Teaching the alphabet to young children. *Young Children, 56,* 34–40.

CHAPTER 5

A Close and Careful Look at Phonological Awareness

Christina M. Cassano

Take care of the sense, and the sounds will take care of themselves.

—LEWIS CARROLL

In 2009, Ingvar Lundberg stated that phonological awareness had perhaps been "over researched" (p. 614). While his assertion was probably correct, given the voluminous corpus of research on the topic accumulated by that time, the discovery that phonological awareness was causally related to reading acquisition was, at one time, revolutionary. In this chapter, I examine how each of three pivotal studies helped shape our understanding of the critical role of phonological awareness in literacy development. These studies include Explicit Syllable and Phoneme Segmentation in the Young Child (Liberman, Shankweiler, Fischer, & Carter, 1974); Effects of an Extensive Program for Stimulating Phonological Awareness in Preschool Children (Lundberg, Frost, & Petersen, 1988); and Learning to Read and Write: A Longitudinal Study of 54 Children from First through Fourth Grades (Juel, 1988).

Before delving into the pivotal studies, I provide some background about phonological awareness. In the sections that follow, I briefly contextualize each study within related research trends and provide a description of each one, along with some reflections about its impact on the field. In the culminating section, I discuss how these studies, in combination with more recent research, continue to influence research and practice, and offer some recommendations.

WHAT PHONOLOGICAL AWARENESS IS, AND WHY IT MATTERS FOR EARLY LITERACY DEVELOPMENT

Phonological awareness (PA) is an oral language skill that is defined as sensitivity to the sounds in spoken words. Whereas the perception of speech sounds is evident in infancy (Eimas, Siqueland, Jusczyk, & Vigorito, 1971), PA refers to the *conscious* awareness of the sound structure of spoken words, apart from word meanings.

Children who are phonologically aware can manipulate spoken language. For example, they can segment sentences into words, words into syllables (e.g., *again* into /a/ - /gain/), and syllables into onsets and rimes (e.g., *cat* into /k/ - /at/) or phonemes (e.g., *back* into /b/ - /a/ - /k/). Advanced levels of PA include the segmentation of spoken words into their smallest units (i.e., phonemes) and the ability to handle complex operations, such as deleting a word's initial or final phoneme (e.g., say *cat* without the /k/ to make *at*; say *keep* without the /p/ to make *key*), which is called phoneme elision, and substituting an initial phoneme (e.g., change /k/ in *cat* to /p/ to make *pat*). A well-documented developmental progression of PA takes into account both the size of the linguistic unit (e.g., Fox & Routh, 1975; Liberman et al., 1974; Treiman & Zukowski, 1991) and the complexity of the task operation, such as segmenting versus blending (e.g., Stahl & Murray, 1994; Stanovich, Cunningham, & Cramer, 1984; Yopp, 1988).

When measured in preschool, PA, particularly at the phoneme level, strongly predicts decoding, which is largely responsible for word reading accuracy in beginning readers (NICHD Early Child Care Research Network, 2005; Storch & Whitehurst, 2002). Although PA does not involve print directly, there is a link between PA and decoding in alphabetic writing systems, because letters represent phonemes in words. Without an awareness of the sound structure of words at the phoneme level, children do not understand how print works and thus can fail to deploy phonics instruction that teachers provide. That is, PA, in conjunction with alphabet knowledge, enables children to understand that graphemes are mapped onto phonemes (i.e., translated into), and that phonemes obtained when phonologically recoding print must be blended to form spoken words that are in the child's oral vocabulary (Adams, 1990; Share, 1995; see also Wharton-MacDonald, Chapter 6, this volume, for further discussion).

Training studies offer the strongest evidence for PA's causal role in learning to read (e.g., Ball & Blachman, 1991; Bradley & Bryant, 1983; Bus & van IJzendoorn, 1999; Lundberg et al., 1988). These results converge on two major findings: First, PA instruction results in higher levels of PA (e.g., Ball & Blachman, 1991; Bradley & Bryant, 1983; Lundberg et al., 1988); second, when phoneme-level instruction is included, reading skill improves (e.g., Bus & van

IJzendoorn, 1999; Ehri, Nunes, Willows, Schuster, Yaghoub, Zadeh, & Shana-han, 2001; Lonigan, Schatschneider, & Westberg, 2008; Lundberg et al., 1988). In addition to its direct effect on decoding, PA also has an indirect effect on reading comprehension, because decoding skill affects reading fluency and flu-ency in turn aids comprehension (Laberge & Samuels, 1974; Storch & White-hurst, 2001).

Phonological awareness is also important for the literacy development of emergent bilinguals (EB). Phonological awareness skills developed in one lan-guage can transfer to another (Chiappe & Siegel, 1999; Durgunoğlu, 2002; Lindsey, Manis, & Bailey, 2003). For example, once a child can attend to sounds in words apart from their referents in one language, this knowledge can be applied to all of the languages the child knows (López & Greenfield, 2004). The transferability of PA, however, is related to the similarities and differences between the languages' phonological structures and writing systems (e.g., Bialy-stok, Luk, & Kwon, 2005; Durgunoğlu, 2002).

THREE PIVOTAL STUDIES ON PHONOLOGICAL AWARENESS

Liberman, Shankweiler, Fischer, and Carter (1974): *Explicit Syllable and Phoneme Segmentation in the Young Child*

During the 1970s, ongoing research in several fields, including cognitive psychology (e.g., Bruner, Oliver, & Greenfield, 1966; Gibson, 1969; Gough, 1972), information processing (e.g., LaBerge & Samuels, 1974), and early lit-eracy development (e.g., Clay, 1967; Goodman, 1973) indicated that learning to read was complex, because it involved several strategic, meaning-making behaviors. Although the belief that reading instruction should not begin until children reached a mental age of 6.5—a norm based on a study by Morphett and Washburn (1931) that still influenced both research and practice in the 1970s—evidence accumulated during the 1960s and 1970s indicated that young children acquired many literacy skills long before attaining this norm (e.g., Chall, Roswell, & Blumenthal, 1963; Cohlert, 1979; Hunt, 1961; Read, 1975). Some of this evidence emerged from studies of the home-based experi-ences of children who had acquired literacy skills beyond what was generally found in most children at the time prior to school entry and the onset of formal reading instruction. This research also sought to explain why some children arrived at school reading or very "ready" to learn to read, while others did not (e.g., Durkin, 1966; Gibson & Levin, 1975; Teale, 1978).

During this same time period, researchers were beginning to explore the relationship between PA and reading (Bond & Dykstra, 1967; Calfee, Lindamood, & Lindamood, 1973; Elkonin, 1963), although the precise rela-tionship was unclear. The 1965 iteration of the Murphy-Durrell Reading

Readiness Analysis included a phoneme subtest, which suggested that the developers considered PA an important prerequisite to reading and thought teachers should determine through testing if children were "ready" for formal instruction (Farr & Anastasiow, 1969). Bond and Dykstra (1967) identified the ability to "discriminate between word sounds" (p. 117) as the second strongest predictor of reading after letter–name knowledge in an analysis of 27 studies on first grade reading. Other researchers provided more anecdotal evidence. For example, observational evidence led Savin (1972) to conclude that first graders who could not read simple text were "unable to analyze syllables into phonemes" and were also "insensitive to rhyme" (p. 321).

The role of maturation remained an important consideration in the research conducted in the 1970s. For example, Bruce (1964) explored "phonetic analysis" abilities in children whose mental ages ranged from 5 to 9 years, using a task that required children to delete a target phoneme in a given word (i.e., phoneme elision). Performance followed a developmental pattern, about which Bruce remarked: "These necessary features of the ability are not attained in discrete steps, but are present in increasing proportion with advancing mental age. Mental age 7+ is indicated as the level at which they first become available in sufficient degree to permit some success on the task" (p. 158).

The ability to analyze spoken words was viewed as far too complex for children who had not yet received any formal reading instruction. Gibson and Levin (1975) asserted that "the evidence is *unequivocal* that children do not come to school with the ability to segment speech at [the phoneme] level although this is not to say that they cannot be taught to recognize phonemes" (emphasis added, p. 120).

Drawing from a series of studies on speech perception, Liberman and colleagues at the Haskins Laboratories (A. M. Liberman, 1970; I. Liberman, 1971; Liberman, Cooper, Shankweiler, & Studdert-Kennedy, 1967) believed that phoneme segmentation was challenging cognitively, because phonemes are not physically perceptible (i.e., acoustically detectable) as syllable units are. Instead, phonemes are often folded into each other (i.e., coarticulated) in spoken words. This "parallel transmission" (Liberman et al., 1967, p. 436) makes it impossible to segment words in the speech stream into a series of single phonemes. Thus, phoneme-level awareness requires children to develop a concrete awareness of a nonconcrete (i.e., abstract) entity. Liberman, Shankweiler, Fisher, and Carter designed a study in 1974 to test their hypothesis that young children would find it far easier to detect syllables than to detect phonemes.

Description of the Study

Forty-six preschoolers, 49 kindergartners, and 40 first graders from Connecticut participated in this study. All children were white and from middle-income families. Those with speech and hearing and/or behavioral issues were excluded. The children were divided into two experimental groups, phoneme segmentation (Group P) and syllable segmentation (Group S), and invited to play a "game." Specifically, each child was asked to repeat the word or sound presented by the researcher and then tap out the appropriate number of segments (e.g., phonemes or syllables) in each one. Training items were included to ensure that the children understood the task requirements.

Stimuli used in the phoneme group were real words consisting of one to three phonemes. Each word was identified as appropriate for 3- to 6-year-olds with the exception of one-segment items, which consisted of a single vowel sound. (See Table 1 in Liberman et al., 1974, for a complete list of the phoneme test items.) Corrective feedback was provided immediately following the child's response, as needed. Children in the syllable group were required to segment real words that ranged in size from one to three syllables. As with the phoneme group, corrective feedback was provided. (See Table 2 in Liberman et al., 1974, for a complete list of the syllable test items.)

Forty six percent of the preschoolers, 48% of the kindergartners, and 90% of the first graders reached the criterion. In other words, nearly half of the preschoolers and kindergartners, and almost all of the first graders successfully segmented the syllables in six consecutive words by the end of the test. None of the preschoolers achieved the criterion on the phoneme task, whereas 17 percent of the kindergartners and 70 percent of the first graders did. The average number of trials required to reach the criterion by kindergartners and first graders was also lower for the syllable task (i.e., 12 and 10, respectively) than for the phoneme task (i.e., 26).

Consistent with the researchers' hypothesis, the results indicated that phoneme segmentation was more difficult than syllable segmentation for preschool, kindergarten, and first-grade children. As noted previously, many child development experts still thought that maturation exerted a strong effect on changes in development, Liberman et al. (1974) hedged about its role.

> We cannot judge from this experiment to what degree these measured increases represent maturational changes and to what extent they may reflect the effects of instruction in reading and writing during the first grade. But whatever the instruction, the findings strongly suggest that a greater level of intellectual maturity is necessary to achieve the ability to analyze words into phonemes than into syllables. (p. 210)

The Liberman group also noted further that, although 46% of the preschoolers had succeeded on the syllable segmentation task, it should not be assumed that all young children can achieve a conscious awareness of syllables without instruction. They suggested that explicit instruction might be required for the development of both phoneme and syllable segmentation. The

Liberman group concluded with a statement that would set the course of PA research for the next two decades:

> It would, of course, be of primary interest to learn in future research whether first grade children who do not acquire phoneme segmentation are, in fact, deficient in reading and writing as well. If it should be found that explicit segmentation of this kind is an important factor in reading disability, we should think . . . that it would be possible (and desirable) to develop this ability by appropriate training methods. (p. 211)

Impact of the Study

The Liberman group was the first to identify a continuum of difficulty of PA related to the size of the linguistic unit. That is, they established empirically that it was easier for children to segment words into larger units (i.e., syllables) than into smaller units (i.e., phonemes). Subsequent research confirmed and extended this continuum by adding onsets and rimes as subsyllabic linguistic units that are more difficult to detect than syllables, but easier than phonemes (e.g., Fox & Routh, 1975; Treiman & Zukowski, 1991).

Some research has shown that when different PA tasks are used, preschoolers can demonstrate phoneme-level skills. In one such study, Lonigan, Burgess, Anthony, and Barker (1998) administered a series of PA tasks, including phoneme-level blending and elision, to 356 middle- and lower-income 2- to 5-year-olds. Trends related to age and socioeconomic status (SES) were observed. Yet, contrary to the Liberman group findings, a moderate percentage of middle-income 2- and 3-year-olds successfully completed the phoneme blending (2.9 and 21.4%, respectively) and elision tasks (2.9 and 10.7%, respectively). In addition to task differences, performance differences between the preschoolers in the Liberman group study and those in Lonigan group study might be attributed to variations in task supports or demands that reduced or increased complexity of the PA tasks used (e.g., multiple-choice answers, picture prompts, motor demands; Cassano & Steiner, 2016). In the Lonigan et al. study, a correct response on the elision and blending tasks required pointing to the correct picture (i.e., picture prompt) from among three choices (i.e., multiple-choice) on over half of the test items. In contrast, a correct response on the phoneme segmentation task in the Liberman et al. study required tapping out the phonemes in a word (i.e., motor demand) correctly on 6 consecutive items to reach the criterion. Thus, a child's perceived level of PA skill can vary depending on the specific requirements of the tasks examined (e.g., Stahl & Murray, 1994; Stanovich, Cunningham, & Cramer, 1984; Yopp, 1988).

It is important to note that the developmental progression of PA skill acquisition does not necessarily imply a stage theory of PA development.

When true stages are evident, lower levels must be mastered in lockstep fashion—that is, each level is a necessary prerequisite for the next. When a developmental sequence does not involve true stages, a child can benefit from exposure to tasks involving more complex skills, while still mastering lower level skills. Although the early research findings on PA would support this second interpretation (e.g., Liberman et al., 1974), the conclusion drawn by many researchers is, instead, that PA development occurs in stages. This assumption is evident in instructional directions provided in PA programs, such as the *Phonological Awareness Book* (Robertson & Salter, 1994, p. 8) which states that children should "reach a level of mastery before moving on." Similarly, instructional guidance found in the curriculum *Phonemic Awareness in Young Children* states that "syllables, for example, should be firmly established before moving on to initial sounds" (Adams, Foorman, Lundberg, & Beeler, 1998, p. 5).

Anthony, Lonigan, Driscoll, Philips, and Burgess (2003) clarified the developmental nature of PA in a study with 947 2- to 5-year-olds. The results indicated that, although children typically achieved syllable-level skills before onset and rime-level skills, and onset and rime-level skills before phoneme-level skills, development occurred in "overlapping stages rather than [in] temporally discrete stages" (p. 481). That is, knowledge at higher levels of PA skill were emerging in children even as they were still mastering the lower levels. This overlapping nature of other areas of development, as compared to stage-like development, has been cited by several other researchers (e.g., Chen & Siegler, 2000; Shrager & Siegler, 1998). (See Rittle-Johnson & Siegler, 1999 for a discussion of the overlapping waves model in contrast to a stage-like model in accounting for children's acquisition of spelling strategies.)

The suggestion from the Liberman et al. (1974) study that maturation might play a role in how children acquire higher levels of PA should be considered with caution. To review, preschoolers could segment words into larger, more accessible units (i.e., syllables) but had difficulty segmenting smaller, abstract units (i.e., phonemes). The Liberman group seemed to suggest that conscious awareness required "intellectual maturity" (i.e., maturation). According to maturational theory (Gesell & Amatruda, 1941), any instruction provided before the child is "ready" could lead to frustration and potential learning issues. Yet, interestingly, Liberman et al. did not recommend that instruction be withheld, which suggests that they were not comfortable taking a strong maturationist stance. Later, the studies by Lonigan et al. (1998) and Anthony et al. (2003) indicated that some children as young as 2 can accurately demonstrate phoneme-level awareness, whereas adult illiterates do not (Morais, Bertelson, Cary, & Alegria, 1986; Morais, Cary, Alegria, & Bertelson, 1979). Taken together, these results suggest that achieving higher levels of PA cannot be attributed solely to intellectual maturity.

Juel (1988): *Learning to Read and Write: A Longitudinal Study of 54 Children from First through Fourth Grades*

In the years that passed between the 1974 Liberman group study and Juel's 1988 study, a growing body of research indicated that performance on a variety of PA tasks predicted reading development (e.g., Helfgott, 1976; Jorm & Share, 1983; Share, Jorm, Maclean, & Matthews, 1984). Torrey (1979) put it this way: "naïve individuals such as children and other illiterates often do not hear phonemes separately, so it is hard for them to form associations between letters and sounds" (p. 126). By the late 1980s, it was apparent from the research that PA was one of the most powerful predictors in reading acquisition, in fact, it was determined to be a better predictor than IQ (Wagner & Torgeson, 1987), a favorite measure used by those with a partiality toward maturation as a strong factor in explaining variations in PA development.

Description of the Study

Juel designed the 1988 study as a follow-up to a larger study conducted with colleagues (Juel, Griffin, & Gough, 1986). The original study followed children from the first through second grades; however, Juel's 1988 study followed the same children through the fourth grade. The 1986 study examined the "simple view of reading" (e.g., Hoover & Gough, 1990), a model that shows how reading comprehension consists of two interrelated processes—decoding and listening comprehension. If either process breaks down, comprehension cannot occur. (See also Roberts, Chapter 2, this volume, for further discussion of the simple view of reading.) Juel and colleagues (1986) paid particular attention to PA's role in the decoding process. In commenting about the 1986 study, Juel (2010) noted the historical consideration of PA in her research:

> It was not common to put phonemic awareness on the table in those days, but in this [1986] study we did. We thought it was a prominent contributor, along with exposure to printed words, to a child's ability to create cipher knowledge. We also thought that whereas the first-grade child might be more dependent on cipher knowledge, the balance would shift in favor of lexical knowledge over time. (p. 15)

One-hundred-twenty-nine children were recruited for the 1986 study from an elementary school in a low-SES area in Austin, Texas. Given the transient nature of the population, only 54 children (i.e., 31 girls and 23 boys) remained in the 1988 study (i.e., through the fourth grade). Twenty-six percent of the children were white, 31% were black, and 23% were Hispanic. An extensive battery of assessments that included both decoding skills (e.g., PA, word recognition) and skills related to comprehension was administered throughout the

4-year study. Data were also collected for IQ, home reading, reading attitude, and print exposure.

Juel's 1988 study examined three, reading-related questions: (1) "Do the same children remain poor readers year after year? (2) What skills do poor readers lack? (3) What factors seem to keep poor readers from improving?" (p. 437). Two similar questions related to writing were also examined, but I do not discuss the findings for those questions here. "Poor readers," as Juel called them (p. 437) were children whose reading comprehension scores fell below the 25th percentile. Regarding the question, *Do the same children remain poor readers year after year?*, 24 of the 29 children categorized as poor readers in first grade remained in the study through fourth grade. Of these, 21 continued to read poorly through fourth grade. Put simply, 88% of the poor readers identified at the end of first grade remained poor readers through fourth grade. In contrast, of the 30 children with at least average reading skills by the end of first grade (i.e., "good readers"), only 4 became poor readers by fourth grade. Thus, good readers in first grade had only a 12% chance of becoming poor readers by the end of the fourth grade.

As for the second question, *What skills do poor readers lack?*, results indicated that poor readers lacked PA upon first grade entry. Specifically, at the beginning of first grade, the mean score on the PA assessment for the poor readers was 4.2, whereas the mean score for the good readers was 21.7. By the conclusion of first grade, the poor readers had a mean score of 18.6 and the good readers had a mean score of 37.5. Put another way, by the end of first grade, the poor readers' level of PA still lagged far behind the level of PA skill that the good readers displayed at first grade entry, despite considerable improvement in PA during the school year.

Given the poor readers' low PA levels, it was not surprising that they also lacked decoding skill. Despite a year of phonics instruction (not PA training), 9 of the poor readers could not read any monosyllabic pseudo words on the decoding measure at the end of first grade. Even by fourth grade, poor readers had not yet achieved the level of decoding skill that good readers had achieved by the end of the second grade. In the fourth grade, the poor readers also lagged behind the good readers in both listening and reading comprehension.

Lastly, as for the question, *What factors seem to keep poor readers from improving?*, Juel identified weak decoding skills as the crucial factor that prevented poor readers from improving their reading skill. She also noted the vast differences in the amount of print exposure between poor and good readers. By counting the sheer number of words in the first-grade basal reader, Juel estimated that good readers had been exposed to nearly twice the number of words as the poor readers, 18,687 and 9,975, respectively. By the end of the fourth grade, Juel reported that good readers had finished the fourth-grade basal, whereas poor readers had only partially completed the third-grade text. She calculated that this difference meant that good readers had been exposed to approximately 178,000 words, compared to 80,000 words for the poor readers. Additionally, responses on the home reading interviews indicated that poor readers were considerably less likely to read outside of the classroom, whereas good readers reported frequent out-of-school reading experiences. Thus, Juel's calculation of differences in print exposure was no doubt an underestimation, because the differences were calculated for reading that took place only in the classroom.

In conclusion, Juel (1988) noted the connection between low decoding skills and the differences in print exposure and reading motivation.

> A vicious cycle seemed evident. Children who did not develop good word-recognition skills in the first grade began to dislike reading and read considerably less than good readers both in and out of school. They thus lost the avenue to develop vocabulary, concepts, ideas and so on. . . . This in turn, may have contributed to the steadily widening gulf between the good and poor readers in reading comprehension. (p. 445)

Thus, children who read less well read less often, whereas the stronger readers continued to improve their skills and acquire new knowledge through reading.

Impact of the Study

Juel's (1988) findings that children who struggled in learning to read did not "catch up" were consistent with the views of other researchers (e.g., Clay, 1979; Lundberg, 1984; Stanovich, 1986). For example, Stanovich (1986) found that issues with PA can cause "delays in early code-breaking progress and initiates the cascade of interacting achievement failures and motivational problems" (p. 393). Spira, Bracken, and Fishel (2005) confirmed and extended Juel's results when they found that the first graders in their study who fell below the 30th percentile in reading had a 70% probability of remaining there or falling lower in reading performance by the end of fourth grade. The Spira group also found that children who "recovered" from first-grade reading failure had higher levels of PA, self-regulation (i.e., ability to attend to instruction and to persist on learning tasks), oral vocabulary (i.e., receptive and expressive levels), and learning-related behaviors. Of note, the children who recovered from initial reading failure did so by the end of second grade (see also Hindin, Chapter 7, this volume)

The lack of reading motivation displayed by the poor readers in Juel's study was also particularly striking. For example, 40% of the participants said that they preferred cleaning to reading. One stated, "I'd rather clean the mold around the bathtub than read" (1988, p. 442). Research that came both before and after Juel's study supports her claim that poor readers are motivated to read less, and, as a result, encounter fewer words. For example, Nagy and Anderson's (1984) estimates of words read by high- and low-achieving readers showed "staggering individual differences in volume of language experience, and therefore, opportunity to learn new words" (p. 328). Cunningham and Stanovich (1990) determined that variations in print exposure were linked to differences in word recognition skills in third and fourth grades.

Despite the finding that poor readers had low levels of PA upon first grade entry, and made slow progress acquiring it, Juel could not determine if PA was causally related to reading acquisition. As with any correlation, the relationship found between PA and reading might have been due to some third variable. The third pivotal study, discussed next, was one of the first to use an experimental design to determine whether systematic and explicit PA instruction can support both PA and reading.

Lundberg, Frost, and Peterson (1988): *Effects of an Extensive Program for Stimulating Phonological Awareness in Preschool Children*

The attention on PA increased rapidly as a growing body of evidence indicated that it was related to success in learning to read. The question that loomed, of course, was whether the relationship was causal (e.g., Bradley & Bryant, 1983; Treiman & Baron, 1983). Bradley and Bryant (1983) were the first to demonstrate a causal link between PA and subsequent reading skill. In their study, 4- and 5-year-olds with low levels of sound categorization skills were divided into four groups and taught to categorize words using: (1) sound categorization only, (2) sound categorization plus letter–sounds, or (3) semantic relations. The fourth group was an unseen control. Over the first year, the children in the two sound categorization groups received 40, individual, instructional sessions that were 10 minutes in length. During the second year of the study, letter–sound instruction was added to one of the sound categorization groups (i.e., sound categorization plus letter sounds). At the end of the 2-year study, the results of reading and spelling measures indicated that children in both sound categorization groups outperformed both control groups on reading and spelling measures. Notably, the sound categorization plus letter–sound instruction group significantly outperformed all 3 groups. The sound categorization only group was consistently ahead of the semantic relations group; however, the differences were not significant.

During the time of the Bradley and Bryant (1983) study, it was widely accepted that some forms of PA could precede literacy instruction (e.g., Liberman et al., 1974; MacLean, Bryant, & Bradley, 1987) and was reciprocally related to reading (Adams, 1990). Morais and colleagues (1979, 1987, 1991a, 1991b), however, had a different view, one based on research with illiterate adults and Chinese and Japanese readers (i.e., readers in non-alphabetic languages). These researchers argued that phoneme-level awareness could only be developed through formal phonics instruction that involved learning letter–sound relationships. Moreover, they believed that the weakness of published PA studies was that they failed to provide information on either letter–sound instruction or children's alphabet knowledge. Morais (1991b) wrote, "I would not be surprised if no child were found who, displaying a high level of segmental analysis ability, would not display also a substantial knowledge of letter sounds" (p. 43).

Other researchers opposed Morais's views that PA was inextricably linked to alphabet knowledge. For example, Lundberg (1991) wrote that the position held by Morais and colleagues suggested that "phonemes are only artifacts within the alphabet script and have no independence outside of the orthography" (p. 48). Lundberg further noted that the presence of phoneme-level awareness in the absence of alphabet knowledge, would provide empirical evidence against Morais's position. Thus, the Lundberg group set out to conduct a study with an intervention of just that kind.

Description of the Study

Although Bradley and Bryant's (1983) highly influential study provided the first evidence that the relationship between PA and reading achievement was causal, Lundberg et al. (1988) had some concerns. Specifically, Bradley and Bryant's training occurred concurrently with school-based reading instruction, thus confounding the two variables. To eliminate this threat to their own study's internal validity, the Lundberg group designed a PA training program to be implemented *before* their participants received any formal reading instruction. The Lundberg group also believed that Bradley and Bryant's training period was too short and that the oddity measure they used tapped alliteration and rhyme awareness, not phoneme-level awareness. In response, they included a longer training period (i.e., daily, 15–20 minute sessions over 8 months) and training and assessments that focused on a broader range of PA skills.

The Lundberg et al. study began in August 1985. It included both an experimental group and a control group. The 235 children (134 boys and 101 girls) in the experimental group were from 12 kindergartens on the island of Bornholm, Denmark. No precise mean age was given, although the children in this group were described as "on average, 6 years old." The control group consisted of 155 kindergartners (75 boys and 80 girls) drawn from 10 kindergartens in Jutland, Denmark. No mean age was given for this group, either. Both groups were comprised of children from low- and middle-SES backgrounds who lived in small, rural areas that were separated geographically to ensure that the children in the control group were not accidentally exposed to the activities used with the experimental group. The children were followed from kindergarten (referred to as preschool) to the beginning of second grade. Lundberg et al. explained that, in Denmark, formal literacy instruction is not provided before first grade. Thus, it was expected that few, if any of the participants, would be reading at the start of their study, although the researchers thought that most of the children would be familiar with a small number of letter names. The important assumption was that "the alphabetic code [was] still a mystery for them" (1988, p. 267).

At both the beginning and the end of the study, the participants in both groups were assessed in prereading skills (i.e., high-frequency words and sentences), alphabet knowledge, language comprehension (i.e., following verbal direction to draw figures), and vocabulary (i.e., labeling pictures of common objects). The PA assessments included rhyme detection; initial phoneme deletion; syllable and phoneme blending; and segmentation of sentences, syllables, and phonemes. During pretesting, one child in the experimental group could already read. Two children in the control group showed some hints of reading ability; however, their scores were too low to qualify them as readers. Pretest scores were equivalent for both groups, with the exception of three phoneme-level tasks (i.e., initial phoneme, phoneme segmentation, and phoneme blending) and the syllable blending task, which favored the control group.

A complete pilot year, in addition to extensive professional development, was provided to the teachers in the training classrooms. When the main study began, the 235 children in the experimental group received 8 months of daily instruction that included metalinguistic games and activities "with the aim of guiding the children to discover and attend to the phonological structure of language" (1988, p. 268). The PA training, later referred to as the Lundberg program, was sequenced carefully: It began with listening games (e.g., verbal and nonverbal sounds), then focused on rhyming (e.g., nursery rhymes, detection, and production), followed by segmenting sentences into words and examining word length. Next, children were taught to segment and blend syllables and, finally, to isolate and identify phonemes. To avoid recency effects at posttesting, activities introduced early in the training were revisited in later sessions. Neither alphabet instruction nor reading instruction was provided.

The progression of tasks in the Lundberg program was deliberate and extremely methodical "to ensure that all children, even those with a minimum of metalinguistic talent, could manage the games with a feeling of success" (p. 269). For example, isolating phonemes in the initial position was introduced beginning in the third month, phoneme blending was introduced in the fifth month and phoneme segmentation of complex words was introduced in the eighth month. Children in the control group received the typical instruction that emphasized social development, not formal literacy instruction.

After the 8-month-long training period, the mean score on the PA test for the experimental group increased from 21.1 to 35.5. In contrast, the mean score for the control group increased from 23.6 to 28.1 (see Table 5.1). Significant differences on the vocabulary and language comprehension assessments were not found. Thus, the effect of the PA training intervention was limited to PA. As Table 5.1 indicates, the differences in means are most notable on the phoneme-level tasks (i.e., initial phoneme deletion and phoneme segmentation) with the exception of phoneme blending. More modest differences were found on the word, rhyming, and syllable tasks.

The long-term effectiveness of the training program was examined during the first grade and again at the beginning of the second grade using assessments in IQ, reading, spelling, and PA. A math test was administered as a control. The children in the experimental group maintained their previous advantage on the PA assessments and also spelled more words correctly compared to the control group across the follow-up period. No significant differences were evident on the word reading or math assessments administered 7 months into the first-grade year. By the start of second grade, however, the trained children outperformed the control group in both reading and spelling.

Impact of the Study

This experimental study provided evidence that PA is causally related to reading. That is, PA instruction provided before the onset of reading instruction positively influenced subsequent reading and writing performance. Three findings from this study have helped to shape early literacy research and instruction: First, the development of phoneme-level awareness appeared to require explicit instruction, because differences between trained and untrained children were strongest for phoneme-level tasks. Second, contrary to Morais's claim (1991a, 1991b) that phoneme-level awareness requires grapheme–phoneme instruction, the Lundberg et al. study demonstrated that it could be developed without a focus on graphemes. In other words, PA had, "an independent status" (Lundberg, 1991, p. 52). Third, the systematic instruction provided in kindergarten had a positive impact on reading and spelling performance at least through the second grade.

Limitations of the Lundberg, Frost, and Peterson Study and Remaining Challenges

Despite the influential findings, the Lundberg et al. (1998) study has been criticized for a number of reasons including: (1) the lack of alphabet instruction; (2) the age of the participants (i.e., 6-year-old "preschoolers"); and (3) the extensive training period. This study, however was the first to demonstrate that higher levels of PA can be achieved when systematic instruction is

TABLE 5.1. Pretest and Posttest Scores on the Phonological Awareness Measure for the Training and Control Groups

Measure	Training group		Control group	
	Pretest	Posttest	Pretest	Posttest
Rhyme detection	15.8	19.1	16.1	18.3
Word segmentation	0.65	1.10	0.60	0.77
Syllable blending	2.06	2.79	1.83	2.41
Syllable segmentation	1.66	2.57	1.61	2.26
Initial phoneme deletion	0.35	4.88	1.15	1.81
Phoneme segmentation	0.39	3.21	1.46	1.73
Phoneme blending	0.16	1.84	0.86	1.05
Total score	21.1	35.5	23.6	28.1

Note. Data from Lundberg et al. (1988).

provided by trained classroom teachers. Subsequent research on these areas of criticism has since confirmed and fine-tuned our understanding of how explicit instruction in PA in early childhood can support children's success in learning to read.

LETTER–SOUND INSTRUCTION

One aim of the Lundberg et al. study was to determine if PA could be developed without letter–sound instruction. Lundberg and Høien (1991) noted that "the fact that phonemic awareness can be developed without using the letters of the alphabet does not necessarily mean that letters are unimportant" (p. 88). We now have compelling evidence that children who receive phoneme-level training *in combination with* letter–sound instruction perform better on subsequent reading and spelling tasks than children who receive phoneme-level awareness training alone (e.g., Ball & Blachman, 1991; Bryant & Bradley, 1983; Lonigan et al., 2008; NICHD Early Child Care Research Network, 2005).

AGE

When children should receive explicit PA instruction is an important consideration. Although Lundberg et al. (1988) is often cited in support of PA training for preschoolers, the children in Denmark do not begin school until the age of 7. Thus, the children who completed their "preschool year" in the study were, on average, 6 years old. This age is considerably older than preschoolers in the United States, who are either 3 or 4 years old during the preschool years and between 5 and 6 years old at the beginning of kindergarten. Because children younger than 4 generally do not master PA skills (e.g., Lonigan, Burgess, & Anthony, 2000; Lonigan et al., 1998) some early learning standards in the United States, such as the California Preschool Curriculum Frameworks, require that explicit and systematic PA instruction begin after age 4 (California Department of Education, 2010).

DURATION

The Lundberg program proceeded slowly and methodically to ensure that all linguistic units (i.e., words, syllables, and phonemes) could be used in training PA. This comprehensive approach appears to be unnecessary. As Table 5.1 indicates, the children in the control group improved on rhyme detection, word and syllable-level tasks without explicit instruction. This evidence suggests that lower-level PA skills can be acquired without specific training. Moreover, subsequent research has shown that, for kindergarten and first grade children, PA can be improved with 5 to 18 hours of instruction that targets phoneme-level awareness (e.g., Ehri et al., 2001).

SITUATING PHONOLOGICAL AWARENESS IN READING DEVELOPMENT

Given the irrefutable evidence that PA is causally related to reading, it is not surprising that considerably more attention has been paid to PA since the publication of the three pivotal works discussed in this chapter. The Google Books Ngram graphic in Figure 5.1 illustrates this increased number of references to both phonological and phonemic awareness.

Although the pivotal works discussed here are not solely responsible for the increase in the attention phonological and phonemic awareness have received, each study has helped to shape our current understandings of PA. Over a half century of research has confirmed that targeting PA can improve word reading accuracy, presumably because children who can manipulate speech sounds better understand how graphemes map to phonemes. Skilled reading, however, requires far more than PA. To decode fluently and accurately, children need other *code-related skills*, including alphabet letter knowledge, the insight of the alphabetic principle, and knowledge of some print conventions (e.g., left to right progression). Without all of these foundational skills, "sounding out" words (i.e., decoding) cannot occur. In addition to decoding, children must also draw meaning from (i.e., comprehend) their texts. Comprehension relies on fluent and accurate decoding in the early phases of reading, but as text becomes more complex, *language-knowledge* that includes deep stores of vocabulary and concept knowledge is essential.

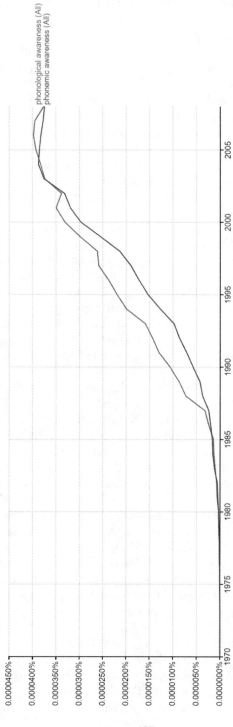

FIGURE 5.1. Frequency of the terms "phonological awareness" and "phonemic awareness" in sources printed between 1970 and 2008 in Google's text corpora.

Although decoding and comprehension are simultaneous and interrelated processes, they vary in the timing of their greatest influence on reading. Code-related skills acquired in PreK and kindergarten predict reading accuracy in the first and second grade when decoding is the major reading challenge and vocabulary and comprehension demands are controlled (e.g., leveled texts). In contrast, PreK and kindergarten levels of oral vocabulary predict reading comprehension, beginning in the third grade, when the comprehension demands of grade-level texts require connecting background knowledge to information in the text and using this combined information to draw inferences (Juel, 2006; NICHD Early Child Care Research Network, 2005; Sénéchal, Ouellette, & Rodney, 2006; Speece et al., 2004; Storch & Whitehurst, 2002).

Some research suggests that early levels of oral vocabulary knowledge are only weakly related to later reading (e.g., Lonigan et al., 2008). However, when oral vocabulary is included in broader measures of language (i.e., combined with listening comprehension, grammatical skill, and other aspects of language), the impact on later reading skill is apparent (Ouellette, 2006; Shanahan, 2016). For example, the National Early Literacy Panel (Lonigan et al., 2008) determined that oral vocabulary alone explained only 9% of the variance in later reading achievement; however, broader, more comprehensive measures of language accounted for approximately 50% of the variance of later reading achievement.

It is important to note that although broader measures of language help to illuminate the impact of early language knowledge on reading skill, research has yet to determine the specific nature of this relationship. It is clear that oral vocabulary predicts current and subsequent performance on both specific PA tasks (DeCara & Goswami, 2002; Metsala, 1999) and comprehensive measures (McDowell, Lonigan, & Goldstein, 2007; Sénéchal et al., 2006; Schwarz, Burnham, & Bowey, 2006; Torppa, Lyytinen, Erskine, Eklund, & Lyytinen, 2010) for children from both high- and low-SES backgrounds. Oral vocabulary and PA also appear to be commensurate skills. For example, 3-, 4-, and 5-year-olds with higher levels of receptive and expressive vocabulary exhibit higher rates of growth in PA (Cassano, 2013; Cassano & Schickedanz, 2015), and toddlers with low levels of expressive vocabulary (i.e., late talkers) had lower scores on PA tasks (e.g., syllable and phoneme deletion, matching initial consonants) at 6 years old compared to typically developing, age-matched peers (Rescola, 2002). Finally, some evidence suggests that targeting oral vocabulary knowledge can result in a "boost" in PA (i.e., crossover effect) in 3- and 4-year-olds who exhibited multiple risk factors (Justice, Chow, Capellini, Flanigan, & Colton, 2003) and in Head Start children (Lonigan, 2007). Although evidence of a crossover effect has been found in only two small studies of "at-risk" children, some researchers (e.g., Lonigan, 2007; Metsala & Walley, 1989) suggest that the origins of PA may be rooted in oral language development.

Oral vocabulary also plays a critical role in recovery from reading failure. Although both Juel (1988) and Spira et al. (2005) determined that reading difficulties are remarkably stable (88 and 70%, respectively), Spira et al. determined that children who *did* recover not only had higher levels of PA and self-regulation in kindergarten than children who did not recover, but also higher levels of both receptive and expressive vocabulary. Perhaps the children who recover compensate for weak decoding skills by relying on their vocabulary knowledge (see also Stanovich, 1984), but it is also possible that low levels of vocabulary present a barrier to the development of PA. Whitely, Smith, and Connors (2007) found that children with low levels of expressive vocabulary to start benefitted less from the intensive PA instruction than did children with higher levels. These researchers thus described low levels of expressive vocabulary as a "limiting factor" in PA interventions.

A major task for early educators, then, is to determine how to help young children efficiently and effectively develop the code-related skills and language-knowledge required for reading, regardless of the specific timing of their greatest effects. Whitehurst and Lonigan (1998) wrote that that "investing resources to improve both code-related and oral language skills" (p. 21) in preschool children may help to prevent reading difficulties in the later years. Although this is sound advice for PreK and kindergarten teachers, evidence suggests that the link between oral language and PA is evident even earlier in development.

PHONOLOGICAL AWARENESS: ORIGINS IN INFANCY

In a series of laboratory studies conducted with infants as young as 7 months, Kuhl (2011) contends that supporting oral language even earlier—that is, during the first year of life—is advantageous to later PA development, because it prompts speech perception, which is strongly related to language and literacy skill in early childhood. Kuhl also observed "strong relationships . . . between infants' early speech perception performance and their later language skills at 18 and 24 months. At 5 years, significant relationships were shown between infants' early speech perception performance and both their language skills and the phonological awareness skills associated with success in learning to read" (p. 138).

Other studies have confirmed the relationship between early language development and later PA knowledge in different populations of young children. In one such study, Torppa et al. (2010) learned that, for Finnish children categorized dichotomously as at-risk for dyslexia or as typically developing, receptive language (including receptive vocabulary) at age 2, predicted PA at age 3 years, 6 months and expressive language (including expressive vocabulary) measured at 3 years, 6 months, predicted PA at age 5. Similarly, in a study that followed verbally precocious children (i.e., early talkers) beginning at 20 months, Crain-Thoreson and Dale (1995) identified mean length of utterance (MLU; a measure of overall language development) at 24 months as a significant predictor of PA at 4 years, 6 months. Taken together, these studies present compelling evidence that the language differences, evident during the early years, can have long term implications for literacy development.

Early language differences are also related to the characteristics of language exposure in social contexts (see Kuhl, 2011, for a review). For example, 6- to 12-month-olds' speech perception abilities were strongly related to the caregiver's use of child-directed speech (i.e., motherese) which emphasizes and exaggerates speech sounds (Liu, Kuhl, & Tsao, 2003) and increases infants' attention (Cooper & Aslin, 1994). Thus, while it is firmly established that caregivers should talk with and read to infants, it might also be the case that playing with sounds intentionally—by exaggerating and emphasizing sounds—supports early speech perception which, in turn, is related to PA. Additional research is required to explore this possibility.

SUPPORTING PHONOLOGICAL AWARENESS
IN PreK AND KINDERGARTEN

Eleanor Gibson (1965) said, "Good pedagogy is based on a deep understanding of the discipline to be taught and the nature of the learning processes involved" (p. 1072). This quote prompts questions about how our understanding of PA should be applied to practice in early childhood settings. Although the section that follows includes recommendations for PreK and kindergarten teachers, it is important to keep in mind that the interactions between speech perception, social interaction, and the characteristics of caregiver speech in infancy and later PA remains underspecified (Kuhl, 2011). It may be that the root cause of phonological awareness difficulties—that is, why some children develop it with apparent ease while others have difficulty, lies in language experiences that occur during infancy. Addressing this question is fundamental to identifying the most effective ways to support PA development in early childhood as well as how to best prevent reading difficulties.

Currently, PA is targeted in early childhood curricula given its impact on word reading skill (Lonigan et al., 2008; National Institute of Child Health and Human Development, 2000) and in the Common Core State Standards (National Governors Association Center for Best Practices and Council of Chief State School Officers [NGA & CCSSO], 2010). This stress on PA instruction might lead early educators to assume that instruction should be emphasized primarily during the PreK and kindergarten years to prepare children to learn to read, and that the other skills, that impact reading comprehension, such as oral vocabulary and content knowledge, can be addressed later in third grade and beyond. These erroneous assumptions can have enduring, negative effects on children's language and literacy development (Dickinson, Golinkoff, & Hirsh-Pasek, 2010; Neuman, 2006). Devoting significant portions of instructional time to PA alone may increase it and subsequent word reading accuracy, but at a high cost, especially if content knowledge, oral vocabulary, and other important components of the early childhood curriculum are given to little attention. The following are practices that support PA in early childhood settings.

Begin and Stay with Phonemes

Despite research indicating that PA develops in overlapping waves, the National Early Literacy Panel's recommends a comprehensive approach to PA in which teachers attend to "children's progress along a developmental continuum of PA, rather than an emphasis on particular PA skills" (Lonigan et al., 2008, p. 79). Lundberg group's (1988) pivotal work confirms that a comprehensive approach *can* be successful in developing PA and *does* contribute to subsequent reading and spelling; *however,* the amount of instructional time consumed by the comprehensive approach is unwise. In Lundberg et al., the children in the control group acquired some rhyme- and syllable-level skills without explicit instruction suggesting that these levels of PA are fairly easy to acquire. Importantly, 4-year-olds can be taught to blend and segment phonemes without first having received syllable-level instruction (Ukrainetz Nuspl, Wilkerson, & Beddes, 2011). In fact, 4- and 5-year-olds who received syllable-level instruction, before phoneme-level, were more likely to confuse syllables and phonemes during the initial phases of phoneme-level instruction than children who received phoneme-level instruction only. Put simply, phoneme-level awareness is not only achievable for 4- and 5-year-olds without prior syllable-level instruction, but seems to proceed more smoothly when children do not need to overcome a learned focus on syllable-level units.

Although Ukrainetz et al. (2011) recommends that early childhood teachers begin PA instruction with phonemes, some teachers might feel more comfortable beginning with syllables because they are accessible units that may help children realize that sounds in words can be manipulated. Children are accustomed to using language meaningfully, and may be somewhat confused at first when asked to set meaning aside and isolate and manipulate sounds in words. If needed, children can learn what is expected in PA tasks by briefly manipulating units that are acoustically easy to detect. This introduction to the nature of PA tasks needs only a few weeks of syllable blending and segmenting, and then the teacher can move on to intra-syllabic units, first initial phonemes and then phonemes in other locations in words (Schickedanz & Collins, 2013). It should also be noted that tasks that require children to clap out syllables pose hidden challenges that can lead teachers to incorrectly assume that children lack syllable segmentation skill. Syllable segmentation activities that require a "vocal-motor match" to the syllables segmented (i.e., a motor activity timed to sync with the child's verbal segmenting) increase the task complexity

(Cassano & Schickedanz, 2015). This problem is remedied easily by requiring children to segment words orally without have to mark them with an added motor response.

Emphasize Oral Language and Concept Knowledge

Early childhood teachers should consider carefully their use of curricula that assume that PA development comes primarily or only from explicit instruction using PA tasks, especially if the amount of time devoted to these tasks leaves little time to foster oral vocabulary and other important content (e.g., math, science, arts). Although a causal relationship between oral language and PA has not been established (i.e., increasing oral vocabulary leads to greater PA development), it is clear that these skills are intricately related (e.g., Dickinson, McCabe, Anastasopoulos, Peisner-Feinberg, & Poe, 2003). Higher levels of oral vocabulary can also help compensate for weak decoding skills (Stanovich, 1984). That is, children can rely on their vocabulary knowledge and context clues to help identify the most likely options when trying to read words in connected text.

Although a complete review of how to support oral language development in early childhood classrooms is beyond the scope of this chapter, suffice it to say that children benefit when teachers and parents *teach* new words intentionally (Wasik & Bond, 2001; Wasik, Bond, & Hindmen, 2006), provide multiple *exposures* to sophisticated words (Collins, 2012; Elley, 1989; Pan, Rowe, Singer, & Snow, 2005), offer word learning *support* (e.g., pointing, labeling, defining; Sénéchal, Thomas, & Monker, 1995; Weizman & Snow, 2001), and engage children in *conversations* about interesting topics (Corrow, Cowell, Doebel, & Koenig, 2012; Klibanoff, Levine, Huttenlocher, Vasilyeva, & Hedges, 2006). Planning content-rich thematic units (i.e., engaging in hands-on explorations and reading age-appropriate informational texts) furthers the development of content knowledge that will ultimately aid in reading comprehension.

Integrate PA with Code-Skill Instruction

To ensure adequate space for all of the important components of early childhood instruction, PA instruction must be intentional, highly efficient, and focused on the types of PA skills that support word reading accuracy. Given the limits of instructional time, combining PA with instruction in other areas can be beneficial, especially when the approach has a strong research foundation. For example, it is well established that PA instruction is facilitated when alphabet knowledge (i.e., instruction on letters and their associated sounds) is included. Given that instructional time is limited, it makes sense to teach these skills together. Children need both PA and alphabet knowledge to understand the alphabetic principle—that is, the insight that letters in printed words represent sounds.

Invented spelling instruction also supports PA in addition to word reading. For example, Ouellette and colleagues (2013) divided 40 kindergarteners from literacy-rich classrooms into two groups: a PA group and an invented spelling group. The PA group received PA instruction including "tasks that are typical of phonological awareness curricula and that have well documented effectiveness" (p. 267). The invented spelling group was "taught to increase the sophistication of their naturally occurring invented spellings" (p. 266). Alphabet knowledge was provided to both groups. After 8 weeks (of two 20-minute sessions per week), both groups made significant gains in PA; however, the invented spelling group outperformed the PA group on a word reading task both immediately after the intervention and at the beginning of first grade. Thus, invented spelling improved the children's literacy outcomes above and beyond the literacy-rich instruction they were already receiving in their kindergarten classrooms (p. 273). These positive results have been replicated with children at risk for reading difficulties (Sénéchal, Ouellette, Pagan, & Lever, 2012) and with prereaders (Ouellette & Sénéchal, 2008).

Invented spelling also provides authentic practice that can support early literacy development because it is *real* writing; children have opportunities to express their thoughts and words meaningfully. When comparing invented spelling to typical PA curricula of the usual sort, Vernon and Ferreiro (1999) noted "Participation in language games may allow children to learn about rhymes and other linguistic phenomena, but . . . the only everyday activities that require segmental phonological awareness are writing and reading. Writing seems to be both an end in itself and an instrument for achieving a specific kind of language knowledge" (p. 411). (See Schickedanz, Chapter 3, this volume, for further discussion on early writing.)

CONCLUSION AND FUTURE DIRECTIONS

The pivotal research conducted by the Liberman (1974) and Lundberg (1988) groups and Juel (1988) helped shape a half century of research on (1) the sequence of PA development, (2) the relationship between PA and reading, and (3) the utility of explicit PA instruction. Although much is now known about PA, questions remain. Some of these questions are about the types of early language experiences that help children deepen their understanding of the segmental nature of spoken language and achieve higher levels of PA skill (i.e., that benefit reading and writing the most). For example, early childhood researchers must continue to examine the instructional approaches that are entrenched in practice, even though other approaches might be more efficient and/or effective. For example, is using a comprehensive approach (i.e., starting with larger units of speech) better than targeting phonemes from the start (Ukrainetz et al., 2011)? We also need research that explores the effectiveness of the oft-cited recommendation of simply exposing children to rhyme, alliteration, and predictable texts to foster PA. It would be useful to know who benefits from this exposure, children with strong oral vocabularies or those who lack a strong language base? Finally, it is important to know if the crossover effect identified by Lonigan (2007) and Justice et al. (2003) (i.e., a boost in PA when oral vocabulary is targeted) is evident with more diverse groups of children.

Questions also remain about the origin and nature of the link between oral language and PA. Oral vocabulary is likely a necessary foundation for acquiring PA, but it would be useful to know if this foundation is sturdier when a child has a good start in oral language during infancy. That is, we might benefit from knowing how oral vocabulary growth and early speech perception, and the importance of child-directed speech on the latter, are interconnected with the development of PA. Studies should, of course, continue to explore how children can compensate for language experiences during infancy that have not been robust. Another question for research to explore is whether having an average or above average vocabulary benefits PA development. If such a benefit exists, a second question is whether a specific type/level of vocabulary knowledge (i.e., receptive, expressive, and definitional) is especially beneficial, and why. A third question is whether a critical vocabulary threshold is needed to prompt the developmental course of PA. In other words, does a vocabulary threshold help explain the progress made by some children in PA development and the lack thereof in others? If it does, time might be better spent on oral vocabulary development before targeted and explicit PA instruction begins.

The pivotal studies discussed in this chapter, along with studies that followed, have revealed a great deal about the essential nature of PA in early literacy development. Early childhood educators can be sure that helping children attend to the sound structure of words is important to their later development of reading and writing. But, of course, given other essential foundations for the early years (e.g., science, the arts, math), efficiency of PA instruction matters. I hope that future work will lead us toward a more nuanced understanding of how to foster PA in the early years, and whether this goal might be accomplished within authentic reading, language, and writing experiences.

REFERENCES

Adams, M. J. (1990). *Beginning to read: Thinking and learning about print.* Cambridge, MA: MIT Press.

Adams, M. J., Foorman, B. R., Lundberg, I., & Beeler, T. (1998). *Phonemic awareness in young children: A classroom curriculum.* Baltimore: Brookes.

Anthony, J. L., Lonigan, C. J., Driscoll, K., Phillips, B. M., & Burgess, S. R. (2003). Phonological sensitivity: A quasi-parallel progression of word structure units and cognitive operations. *Reading Research Quarterly, 38*(4), 470–487.

Ball, E. W., & Blachman, B. A. (1991). Does phoneme awareness training in kindergarten make a difference in early word recognition and developmental spelling? *Reading Research Quarterly, 26*(1), 49–66.

Bialystok, E., Luk, G., & Kwan, E. (2005). Bilingualism, biliteracy, and learning to read: Interactions among languages and writing systems. *Scientific Studies of Reading, 9*(1), 43–61.

Bond, G. L., & Dykstra, R. (1967). The cooperative research program in first-grade reading instruction. *Reading Research Quarterly, 2*(4), 5–142.

Bradley, L., & Bryant, P. (1983). Categorizing sounds and learning to read: A causal connection. *Nature, 301,* 419–421.

Bruce, D. (1964). The analysis of word sounds by young children. *British Journal of Educational Psychology, 34,* 158–170.

Bruner, J. S., Oliver, R., & Greenfield, P. (1966). *Studies in cognitive growth.* New York: Wiley.

Bus, A. G., & van IJzendoorn, M. H. (1999). Phonological awareness and early reading: A meta-analysis of experimental training studies. *Journal of Educational Psychology, 91*(3), 403–414.

Calfee, R. C., Lindamood, P., & Lindamood, C. (1973). Acoustic-phonetic skills and reading: Kindergarten through twelfth grade. *Journal of Educational Psychology, 64*(3), 293–298.

California Department of Education (2010). California Preschool Curriculum Framework (Vol. 1). Retrieved from *www.cde.ca.gov/sp/cd/re/psframework.asp.*

Cassano, C. M. (2013). An examination of growth in vocabulary and phonological awareness in early childhood: An individual growth model approach (Doctoral dissertation). Retrieved from *https://open.bu.edu/handle/2144/10955.*

Cassano, C. M., & Schickedanz, J. A. (2015). An examination of the relations between oral vocabulary and phonological awareness in early childhood. *Literacy Research: Theory, Method, and Practice, 64,* 227–248.

Chall, J. S., Roswell, F. G., & Blumenthal, S. H. (1963). Auditory blending ability: A factor in success in beginning reading. *The Reading Teacher, 17,* 113–118.

Chen, Z., & Siegler, R. S. (2000). Overlapping waves theory. *Monographs of the Society for Research in Child Development, 65*(2), 7–11.

Clay, M. M. (1967). The reading behavior of five-year-old children: A research report. *New Zealand Journal of Educational Studies, 2*(1), 11–31.

Clay, M. M. (1979). *What did I write?: Beginning writing behaviour.* Portsmouth, NH: Heinemann.

Cohlert, M. (1979). When can children learn to read—and when can they be taught? In T. G. Waller & G. E. MacKinnon (Eds.), *Reading research: Advances in theory and practice* (pp. 1–30). New York: Academic Press.

Collins, M. F. (2012). Sagacious, sophisticated, and sedulous: The importance of discussing 50-cent words with preschoolers. *Young Children, 67*(5), 66.

Cooper, R. P., & Aslin, R. N. (1990). Preference for infant-directed speech in the first month after birth. *Child Development, 61*(5), 1584–1595.

Corrow, S. L., Cowell, J., Doebel, S., & Koenig, M. A. (2012). How children understand and use other people as sources of knowledge. In A. M. Pinkham, T. Kaefer, & S. B. Neuman (Eds.), *Knowledge development in early childhood: Sources of learning and classroom implications* (pp. 35–51). New York: Guilford Press.

Crain-Thoreson, C., & Dale, P. S. (1992). Do early talkers become early readers?: Linguistic precocity, preschool language, and emergent literacy. *Developmental Psychology, 28,* 42–49.

Cunningham, A. E., & Stanovich, K. E. (1990). Assessing print exposure and orthographic processing skill in children: A quick measure of reading experience. *Journal of Educational Psychology, 82*(4), 733–740.

DeCara, B., & Goswami, U. (2002). Similarity relations among spoken words: The special status of rimes in English. *Behavior Research Methods, Instruments, and Computers, 34*(3), 416–423.

Dickinson, D. K., Golinkoff, R. M., & Hirsh-Pasek, K. (2010). Speaking out for language: Why language is central to reading development. *Educational Researcher, 39*(4), 305–310.

Dickinson, D. K., McCabe, A., Anastopoulos, L., Reisner-Feinberg, E. S., & Poe, M. D. (2003). The comprehensive language approach to early literacy: The interrelationships among vocabulary, phonological sensitivity, and print knowledge among preschool-aged children. *Journal of Educational Psychology, 95*(3), 465–481.

Durgunoğlu, A. Y. (2002). Cross-linguistic transfer in literacy development and implications for language learners. *Annals of Dyslexia, 52*(1), 189–204.

Durkin, D. (1966). *Children who read early.* New York: Teachers College Press.

Ehri, L. C., & Nunes, S. R. (2002). The role of phonemic awareness in learning to read. In A. E. Farstrup & S. J. Samuels (Eds.), *What research has to say about reading instruction* (3rd ed., pp. 110–139). Newark, DE: International Reading Association.

Ehri, L. C., Nunes, S. R., Willows, D. M., Schuster, B. V., Yaghoub-Zadeh, Z., & Shanahan, T. (2001). Phonemic awareness instruction helps children learn to read: Evidence from the National Reading Panel's meta-analysis. *Reading Research Quarterly, 36*(3), 250–287.

Eimas, P. D., Siqueland, E. R., Juscyk, P., & Vigorito, J. (1971). Speech perception in infants. *Science, 171,* 303–306.

Elkonin, D. B. (1963). The psychology of mastering the elements of reading. In B. Simon & J. Simon (Eds.), *Educational psychology in the U.S.S.R.* (pp. 165–179). London: Routledge & Kagan.

Elley, W. B. (1989). Vocabulary acquisition from listening to stories. *Reading Research Quarterly, 24*(2), 174–187.

Farr, R., & Anastasiow, N. (1969). *Tests of reading readiness and achievement: A review and evaluation.* Newark, DE: International Reading Association.

Fox, B., & Routh, D. K. (1975). Analyzing spoken language into words, syllables, and phonemes: A developmental study. *Journal of Psycholinguistic Research, 4*(4), 331–342.

Gesell, A., & Amatruda, C. S. (1941). *Developmental diagnosis: Normal and abnormal child development.* Oxford, UK: Hoeber.

Gibson, E. J. (1965). Learning to read. *Science, 148,* 1066–1072.

Gibson, E. J. (1969). *Principles of perceptual learning and development.* East Norwalk, CT: Appleton-Century-Crofts.

Gibson, E. J., & Levin, H. (1975). *The psychology of reading.* Cambridge, MA: MIT Press.

Goodman, K. S. (1973). Miscues: Windows on the reading process. In K. S. Goodman

(Ed.), *Miscue analysis: Applications to reading instruction* (pp. 3–14). Urbana, IL: National Council of Teachers of English.

Gough, P. B. (1972). One second of reading. *Visible Language, 6*(4), 291–320.

Helfgott, J. A. (1976). Phonemic segmentation and blending skills of kindergarten children: Implications for beginning reading acquisition. *Contemporary Educational Psychology, 1*(2), 157–169.

Hoover, W. A., & Gough, P. B. (1990). The simple view of reading. *Reading and Writing, 2*(2), 127–160.

Hunt, J. M. V. (1961). *Intelligence and experience.* New York: Ronald Press.

Jorm, A. F., & Share, D. L. (1983). An invited article: Phonological recoding and reading acquisition. *Applied Psycholinguistics, 4*(2), 103–147.

Juel, C. (1988). Learning to read and write: A longitudinal study of 54 children from first through fourth grades. *Journal of Educational Psychology, 80*(4), 437–447.

Juel, C. (2006). The impact of early school experiences on initial reading. In D. K. Dickinson & S. B. Neuman (Eds.), *Handbook of early literacy research* (Vol. 2, pp. 410–426). New York: Guilford Press.

Juel, C. (2010). Taking a long view of reading development. In M. G. McKeowan & L. Kucan (Eds.), *Bringing reading research to life* (pp. 11–32). New York: Guilford Press.

Juel, C., Griffith, P. L., & Gough, P. B. (1986). Acquisition of literacy: A longitudinal study of children in first and second grade. *Journal of Educational Psychology, 78*(4), 243–255.

Justice, L. M., Chow, S. M., Capellini, C., Flanigan, K., & Colton, S. (2003). Emergent literacy intervention for vulnerable preschoolers: Relative effects of two approaches. *American Journal of Speech–Language Pathology, 12*(3), 320–332.

Klibanoff, R. S., Levine, S. C., Huttenlocher, J., Vasilyeva, M., & Hedges, L. V. (2006). Preschool children's mathematical knowledge: The effect of teacher "math talk." *Developmental Psychology, 42*(1), 59–69.

Kuhl, P. K. (2011). Early language learning and literacy: Neuroscience implications for education. *Mind, Brain, and Education, 5*(3), 128–142.

LaBerge, D., & Samuels, S. J. (1974). Toward a theory of automatic information processing in reading. *Cognitive Psychology, 6*(2), 293–323.

Liberman, A. M. (1970). The grammars of speech and language. *Cognitive Psychology, 1*(4), 301–323.

Liberman, A. M., Cooper, F. S., Shankweiler, D. P., & Studdert-Kennedy, M. (1967). Perception of the speech code. *Psychological Review, 74*(6), 431–461.

Liberman, I. Y. (1971). Basic research in speech and lateralization of language: Some implications for reading disability. *Bulletin of the Orton Society, 23*(1), 71–87.

Liberman, I. Y., Shankweiler, D., Fischer, F. W., & Carter, B. (1974). Explicit syllable and phoneme segmentation in the young child. *Journal of Experimental Child Psychology, 18*(2), 201–212.

Lindsey, K. A., Manis, F. R., & Bailey, C. E. (2003). Prediction of first-grade reading in Spanish-speaking English-language learners. *Journal of Educational Psychology, 95*(3), 482–494.

Liu, H. M., Kuhl, P. K., & Tsao, F. M. (2003). An association between mothers' speech clarity and infants' speech discrimination skills. *Developmental Science, 6*(3), F1–F10.

Lonigan, C. J. (2007). Vocabulary development and the development of phonological awareness skills in preschool children. In R. K. Wagner, A. E. Muse, & K. R. Tannenbaum (Eds.), *Vocabulary acquisition: Implications for reading comprehension* (pp. 15–31). New York: Guilford Press.

Lonigan, C. J., Burgess, S., & Anthony, J. (2000). Development of emergent literacy and early reading skills in preschool children: Evidence from a latent-variable longitudinal study. *Developmental Psychology, 36*(5), 596–613.

Lonigan, C. J., Burgess, S. R., Anthony, J. L., & Barker, T. A. (1998). Development of phonological sensitivity in 2- to 5-year-old children. *Journal of Educational Psychology, 90*(2), 294–311.

Lonigan, C. J., Schatschneider, C., & Westberg, L. (2008). Identification of children's skills and abilities linked to later outcomes in reading, writing, and spelling. In *Developing Early Literacy: Report of the National Early Literacy Panel* (pp. 55–106). Washington, DC: National Institute for Literacy.

López, L. M., & Greenfield, D. B. (2004). The cross-language transfer of phonological skills of Hispanic Head Start children. *Bilingual Research Journal, 28*(1), 1–18.

Lundberg, I. (1984, August). Learning to read. *School Research Newsletter.* Stockholm, Sweden: National Board of Education.

Lundberg, I. (1991). Phonemic awareness can be developed without reading instruction. In S. A. Brady & D. P. Shankweiler (Eds.), *Phonological processes in literacy: A tribute to Isabelle Y. Liberman* (pp. 47–53). Hillsdale, NJ: Erlbaum.

Lundberg, I. (2009). Early precursors and enabling skills of reading acquisition. *Scandinavian Journal of Psychology, 50*(6), 611–616.

Lundberg, I., Frost, J., & Petersen, O. (1988). Effects of an extensive program for stimulating phonological awareness in preschool children. *Reading Research Quarterly, 23*, 263–284.

Lundberg, I., & Høien, T. (1991). Initial enabling knowledge and skills in reading acquisition: Print awareness and phonological segmentation. In D. J. Sawyer & B. J. Fox (Eds.), *Phonological awareness in reading: The evolution of current perspectives* (pp. 73–96). New York: Springer.

Maclean, M., Bryant, P., & Bradley, L. (1987). Rhymes, nursery rhymes, and reading in early childhood. *Merrill–Palmer Quarterly, 33*, 255–281.

Martins, M. A., & Silva, C. (2006). The impact of invented spelling on phonemic awareness. *Learning and Instruction, 16*(1), 41–56.

McDowell, K. D., Lonigan, C. J., & Goldstein, H. (2007). Relations among socioeconomic status, age, and predictors of phonological awareness. *Journal of Speech, Language, and Hearing, 50*, 1079–1092.

Metsala, J. L. (1999). Young children's phonological awareness and nonword repetition as a function of vocabulary development. *Journal of Educational Psychology, 91*, 3–19.

Metsala, J. L., & Walley, A. C. (1998) Spoken vocabulary growth and the segmental restructuring of lexical representations: Precursors to phonemic awareness and early reading ability. In J. L. Metsala & L. C. Ehri (Eds.), *Word recognition in beginning literacy* (pp. 89–120). Mahwah, NJ: Erlbaum.

Morais, J. (1991a). Constraints on the development of phonemic awareness. In S. A. Brady & D. P. Shankweiler (Eds.), *Phonological processes in literacy: A tribute to Isabelle Y. Liberman* (pp. 5–27). Hillsdale, NJ: Erlbaum.

Morais, J. (1991b). Phonological awareness: A bridge between language and literacy. In D. J. Sawyer & B. J. Fox (Eds.), *Phonological awareness in reading: The evolution of current perspectives* (pp. 31–71). New York: Springer.

Morais, J., Bertelson, P., Cary, L., & Alegria, J. (1986). Literacy training and speech segmentation. *Cognition, 24*(1), 45–64.

Morais, J., Cary, L., Alegria, J., & Bertelson, P. (1979). Does awareness of speech as a sequence of phones arise spontaneously? *Cognition, 7,* 323–331.

Morphett, M. V., & Washburne, C. (1931). When should children begin to read? *The Elementary School Journal, 31*(7), 496–503.

Nagy, W. E., & Anderson, R. C. (1984). How many words are there in printed school English? *Reading Research Quarterly, 19,* 304–330.

National Governors Association Center for Best Practices & Council of Chief State School Officers. (2010). *Common core state standards in English language arts, history/social studies, science, and technical subjects.* Washington, DC: Author.

National Institute of Child Health and Human Development. (2000). *Report of the National Reading Panel.* Washington, DC: U.S. Government Printing Office

Neuman, S. B. (2006). The knowledge gap: Implications for early education. In D. K. Dickinson & S. B. Neuman (Eds.), *Handbook of early literacy research* (Vol. 2, pp. 29–40). New York: Guilford Press.

NICHD Early Child Care Research Network. (2005). Pathways to reading: The role of oral language in the transition to reading. *Developmental Psychology, 41*(2), 428–442.

Ouellette, G. P. (2006). What's meaning got to do with it: The role of vocabulary in word reading and reading comprehension. *Journal of Educational Psychology, 98*(3), 554–556.

Ouellette, G., & Sénéchal, M. (2008). Pathways to literacy: A study of invented spelling and its role in learning to read. *Child Development, 79*(4), 899–913.

Ouellette, G., Sénéchal, M., & Haley, A. (2013). Guiding children's invented spellings: A gateway into literacy learning. *Journal of Experimental Education, 81*(2), 261–279.

Pan, B. A., Rowe, M. L., Singer, J. D., & Snow, C. E. (2005). Maternal correlates of growth in toddler vocabulary production in low-income families. *Child Development, 76*(4), 763–782.

Read, C. (1975). *Children's categorization of speech sounds in English.* Urbana, IL: National Council of Teachers of Reading.

Rescorla, L. (2002). Language and reading outcomes to age 9 in late-talking toddlers. *Journal of Speech, Language, and Hearing Research, 45*(2), 360–371.

Richgels, D. J. (2001). Invented spelling, phonemic awareness, and reading and writing instruction. In S. B. Neuman & D. K. Dickinson (Eds.), *Handbook of early literacy research* (Vol 1, pp. 142–155). New York: Guilford Press.

Rittle-Johnson, B., & Siegler, R. S. (1999). Learning to spell: Variability, choice, and change in children's strategy use. *Child Development, 70,* 332–348.

Robertson, C., & Salter, W. (1995). *The phonological awareness book.* East Moline, IL: LinguiSystems.

Savin, H. B. (1972). What the child knows about speech when he starts to read. In J. F. Kavanaugh & I. G. Mattingly (Eds.), *Language by ear and by eye* (pp. 319–326). Cambridge, MA: MIT Press.

Schickedanz, J. A., & Collins, M. F. (2013). *So much more than the ABCs: The early phases of reading and writing.* Washington, DC: National Association for the Education of Young Children.

Schwarz, I. C., Burnham, D., & Bowey, J. A. (2006). Phoneme sensitivity and vocabulary size in 2½- to 3-year-olds. In *Proceedings of the 11th Australian International Conference on Speech Science and Technology,* 142–147.

Sénéchal, M., Ouellette, G., Pagan, S., & Lever, R. (2012). The role of invented spelling on learning to read in low-phoneme awareness kindergartners: A randomized-control-trial study. *Reading and Writing, 25*(4), 917–934.

Sénéchal, M., Ouellette, G., & Rodney, D. (2006). The misunderstood giant: On the predictive role of early vocabulary to future reading. In D. K. Dickinson & S. B. Neuman (Eds.), *Handbook of early literacy research* (Vol. 2, pp. 173–182). New York: Guilford Press.

Sénéchal, M., Thomas, E., & Monker, J. (1995). Individual differences in 4-year-old children's acquisition of vocabulary during storybook reading. *Journal of Educational Psychology, 87*(2), 218–229.

Shanahan, T. (2016). Thinking with research: Research changes its mind (again). *The Reading Teacher, 70*(2), 245–248.

Share, D. L. (1995). Phonological recoding and self-teaching: Sine qua non of reading acquisition. *Cognition, 55*(2), 151–218.

Share, D. L., Jorm, A. F., MacLean, R., & Matthews, R. (1984). Sources of individual differences in reading achievement. *Journal of Educational Psychology, 76,* 1309–1324.

Shrager, J., & Siegler, R. S. (1998). SCADS: A model of children's strategy choices and strategy discoveries. *Psychological Science, 9*(5), 405–410.

Speece, D. L., Ritchey, K. D., Cooper, D. H., Roth, F. P., & Schatschneider, C. (2004). Growth in early reading skills from kindergarten to third grade. *Contemporary Educational Psychology, 29*(3), 312–332.

Spira, E. G., Bracken, S. S., & Fischel, J. E. (2005). Predicting improvement after first grade reading difficulties: The effects of oral language, emergent literacy, and behavior skills. *Developmental Psychology, 41*(1), 225–234.

Stahl, S. A., & Murray, B. A. (1994). Defining phonological awareness and its relationship to early reading. *Journal of Educational Psychology, 86*(2), 221–234.

Stanovich, K. E. (1984). The interactive–compensatory model of reading: A confluence of developmental, experimental, and educational psychology. *Remedial and Special Education, 5*(3), 11–19.

Stanovich, K. E. (1986). Matthew effects in reading; Some consequences of individual differences in the acquisition of literacy. *Reading Research Quarterly, 21,* 360–406.

Stanovich, K. E., Cunningham, A. E., & Cramer, B. B. (1984). Assessing phonological awareness in kindergarten children: Issues of task comparability. *Journal of Experimental Child Psychology, 38,* 175–190.

Storch, S. A., & Whitehurst, G. J. (2002). Oral language and code-related precursors to reading: Evidence from a longitudinal structural model. *Developmental Psychology, 38*(6), 934–947.

Teale, W. (1978). Positive environments for learning to read: What studies of early readers tell us. *Language Arts, 55*(8), 922–932.

Torppa, M., Lyytinen, P., Erskine, J., Eklund, K., & Lyytinen, H. (2010). Language development, literacy skills, and predictive connections to reading in Finnish children with and without familial risk for dyslexia. *Journal of Learning Disabilities, 43*(4), 308–321.

Torrey, J. (1979). Early readers. In T. G. Waller & G. E. MacKinnon (Eds.), *Reading research: Advances in theory and practice* (pp. 115–144). New York: Academic Press.

Treiman, R., & Baron, J. (1983). Phonemic-analysis training helps children benefit from spelling-sound rules. *Memory and Cognition, 11*(4), 382–389.

Treiman, R., & Zukowski, A. (1991). Levels of phonological awareness. In S. A. Brady & D. P. Shankweiler (Eds.), *Phonological processes in literacy: A tribute to Isabelle Y. Liberman* (pp. 67–83). Hillsdale, NJ: Erlbaum.

Ukrainetz, T. A., Nuspl, J. J., Wilkerson, K., & Beddes, S. R. (2011). The effects of syllable instruction on phonemic awareness in preschoolers. *Early Childhood Research Quarterly, 26,* 50–60.

Vernon, S., & Ferreiro, E. (1999). Writing development: A neglected variable in the consideration of phonological awareness. *Harvard Educational Review, 69*(4), 395–416.

Wagner, R. K., & Torgesen, J. K. (1987). The nature of phonological processing and its causal role in the acquisition of reading skills. *Psychological Bulletin, 101*(2), 192.

Wasik, B. A., & Bond, M. A. (2001). Beyond the pages of a book: Interactive book reading and language development in preschool classrooms. *Journal of Educational Psychology, 93*(2), 243–250.

Wasik, B. A., Bond, M. A., & Hindman, A. (2006). The effects of a language and literacy intervention on Head Start children and teachers. *Journal of Educational Psychology, 98*(1), 63.

Weizman, Z. O., & Snow, C. E. (2001). Lexical input as related to children's vocabulary acquisition: Effects of sophisticated exposure and support for meaning. *Developmental Psychology, 37*(2), 265–279.

Whitehurst, G. J., & Lonigan, C. J. (1998). Child development and emergent literacy. *Child Development, 69*(3), 848–872.

Whiteley, H. E., Smith, C. D., & Connors, L. (2007). Young children at risk of literacy difficulties: Factors predicting recovery from risk following phonologically based intervention. *Journal of Research in Reading, 30*(3), 249–269.

Yopp, H. K. (1988). The validity and reliability of phonemic awareness tests. *Reading Research Quarterly, 23*(2), 159–177.

CHAPTER 6

The Role of Word Recognition in Beginning Reading

Getting the Words off the Page

Ruth M. Wharton-McDonald

Oh, magic hour, when a child first knows she can read printed words!

—FRANCIE in Betty Smith's
A Tree Grows in Brooklyn

The process of becoming a reader has been the subject of intense debate for more than a century. Children who learn to read fluently with comprehension grow into adults who enjoy a higher quality of life and are able to participate fully in a democracy. Those who do not learn to read become adults who are more likely to live in poverty and are less likely to vote (National Center for Education Statistics, 2002). Increasingly, literacy is being considered as a basic civil right (Greene, 2008; Plaut, 2009; Winn, Behizadeh, Duncan, Fine, & Gadsden, 2011). Kofi Annan, former Secretary-General of the United Nations has argued that "literacy unlocks the door to learning throughout life, is essential to development and health, and opens the way for democratic participation and active citizenship." The trajectory of those outcomes begins at birth, but takes a major step forward when children are able to look at a page of text and accurately identify the words.

THREE PIVOTAL PIECES ON EARLY WORD RECOGNITION

Readers who are familiar with my work (e.g., Pressley, Allington, Wharton-McDonald, Block, & Morrow, 2001; Wharton-McDonald, 2008; Wharton-McDonald & Williamson, 2002) know that I spend a lot of time in classrooms in the company of young children who are making their early forays into reading and writing. My research has focused on teacher practices and student perspectives. So when I was asked to delve into these three pieces with an emphasis on the theoretical processes used to identify individual words, I felt a little out of my element. The reader will notice that my analyses of these studies and their implications tend to focus on instructional practice. Nonetheless, I hope I have done justice to these hugely influential contributions to our understandings of beginning reading development.

The first pivotal piece (Stanovich, 1980) was an early contribution to the "reading wars," which, in its extreme, pitted the defenders of bottom-up ("code-based") theorists—those who emphasized the role of decoding in word identification—against the top-down ("meaning-based," whole language) theorists, who argued for the primacy of meaning and context in identifying unfamiliar words. Psychologist Keith Stanovich demonstrated that readers use *both* types of processes, and that readers with deficits one in type (e.g., decoding) can compensate by relying on processes of the other type (e.g., semantic context). The second pivotal piece, the book by Marilyn Jager Adams (1990), was commissioned by the federal government to identify the most effective way to teach phonics to American children. In the book, Adams went well beyond her mandate, reporting in depth on phonics instruction as promised, but also laying the groundwork for an intensifying focus on phonological awareness (PA) *and* recommendations for balanced literacy instruction. Finally, as researchers and educators continued to dispute the role of decoding in early reading development, the article by Share (1995) proposed a hypothesis to explain how young readers proceed from PA (spotlighted by Adams) to decoding and ultimately automatic word recognition. Share's focus on the role of PA as an essential component in word recognition has had a lasting impact on early instruction.

Stanovich (1980): *It's Not Either/Or—Readers Use Top-Down and Bottom-Up Strategies to Recognize Words, but They Do It Differently*

In the late 1970s, the field of early reading was dominated by the great debate (e.g., Chall, 1967/1983; Smith, 1971): Was reading essentially a process of meaning making, in which readers made use of decoding and word recognition skills only as needed (e.g., Goodman, 1965, 1976, 1986; Smith, 1971, 1979)? Or were those bottom-up skills the essential building blocks of reading—without which the edifice of skilled reading could not stand?

Existing models favored one source of input over another. For example, serial-stage models suggested that the beginning reader processes information from the bottom up, beginning with recognizing orthographic patterns, converting the patterns to sounds, and ultimately attaining meaning. Thus, beginning readers (or older, struggling readers) would be unable to access top-down processes, such as the use of context to aid in word recognition—until they had successfully decoded the word. According to these theories, there was no mechanism by which higher-level processes could affect lower levels. These theories predicted that poor readers would expend all of their cognitive energy on decoding and would essentially ignore context.

The top-down models (e.g., Goodman, 1976; Levin & Kaplan, 1970; Smith, 1971, 1973) described the reader as being constantly engaged in hypothesis testing as she or he proceeds through text. That is, the skilled reader[1] develops hypotheses about upcoming words by sampling only a few features of the words and then deciding on the word based on these context-generated hypotheses. Such models argued that poor readers' difficulties with comprehension were the result of too much reliance on visual patterns and cues at the word level and ignoring the syntactic and semantic information provided by context. (For example, a beginning reader encountering the word *black* stops to process each letter and sound and reassembles them to decode the word, rather than attending to the fact that the story is about Halloween, and the word that follows is *cat*.) Levin and Kaplan (1970, p. 132) described the fluent reader as one who "continually assigns tentative interpretations to a text or message and then checks these interpretations." As the material is grammatically or semantically constrained, the reader is able to formulate correct hypotheses about what will come next. When the prediction is confirmed, the material covered by that prediction can be more easily processed and understood. According to Smith, "guessing . . . is not just a preferred strategy for beginners and fluent readers alike; it is the most efficient manner in which to read and learn to read" (1979, p. 67). Top-down models presented poor readers as "slaves to print"—unable to make adequate use of contextual cues to identify an unfamiliar word because they were so focused on the letters and sounds. According to these theories, the readers' difficulty with comprehension was the result of over-attention to print.

In short, in the top-down model the skilled reader begins with meaning-based hypotheses and then attempts to verify them by processing the stimulus (the features of the word), whereas in the bottom-up model the reader begins

---

[1] The deficit-based language of "poor," "unskilled," "struggling," and "good" or "skilled" readers has become less common, having been replaced by terms like "striving" and "successful" readers; I maintain the older language here in order to accurately represent the original Stanovich article, written in 1980.

with the stimulus and then works her or his way up to the meaning. It is important to recognize that "context" can refer to two different types of effects: Context can be used to facilitate memory and higher-order comprehension of text (e.g., Bransford & Johnson, 1973), or it can be used to facilitate ongoing word recognition during reading. It is this latter use of context that Stanovich was interested in studying.

Reviewing the literature, Stanovich (1980) reported that although skilled readers did indeed use context to support their higher-order comprehension of text (making predictions or inferences, for example), their word recognition processes were so rapid and automatic that they did not *need* to rely on context to recognize individual words. Skilled readers' automaticity in word recognition thus left them with more cognitive attention to focus on higher-order comprehension. Stanovich has referred to the rapid automatic word recognition of skilled readers as "one of the most consistent and well replicated [findings] in all of reading research" (1993–1994, p. 282). Moreover, a number of studies found that when attempting to read individual words, less-skilled readers were more dependent on the surrounding context for word recognition than were the skilled readers (Stanovich, West, & Freeman, 1981; West & Stanovich, 1978). The process of using context to identify words, however, comes at a cost. First, it is a slower process (Mitchell & Green, 1978); strong readers rely on automatic word recognition because it is faster. Second, it is prone to errors; relying on context can easily lead the reader astray. And third, it uses attentional capacity, reducing cognitive resources available for the comprehension of larger units of text. Thus, poor readers, with more time (relying on context), can get the words off the page, but they may then struggle to understand what the words mean when they are all put together.

Stanovich (1980) sought to explain developmental and individual differences in the use of context to facilitate word recognition. His interest lay in the interaction of bottom-up (stimulus-based) processing and top-down (context-based) processing and in the ways the interaction changes as readers develop fluency. Stanovich presented evidence for contextual effects in the opposite direction of what would be expected from Smith's (1979) hypothesis. Contrary to Smith's hypothesis, contextual effects actually *diminish* as readers develop fluency: It is the skilled readers who rely more on the features of the word and less-skilled readers who depend on context to figure out what the word might be.

Stanovich's interactive–compensatory model recognized both sets of processes as essential and as part of a compensatory system in which deficits in one set of processes (e.g., the bottom-up processing of orthographic information) could be compensated for by the other set of processes (such as the top-down use of context). While the system allows for compensatory application of the processes, it remains the case that the faster, more efficient way to identify a word is through the application of orthographic and phonemic input derived from the word itself.

Beyond Stanovich: The Goal Is Automaticity, and Earlier Is Better

A major outcome of the interactive–compensatory model was to pose a significant challenge to Smith's (1971, 1973, 1979) and Goodman's (1976) "psycholinguistic guessing game" model of beginning reading processes. The psycholinguistic theory posited that skilled readers use the syntax and semantics of language to generate hypothetical "guesses" for an unknown word. The fact that the trend in contextual effects actually runs in the opposite direction posed a significant challenge to the theory. Moreover, the fact that beginning readers only use context as a means for *compensating* for deficits in automatic word recognition reinforced arguments for the essential role of decoding and word recognition skills in early reading instruction. Stanovich (1980, 2000) provided evidence that efficient word recognition is a prerequisite to good reading comprehension. Readers who develop automaticity early on can recognize words much more rapidly and are able to direct their cognitive attention to making meaning from the words (Adams, 1990; Perfetti, 1985; Stanovich, 1980). Thus, while context plays an important role in strong readers' higher-order comprehension, it is not the primary process by which strong readers identify individual words.

Moreover, while the link is indirect, Stanovich's interactive–compensatory theory of word recognition also played a role in his conceptualization of the "Matthew Effect" (Stanovich, 1986): the term used to describe the snowballing impact of early success in reading, in which "the rich get richer"—and "the poor get poorer." Children who experience early success in reading, developing fast, automatic word recognition skills, read more and are subsequently exposed to more print; they have more opportunities to decode and identify words; they develop reading fluency; reading is thus meaningful and enjoyable and they read more; increased reading leads to an increase in their vocabularies—and all of this supports improved comprehension and strengthens their motivation to read. Readers who are thus motivated and successful continue to be more likely to read and to show growth in all of these areas. The Matthew Effect has been used to explain the growing disparities between the "haves" and the "have nots" across academic domains, because in the words of one 9-year-old: "Reading affects everything you do" (Stanovich, 1986, p. 390). The Matthew Effect continues to exert pressure on teachers to ensure early success for their young students in order to set them on the path of growth (literacy richness) as opposed to the path of failure (in which the poor get poorer).

Adams (1990): *Phonics Is an Essential Component of Early Reading Instruction—but It Is Only One Component*

In 1986, Congress mandated the Department of Education to "provide guidance as to how schools might maximize the quality of phonic [sic] instruction in beginning reading programs" (Adams, 1990, p. 29). Marilyn Jager Adams, a cognitive psychologist working with the Center for the Study of Reading, was enlisted to review the existing research and address the mandate; *Beginning Reading: Thinking and Learning about Print* was the result. In the book, Adams undertook a massive review of the existing findings, covering 20 years of basic and applied research on models of reading and word identification, phonemic awareness and phonics, reading development, and instructional models— including the controversies surrounding phonics instruction—and the educational context in which it all unfolds for children. The book was hailed as "the most complete review, within a single cover" of the expanding knowledge of reading processes, controversies surrounding phonics instruction, and related research and issues in early reading instruction (Pearson, 1990, p. vi).

Understanding Basic Processes

In explaining the complexities of the reading process, Adams described a (later oft-cited) model of multiple processors that contribute to a reader's identification and understanding of the printed word. She began with an *orthographic processor,* which receives input directly from the written page. It contains all of the individual and combination letter units known to the reader. Readers acquire familiarity with these units, or spelling patterns, through multiple encounters with them: the more encounters they have, the stronger the connections and the resulting facilitation—among individual units. Thus, when the experienced reader encounters the letter *t* on the page, all of the letters that might follow a *t* in English are facilitated; those that occur frequently (such as *h* or *a*) are strongly facilitated; others occurring less frequently (such as *c* or *l*) are only weakly activated. Some (such as *j* or *q*) are not activated at all.

The orthographic processor has bidirectional relationships with both a *phonological processor* and a *meaning processor.* The *phonological processor* attends to the auditory representation of the letters or words. Thus, the orthographic processor sends information to the phonological processor, which determines the pronounceability of the letter combinations, and sends back excitatory or inhibitory stimulation to the orthographic processor. These two processors are working in concert to send input to the *meaning processor,* which works to determine whether the pronounceable letter string makes sense as a real word. Simultaneously, the meaning processor sends information to the orthographic and phonological processors, which use the information to predict a word that makes sense. All three processors are interconnected, so that at any given time they are all working on the same set of letters. For beginning readers, Adams suggested that the orthographic and phonological processors work together to generate a pronounceable word, and then the meaning processor determines whether the word is real—that is, whether it makes sense. For more skilled readers, however, it would be possible to go directly from the orthographic processor to the word's meaning and bypass the phonological processor: the skilled reader can activate the meaning of a word just as quickly as its sound.

The final component in Adams's model is a *context processor*, which, at the "top" of the system, interacts with the meaning processor to determine whether the possible words make sense in the context of the text. The context processor "is in charge of constructing a coherent, ongoing interpretation of the text" (Adams, 1990, p. 138). It thus facilitates the perception of contextually appropriate words, as well as the contextually appropriate interpretation of words that are ambiguous or diffuse. In texts that are highly predictive, such as *Brown Bear, Brown Bear, What Do You See?* (Martin, 1983) or *Green Eggs and Ham* (Geisel, 1960), the meaning processor will receive strong facilitation from the context processor. Note that Adams's model begins with the orthographic and phonological processors—letters and sounds—but necessarily includes the meaning and context processors as well in explaining basic reading processes. Moreover, consistent with Stanovich (1980), Adams reiterated the findings that context exerts a stronger effect on the word identification performance of younger and less skilled readers than it does on older, more skilled readers.

Instructional Considerations

As I noted earlier, Adams's primary obligation to the Center for the Study of Reading was to evaluate the evidence related to phonics instruction in beginning reading. Consistent with Jeanne Chall's (1967/1983) classic analysis, Adams (1990) concluded unequivocally that systematic phonics is an essential component of effective reading instruction. The foundation for deriving meaning from text is the automaticity with which skilled readers recognize words. Automatic word recognition "allows them to devote their conscious attention and effort to the meaning and significance of the text" (Adams, 1991, p. 207). And phonics instruction, she found, was the surest way to develop automaticity.

In the process of understanding the role of word recognition in beginning reading, Adams delved deeply into the phonological prerequisites of phonics instruction, concluding that, "only those prereaders[2] who acquire awareness of phonemes . . . learn to read successfully" (1990, p. 293). Her book highlighted research demonstrating the multiple levels of phonemic awareness development, ranging from knowledge of nursery rhymes (the most primitive level) to the manipulation of individual phonemes. She underscored the relationship

---

[2] Adams (1990) uses the term "prereader" throughout the book to refer to young children who are still developing the processes of conventional reading. She was widely criticized for avoiding the terms "emergent reader" and "emergent literacy," despite their widespread use at the time. According to Adams et al. (1991), she chose the "archaic" term "prereader" as a rhetorical move, rather than as a deliberate rejection of the term "emergent reader."

between phonemic awareness and early reading and spelling and emphasized the apparent advantage of teaching letters and sounds *together* (Bradley & Bryant, 1983; see also Cassano, Chapter 5, this volume).

While Adams's book devoted a great deal of attention to the understanding of word identification processes—and sound–symbol correspondences in particular—she was always clear that phonics instruction is just one part of teaching children to read: It is a necessary but not sufficient set of skills and strategies. The book is replete with frequent reminders that these essential skills are best learned in the context of real reading and writing. For example, in her chapter titled "The Proper Place of Phonics," Adams wrote that young children

> should have a solid sense of [reading's] various functions—to entertain, inform, communicate, record—and the potential value of each such function to their own selves. All such awarenesses are powerfully fostered by reading aloud to children—by engaging them regularly and interactively in the enjoyment and exploration of print. (1990, p. 411)

This perspective differentiates the book from its historical predecessors (e.g., Bond & Dykstra, 1967; Chall, 1967/1983; Stebbins, St. Pierre, Proper, Anderson, & Cerva, 1977), which, according to Allington, maintained a much narrower focus on phonics and word-level reading (in Adams et al., 1991).

In fact, despite criticisms (e.g., Adams et al., 1991) that Adams overemphasized phonics and advocated an all-phonics, drill-and-kill curriculum, her book was essentially an appeal for a balanced, child-focused approach to early reading instruction: one that deliberately includes systematic, explicit phonics instruction, but that does so in the context of real reading and with attention to children's interests. Indeed, she explicitly refrained from making pedagogical recommendations, concluding in her last chapter that "there can be no such thing as a universal method" (Adams, 1990, p. 423).

Children's Unequal Preparation to Succeed

Finally, *Beginning to Read*'s spotlight on the large and widening gap between the "haves" and the "have nots" among American students was a significant contribution to the field. Given the power of oral language, concepts of print, PA, and letter–name knowledge to predict and support early success in reading, Adams raised the issue of how to educate children who began school *without* such skills and understandings. She compared children who arrived at first grade with thousands of hours of literacy preparation to those who began school with many fewer such experiences. She cited studies by Allington (1983, 1989a, 1989b), in which schools with higher proportions of "at risk" children from low-income families—those who need *more* reading time in order to catch up—actually spent 20 minutes *less* per day on reading. Moreover, she lamented an educational system in which "characteristically, low achievers are given less classroom opportunity than their on-schedule peers to read text or to read text independently" (Adams, 1990, p. 417). Still worse, she pointed out, when low-achieving students *were* given opportunities to read, it was typically done in round-robin style, with the consequence that they also wound up reading far fewer words, stories, and books than their high-achieving peers. In identifying these challenges, Adams suggested issues far greater than "phonics or no phonics" instruction—and she summoned her readers—and the broader educational community—to step up and address them.

Reverberations of the Adams Study

As predicted (see Editors' Note, Adams et al., 1991, p. 370; Pearson, 1990), *Beginning to Read* was of great interest to—and highly controversial within—the reading community. Despite Adams's espoused wishes to the contrary, the book served to reinforce the ongoing reading wars, in which whole language critics focused on her strong support for phonics instruction, and code-based proponents all but ignored her reminders of the critical importance of engaging reading experiences. Adding to the polarization was the fact that many interested educators and policymakers did not read the book, but rather opted for the much shorter "Summary" version prepared by other authors from the Center for the Study of Reading (Stahl, Osborn, & Lehr, 1990). In an effort to make Adams's book more accessible to a wider audience, the authors reorganized the presentation of findings somewhat and eliminated a great deal of information. The result was a streamlined version that could easily be interpreted as in favor of phonics, and not much else. The text was cited repeatedly in publications that were used to defend legislation in California (California Department of Education, 1996) and Texas (Texas Education Agency, 1997), requiring phonemic and PA instruction and restricting beginning readers to the use of decodable texts as part of a heavy emphasis on early-grades phonics instruction. (Interestingly, the other frequently cited work was Stanovich's [1986] article on the Matthew Effect.) For more on the legislation of decodable text in early reading instruction, see page 154.

But in seeking a middle ground between the hard-core extremes in the reading wars, Adams's book also led to increased calls for balanced instruction and to a new kind of classroom-based research designed to investigate how expert teachers were putting research-based practices into action to promote early literacy development. In a 1991 interview, Adams claimed that despite accusations that the book was dense and difficult for some to read, she had in fact written it for first-grade teachers more than any other audience, stating that first-grade teachers have "the most difficult job in the world" (Adams, 1991, p. 212). Rather than constrain instructional methods or promote drill-and-kill phonics worksheets, she hoped that the book would, "directly or indirectly help to create the kind of support that will let teachers work most flexibly and most confidently" (National Council of Teachers of English, 1991, p. 212). The book indirectly challenged researchers to investigate classroom practices with the goal of better understanding how to combine the essential components of reading instruction in ways that developed skill and strategies *and* engaged young children so that they not only could read, but also wanted to read.

Rejecting laboratory-based research into basic processes, some scholars began using qualitative methods to investigate the practices of expert reading teachers. Michael Pressley and his colleagues were among the first to conduct such classroom-based research and to document the ways in which teachers in first and fourth grades were implementing balanced reading instruction (e.g., Allington & Johnston, 2002; Pressley et al., 2001; Wharton-McDonald, Pressley, & Mistretta, 1998). These investigators demonstrated that the most effective teachers (those whose students were consistently reading more challenging books, writing more coherent pieces, and exhibiting the highest levels of engagement) did, in fact, teach phonics and word recognition skills. *And* they did it in the context of meaningful reading and writing activities. Such qualitative classroom studies and related teacher survey studies (e.g., Baumann, Hoffman, Moon, & Duffy-Hester, 1998) confirmed that while researchers continued to wage the reading wars, great teachers were already implementing balanced instruction.

Share (1995): *Beginning Readers Teach Themselves the Orthographic Structures Required for Word Recognition*

By the mid-1990s, the central role of word recognition in early reading development was accepted by the vast majority of the literacy community. While teachers and scholars continued to study and debate instructional methods, there was general agreement that in order to become successful, beginning readers needed a foundation of phonemic awareness and PA and the ability to quickly identify words in print. Research continued to demonstrate that differences in the ability to identify unfamiliar words accounted for much of the variation in beginning reading success, including success in reading comprehension (Rispens, 1990; Stanovich, 1991). What was (and is) still undetermined was the process by which beginning readers acquired this ability.

David Share (1995) reasoned that there were a number of possible ways for the reader to build the orthographic lexicon, that is, those words that the reader could identify rapidly and automatically; they included contextual guessing, direct instruction, or the process of phonological recoding itself. Stanovich (1980, 1984) had already demonstrated that while contextual guessing was favored by struggling readers, the process was too inefficient and slow to be the primary means of the typically developing reader. Since the most challenging words in a text are likely to be those that contain the most meaning, the reader who relies solely on context is at a circular disadvantage: She needs the unfamiliar word to build context in order to *use* context to guess the word (Finn, 1977–1978). Likewise, mastering the enormous number of orthographic combinations in printed English through direct instruction would simply be too inefficient. Nagy and Anderson (1984) estimated that school English includes upward of 88,500 distinct word families—and the likelihood that a developing reader could master even a fraction of this "orthographic avalanche" seemed remote (Share, 1990, p. 153).

Based on earlier work with Anthony Jorm, Share (1995) proposed a hypothesis that viably explained both word identification and the mechanism by which the Matthew Effect got rolling. Share's hypothesis suggested that beginning readers develop the ability to recognize orthographic patterns and words through successful experiences of phonologically recoding them. According to Share, the process of phonological recoding (translating print to sound) is in fact a self-teaching process, "enabling the learner to acquire the detailed orthographic representations necessary for rapid, autonomous, visual word recognition" (p. 152). That is, each time the learner encounters an unfamiliar word or letter pattern, he has an opportunity to acquire word-specific orthographic information. When these encounters are successful, the reader's knowledge is reinforced, and he is subsequently more likely to apply the information in future encounters. The self-teaching hypothesis thus conceptualizes the developmental role of recoding (sounding out) as *item based*, rather than *stage based*. Each time the reader has a successful encounter with a word, she learns specific information about the word's orthography. According to Share, "the process of word recognition will depend primarily on the frequency [with] which a child has been exposed to a particular word together, of course, with the nature and success of item identification" (p. 155). Moreover, he proposed that the self-teaching opportunities provided by phonological recoding are effective not only for the beginning reader but "throughout the entire ability range" (p. 156). Thus, as readers develop their abilities, their recoding process becomes increasingly complex—increasingly "lexicalized,"—as their growing orthographic knowledge imposes constraints on a word's possibilities. Beginning readers may start out by attending to individual letter–sound correspondences, but over time and with experience, they learn to attend to details such as positional or morphemic constraints (Share, 1995; Gillon, 2017).

Notably, while Share acknowledged the role of orthographic knowledge, he argued that it is the phonological recoding that is the primary process; the storage and retrieval of orthographic knowledge are secondary. Because decoding is dependent on PA—being able to identify, isolate, and manipulate the sounds of language—acquiring PA skills constitutes the primary process in the self-teaching hypothesis.

Share's theory helped to explain the phenomenon whereby readers are more successful with words they encounter frequently, regardless of whether the words are actually "high-frequency" words. Consistent with an item-based model, Treiman (1993) found that first graders were more likely to accurately spell words that they had frequently encountered in print. This was true whether or not the word's spelling was perceived to be difficult; it was the child's *actual encounters with the words* that determined learning.

Share's (1995) work emphasized PA's foundational role in the development of independent, conventional reading. Given the importance of recoding in word identification, children who struggle with PA will also struggle in their early attempts at decoding; they will thus be exposed to fewer words and opportunities for self-teaching of basic orthographic structures. Increasingly, they will be less likely to encounter more complex grapheme–phoneme relationships; again, they will have fewer occasions for self-teaching. With limited ability to identify words on the page, these readers will tend to be dysfluent, will be exposed to fewer new vocabulary words, and thus, will struggle with comprehension and perhaps, most important, motivation. Thus, according to Share's model, the Matthew Effect begins with PA and the subsequent ability to recode print to sound.

Reverberations of the Self-Teaching Hypothesis

The self-teaching effect has subsequently been explored by many other researchers with a range of populations. It has been demonstrated in children from first through fifth grades (Cunningham, 2006; Share, 2004) and in oral and silent reading (Bowey & Muller, 2005; deJong & Share, 2007; deJong et al., 2009).

On the heels of Adams's (1990) book, situating phonemic awareness and PA at the root of decoding, Share's emphasis on the critical role of phonological recoding led to a heavy emphasis on instruction for young children. A proliferation of preschool and kindergarten literacy programs, featuring exercises, activities, and assessments intended to boost children's ability to identify and manipulate the sounds of English, ensued. Adams was among the authors who created classroom curricula for developing phonemic awareness (Adams, Foorman, Lundberg, & Beeler, 1998; McCormick, Throneburg, & Smitley, 2002).

While Share did not begin to make instructional recommendations in his work, his model proposed that readers acquire the most knowledge about the orthographic structure of words incidentally while reading independently (Cunningham, 2006; Share, 1995). An implied extension to practice, there-fore, would seem to be to maximize "incidental" exposures by having readers spend time with decodable texts, in which they have the greatest incidence of successful encounters with predictable orthographic patterns (i.e., the child who is learning that the vowel digraph "oa" most often makes the /ō/ sound might benefit from reading sentences such as "Come *aboard*! My *boat* will *float*; I use my *oars* to row for the *coast*"). As noted earlier, the states of California (California Department of Education, 1996) and Texas (Texas Education Agency, 1997) legislated the exclusive use of decodable texts in the first grade not long after the self-teaching hypothesis was formally elaborated in Share's (1995) article. A more careful reading of his piece, however, suggests a more moderate approach. According to Share, when the reader is immersed in "natural text" (note that he does not even consider the constrained texts legislated by California and Texas), there will be many words that are familiar based on their high-frequency occurrences and a smaller number of words that will require the more resource-draining recoding process. "Too great a number of unfamiliar words," he writes, "will disrupt ongoing comprehension processes by siphoning off available cognitive resources (Perfetti, 1985), but the occasional novel string will provide relatively unintrusive self-teaching opportunities" (p. 158). Note the use of the word "occasional": Share specifies that self-teaching opportunities should be at the "cutting edge" of reading acquisition—for both beginning and skilled readers—"enabling a gradual, unobtrusive expansion of the orthographic lexicon." Thus, Share's article implies that beginning readers benefit from systematic opportunities to practice, but they do not necessarily need the constraints of all decodable text.

One possible approach to providing the "occasional" encounters with novel strings of letters (words) in the context of otherwise familiar print would be to promote the use of texts at a child's independent reading level. A number of prominent researchers have reported that developing readers benefit from extensive reading in which they experience high levels of accuracy (Allington, 2002; Betts, 1946; Ehri, Dreyer, Flugman, & Gross, 2007). Their recommendations seem to be in line with Share's argument for occasional encounters.

CONCLUSION: COLLECTIVE IMPLICATIONS FOR BEGINNING READING INSTRUCTION

The three pivotal studies described in this chapter highlighted the importance of ensuring multiple opportunities to develop word recognition skills as the foundation for fluent, comprehensive reading. Stanovich's (1980) interactive–compensatory model has clear implications for early instruction. If the ability to identify words in print—and to do so rapidly (automatically)—is an essential process in developing reading, then beginning readers must receive strong instruction in decoding and word recognition. An essential goal of early reading instruction should be rapid recognition *in order that the reader will be able to devote conscious attention to comprehension of the text.* This goal is different from rapid recognition for the sake of rapid recognition. Stanovich's work does not assign any value to the rapid pronunciation of word lists—or even sentences, such as on the Dynamic Indicators of Basic Early Literacy Skills (DIBELS) assessment. Skilled readers demonstrate automaticity in the service of higher-order comprehension.

Adams's (1990) review reconfirmed the essential importance of decoding and word recognition in beginning reading instruction; she emphasized the need for explicit and systematic phonics instruction. But Adams also made it clear that word recognition is only one part of a very complex process, and that beginning readers must understand the functions of print—and they must be motivated to *want* to read.

Share's (1995) self-teaching hypothesis suggests that students need plenty of opportunities to recode the orthographic patterns of written English. It has been argued (and even legislated) that this must be done in the context of decodable text, but a careful read of his (1995) piece suggests that exclusive use of decodable text is not necessary and, indeed, perhaps not even desirable. Again, novice readers need opportunities to practice and thus master the patterns of recoding, but Share's own writing indicates that this can be done in the context of "natural text" (p. 158).

All three of these pieces emphasize the critical role of automatic word recognition in skilled reading. And the work of all three authors implicates the value of accomplishing this in the context of a balanced, motivating instructional environment. While rapid word identification is the foundation of skilled reading, it is only the foundation; it is not actually reading. In a basic explanation of why Reading First policies failed to yield expected gains, Cunningham (2017) reminds us that the foundations of reading must not be mistaken for the whole building. Thoughtful, enjoyable, informative reading rests on a foundation of word recognition. But raising the building itself involves a great deal more.

A Final Caveat

There has been a recurring assumption in the field that the essential struggle for beginning readers is to get the words off the page; that once these readers have identified the words, they will immediately access the words' meanings and comprehension will follow. Stanovich (1980), for example, cites two studies in which word recognition automatically leads to meaning activation for young children (Ehri, 1977; Stanovich, 1986). More recently, though, scholars have questioned this assumption, with attention paid to both early-grade texts and student demographics. Mesmer, Cunningham, and Hiebert (2012), for example, point out that the phonetically regular words appearing in decodable texts may not be known to the young readers. For example, "pigs doing *jigs* eating *figs*" may be decodable, but may still be incomprehensible to young readers learning English or those with limited vocabularies. Some research indicates that up to 50% of words in early-grade texts may be unknown to children (Foorman, Francis, Davidson, Harm, & Griffin, 2004). Chapter 1 in this volume reviews the work of Hart and Risley (1995) documenting the enormous vocabulary gap between children of different socioeconomic backgrounds before they even begin school. An overemphasis on phonological recoding and word recognition ignores the essential issue of whether the reader understands the words she is reading. The words are the means to an end; ultimately, the goal is understanding and being able to do something with the meaning they convey.

REFERENCES

Adams, M. J. (1990). *Beginning to read: Thinking and learning about print.* Cambridge, MA: MIT Press.

Adams, M. J. (1991). A talk with Marilyn Adams (no author listed). *Language Arts, 68,* 206–212.

Adams, M., Allington, R., Chaney, J., Goodman, Y., Kapinus, B., McGee, L. M., . . . Williams, J. P. (1991). Beginning to read: A critique by literacy professionals and a response by Marilyn Jager Adams. *The Reading Teacher, 44*(6), 370–395.

Adams, M. J., Forman, B. R., Lundberg, I., & Beeler, T. (1998). *Phonemic awareness in young children: A classroom curriculum.* Baltimore: Brookes.

Allington, R. L. (1983). The reading instruction provided readers of different reading abilities. *Elementary School Journal, 83,* 95–107.

Allington, R. L. (1989a). Coherence or chaos?: Qualitative dimensions of the literacy instruction provided low-achievement children. In A. Gartner & D. Lipsky (Eds.), *Beyond separate education.* Baltimore: Brookes.

Allington, R. L. (1989b). How policy and regulation influence instruction for at-risk learners: Why poor readers rarely comprehend well. In B. F. Jones & L. Idol (Eds.), *Dimensions of thinking and cognitive instruction.* Mahwah, NJ: Erlbaum.

Allington, R. L. (2002). What I've learned about effective reading instruction from a decade of studying exemplary elementary classroom teachers. *The Phi Delta Kappan, 83,* 40–47.

Allington, R. L., & Johnston, P. H. (2002). *Reading to learn: Lessons from exemplary fourth-grade classrooms.* New York: Guilford Press.

Baumann, J. F., Hoffman, J. V., Moon, J., & Duffy-Hester, A. M. (1998). Where are teachers' voices in the phonics/whole language debate?: Results from a survey of U.S. elementary classroom teachers. *The Reading Teacher, 51,* 636–650.

Betts, E. A. (1946). *Foundations of reading instruction: With emphasis on differentiated guidance.* Oxford, UK: American Book Company.

Bond, G. L., & Dykstra, R. (1967). The cooperative research program in first-grade reading instruction. *Reading Research Quarterly, 2,* 5–142.

Bowey, J. A., & Muller, D. (2005). Phonological recoding and rapid orthographic learning in third-graders' silent reading: A critical test of the self-teaching hypothesis. *Journal of Experimental Child Psychology, 92,* 203–219.

Bradley, L., & Bryant, P. E. (1983). Categorizing sounds and learning to read—A causal connection. *Nature, 301,* 419–421.

Bransford, J. D., & Johnson, M. K. (1973). Consideration of some problems in comprehension. In W. G. Chase (Ed.), *Visual information processing* (pp. 383–438). New York: Academic Press.

California Department of Education. (1996). *Teaching reading: A balanced, comprehensive approach to teaching reading in prekindergarten through grade three.* Sacramento, CA: Author.

Chall, J. S. (1983). *Learning to read: The great debate.* New York: McGraw-Hill. (Original work published 1967)

Cunningham, A. E. (2006). Accounting for children's orthographic learning while reading text: Do children self-teach? *Journal of Experimental Child Psychology, 95,* 56–77.

Cunningham, A. E., & Stanovich, K. E. (2001). What reading does for the mind. *Journal of Direct Instruction, 1*(2), 137–149.

deJong, P. F., Bitter, D. J. L., van Setten, M., & Marinus, E. (2009). Does phonological recoding occur during silent reading, and is it necessary for orthographic learning? *Journal of Experimental Child Psychology, 104,* 267–282.

deJong, P. F., & Share, D. L. (2007). Orthographic learning during oral and silent reading. *Scientific Studies of Reading, 11,* 55–71.

Ehri, L. C. (1977). Do adjectives and functors interfere as much as nouns in naming pictures? *Child Development, 48,* 697–701.

Ehri, L. C., Dryer, L. G., Flugman, B., & Gross, A. (2007). Reading rescue: An effective tutoring intervention model for language minority students who are struggling readers in first grade. *American Educational Research Journal, 44,* 414–448.

Finn, P. J. (1977–1978). Word frequency, information theory, and cloze performance: A transfer feature theory of processing in reading. *Reading Research Quarterly, 23,* 510–537.

Foorman, B. R., Francis, D. J., Davidson, K. C., Harm, M. W., & Griffin, J. (2004). Variability in text features in six grade 1 basal reading programs. *Scientific Studies of Reading, 8,* 167–197.

Geisel, T. (1960). *Green eggs and ham.* Boston: Random House.

Gillon, G. T. (2017). *Phonological awareness: From research to practice* (2nd ed.). New York: Guilford Press.

Goodman, K. (1965). A linguistic study of cues and miscues in reading. *Elementary English, 42,* 639–643.

Goodman, K. (1976). Reading: A psycholinguistic guessing game. In H. Singer & R. Ruddell (Eds.), *Theoretical models and processes of reading* (2nd ed., pp. 497–508). Newark, DE: International Reading Association.

Goodman, K. (1986). *What's whole in whole language?* Portsmouth, NH: Heinemann.

Greene, S. (2008). Introduction. In S. Greene (Ed.), *Literacy as a civil right: Reclaiming social justice in literacy teaching and learning* (pp. 1–25). New York: Peter Lang.

Hart, B., & Risley, T. R. (1995). *Meaningful differences in the everyday experiences of young American children.* Baltimore: Brookes.

Levin, H., & Kaplan, E. L. (1970). Grammatical structure and reading. In H. Levin & J. Williams (Eds.), *Basic studies in reading* (pp. 119–133). New York: Basic Books.

Martin, B. M., Jr. (1983). *Brown bear, brown bear, what do you see?* New York: Henry Holt.

McCormick, C. E., Throneburg, R. N., & Smitley, J. M. (2002). *A sound start: Phonemic awareness lessons for reading success.* New York: Guilford Press.

Mesmer, H. A., Cunningham, J. W., & Hiebert, E. H. (2012). Toward a theoretical model of text complexity for the early grades: Learning from the past, anticipating the future. *Reading Research Quarterly, 47,* 235–258.

Mitchell, D. C., & Green, D. W. (1978). The effects of context and content on immediate processing in reading. *Quarterly Journal of Experimental Psychology, 30,* 609–636.

Nagy, W. E., & Anderson, R. C. (1984). How many words are there in printed school English? *Reading Research Quarterly, 19,* 357–366.

National Council of Teachers of English. (1991). A talk with Marilyn Adams. *Language Arts, 63,* 206–212.

Pearson, P. D. (1990). Forward: How I came to know about beginning to read. In M. J. Adams, *Beginning to read: Thinking and learning about print* (pp. v–viii). Cambridge, MA: MIT Press.

Perfetti, C. (1985). *Reading ability.* New York: Oxford University Press.

Plaut, S. (Ed.). (2009). *The right to literacy in secondary schools: Creating a culture of thinking.* New York: Teachers College Press.

Pressley, M., Allington, R., Wharton-McDonald, R., Block, C., & Morrow, L. (2001). *Learning to read: Lessons from exemplary first-grade classrooms.* New York: Guilford Press.

Rispens, J. (1990). Comprehension problems in dyslexia. In D. Balota, G. Flores d'Arcias, & K. Rayner (Eds.), *Comprehension processes in reading* (pp. 603–620). Mahwah, NJ: Erlbaum.

Share, D. L. (1995). Phonological recoding and self-teaching: Sine qua non of reading acquisition. *Cognition, 55,* 151–218.

Share, D. L. (2004). Orthographic learning at a glance: On the time course and developmental onset of self-teaching. *Journal of Experimental Child Psychology, 87,* 267–298.

Smith, F. (1971). *Understanding reading: A psycholinguistic analysis of reading and learning to read.* Mahwah, NJ: Erlbaum.

Smith, F. (1973). *Psycholinguistics and Reading.* New York: Holt, Rinehart and Winston.

Smith, F. (1979). *Reading without nonsense.* New York: Teachers College Press.

Stahl, S., Osborn, J., & Lehr, F. (1990). *Beginning to read: Thinking and learning about print: A summary.* Urbana, IL: Center for the Study of Reading and The Reading Research and Education Center.

Stanovich, K. E. (1980). Toward an interactive–compensatory model of individual differences in the development of reading fluency. *Reading Research Quarterly, 12,* 32–71.

Stanovich, K. E. (1984). The interactive–compensatory model of reading: A confluence of developmental, experimental, and educational psychology. *Remedial and Special Education, 5*(3), 11–19.

Stanovich, K. E. (1986). Matthew effects in reading: Some consequences of individual differences in the acquisition of literacy. *Reading Research Quarterly, 21,* 360–407.

Stanovich, K. E. (1991). Word recognition: Changing perspectives. In R. Barr, M. L. Kamil, P. Mosenthal, & P. D. Pearson (Eds.), *Handbook of reading research* (Vol. 2, pp. 418–452). New York: Longman.

Stanovich, K. E. (1993–1994). Romance and reality. *The Reading Teacher, 47,* 280–291.

Stanovich, K. E., West, R. F., & Freeman, D. J. (1981). A longitudinal study of sentence context effects in second-grade children: Tests of an interactive–compensatory model. *Journal of Experimental Child Psychology, 32*, 185–199.

Stebbins, L. B., St. Pierre, R. G., Proper, E. C., Anderson, R. B., & Cerva, T. R. (1977). *Education as experimentation: A planned variation model* (Vol. IV-A), *An evaluation of Project Follow Through*. Cambridge, MA: Abt Associates.

Texas Education Agency (1997). *Beginning reading instruction: Components and features of a research-based reading program*. Austin, TX: Author.

Treiman, R. (1993). *Beginning to spell*. New York: Oxford University Press.

West, R. F., & Stanovich, E. E. (1978). Automatic contextual facilitation in readers of three ages. *Child Development, 49*, 717–727.

Wharton-McDonald, R. (2008). The dynamics of flexibility in effective literacy teaching. In K. Cartwright (Ed.), *Flexibility in literacy processes and instructional practice: Implications of developing representational ability for literacy teaching and learning*. New York: Guilford Press.

Wharton-McDonald, R., Pressley, M., & Mistretta, J. (1998). Literacy instruction in nine first-grade classrooms: Teacher characteristics and student achievement. *The Elementary School Journal, 99*, 101–128.

Wharton-McDonald, R., & Williamson, J. (2002). Focus on the real and make sure it connects to kids' lives. In R. Allington & P. Johnston (Eds.), *Reading to learn: Lessons from exemplary fourth-grade classrooms* (pp. 78–98). New York: Guilford Press.

Winn, M. T., Behizadeh, N., Duncan, G., Fine, M., & Gadsden, V. (2011). The right to be literate: Literacy, education, and the school-to-prison pipeline. *Review of Research in Education, 35*, 147–173.

CHAPTER 7

Engagement, Motivation, Self-Regulation, and Literacy Development in Early Childhood

Alisa Hindin

Although no curriculum can ensure that every child
will succeed immediately at the complex task of reading,
strengthening children's emergent literacy skills and
behavioral aptitude may improve their potential for resilience
should they confront early reading difficulties.
—E. G. SPIRA, S. S. BRACKEN, and
J. E. FISCHEL (2005, p. 233)

It is independent reading time in Ms. Tyler's fourth-grade class. As I look around, I take particular notice of Miley, Xavier, and Connor. Xavier is sitting at his desk with his knees up fully engrossed in *Space Case* by Stuart Gibbs. Miley is quickly flipping through *Wonderstruck* by Brian Selznick, going back to carefully examine the sections of the book that contain only pictures. Connor has yet to open his book and is spending his time erasing marks on his desk. At first glance, it is impossible to know why there is such a difference in these children's reading behaviors, but it is clear that Connor is not at all engaged with the reading task.

Independent reading time in many classrooms is a time during which children can select books of interest to read that provide appropriate challenge. When children are off-task during independent reading, it may be because they have not found a suitable book or they might just be having a difficult day. Yet, for Connor, this off-task behavior is a frequent occurrence. In fact, Connor's teachers noted his difficulties with focusing and attention since he began school. As far back as preschool, Connor had trouble paying attention and listening to directions. He struggled with turn-taking and transitioning from one task to another. Even though Connor entered kindergarten recognizing his letters and exhibiting a strong vocabulary, reading did not come easily to him. His first- and second-grade teachers reported that he was difficult to engage in reading-related tasks. As a fourth grader, Connor appears unmotivated and distracted frequently. His challenges with reading and his reluctance to read have resulted in his reading less than many of his peers throughout early elementary school. Researchers have shown that these missed opportunities to practice reading often result in continued and exacerbated struggles with reading (Allington, 2009; Juel, 1988).

By the time children reach fourth grade, it can be challenging to significantly improve their reading performance. In fact, researchers have found that children's reading performance is fairly stable over time and that children who struggle with reading early in their elementary school years continue to struggle throughout their schooling (i.e., Foorman, Francis, Shaywitz, Shaywitz, & Fletcher, 1997; Juel, 1988; Stanovich, 1986; Stuart, Masterson, & Dixon, 1999). There has been considerable research on early predictors of reading difficulties, such as phonemic awareness, alphabet knowledge, and vocabulary skills (e.g., Dickinson, McCabe, Anastasopoulos, Peisner-Feinberg, & Poe, 2003; Lonigan, Burgess, & Anthony, 2000; Wagner et al., 1997). Yet, these emergent literacy skills only show part of the picture. Many children, like Connor, have little difficulty acquiring emergent literacy skills. Nonetheless, because of difficulties with self-regulation and motivation, their performance in literacy suffers in both the early and later grades.

THREE PIVOTAL PIECES ON MOTIVATION, ENGAGEMENT, AND SELF-REGULATION

This chapter addresses three pivotal works that have been particularly influential in the areas of motivation, engagement, and self-regulation, including publications by Guthrie and Wigfield (2000), Blair (2002), and Spira, Bracken, and Fischel (2005). One quick measure of their influence can be seen in the sheer number of citations to their work. For example, according to Google Scholar, Blair's (2002) article has been cited more than 1,500 times. Similarly, Guthrie and Wigfield's (2000) chapter has been cited over 1,800 times. The newest of the three publications, written by Spira and colleagues (2005) has already been cited approximately 200 times.

Situating these works within the historical context is challenging; although they address cognitive, social, and affective aspects of learning, they do so in very distinct ways. For example, one of the three pivotal works, Guthrie and Wigfield (2000), is a book chapter in which the authors present a model depicting the multiple factors that influence children's engagement in literacy. They present their work in relation to prior research on motivation and engagement in learning. They trace the historical antecedents of their theory back to Dewey for a more general view of learning and cite a study by Gray and Monroe on reading motivation that was conducted in 1929.

There were many studies of motivation and literacy prior to Guthrie's and Wigfield's model, yet research in the area of engagement and motivation in reading has increased significantly since their study was published. An ERIC database search by year for peer-reviewed publications on either engagement or motivation in reading or literacy shows this substantial increase (see Figure 7.1). From 1990 to 1995, there were close to 50 articles per year on this topic. Yet, beginning in 2001, this number doubles to more than 100 articles per year, followed by a steady rise from 2008 to 2012, a year in which a peak of more than 450 articles on this topic was reached. Although counting citations is far from a perfect measure of the impact of research, it does provide a useful indicator of the extent to which the research topic has grown.

Although the other articles by Blair (2002) and Spira and colleagues (2005) address the social, cognitive, and affective aspects of learning, they also consider the ways these early skills connect with children's school readiness. As such, we can view their work in relation to school readiness research, policies, and practices in early childhood. The topic of school readiness was described before the early 2000s, but it became more prevalent as a subject of research between 2004 and 2016. In searching the ERIC database for peer-reviewed

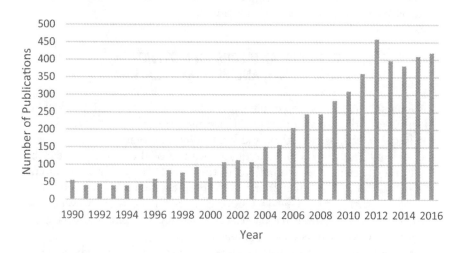

FIGURE 7.1. Peer-reviewed publications on motivation and engagement.

articles on school readiness by year, the clear growth in research devoted to this topic is evident beginning in the year 2005 (see Figure 7.2). Between the years 1990 and 2004, there were fewer than 30 publications that focused on school readiness, and this number more than doubles by the year 2006.

There were also significant changes in educational policy that coincided with the time frame in which these articles were published. At the time of publication, educational policies in the United States had shifted to a clear emphasis on standards and achievement. Some of the impetus for this move‑ ment came from the enactment in 1994 of Goals 2000 (U.S. Congress, 1994), a nationwide initiative that stated that by the year 2000 all children were to begin school "ready to learn." This was followed in 2002 by the No Child Left Behind Act, which further increased schools' accountability. These policies also correlated with the development of statewide preschool learning standards and the further development of assessments and screening of children's skills for kindergarten entry.

The growth of research on motivation and school readiness since the pub‑ lication of these three studies is a clear indicator of their importance to the field of early literacy research. These three publications broaden early literacy research and theory by including theoretical models and research studies that highlight the affective and cognitive processes that influence children's read‑ ing development and performance. The section that follows includes a brief overview of each of the three works, a description of their impact on the field, and implications for practice.

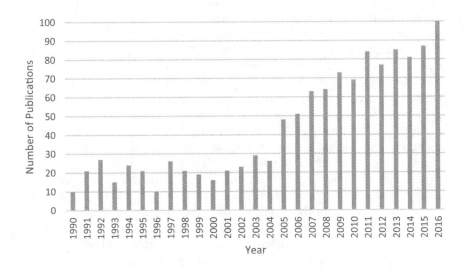

FIGURE 7.2. Peer-reviewed publications on school readiness.

Guthrie and Wigfield (2000): *A Model of Engagement in Literacy*

Guthrie and Wigfield (2000) significantly advanced the field of early literacy research with their presentation of a cohesive model for engaged reading that considers readers' knowledge, skills, and experiences as critical factors for engagement. This model depicts three essential outcomes of literacy engagement: achievement, knowledge, and practices. The outcomes are placed in the center of the model and are surrounded by the four factors that affect these outcomes, which include social interactions, motivation, conceptual knowledge, and strategy use. The authors explain how these factors work together to influence engagement. They write, "Engaged readers in the classroom or elsewhere coordinate their strategies and knowledge (cognition) within a community of literacy (social) in order to fulfill their personal goals, desires, and intentions (motivation)" (2000, p. 404).

According to Guthrie and Wigfield (2000), motivation is the key component for engaged readers, and is the factor that "activates" the learner. They posit that motivation can be internally or externally activated, and that a child's motivation for a particular task is affected by his or her self-efficacy for the task (i.e., confidence in his or her ability). They emphasize that motivation is not fixed and can fluctuate depending on the context as well as on a child's age. Since motivation is what "propels students to choose to read," it is essential for children's achievement (2000, p. 417).

In their model, these central facets of engagement are surrounded by external factors that influence children's level of engagement (i.e. learning goals and knowledge, real-world interactions, autonomy support, interesting texts, strategy instruction, collaboration, rewards and praise, evaluation, and teacher involvement). By including contextual factors that influence children's motivation, the model helps demonstrate the ways classroom supports can enhance children's engagement in literacy. Some examples of these factors are having teachers who value understanding (knowledge goals), instead of learning that prioritizes correct answers; having a range of texts that will interest all children; providing meaningful choices so that children can be more autonomous; teaching children strategies for comprehending texts; and making connections between the real world and instruction and interconnecting different aspects of instruction. Guthrie and Wigfield (2000) also assert that assessments can either foster or inhibit engagement and maintain that teachers should give positive feedback in a thoughtful manner.

Although many of the examples that these authors provide for creating classrooms that foster literacy engagement are more easily adapted to elementary schools, these same principles also can be applied to early childhood classrooms. For instance, after reading about habitats, teachers can help engage kindergartners through real-world interactions by asking them to create a habitat for a class pet. Similarly, teachers can focus on understanding during a read-aloud by asking children to draw connections to the text with examples from their own experiences.

Further Research: Engagement and Motivation

Guthrie and Wigfield's model (2000) clarified our understanding of what it means to be an "engaged" learner. As Alexander and Fox (2004) explain, their work shaped our thinking about learning with a "reconceptualization of the student as engaged or motivated" (p. 51). Their work is also referenced by researchers who are investigating the connection between engagement and reading performance (August, Carlo, Dressler, & Snow, 2005; Lutz, Guthrie, & Davis, 2006). For example, Hughes, Luo, Kwok, and Loyd (2008) investigated whether children's level of "effortful engagement" alone served as a predictor of future literacy achievement and found that it contributes significantly to children's math and literacy performance. Pearson, Cervetti, and Tilson (2008) reference Guthrie and Wigfield's work when describing their own framework for the mindful engagement necessary for reading for understanding. Moreover, Guthrie and Wigfield's (2000) theory of literacy engagement is often cited as foundational to the literature on motivation, and at times, the terms are used in interchangeably (Alexander & Fox, 2004; Gambrell, 2011; Klingner, 2005).

Although there are numerous studies that assess interventions designed to improve engagement in learning, they typically involve older students rather than children in early childhood settings (Felner, Seitsinger, Brand, Burns, & Bolton, 2007; Reyes, Brackett, Rivers, White, & Salovey, 2012; Wigfield, Guthrie, Tonks, & Perencevich, 2004). For example, in an extension of their earlier theoretical model, Wigfield and colleagues (2004) examined the effectiveness of two instructional programs, Concept Oriented Reading Instruction (CORI) and Strategy Instruction, on third-graders' motivation. Whereas the Strategy Instruction program primarily focuses on teaching comprehension strategies, the researchers found that the CORI program effectively improved motivation through the matching of "hands-on" science activities with engaging texts. In connecting with the earlier model, CORI also promotes peer collaboration and autonomy support by creating opportunities for children to work together and ask their own questions. Felner et al. (2007) report on the effectiveness of creating smaller learning communities within larger middle and high schools to improve engagement and achievement. In another study of older elementary school children, researchers have uncovered a relationship between classroom emotional climate and both engagement and academic achievement (Reyes et al., 2012).

The lack of research on engagement in learning in early childhood may be partially explained by the difficulties in measuring engagement in the younger years. Many existing measures of motivation are self-report questionnaires that are designed for somewhat older students. For example, the Motivation to Read

Survey was created with second through sixth graders in mind (Malloy, Marinak, Gambrell, & Mazzoni, 2013). Yet, with new surveys that are being developed for younger students, research in this area may expand (i.e., Marinak, Malloy, Gambrell, & Mazzoni, 2015).

Blair (2002): *A Neurobiological Model of Self-Regulation*

Whereas Guthrie and Wigfield (2000) focus on the role of engagement in children's readiness to learn, Blair (2002) created what he describes as "a neurobiological model of self-regulation" that focuses on the ways that self-regulation develops and influences children's school readiness. Although Blair does not depict his model graphically, he describes the underlying theories and research that support his conceptualization of the links between self-regulation and school readiness. Blair's (2002) definition of self-regulation includes the regulation of emotions and cognition, both of which he asserts are essential for learning. As Blair explains, "Whether defined as the regulation of emotion in appropriate social responding or the regulation of attention and selective strategy use in the execution of cognitive tasks, self-regulatory skills underlie many of the behaviors and attributes that are associated with successful school adjustment" (p. 112).

Blair positions self-regulation under the umbrella of executive functioning, which he defines as the combination of "working memory," "attention," and "inhibitory control." He asserts that self-regulation is not a fixed skill but evolves over time, beginning as early as infancy, and varying depending on environmental inputs. In keeping with the idea that children's self-regulation is influenced by the environment, Blair (2002) highlights the changeable nature of children's emotionality, and thus cautions against a fixed categorization of children's temperament.

> My goal in relating emotionality to school readiness through executive cognition is not to define distinct temperament types or to equate school readiness with a particular temperamental style per se. It is to identify individual differences in certain aspects of behavior that are labeled as temperamental in order to outline how they may be related to the development of the skills and abilities that underlie adaptation to the socially defined role of student. (p. 118)

Given the "plasticity" of self-regulation, Blair proposes that children's temperament can change from one context to another. In his view, children in a supportive environment would be less likely to be emotionally reactive.

At the heart of Blair's (2002) theory is the idea that self-regulatory skills are essential for school readiness. Instead of conceptualizing school readiness as a function of only emergent literacy or math skills, he broadens the concept of readiness by adding self-regulatory skills that can be measured and used as predictors of later academic success. In proposing the concept of school "readiness," he takes into account the many factors that influence children's use self-regulation strategies. As he describes "only keeping in mind that readiness is a multidimensional construct involving family, peer, school, and community levels of influence will the value of the neurodevelopmental perspective on self-regulation become apparent" (Blair, 2002, p. 112).

By combining research from various disciplines, including education, psychology, neuropsychology, physiology, and neuroscience, Blair constructs a comprehensive view of the development of self-regulation skills. In doing so, he cites a wide range of studies addressing such areas as emotionality, teachers' reports of children's readiness, metacognition, neural connectivity, and early interventions. Additionally, by recognizing the variability of children's self-regulatory skills and the role of children's environment, Blair's (2002) theory, like that of Guthrie and Wigfield (2000), can inform educational practice. Although he does not include specific classroom recommendations, he advocates for preschool classrooms that, " . . . promote the attention and cognitive self-regulation needed for both social and cognitive adaptation to the classroom" (p. 119). He suggests that preschool programs teach children "problem solving" steps that they could use to think through a situation before reacting impulsively. The influence of Blair's work is evident in preschool intervention studies on improving children's self-regulation skills, such as the Preschool PATHS Curriculum, which includes prescribed lessons that employ examples through stories and puppets that show children good behavioral models (Bierman et al., 2008).

Further Research: Self-Regulation and Readiness

Blair's (2002) model of self-regulation continues to be cited as a pivotal theory that demonstrates the relationship between children's early self-regulatory abilities and their future academic success (see Bierman et al., 2008; Bodrova & Leong, 2006; McClelland & Cameron, 2012; Raver, Carter, McCoy, Roy, Ursache, & Friedman, 2012; Sasser, Bierman, & Heinrichs, 2015; Skibbe, Connor, Morrison, & Jewkes, 2011). Additionally, Blair's work is often referenced for the purpose of establishing the connections between school readiness and self-regulation (i.e., Bierman et al., 2008; Russell, Lee, Spieker, & Oxford, 2016). In their review of the literature on self-regulation, McClelland and Cameron (2012) lend further support for the finding that self-regulation is predictive of academic performance when they assert "Overall self-regulation—assessed by measures that require the integration of inhibitory control, attentional flexibility, and working memory—is also predictive of academic success, with predictive coefficients ranging from .21 to .54" (p. 138).

Subsequent research on self-regulation includes studies of contextual factors that may influence children's skills. For example, Dieterich, Assel, Swank, Smith, and Landry (2006) examined the relationships between children's early language development, parent–child verbal interactions, and children's reading performance. Researchers have also investigated the relationship between infant–caregiver relationships and the self-regulation skills of children in preschool (Russell et al., 2016). Skibbe et al. (2011) investigated whether the number of years in preschool made a difference in children's early literacy and self-regulation skills.

The continued relevance of self-regulation can also be shown in studies of executive functioning skills. Zhou, Chen, and Main (2012, p. 117) assert that both the terms *executive function* and *effortful control* should be viewed as a "framework" for studying self-regulation, and find overlapping descriptions in the research that uses both terms interchangeably. For example, Sasser and colleagues (2015) examined the predictive value of executive functioning skills in preschool and kindergarten, but their definition of these skills overlaps with Blair's (2002) description of self-regulation skills. According to these authors, executive functioning includes "working memory, inhibitory control, and attention set-shifting skills" (Sasser et al., 2015, p. 70). Raver, Carter, McCoy, Roy, Ursache, and Friedman (2012) describe executive function as the cognitive domain of self-regulation and as differentiated from the emotional aspects of regulation. According to these researchers, executive functioning studies focus on the cognitive aspects of self-regulation, whereas studies of effortful control target the emotional components of self-regulation.

Convinced of the importance of early self-regulation skills, many researchers have assessed the effectiveness of different interventions designed for children who are considered at risk in the preschool years (Bierman et al., 2008; Bodrova & Leong, 2006; Domitrovich, Cortes, & Greenberg, 2007; Raver et al., 2012). For example, Bodrova, and Leong (2006) review two promising interventions for increasing children's readiness for kindergarten. These programs, Tools of Mind and the Scaffolded Early Literacy Program, were both implemented in Head Start classrooms. Similarly, in Switzerland, Röthlisberger, Neuenschwander, Cimeli, Michel, and Roebers (2012) implemented a small-group intervention for preschool and kindergarten children that led to improvement in children's executive functioning skills, including *working memory, interference control,* and *cognitive flexibility.* In their meta-analyisis, Reid, Trout, and Schartz (2005) found that programs that teach children with ADHD self-regulation were effective for helping develop positive learning behaviors.

Spira, Bracken, and Fischel (2005): *Behavioral and Social Skills as Predictors*

The third pivotal article differs from the prior two in that it is an empirical research study rather than a theoretical work. In this longitudinal study, Spira and colleagues (2005) researched the predictive nature of children's early skills on their later reading performance. More specifically, they were investigating which emergent literacy and behavioral skills predicted children's reading performance in fourth grade. Language and literacy skills, such as phonemic awareness, letter recognition, expressive and receptive language, and concepts about print, were assessed. Yet, what distinguished this study from others at the time was that these researchers examined children's behavioral, attentional, and social skills in addition to emergent literacy and language skills.

Data collection began with a group of kindergarten children in Head Start classrooms; the study used data from only those children who fell below the national norms on assessments of literacy skills (below the 30th percentile) at the end of first grade. Data were collected each year through fourth grade, and the researchers conducted several analyses to pinpoint the early predictors of reading performance. Based on these analyses, Spira et al. (2005) found that several kindergarten measures, including measures of "emergent literacy, expressive language, and classroom behavior," were highly predictive (p. 230). The addition of classroom behavior to the list of early predictors of later reading performance is one of the important ways this study advanced the research in early literacy.

Additionally, the researchers examined correlations between scores at each grade level and children's reading performance at the end of fourth grade. One finding from this analysis was that second-grade scores were good predictors of fourth-grade reading performance. These scores predicted greater than 70% of the variance in performance at third grade. This percentile was much higher than the predictive value of the first-grade scores, which only accounted for "19% of the variance in the second-grade reading scores" (p. 230).

In another set of analyses, Spira et al. (2005) focused on a subset of students who they termed "improvers" because they scored at a higher percentile (greater than 30%) on measures at the fourth-grade level than the other students in the study. Keeping in mind that all students in the initial analyses were performing below national norms and that based on overall trends these students would remain low performing in fourth grade, the higher scores meant that the students in the new analyses had deviated from the trend and were performing better than might be predicted. By focusing their analyses on this population, these researchers hoped to isolate specific factors, including behavioral indicators, that could potentially mediate against reading difficulties in fourth grade. As they explain, "The ultimate goal was to isolate those skills that may act as buffers against long-term reading failure and, thus, to aid in the construction of future interventions targeting children who experience initial difficulties with reading" (p. 226). They found that language, emergent literacy, and behavioral skills all served as powerful predictors. More specifically, they explain:

> Simple correlations between kindergarten skills and growth indicated that those children who had relative strength in phonological awareness, oral

language, print knowledge, letter–word identification, and classroom behavior in kindergarten were more likely to show improvement after encountering initial reading difficulties in first grade. (Spira et al., 2005, p. 230)

The finding that children's kindergarten behavioral skills help to forecast their future reading performance provides evidence for Blair's (2002) assertion that self-regulation skills are an important factor in school readiness. Although Spira et al. do not use the term "self-regulation" to describe these behavioral skills, they address this construct when they discuss children's "behavioral control," and their evidence documenting the importance of self-regulation to academic performance is acknowledged in subsequent literature (Allan & Lonigan, 2011; Lin, Morgan, Hillemeier, Cook, Maczuga, & Farkas, 2013; Paratore, Cassano, & Schickedanz, 2011).

Spira et al. (2005) do not include specific recommendations for classroom practice, but they do advocate for interventions to support learning for children who struggle with these skills. As they explain, "Children with poor social and/or behavioral skills in kindergarten should be targeted for intervention efforts aimed at facilitating their classroom adjustment and developing their adaptive skills before they encounter significant difficulties in elementary school" (p. 232). They conclude that, although children's negative behaviors are possibly a result of struggles with learning to read, their behavioral assessments occurred before reading instruction began, leading them to conclude that the behaviors were negatively affecting children's learning. Therefore, the need for early behavioral interventions is critical for literacy achievement, and is especially necessary for students who display difficulties with both emergent literacy skills and behavior in kindergarten. Spira et al. (2005) note the toll that behavioral difficulties take on children's academic performance when they state, "Behavioral problems may place children with reading difficulties at increased risk for continued failure by interfering with the ability to focus on and benefit from further instruction" (p. 332). Therefore, interventions for children's readiness should include focusing on behavior and self-regulation so that children can be in the best position to acquire the needed skills.

Further Research: Behavioral and Social Skills as Predictors

Spira et al.'s (2005) work has been cited in the literature that describes the stability of reading performance over time (Connor, Morrison, & Underwood, 2007; Kent, Wanzek, & Al Otaiba, 2012; Wadsworth, DeFries, Olson, & Willcutt, 2007). One of the unique contributions of this study is that it helped to establish the connection between young children's behaviors, regulation skills, their reading performance, and their early behaviors and long-term reading outcomes (Allan & Lonigan, 2011; Kwok, Hughes, & Luo, 2007; Nathan & Rucklidge, 2011; Paratore et al., 2011).

Researchers have continued to study the social and behavioral factors that can predict later literacy difficulties. Stipek and Miles (2008) linked early aggressive behavior in school with lower school achievement. These factors have also been highlighted in research that studied children's relationships with their teachers (Hughes et al., 2008; Stipek & Miles, 2008). In addition to identifying the factors that predict reading difficulties, researchers have also looked into other affective factors, such as children's resilience, as predictive of later reading performance (Kwok et al., 2007).

This research also spurred several interventions efforts to enhance children's social and behavioral skills in order to improve their school readiness. For example, Bierman et al. (2008) measured the effectiveness of the program developed in partnership with Head Start—REDI (Research based, Developmentally informed), which was created to improve children's readiness for kindergarten. The REDI program targeted language and literacy skills as well as social–emotional development. Domitrovich et al. (2007) examined the results of PATHS, a program that also fostered preschoolers' social–emotional development. In another study of a Head Start intervention, Raver and colleagues (2012) examined the results of the Chicago School Readiness Project (CSRP), which was aimed particularly at improving children's self-regulation skills.

IMPLICATIONS FOR PRACTICE OF THE THREE PIVOTAL STUDIES

These three studies have substantially influenced the field of literacy research and practice, as they helped to set in motion other research on predictive factors for children's literacy performance that go beyond emergent literacy skills, such as phonemic awareness, letter identification, and language skills. By placing a new emphasis on motivation, engagement, and self-regulation, these studies helped expand the research agenda, as can be seen in Alexander's and Fox's (2004) description of this time period as the "era of engaged learning." Moreover, they helped to set the stage for future research on ways of enhancing at-risk children's self-regulation and engagement as early as preschool.

One implication of this work is evident in the policies and standards that have been developed for early childhood. For example, the framework for Head Start prominently features the concept of self-regulation. As described in the framework, "The Approaches to Learning domain incorporates emotional, behavioral, and cognitive self-regulation under a single umbrella to guide teaching practices that support the development of these skills" (U.S. Department of Health and Human Services, 2015, p. 10). Self-regulation is also included as one of the developmentally appropriate practices approved by the National Association for the Education of Young Children for the first time in 2009 (Copple & Bredekamp, 2009).

These pivotal works have also led to research-based recommendations for classroom practices that aim to foster children's self-regulation, engagement, and motivation. For example, Bodrova, Germeroth, and Leong (2013), Copple and Bredekamp (2009), and Whitebread, Coltman, Jameson, and Lander (2009) have recommended engaging young children in dramatic play as a means of improving self-regulation. Researchers also recommend classroom practices for improving kindergarten children's self-regulatory ability through direct instruction, modeling, scaffolding, and providing many opportunities to practice (Bodrova & Leong, 2008; Florez, 2011).

Guthrie and Wigfield's (2000) model of engagement also encourages a number of suggestions for classroom practice that have a demonstrated impact on children's engagement. For example, in an early childhood classroom, the teacher could include a variety of interesting texts for read-alouds and provide children with meaningful choices in their learning. Engagement and motivation can also be enhanced through integrating literacy with other content areas and through offering meaningful social interactions around texts (Malloy, 2015; Pearson et al., 2008).

Finding ways to further children's success in literacy is a high priority, and by examining the ways motivation, engagement, and self-regulation can stimulate learning, we can better support children. Yet, a cautionary note should be sounded to make sure that the research and development of assessments of school readiness policies do not serve as gatekeeping mechanisms whereby children deemed not ready would be prevented from progressing in school. Assessments of readiness should not be used for "high-stakes" decisions, but rather as indicators of ways to improve (Denham, 2006).

Further confounding the potential impact of these readiness assessments are the significant changes to kindergarten expectations and practices, which are illustrated by those who categorize kindergarten as the "new first grade." According to Bassok, Latham, and Rorem (2016), kindergarten teachers' expectations for the skills and knowledge children should have when entering kindergarten dramatically increased from the year 1998 to 2010 in every readiness category that was assessed (i.e., knowing the alphabet, knowing the names of colors, counting to 20, following directions, and sitting still and paying attention). Rather than focusing on creating contexts for children to gain self-regulation skills and motivation for learning, kindergarten classrooms have become more focused on literacy skills and math drills. With too much emphasis on these content-area skills, children may miss out on opportunities to expand their needed skills in self-regulation.

CONCLUSION

The pivotal works discussed in this chapter have helped to shape the field in important ways. First, they help highlight the significance of engagement, motivation, and self-regulation for children's literacy learning. This is especially critical in today's educational climate where teachers are under tremendous pressure to demonstrate children's literacy success in meeting grade-level standards. Given this context, teachers may cast aside developing motivational lessons in favor of skill-based, direct instruction. Similarly, modeling and teaching children successful strategies for self-regulation may not seem as important as practicing reading skills. Yet, by pushing motivation and self-regulation aside, teachers risk further exacerbating potential academic difficulties.

The following recommended practices are based on the pivotal studies discussed in this chapter and on subsequent research that will help foster motivation, engagement, and self-regulation in early childhood classrooms.

• *Connect learning opportunities with children's interests and experience.* Whether teachers are selecting texts for whole-class readings or planning experiences to expand content knowledge, it is important that they consider children's interests. Interest surveys administered at the beginning of the school year can serve as a useful starting point for learning about children's interests. During the year, Seitz (2006) recommends that teachers look for "sparks" or "phenomena, conversations—anything that provokes deeper thought" (p. 2). Teachers can also create sparks by giving children experiences that interest and engage them in meaningful learning.

• *Provide opportunities for children to learn together.* School days should include multiple activities and routines that enable children to collaborate and share their learning with one another. When children to work together on problems that arise during child-directed play (e.g., in a block center or in a play kitchen), they are learning self-regulation skills. Teachers can buttress children's developing social skills by joining at times to model and support turn-taking and listening skills. Opportunities to collaborate (e.g., working together to paint a nature mural or to plant a garden) foster children's motivation for learning and engagement in school tasks.

• *Understand your students' self-efficacy beliefs related to reading and writing.* Believing in one's own ability to succeed at a task is an essential component of motivation. Teachers must intentionally scaffold classroom reading and writing tasks so that children feel successful. Surveys, such as the Me and My Reading Profile, are useful in gathering an initial snapshot of children's views of their abilities and of their interest in reading and help teachers design instruction that will stimulate children's motivation in literacy (Marinak et al., 2015).

• *Partner with parents.* Parents can be a tremendous resource for helping teachers learn more about their children. Parent surveys can shed light on children's interests, hobbies, favorite books, and activities. This information can be useful for planning motivational instructional activities because they connect to children's prior knowledge, interests, and experiences. Similarly, informing families about classroom activities and routines and suggesting activities that support school-based learning targets fosters the kinds of home–school collaboration that are vital. These collaborations are interesting to children because they realize that what they are learning in school connects with their lives outside of school (Hindin & Mueller, 2016). For example, when shopping, parents can make a game of pointing out words in the supermarket that start with the classroom sounds of the week to motivate them to find more words than their parents or siblings.

• *Intentionally support the development of self-regulation.* Since self-regulation plays an essential role in academic success, teachers should look for opportunities to enhance children's developing skills through modeling and scaffolding (Florez, 2011). Over time, teachers can gradually withdraw adult support as children begin to regulate their own thinking, attention, behavior, and motivation independently. Opportunities for practicing these essential skills should include free and guided play, teacher-mediated social–dramatic play, and small- and whole-group activities.

REFERENCES

Alexander, P. A., & Fox, E. (2004). A historical perspective on reading research and practice. *Theoretical Models and Processes of Reading, 5,* 33–68.

Allan, N. P., & Lonigan, C. J. (2011). Examining the dimensionality of effortful control in preschool children and its relation to academic and socioemotional indicators. *Developmental Psychology, 47*(4), 905.

Allington, R. L. (2009). If they don't read much . . . 30 years later. In E. H. Hiebert (Ed.), *Reading more, reading better* (pp. 30–54). New York: Guilford Press.

August, D., Carlo, M., Dressler, C., & Snow, C. (2005). The critical role of vocabulary development for English language learners. *Learning Disabilities Research and Practice, 20*(1), 50–57.

Bassok, D., Latham, S., & Rorem, A. (2016). Is kindergarten the new first grade? *AERA Open, 2*(1), 1–31.

Bierman, K. L., Domitrovich, C. E., Nix, R. L., Gest, S. D., Welsh, J. A., Greenberg, M. T., . . . Gill, S. (2008). Promoting academic and social-emotional school readiness: The Head Start REDI program. *Child Development, 79*(6), 1802–1817.

Blair, C. (2002). School readiness: Integrating cognition and emotion in a neurobiological conceptualization of children's functioning at school entry. *American Psychologist, 57*(2), 111–127.

Bodrova, E., Germeroth, C., & Leong, D. J. (2013). Play and self-regulation: Lessons from Vygotsky. *American Journal of Play, 6*(1), 111–123.

Bodrova, E., & Leong, D. J. (2006). Self-regulation as a key to school readiness. In M. J. Zaslow & I. Martinez-Beck (Eds.), *Critical issues in early childhood professional development* (pp. 203–224). Baltimore: Brookes.

Bodrova, E., & Leong, D. J. (2008). Developing self-regulation in kindergarten: Can we keep all the crickets in the basket? YC Young Children, 63(2), 56–58.

Connor, C. M., Morrison, F. J., & Underwood, P. S. (2007). A second chance in second grade: The independent and cumulative impact of first- and second-grade reading instruction and children's letter-word reading skill growth. Scientific Studies of Reading, 11(3), 199–233.

Copple, C., & Bredekamp, S. (2009). Developmentally appropriate practice in early childhood programs serving children from birth through age 8. Washington, DC: National Association for the Education of Young Children.

Denham, S. A. (2006). Social-emotional competence as support for school readiness: What is it and how do we assess it? Early Education and Development, 17(1), 57–89.

Dickinson, D. K., McCabe, A., Anastasopoulos, L., Peisner-Feinberg, E. S., & Poe, M. D. (2003). The comprehensive language approach to early literacy: The interrelationships among vocabulary, phonological sensitivity, and print knowledge among preschool-aged children. Journal of Educational Psychology, 95(3), 465–481.

Dieterich, S. E., Assel, M. A., Swank, P., Smith, K. E., & Landry, S. H. (2006). The impact of early maternal verbal scaffolding and child language abilities on later decoding and reading comprehension skills. Journal of School Psychology, 43(6), 481–494.

Domitrovich, C. E., Cortes, R. C., & Greenberg, M. T. (2007). Improving young children's social and emotional competence: A randomized trial of the preschool "PATHS" curriculum. Journal of Primary Prevention, 28(2), 67–91.

Felner, R. D., Seitsinger, A. M., Brand, S., Burns, A., & Bolton, N. (2007). Creating small learning communities: Lessons from the project on high-performing learning communities about "what works" in creating productive, developmentally enhancing, learning contexts. Educational Psychologist, 42(4), 209–221.

Florez, I. R. (2011). Developing young children's self-regulation through everyday experiences. YC Young Children, 66(4), 46.

Foorman, B. R., Francis, D. J., Shaywitz, S. E., Shaywitz, B. A., & Fletcher, J. M. (1997). The case for early reading intervention. In B. Blachman (Ed.), Foundations of reading acquisition and dyslexia: Implications for early intervention (pp. 243–264). Mahwah, NJ: Erlbaum.

Gambrell, L. B. (2011). Seven rules of engagement: What's most important to know about motivation to read. The Reading Teacher, 65(3), 172–178.

Guthrie, J. T., & Wigfield, A. (2000). Engagement and motivation in reading. In M. L. Kamil, P. B. Mosenthal, P. D. Pearson, & R. Barr (Eds.), Handbook of reading research (Vol 3, pp. 403–422). Mahwah, NJ: Erlbaum.

Hindin, A., & Mueller, M. F. (2016). Getting parents on board: Partnering to increase math and literacy achievement, K–5. New York: Routledge.

Hughes, J. N., Luo, W., Kwok, O.-M., & Loyd, L. K. (2008). Teacher–student support, effortful engagement, and achievement: A 3-year longitudinal study. Journal of Educational Psychology, 100(1), 1–14.

Juel, C. (1988). Learning to read and write: A longitudinal study of 54 children from first through fourth grades. Journal of Educational Psychology, 80, 437–447.

Kent, S. C., Wanzek, J., & Al Otaiba, S. (2012). Amount of time in print reading in general education kindergarten classrooms: What does it look like for children at-risk for reading difficulties? *Learning Disabilities Research and Practice, 27*(2), 56–65.

Klingner, J., Artiles, A. J., Kozleski, E., Harry, B., Zion, S., Tate, W., . . . Riley, D. (2005). Addressing the disproportionate representation of culturally and linguistically diverse children in special education through culturally responsive educational systems. *Education Policy Analysis Archives, 13*(38), 1–40.

Kwok, O. M., Hughes, J. N., & Luo, W. (2007). Role of resilient personality on lower achieving first grade children's current and future achievement. *Journal of School Psychology, 45*(1), 61–82.

Lin, Y. C., Morgan, P. L., Hillemeier, M., Cook, M., Maczuga, S., & Farkas, G. (2013). Reading, mathematics, and behavioral difficulties interrelate: Evidence from a cross-lagged panel design and population-based sample of US upper elementary students. *Behavioral Disorders, 38*(4), 212–227.

Lonigan, C. J., Burgess, S. R., & Anthony, J. L. (2000). Development of emergent literacy and early reading skills in preschool children: evidence from a latent-variable longitudinal study. *Developmental psychology, 36*(5), 596.

Lutz, S. L., Guthrie, J. T., & Davis, M. H. (2006). Scaffolding for engagement in elementary school reading instruction. *Journal of Educational Research, 100*(1), 3–20.

Malloy, J. A. (2015). New insights on motivation in the literacy classroom. In S. R. Parris & K. Headley (Eds.), *Comprehension instruction: Research-based best practices* (pp. 147–161). New York: Guilford Press.

Malloy, J. A., Marinak, B. A., Gambrell, L. B., & Mazzoni, S. A. (2013). Assessing motivation to read. *The Reading Teacher, 67*(4), 273–282.

Marinak, B. A., Malloy, J. B., Gambrell, L. B., & Mazzoni, S. A. (2015). Me and my reading profile. *The Reading Teacher, 69*(1), 51–62.

McClelland, M. M., & Cameron, C. E. (2012). Self-regulation in early childhood: Improving conceptual clarity and developing ecologically valid measures. *Child Development Perspectives, 6*(2), 136–142.

Nathan, K. M., & Rucklidge, J. J. (2011). Potential moderators of psychosocial problems in children with reading difficulties. *New Zealand Journal of Psychology, 40*(1), 19–28.

Paratore, J. R., Cassano, C. M., & Schickedanz, J. A. (2011). Supporting early (and later) literacy development at home and at school In M. L. Kamil, P. D. Pearson, E. B. Moji, & P. P. Afflerbach (Eds.), *Handbook of reading research* (Vol. 4, pp. 107–135). New York: Routledge.

Pearson, P. D., Cervetti, G. N., & Tilson, J. L. (2008). Reading for understanding, In L. Darling-Hammond, B. Barron, P. D. Pearson, A. H. Schoenfeld, E. K. Stage, T. D. Zimmerman, . . . J. L. Tilson (Eds.), *Powerful learning: What we know about teaching for understanding* (pp. 71–112) San Francisco: Wiley.

Raver, C. C., Carter, J. S., McCoy, D. C., Roy, A., Ursache, A., & Friedman, A. (2012). Testing models of children's self-regulation within educational contexts: Implications for measurement. *Advances in Child Development and Behavior, 42*, 245–270.

Reid, R., Trout, A. L., & Schartz, M. (2005). Self-regulation interventions for children with attention deficit/hyperactivity disorder. *Exceptional Children, 71*(4), 361.

Reyes, M. R., Brackett, M. A., Rivers, S. E., White, M., & Salovey, P. (2012). Classroom emotional climate, student engagement, and academic achievement. *Journal of Educational Psychology, 104*(3), 700.

Röthlisberger, M., Neuenschwander, R., Cimeli, P., Michel, E., & Roebers, C. M. (2012). Improving executive functions in 5- and 6-year-olds: Evaluation of a small group intervention in prekindergarten and kindergarten children. *Infant and Child Development, 21*(4), 411–429.

Russell, B. S., Lee, J. O., Spieker, S., & Oxford, M. L. (2016). Parenting and preschool self-regulation as predictors of social emotional competence in 1st grade. *Journal of Research in Childhood Education, 30*(2), 153–169.

Sasser, T. R., Bierman, K. L., & Heinrichs, B. (2015). Executive functioning and school adjustment: The mediational role of pre-kindergarten learning-related behaviors. *Early Childhood Research Quarterly, 30*, 70–79.

Seitz, H. J. (2006). The plan: Building on children's interests. *Young Children on the Web*, 1–5.

Skibbe, L. E., Connor, C. M., Morrison, F. J., & Jewkes, A. M. (2011). Schooling effects on preschoolers' self-regulation, early literacy, and language growth. *Early Childhood Research Quarterly, 26*(1), 42–49.

Spira, E. G., Bracken, S. S., & Fischel, J. E. (2005). Predicting improvement after first-grade reading difficulties: The effects of oral language, emergent literacy, and behavior skills. *Developmental Psychology, 41*(1), 225–234.

Stanovich, K. E. (1986). Matthew effects in reading: Some consequences of individual differences in the acquisition of literacy. *Reading Research Quarterly, 21*, 360–405.

Stipek, D., & Miles, S. (2008). Effects of aggression on achievement: Does conflict with the teacher make it worse? *Child Development, 79*(6), 1721–1735.

Stuart, M., Masterson, J., & Dixon, M. (1999). Learning to read words turns listeners into readers: How children accomplish this transition. In J. Oakhill & R. Beard (Eds.), *Reading development and the teaching of reading* (pp. 109–130). Malden, MA: Blackwell.

U.S. Congress. (1994). Goals 2000: Educate America Act. H. R. 1804. Retrieved from *www2.ed.gov/legislation/GOALS2000/TheAct/index.html*.

U.S. Department of Health and Human Services. (2015). *Head Start early learning outcomes framework: Ages birth to five*. Washington, DC: Administration for Children & Families.

Wadsworth, S. J., DeFries, J. C., Olson, R. K., & Willcutt, E. G. (2007). Colorado longitudinal twin study of reading disability. *Annals of Dyslexia, 57*(2), 139–160.

Wagner, R. K., Torgesen, J. K., Rashotte, C. A., Hecht, S. A., Barker, T. A., Burgess, S. R., . . . Garon, T. (1997). Changing relations between phonological processing abilities and word-level reading as children develop from beginning to skilled readers: A 5-year longitudinal study. *Developmental Psychology, 33*, 468–479.

Whitebread, D., Coltman, P., Jameson, H., & Lander, R. (2009). Play, cognition and self-regulation: What exactly are children learning when they learn through play? *Educational and Child Psychology, 26*(2), 40.

Wigfield, A., Guthrie, J. T., Tonks, S., & Perencevich, K. C. (2004). Children's motivation for reading: Domain specificity and instructional influences. *Journal of Educational Research, 97*(6), 299–310.

Zhou, Q., Chen, S. H., & Main, A. (2012). Commonalities and differences in the research on children's effortful control and executive function: A call for an integrated model of self-regulation. *Child Development Perspectives, 6*(2), 112–121.

PART III

HOME AND COMMUNITY LITERACY EXPERIENCES OF CHILDREN

Starting Them Young

How the Shift from Reading Readiness to Emergent Literacy Has Influenced Preschool Literacy Education

William H. Teale, Emily Brown Hoffman,
Colleen E. Whittingham, and Kathleen A. Paciga

School systems work on a fixed schedule, and human
development doesn't.

—FRED ROGERS

This chapter examines the influence of two pivotal studies on the organization and aims of early literacy education in preschools today. The discussion centers on the U. S. educational context, but educational applications of the ideas spurred by these studies can be seen in a many other countries around the world. We specifically frame the changing theories and practices of preschool literacy around the movement away from reading readiness toward emergent literacy that occurred beginning in the 1940s and continuing until the present. We find this changeover to be key to understanding how thinking about young children and literacy has evolved over three quarters of a century.

From	*To*
A belief that children are ready to read once they have attained sufficient mental development	A belief that literacy learning starts with children's earliest encounters with text
A focus on learning to read	A focus on literacy development

From	*To*
Prescribed reading readiness curriculum and instruction	Child-centered activities that emphasize oral language and authentic, goal-oriented uses of print
Early literacy conceived of as a set of cognitive skills to be learned	Early literacy conceived of as developing competency in a range of social and cultural uses of print
Little attention to the physical literacy environment in the classroom	Focused attention on the presence and organization of literacy materials throughout the classroom
Little emphasis on the social literacy environment—including teacher–student verbal exchanges around literacy	Targeted teacher attention to their verbal interactions with children around print- and language-based experiences, as well as on the social opportunities for children to participate in activities mediated by various forms of literacy
Limited emphasis on early literacy in preschool education	Widespread support for preschool programs that have early learning goals emphasizing language and literacy

We discuss Almy's (1949) book, based on her doctoral dissertation, and Teale and Sulzby's (1996) volume by situating each in a historical context, describing its content, and tracing its impact on the organization and aims of preschool literacy education. We conclude by reflecting on the relationships between the two studies and speculating on their continuing future influence.

TWO PIVOTAL STUDIES ON PRESCHOOL LITERACY INSTRUCTION

Almy (1949): *Children's Experiences Prior to First Grade and Success in Beginning Reading*

The first pivotal study discussed in this chapter is Milly Almy's dissertation research that was conducted at Columbia University as part of her doctoral degree requirements for the Faculty of Philosophy. She received her degree in 1948, and Teachers College Columbia University Bureau of Publications published the dissertation in full as a book in 1949 as part of the series *Columbia's Contributions to Education*.

Description of the Study

To grasp the significance of how this research study contributed to the field of early literacy, it is important to understand two relevant aspects of the context out of which it arose: early childhood education in the United States during the 1930s and 1940s and the prevailing approach to conducting educational research at the time.

Millie Almy's entire career, until she retired from the University of California, Berkeley, in 1980, was devoted to early childhood education. She was particularly concerned with the mental and social–emotional development of young children. Especially during the 1920s through the 1940s, but also continuing beyond that era to the present day, the purpose of early childhood education has been widely discussed: to what extent should it focus on social–emotional learning and to what extent, academic development (Meisels & Shonkoff, 2000; Shonkoff & Meisels, 1990)? An integral part of this discussion has been the role of play (as compared to some form of instruction) in young children's classroom experiences. The topic of reading education has been a central part of such discussions because literacy was (and continues to be) so fundamental to school achievement. Historically, readiness to read also stood as a kind of dividing line between preschool and the subsequent primary grades education. Roma Gans, a reading education faculty member at Teachers College, who was on Almy's dissertation committee, noted the "dichotomy . . . between the *play* years and *formal learning* years" (Gans, 1948, p. 12) and the sharp differences between the preschool and primary grades in instructional approaches and goals, and even the language used to describe children's work.

In the introduction to her book, Almy contextualizes the then-current debate around the concept of reading readiness—the idea that children are dubbed "ready to read" at a certain chronological age/mental age (see Morphett & Washburne, 1931). At the time, teaching based on reading readiness called for withholding formal beginning reading instruction because it was thought that teaching before a child was mentally ready would have detrimental effects. It was considered far better to wait until the child matured to the point at which instruction could be effective. As a result, parents and teachers were actively discouraged from formally engaging in any reading instruction prior to the onset of first grade.

Almy argued that this point of view was too simplistic, asserting instead that children's readiness for, and success in, reading instruction also depended on other factors. She called attention to other influences, such as whether the child completed nursery school and/or kindergarten, the environment for learning created in the school and classroom, individual child differences and interests, and—especially—the child's experiences with reading materials and activities prior to first grade. Furthermore, she maintained, the child's earlier experiences were singularly important, even given the diverse types of pro-grams and emphases in curricular experiences that existed in first grades at the time.

Almy seemed to have realized that to understand the relationships among the aforementioned factors and a child's success in beginning to read in first grade, one needed to describe the interactions that actually occurred in the home. But—because of the prevailing approach at the time to conducting educational research—she would likely not have considered using anthropological methods to investigate the issue. Instead, in keeping with the view that educational research depended on quantitative methods to achieve rigor, Almy employed a range of measurements and then analyzed correlations among the variables she previously identified.

True to the parameters of quantitative enquiry, Almy's study involved a substantial number of participants: 106 child and parent participants from half-day first-grade programs in one town in New York State. Her hypotheses were: "Learning to read in first grade is positively related to the number of responses to opportunities for reading the child makes prior to first grade entrance," and "The kinds of activities in which the child participates influences his approach to learning to read in first grade" (p. 18). To test them, Almy interviewed parents to discuss their children's play-based and formal experiences with language, reading, and writing—ranging from materials to social interactions—and also included parents' assessment of their children's success with reading. Interviews she conducted with children served to triangulate parent reports and to appraise their dispositions for reading and reading accomplishment.

Almy then quantified data from the parent and child interviews (e.g., a parent who automatically answered "reading" to the question "What does he like about first grade?" earned 1 credit, and no mention of reading earned no credit) and correlated those indicators of the home reading environment with two achievement measures, the subtests from the Gates Primary Reading Test of Word Recognition and of Sentence Reading (Gates, 1942) and an assessment of the children's mental age. The information from these data sources was used to generate a series of correlation matrices.

Almy concluded that "success in beginning to read is positively related to the number of the child's reading experiences prior to first grade" and that "there is no evidence in the group studied of a significant relationship between either mental age or occupational level and success in beginning to read" (p. 64). Her interview data confirmed that children's experiences of read-ing instruction before first grade varied, and pointed to considerable parental attentiveness to reading prior to the start of first grade as a determining factor. In the final section of her book, Almy included several comparative cases of dyads of children in each of three identified categories: "bright, average, and dull" groups for reading instruction. Here she presented descriptive quantita-tive data, such as the child's biological age, mental age, parent occupation, teacher's rating, and the total responses to opportunities to read to compare children. More important, she also provided thick, detailed descriptions of each child's experiences to illustrate the importance of honoring the needs and wishes of the child, as both are related to his or her success in beginning reading. For example, she compared the home teaching experiences of Marie and Tina, two children in the "dull group."

> Both mothers tried to teach the children to read. Tina's mother indicated that the whole family taught certain words and letters, that they bought her alphabet books and coloring books with special directions. She was concerned over the fact that she would like to help her but did not know modern teaching methods. Marie's mother also tried to teach her to read but when she found she was only interested in her name she dropped attempts to teach her the rest of the letters. She was amazed at how well she was doing in first grade with no earlier interest in letters and words. (Almy, 1949, p. 105)

The inclusion of case-specific and anthropologic illustrations of children's backgrounds embedded in unique family units and used in conjunction with purely quantitative correlations is arguably what is most pivotal about Almy's research. Her conclusion was that "the teacher must know not only what experiences the child has had, but also, so far as she is able, what their significance for him has been and how she can best build on them" (p. 108).

Impact of the Study

There are no citation index entries for Almy's book, no h-index indicating how often Almy's publication has been cited by others, and no Google Scholar source to examine. How do we then gauge the significance of a book published in 1949, and of an educator who was most active in her academic career in the through the 1960s until she retired in 1980 after she wrote her last major work, a coauthored book in 1979 (Almy & Genishi, 1979)?

In fact, it is extremely rare to find any reference to Almy or her 1949 book in virtually any publication on early literacy today. Searching early literacy methods texts (e.g., Morrow, 2015; Vukelich, Christie, & Enz, 2011); a variety of edited volumes on early literacy (e.g., *Achieving Excellence in Preschool Literacy Instruction* [Justice & Vukelich, 2008], *Literacies in Early Childhood* [Makin, Jones-Díaz, & McLachlan, 2007], *Early Childhood Literacy* [Shanahan & Lonigan, 2013]); as well as the *Handbook of Early Literacy Research* (Neuman & Dickinson, 2001, 2011; Dickinson & Neuman, 2006); and the first three volumes of the *Handbook of Reading Research* (Pearson et al., 1984; Barr et al., 1996; Kamil, Mosenthal, Pearson, & Barr, 2000) yielded no reference to *Children's Experiences Prior to First Grade and Success in Beginning Reading.*

Likewise no reference to Almy's book can be found in contemporary publications focused on preschool and early childhood education (e.g., *Handbook of Early Childhood Education* [Pianta, Barnett, Justice, & Sheridan, 2012] and the *International Handbook of Early Childhood Education* [Fleer & van Oers, 2018]).

In what ways, then, could *Children's Experiences Prior to First Grade and Success in Beginning Reading* be said to be both pivotal and influential with respect to the organization and aims of preschool education? The short answer is that Almy's book had its greatest impact on the practice of early childhood education during the two to three decades immediately following its publication. To gain a deeper understanding of the reasons why, let us consider two threads in the preschool education story.

1. Preschool education in the 1940s and now, and
2. The impact that early literacy learning and teaching as emergent literacy had on preschool education.

PRESCHOOL EDUCATION: THEN AND NOW

Prior to Almy's 1949 work, preschool education had ebbed and flowed as an institution in the United States. During the 1920s and 1930s substantial philanthropic investment was made in the study of child development, parent training, and early childhood workforce training. This investment led to the creation of nursery schools for children from 2 to 4 years of age. Group-play activities in these schools focused especially on social–emotional development and on helping children with their "social responsibilities" (Whipple, 1929). In 1914 Caroline Pratt established the City and Country School in New York City, which rebelled against formalized practices for young children and instituted more play-based activities that emphasized children's lived experiences. Her program for young children integrated block play, field trips, and few, if any, books (described in Pratt, 2014, and pictured in Figure 8.1). Almy endorsed Pratt's approach to early education, championing experience-based and play-based instruction throughout her career.

As Almy conducted her research after World War II, a period that saw the extension of federal support for child care and the increased growth of kindergartens, the first structured preschool curriculum emerged as an attempt to systematize early education to better prepare students for formal school (Cahan, 1989). The curriculum consisted of lists of activities covering the knowledge and behaviors considered prerequisites for entering school—in health, spirituality and aesthetics, leisure, citizenship, human relationships, economics, and vocational responsibilities—but were not especially academically focused. These activities were thought to be best implemented in the home by the children's caretakers since it was believed that the state bore no responsibility for

FIGURE 8.1. Early learning classroom in Caroline Pratt's City and Country School. Photo by George W. Harting. Copyright © 2014 City and Country School. Courtesy of City and Country School Archives.

the education of young children (Pierce, 1952). Thus, it should come as no surprise that Almy's research into the nature of preschool experiences relied on parent and child informants rather than on preschool teachers.

Almy's study and her subsequent work planted the idea that young preschool children were indeed having experiences in their home that related to their learning to read when they later encountered reading instruction in school. This finding had important implications for how first-grade teachers needed to think about how they were teaching reading, but it also set the stage for later research into what curriculum should be followed in early childhood classrooms, as preschool education became more and more prevalent in the 1960s and the years beyond.

In 1965, as part of the national War on Poverty intended to break the cycle of failure experienced by many Americans from economically stressed homes and communities, President Lyndon Johnson inaugurated Head Start (Barnett & Friedman-Krauss, 2016), a program that provided health care, social services, and educational opportunities to preschoolers and their families. Preschool education funded by the federal and state governments has steadily increased since then, fueled largely by a plethora of studies that reflect a range of perspectives (from that of neurological research, to economic-impact analyses, to studies of the cognitive impacts of preschool, and more) showing that high-quality early education is a success and results in economic and social benefits for the nation (e.g., García, Heckman, Leaf, & Prados, 2016; Smith & James, 1975).

Programs like Head Start employed scripted instructional strategies based on behaviorist research (e.g., *DISTAR* [Engelmann & Bruner, 1974]) that addressed early language development in the classroom. Today, research stressing the role of social interaction and the importance of the child's prior experiences and knowledge has led to preschool instructional practices that eschew the drill and practice of isolated skills and instead emphasize a range of "hands-on/minds-on" developmentally appropriate activities that foster both children's social–emotional and academic competencies. Such instructional methods reflect what Almy championed throughout her career.

Emergent Literacy and the Preschool

The transition to an emergent literacy perspective was a progressive one. Emergent literacy grew out of a sociocultural view of learning and development that reinforced the idea of children as coconstructors of their language and literacy and recognized the value of engaging in literacy work with young children rather than merely following a prescribed curriculum. An emergent literacy approach privileges children's prior experiences and access to literacy materials in home and in schoollike environments. The theoretical shift toward emergent literacy and its associated implications for pedagogy and policy in the early years prompted an orientation toward what Almy had identified in her research: the importance of children's learning environments, particularly their access to literacy materials, such as books and writing tools, in the immediate environment.

The changes that flowed from an emergent literacy orientation have only multiplied over the past three decades. What was once in the 1980s a new way of conceptualizing early reading and writing has now become commonplace, as any survey of early learning standards, preschool programs, research studies, or early childhood methods textbooks would show. Almy's study is rarely cited by today's emergent literacy researchers or those writing curricula, textbooks, or articles about early literacy instructional practices. But Almy's influence is evident in the attention to integrating literacy into young children's everyday, purposeful activities in the classroom and orchestrating instruction in ways that take into account children's early experiences in life, and with print in particular.

Teale and Sulzby (1986): *Emergent Literacy: Writing and Reading*

The second pivotal study discussed in this chapter is *Emergent Literacy: Writing and Reading*. It is an edited volume consisting of

- An introductory chapter written by William Teale and Elizabeth Sulzby that provides a conceptual and historical context for the book, and
- Eight chapters representing the work of prominent researchers who, during the early 1980s, were leading figures in the study of early literacy learning.

Emergent Literacy: Writing and Reading was the pivotal work that introduced the term *emergent literacy* to the field of literacy education overall and that made a research-based case for the need to reconceptualize the literacy development of young children.

The book followed on the heels of great research activity in studies of first-language development that employed direct and sustained observation of children in their home environments (e.g., Brown, 1973). Reading researchers examining preschool and kindergarten children's learning drew upon such studies heavily. Its publication also occurred in conjunction with a change in educational research methodology. In addition to the quantitative paradigm that had been *the* approach used by researchers (and was, for example, characteristic of Almy's work), this change legitimized approaches from the fields of anthropology and social psychology that employed rigorous observational, qualitative methodologies and emphasized a sociocultural/constructivist perspective.

The research featured in Teale and Sulzby (1986) also built upon work by Durkin (1966) (see Schickedanz, Chapter 3, this volume) and Clark (1976), who had examined the reading development of "exceptional" children—that is, "early readers" who had learned to read conventionally before going to school. The early reader work served as a touchstone for extending the examination of literacy beyond precocious children to the full range of preschoolers. Hence, studies of children's understandings of environmental print (e.g., Harste, Burke, & Woodward, 1982), early writing (e.g., Bissex, 1980), and home and community literacy experiences (e.g., Heath, 1980, 1983) also served as context for the volume.

In the larger societal context at the time *Emergent Literacy* was published, Head Start had been in existence for two decades. Also, attending preschool was becoming the norm, not only among children from lower-income families served by federal and state programs, but also among the growing number of children whose mothers, either by choice or out of economic necessity, were entering the workforce.

Description of the Volume

Teale and Sulzby (1986) captured the rethinking of the early literacy field taking place during the late 1970s and early 1980s. They invited the contributors represented in this book to write chapters that simultaneously would address their own work over the past few years and also contextualize it within the evolving climate that was reconceptualizing early literacy. As the editors reviewed the incoming chapters and worked on writing the introductory chapter to the volume, they held many discussions about what vision they intended for the book and what title to give it. Should a new term be used, or should the existing terminology for young children's literacy learning be repurposed? In retrospect, it might be said that the resulting volume became a manifesto for emergent literacy that significantly altered prevailing thinking about children's literacy development In 1966 Marie Clay had used the term "emergent reading behaviour" in her doctoral dissertation, but there was no extant use of the term *emergent literacy* to speak of in the field. In the end, Teale and Sulzby decided that the term *emergent* best described what research revealed about development and had the potential to reshape practitioner thinking. And so, the title of the book became *Emergent Literacy*.

In their introduction to the 1986 volume, Teale and Sulzby explained that over the prior three-quarters of a century, approaches to teaching young children to read and write had moved "from benign neglect to reading readiness" (p. viii). The reading readiness paradigm held that children became "ready" to learn to read only when they had reached a certain developmental level (represented by a mental age of 6 years, 6 months) and that educators and adults in general should delay teaching children to read until that time arrived. Grounded in research conducted in the decade before their book was published, Teale and Sulzby posited instead that reading does not begin only when children master "pre-reading" skills or subskills. They pointed out that research evidence stemming from systematic observational and structured interview techniques had accumulated to the point of convincingly indicating that children engage in legitimate literacy behaviors and development virtually from birth. They concluded, " . . . it is not reasonable to point to a time in a child's life when literacy begins. Rather at whatever point we look, we see children in the process of becoming literate, as the term *emergent* indicates" (p. xix).

Emergent Literacy is a compilation of several different perspectives on what the contributing researchers believed was important to discuss at the time. The contributors' approaches can be characterized in three ways.

Some of them reported results from their own specific research studies.

- Ferreiro described two case studies, conducted over a 2-year period, of young children's developing knowledge about writing.
- Sulzby presented descriptions of three 6-year-olds' developing notions of

oral and written language as revealed in oral discussion of and written responses to a shared activity.

- McCormick and Mason shared the results of a traditionally designed early intervention study that employed emergent literacy perspectives on preschool children's acquisition of print knowledge.
- Teale detailed the results from a longitudinal observational study of the daily home literacy experiences of preschool children from three cultural groups.

Other contributors analyzed a series of previous research studies.

- Goodman used the results from previous studies of environmental print, book handling, children's writing, and metalinguistic awareness that she and her doctoral students conducted to draw conclusions about what she termed the five "roots of literacy" for young children.
- Snow and Ninio merged their previously separate lines of research on mother–child interactions and language acquisition (Snow) and joint adult–child picture book reading (Ninio) to discuss how children learn seven "contracts of literacy" because of participation in book reading activities.

Still others took less traditional approaches, sharing small samples from larger data sets to emphasize critical points.

- Heath discussed her seminal work in the communities of the Piedmont Carolinas with a focus on adult–child talk within the context of the family and the culture of the community.
- Taylor presented data to better understand how parents and children have come to engage in joint book reading to construct not only stories in books but also, Taylor argued, the family itself.

Thus, the book delivered not so much a specific message as it captured a new perspective on early literacy learning, which stressed that " . . . children's early reading and writing behaviors are not pre-anything but are integral parts of a language process which is in a state of becoming" (p. xix).

Impact of the Volume

A Google Books Ngram graphic, shown in Figure 8.2, captures the impact that the research on emergent literacy has had on how researchers conceptualize young children's literacy development.

We by no means claim that *Emergent Literacy* was solely responsible for the seismic shift that took place in the prevailing view of early literacy learning

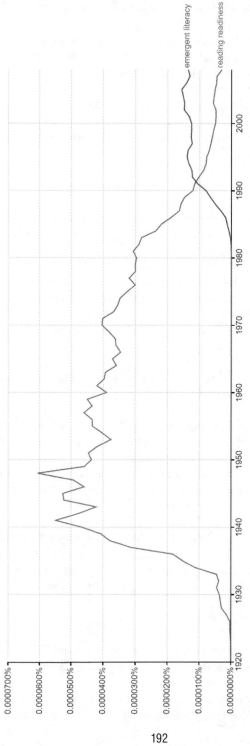

FIGURE 8.2. Frequency of occurrence of the terms *reading readiness* and *emergent literacy* found in sources printed between 1920 and 2008 in Google's text corpora.

and teaching and its resulting implications for the organization and aims of preschool education, but there is ample evidence that its role among scholars was and is significant. The book was widely cited among researchers during the decade following its publication, and it was frequently used as a touchstone text in doctoral seminars on early literacy. It has remained in print (now digitally) for over 30 years, and citation patterns by year (see *https://goo.gl/Jfxa9V*) illustrate that the book continues to be cited up to the present.

With respect to practice, Teale and Sulzby launched an international conversation about how and when children begin to engage in literate practices. Their emergent literacy paradigm foundationally altered how we think about early literacy instruction. By making connections between the purposes of literacy instruction in preschool (teaching young children to read and write and not just waiting for them to reach a certain developmental age) and what type of instruction that entails, the book set in motion preschool emergent literacy instructional practices that are followed today. Instructional practices that now seem commonplace—and, indeed, even common sense in current early childhood classrooms (e.g., engaging in interactive read-alouds, encouraging young children to write, incorporating literacy experiences into children's dramatic play)—were introduced after educators changed from a reading-readiness state of mind to one anchored in emergent literacy. At the core of this shift was the idea that reading and writing needed to be appropriately taught in preschool settings.

Child and adult interactions now were known to be the crux of early learning achievement (e.g., Pianta, Howes, Burchinal, Bryant, Clifford, Early, & Barbarin, 2005; Pianta, Mashburn, Downer, Hamre, & Justice, 2008; Pianta et al., 2014). Such interactions, cited in the meta-analysis conducted by the National Early Literacy Panel (2008) and even discussed in Almy's (1949) text, were now viewed in a new light due to the emergent literacy paradigm that emphasized the role that daily interactions between caregivers and children played in children's becoming conventionally literate. Emergent literacy classroom instruction was not envisioned as targeting formal reading instruction, as traditionally found in beginning reading programs. Instead, it emphasized finding more opportunities for children to authentically interact with text (in its variety of forms) in engaging, child-centered activities. Teale (1995) offers an abridged discussion of emergent literacy instructional concepts that contested the instructional concepts of reading readiness. He focused on how to align preschool programs with emergent literacy concepts, such as involving children in literate activities from the first day of school, creating print-rich environments in classrooms, making written language a purposeful part of the school day, and involving children in goal-directed written language activities.

Initially, in the 1980s and early 1990s, the emergent literacy paradigm impacted kindergarten curriculum. As kindergarten movement to implement emergent literacy practices grew, and as the research on implementation became widespread, basal reading teachers took note and moved away from the instructional paradigms represented in their teachers' manuals toward an emergent literacy approach for kindergarten and even for early first grade.

Subsequently, emergent literacy became a more common practice in preschools. Currently preschool curriculum programs, such as The Creative Curriculum (CC), attend to foundational early literacy skills, like listening comprehension, phonological awareness (PA), and composing in writing, but that had not always been the case. When first introduced in 1978, CC attained widespread adoption because it emphasized play environments, student choice, and center activities. Accompanied by a document called "Room Arrangement as a Teaching Strategy," the initial CC curriculum included *Blocks, Table Toys, House Corner,* and *Art* (*https://teachingstrategies.com/company/history/*). There was almost no intentional instruction in literacy written into the document. Rather, CC was based on the notion that what was needed was to give children the right materials to interact with, and that would be sufficient for them to develop early knowledge, basic skills, and social–emotional awareness. As a result, preschool teachers' lesson planning from that time until relatively recently tended to revolve around the materials supplied to children in each center, but paid comparatively little attention to planning for teacher–child interactions or interactions between children that would improve student competencies.

Eventually, a "push down" of academic goals occurred in the preschool years—if we no longer needed to wait to teach early reading and writing concepts, then we needed to introduce them, and the earlier the better. Such attitudes prompted the developers of CC to respond. In 1998 Teaching Strategies released the *Creative Curriculum Developmental Continuum for 3–5,* a formal outline of what students should be learning in preschool. Along with social–emotional, physical, and cognitive goals, the curriculum also included a language development category that included specific attention to speaking, listening, reading, and writing goals emphasized in emergent literacy instruction. Later, in 2010, *Teaching Strategies GOLD,* the assessment component of CC that documented student achievement, was introduced the same year that Head Start revised its performance standards to include emergent literacy goals.

Teale and Sulzby (1986) argued that "all the authors represented in this volume are deeply concerned with the interface between research and policy, whether it be day care, preschool, or school policy, home intervention policy, or larger issues of governmental/social policy" (p. xxi). This appeal to pay attention to policy played itself out in a number of ways since the 1980s, as the impact of the emergent literacy paradigm grew. Policies nationwide increasingly coalesced around the idea that children should be supported in learning how to read and write during the preschool years.

- In the late 1980s, programs such as Reach Out and Read, the Children's Literacy Initiative, and even the popular Sesame Street program reflected the increasing focus on early literacy.
- In the late 1990s, the (then) International Reading Association and the National Association for the Education of Young Children issued a joint statement in *Young Children* entitled "Learning to Read and Write: Developmentally Appropriate Practices for Young Children."
- Such developments aligned with 1997 White House Conference on Early Childhood Development and Learning, which highlighted new scientific findings on brain development in young children.
- As just mentioned, in 2010, the Head Start Child Development and Early Learning Framework, a document that focused on positive outcomes for 3- to 5-year-olds, reflected "literacy knowledge and skills" for the first time.

Today, emergent literacy has become the paradigm followed by the vast majority of preschool programs. Enlightened preschools are centrally concerned with both *how* children are learning and *what* children are learning in terms of both early reading and early writing concepts and skills.

CONCLUSION

This chapter focused on the changes that have occurred in the approach to and aims of preschool literacy from the 1940s to the present. We have discussed two pivotal publications, Almy's *Children's Experiences Prior to First Grade and Success in Beginning Reading* and Teale and Sulzby's edited volume, *Emergent Literacy: Writing and Reading*, in the context of the shift that took place from a reading-readiness conception of children's early literacy development to an emergent-literacy perspective. These two publications were not solely responsible for the momentous sea change in how early literacy is viewed and researched and in how preschool curriculums have been transformed. Many other influences from early literacy scholarship and from enlightened classroom practices that pushed the field to where it is today also played a role.

But the two works serve as important markers on the path. Almy's research examined children and their families in an attempt to clarify misconceptions that were guiding the early literacy instruction of the time. Teale and Sulzby brought together the perspectives of various contributors, who were developing new theories and practical recommendations that, over the decade and a half following the book's publication, would fundamentally alter how we think about young children's literacy learning and what has become recommended practice in the preschool classroom.

As we think about the pivotal works of Almy and Teale and Sulzby in relation to where the field of preschool literacy is headed, what are the take-away messages? First, in the field as a whole, the emergent literacy perspective is strong and will remain so in the future. But it is also changing in light of new theories and research. We began this chapter with a from-then-to-now framework. Let us end with a from-now-to-next proposal for changes that we believe need to be accomplished to align practice and policy with the principles of emergent literacy inherent in the work of Almy, Teale, and Sulzby. We note five especially important areas in which preschool literacy education should be reshaped in future years.

Now	*Next*
American preschools are currently experiencing "academic pushdown," as there is more pressure to offer instruction in literacy and mathematics (Bassok, Latham, & Rorem, 2016). In many instances the result has been a focus on constrained skills (alphabet knowledge, PA, letter–sound correspondences) and a de-emphasis on, or squeezing out of, play and the arts from the daily curriculum (Moser, 2015).	There will be a concerted movement among teachers and administrators well-grounded in early childhood to maintain high academic expectations through intentional instruction embedded in developmentally appropriate literacy experiences, such as centers-based play that is grounded in authentic, goal-directed contexts that are of high interest to children (see Wohlwend, 2008; Dyson, 2003; Rowe, 1998; Hoffman, Paciga, & Teale, 2014, for examples).
Digital media have invaded the early childhood marketplace, and increased emphasis has been placed on preschool as the place to start children on the road to becoming competent at operating in digital spaces. But often the literacy content of these experiences and instructional products is targeted at constrained skills.	Teachers (and parents) will become more discerning consumers of apps and smarter about embedding technology in early childhood classrooms in ways that are not glorified workbooks or about the technology itself. Instead, using technological tools to create, problem solve, interact, and collaborate with both the tool and with other people will be emphasized in order to add innovative dimensions to early-childhood classroom learning.

Now

Vocabulary, vocabulary, vocabulary. Hart and Risley's (1995, 2003) work currently dominates the conversation about preschool language development, in its emphasis on quantity over quality. Adoption of this work has created preschool initiatives that decontextualize language use, focusing teacher and parent attention on "how many" words are heard or spoken.

In many instances, preschool has become its own island. Preschool teachers and assistants in classrooms who teach in elementary schools do not typically engage in schoolwide professional trainings, and those who work in child-care centers often have little connection to the elementary schools their students will attend.

Preschool teachers and administrative heads (school principals, center directors) frequently have little background in evidence-based early literacy curriculum and instruction.

Next

Emphasis on early oral language and vocabulary development will rightfully continue, but with appropriate resistance to ideas like the 30-million word gap. Instead the value of home language experiences of all kinds will be recognized, and the centrality of context and culture will be emphasized as an important basis for instruction, thereby enhancing the quality of teacher–child, parent–child, and child–child language interactions.

Schools, communities, and states will implement curricular, instructional, and professional learning coherence in literacy across the preschool to second-grade spectrum. School and center initiatives, as well as district and state policies, will make this coherence a priority and a reality.

Preparation programs in colleges and universities for school principals and directors will purposely embed early literacy leadership into their standards and required course content. Schools, centers, and family day care organizations will develop robust professional learning opportunities for currently practicing leaders to gain expertise in evidence-based early literacy leadership strategies.

The 1980s and early 1990s were revolutionary in many respects for the field of preschool literacy. Those changes were built upon the foundation set by scholar–practitioners like Millie Almy, and taken up by a host of other scholars, such as those represented in the volume edited by Teale and Sulzby. Research in the years since that time has continued to extend the revolution, by advancing our knowledge of sound emergent-literacy pedagogies and by responding to the ever-changing contexts in which children learn. Current challenges, including the "academic pushdown," professional isolation, and the often limited early-literacy capacity of school leaders, stymie opportunities to achieve the vision inherent in an emergent literacy perspective. In identifying these challenges, it is our hope that scholars today and practitioners in the next generation continue in the trailblazing spirit of Almy, Sulzby, Teale, and others in moving the field in a progressive direction.

ACKNOWLEDGMENTS

This chapter was supported with resources from the UIC Center for Literacy, under the leadership and mentorship of the late William H. Teale (1947–2018). Each of the coauthors has worked for the UIC Center for Literacy and has been blessed to call Bill her mentor, colleague, and friend. P. David Pearson suggested that "every time we put a book in the hands of a 4-year-old, we honor Bill's legacy." We hope this chapter both honors and contributes to Bill's legacy too, of which we are eternally grateful to have been a part.

REFERENCES

Almy, M. (1949). *Children's experiences prior to first grade and success in beginning reading.* New York: Bureau of Publications, Teachers College, Columbia University.

Almy, M., & Genishi, C. (1979). *Ways of studying children: An observation manual for early childhood teachers.* New York: Teachers College Press.

Barnett, W. S., & Friedman-Krauss, A. H. (2016). *State(s) of Head Start.* New Brunswick, NJ: National Institute for Early Education Research.

Barr, R., Kamil, M., Mosenthal, P., & Pearson, P. D. (Eds.). (1996). *Handbook of reading research* (Vol. II). Mahwah, NJ: Erlbaum.

Bassok, D., Latham, S., & Rorem, A. (2016). Is kindergarten the new first grade? *AERA Open, 1*(4), 1–31.

Bissex, G. L. (1980). *GNYS AT WRK: A child learns to write and read.* Cambridge, MA: Harvard University Press.

Brown, R. (1973). *A first language: The early stages.* Cambridge, MA: Harvard University Press.

Cahan, E. D. (1989). *Past caring: A history of U.S. preschool and education for the poor, 1820–1965.* New York: National Center for Children in Poverty.

Clark. M. M. (1976). *Young fluent readers: What can they teach us?* London: Heinemann Educational Books.

Clay, M. M. (1966). *Emergent reading behaviour.* Unpublished doctoral dissertation. University of Auckland, Auckland, New Zealand.

Dickinson, D. K., & Neuman, S. B. (Eds.). (2006). *Handbook of early literacy research* (Vol. 2). New York: Guilford Press.

Durkin, D. (1966). *Children who read early.* New York: Teachers College Press.

Dyson, A. H. (2003). *The brothers and sisters learn to write: Popular literacies in childhood and school culture.* New York: Teachers College Press.

Engelmann, S., & Bruner, E. C. (1974). *Distar Reading I: An instructional system* (2nd ed.). Chicago: Science Research Associates.

Fleer, M., & van Oers, B. (2018). *International handbook of early childhood education.* Berlin: Springer.

Gans, R. (1948). Young children at the turn of this era. In N. Henry (Ed.), *The forty-sixth yearbook of the National Society for the Study of Education: Part 2—Early childhood education* (pp. 6–13). Chicago: University of Chicago Press.

García, J. L., Heckman, J. J., Leaf, D. E., & Prados, M. J. (2016). *The life-cycle benefits of an influential early childhood program.* Working Paper 22993. Cambridge, MA: National Bureau of Economic Research.

Gates, A. I. (1942). *Manual of directions: Gates Primary Reading Tests (grade I and first half of grade II).* New York: Bureau of Publications, Teachers College, Columbia University.

Harste, J. C., Burke, C. L., & Woodward, V. A. (1982). Children, their language and world: Initial encounters with print. In J. Langer & M. Smith-Burke (Eds.), *Reader meets author: Bridging the gap.* Newark, DE: International Reading Association.

Hart, B., & Risley, T. R. (1995). *Meaningful differences in the everyday experience of young American children.* Baltimore: Brookes.

Hart, B., & Risley, T. R. (2003). The early catastrophe: The 30 million word gap by age 3. *American Educator, 27,* 4–9.

Heath, S. B. (1980). The functions and uses of literacy. *Journal of Communication, 30,* 123–133.

Heath, S. B. (1983). *Ways with words: Language, life, and work in communities and classrooms.* Cambridge, UK: Cambridge University Press.

Hoffman, J. L., Paciga, K. A., & Teale, W. H. (2014). *Common Core State Standards and early childhood literacy instruction: Confusions and conclusions* (UIC Center for Literacy Research Paper). Chicago: UIC Center for Literacy.

Justice, L., & Vukelich, C. (Eds.). (2008). *Achieving excellence in preschool literacy instruction.* New York: Guilford Press.

Kamil, M., Mosenthal, P., Pearson, P. D., & Barr, R. (Eds.). (2000). *Handbook of reading research* (Vol. 3). Mahwah, NJ: Erlbaum.

Makin, L., Jones-Díaz, C., & McLachlan, C. (2007). *Literacies in childhood: Changing views, challenging practice.* Sydney, Australia: Elsevier.

Meisels, S., & Shonkoff, J. (2000). Early childhood intervention: A continuing concept. In J. Shonkoff & S. Meisels (Eds.), *Handbook of early childhood intervention* (pp. 3–31). Cambridge, UK: Cambridge University Press.

Morphett, M. V., & Washburne, C. (1931). When should children begin to read? *The Elementary School Journal, 31,* 496–508.

Morrow, L. M. (2015). *Literacy development in the early years: Helping children read and write* (8th ed.). New York: Pearson.

Moser, L. (2015, December 21). If academics-focused preschool is "crushing our kids," what's the alternative? *Slate.* Retrieved from *www.slate.com.*

National Early Literacy Panel. (2008). *Developing early literacy: Report of the National Early Literacy Panel.* Washington, DC: National Institute for Literacy.

Neuman, S. B., & Dickinson, D. K. (2001). *Handbook of early literacy research*. New York: Guilford Press.

Neuman, S. B., & Dickinson, D. K. (2011). *Handbook of early literacy research* (Vol. 3). New York: Guilford Press.

Pearson, P. D., Barr, R., Kamil, M. L., & Mosenthal, P. B. (Eds.). (1984). *Handbook of reading research* (Vol. 1). New York: Longman.

Pianta, R. C., Barnett, W. S., Justice, L. M., & Sheridan, S. M. (Eds.). (2012). *Handbook of early childhood education*. New York: Guilford Press.

Pianta, R. C., Burchinal, M., Jamil, F., Sabol, T., Grimm, K., Hamre, B., . . . Howes, C. (2014). A cross-lag analysis of longitudinal associations between preschool teachers' instructional support identification skills and observed behavior. *Early Childhood Research Quarterly, 29*(2), 144–154.

Pianta, R., Howes, C., Burchinal, M., Bryant, D., Clifford, R., Early, D., & Barbarin, O. (2005). Features of pre-kindergarten programs, classrooms, and teachers: Do they predict observed classroom quality and child-teacher interactions? *Applied Developmental Science, 9*(3), 144–159.

Pianta, R. C., Mashburn, A. J., Downer, J. T., Hamre, B. K., & Justice, L. (2008). Effects of web-mediated professional development resources on teacher–child interactions in pre-kindergarten classrooms. *Early Childhood Research Quarterly, 23*(4), 431–451.

Pierce, P. R. (1952). Chicago's preschool curriculum. *The Elementary School Journal, 53*(3), 138–143.

Pratt, C. (2014). *I learn from children: An adventure in progressive education* [Kindle ed.]. New York: Grove/Atlantic.

Rowe, D. W. (1998). The literate potentials of book-related dramatic play. *Reading Research Quarterly, 33*(1), 10.

Shanahan, T., & Lonigan, C. J. (2013). *Early childhood literacy: The National Early Literacy Panel and beyond*. Baltimore: Brookes.

Shonkoff, J. P., & Meisels, S. J. (1990). Early childhood intervention: The evolution of a concept. In S. J. Meisels & J. P. Shonkoff (Eds.), *Handbook of early childhood intervention* (pp. 3–31). New York: Cambridge University Press.

Smith, G., & James, T. (1975). The effects of preschool education: Some American and British evidence. *Oxford Review of Education, 1*(3), 223–240.

Teale, W. H. (1995). Young children and reading: Trends across the twentieth century. *Journal of Education, 177*(3), 95–127.

Teale, W. H., & Sulzby, E. (Eds.). (1986). *Emergent literacy: Writing and reading*. Norwood, NJ: Ablex.

Vukelich, C., Christie, J., & Enz, B. J. (2011). *Helping young children learn language and literacy: Birth through kindergarten* (3rd ed.). New York: Pearson.

Whipple, G. (Ed.). (1929). *National Society for the Study of Education twenty-eighth yearbook: Preschool and parental education*. Bloomington, IL: Public School Publishing.

Wohlwend, K. E. (2008). Kindergarten as nexus of practice: A mediated discourse analysis of reading, writing, play, and design in an early literacy apprenticeship. *Reading Research Quarterly, 43*(4), 332–334.

CHAPTER 9

Storybook Reading

Insights from Hindsight

Molly F. Collins

The book to read is not the one that thinks for you but the one that makes you think.

—HARPER LEE

Reading stories to young children has been among the most extensively studied instructional practice in the early years with research now having spanned many decades (Irwin, 1960; Ninio & Bruner, 1978). In their inquiries, researchers have explored the participants involved (e.g., children, parents, and educators), the books (e.g., genre and complexity) and the contexts (e.g., home, school, community; dyads and large and small groups) used, and the outcomes (e.g., literacy skills, language development, comprehension), as well as variables related to these (e.g., interactions between reader and child/children, children's motivation, and initial language status). Investigative modalities have ranged from case studies to randomized control trials, and researchers have come from many academic fields (e.g., education, language and linguistics, developmental psychology, special education, communication sciences, neurobiology). The inclusion of reviews and meta-analyses of storybook reading to young children in a wide range of handbooks and reports (Dickinson & Neuman, 2011; National Early Literacy Panel, 2008; National Reading Panel, 2000) indicates its significance, as does its inclusion in learning standards (e.g., National Governors Association Center for Best Practices, Council of Chief State School Officers [NGA & CCSSO], 2010) and curriculum guidelines, and has influenced the content of commercial curricula (e.g., Dodge, Colker, & Heroman, 2010; Jumpstart for Young Children, Inc., 2018; Neuman, Snow, & Canizares, 2010; Schickedanz & Dickinson, 2005).

THREE PIVOTAL STUDIES ON STORYBOOK READING

This chapter focuses on early research on reading aloud to preschoolers. Each of the three pivotal studies selected for this chapter has been critical to our understanding of reading aloud to preschoolers, in part because they asked the right questions at the right time. The studies held substantial potential for shaping research and practice and laid the conceptual groundwork for deeper understanding of the relationship between storybook reading with preschoolers and later reading achievement. Of course, some current practices do not reflect messages that are found in the pivotal research; what now appear to have been detours and side roads looked like neither at the time. Understanding the trajectory of storybook reading's contribution to early literacy can illuminate the road already traveled, as well as the road ahead in helping children learn (and love) to read.

The pivotal studies selected for this chapter are discussed in chronological order to provide a historical trace for each within the body of research available at the time and to indicate how the studies cohere and add to our knowledge. I start the discussion of each pivotal study with the historical context in which it was undertaken, including reference to theoretical underpinnings. I then comment briefly about the researchers' motivations before describing the study's research questions, methods, and findings. I end each discussion with an overview of the study's impact on the field and a few take-away messages. Following the discussion of the three pivotal pieces, I present a concluding section that features a synthesis of the studies' contributions, proposes a new direction for storybook reading instruction and research, and offers some action steps for teachers, administrators, and educational researchers.

Cochran-Smith (1984): *The Making of a Reader*

Historical Context

In *The Making of a Reader* (1984), Marilyn Cochran-Smith includes the contributions of social and contextual factors nascent to home and school experiences. Most of the storybook research prior to Cochran-Smith's study had focused on children's experiences with books at home (Teale, 1981). The field was becoming aware that parents communicated important literacy knowledge to children in the story reading setting and that children who had early book reading experience at home often had higher rates of success in learning to read in school than children without this experience. The extant research was less informative about how young children actually acquired language and literacy knowledge. Comprehension research was concurrently rife with methodological or theoretical problems, such as the use of inauthentic experiences with books or inadequate research questions. For example, experimental studies were not conducted in natural settings, and the stories that were contrived for experimental purposes had a story script but no illustrations and were read aloud by a researcher or played via an audiotape. In other words, naturally-occurring contexts, such as parents reading at home and picture books that were representative of books used by children, were not used in the research.

Other problems in the research conducted at this time arose from researchers' view of text comprehension by young children as a nonconstructive process. Or, infrequently, the researcher valued the adult's role as important to fostering a young child's sense-making but discounted and thus ignored children's responses to questions and comments and focused singularly on adult talk. At the same time, evidence provided by other researchers suggested that the preliterate child developed an understanding of print at home, prior to formal schooling (Crago & Crago, 1976; Heath, 1983; Scollon & Scollon, 1981) and that the process involved substantial construction of meaning about print by the child in contexts where the adult behaved in ways that aided it. Findings from these naturalistic studies, coupled with the deficiencies of extant comprehension research, undoubtedly inspired Cochran-Smith's call for inquiry into the ways that adults support children in making inferences about stories during read-aloud sessions and influenced the ways in which she set out to describe teacher–child interactions during story reading in preschool. (Cochran-Smith also described and analyzed data from writing activities; however, only information from read-aloud experiences is reported here.)

Description of the Study

The 15 participants were the children, parents, and a classroom teacher at Maple Nursery School (MNS), a private preschool serving middle-class families living in a residential neighborhood of Philadelphia. For 18 months, Cochran-Smith collected information on the story reading and literacy activities of children in the classroom through observations which comprised both an exploratory (90 hours) and a formal (200 hours) phase. Story reading, including all interactions between the teacher and the children, and book-related conversations prior to and immediately after a book was read, were audiotaped. Handwritten notes provided details about the setting, including the participants, nonverbal behaviors during the reading session, and the book's text and conversations that took place during the reading of the book and after.

Transcriptions of 100 story-reading sessions were prepared from these sources of input and contained text reading; all verbal exchanges before, during, and after the reading; descriptions of text and pictorial representations;

and participants' nonverbal behavior. All information was embedded in the transcripts in chronological order. These transcripts were used as the main source of data from which she categorized three types of meaning-making inter-actions: (1) readiness routines of preparing for and participating in reading, (2) life-to-text interaction sequences aimed at helping children make sense of story events, and (3) text-to-life interaction sequences focused on helping children apply the books' themes and messages to life (see Table 9.1). Cochran-Smith also collected anecdotal information from the teacher, which included her pur-poses for story reading, the general educational goals of the nursery school, the roles of parents and teachers in the school, and specific nursery school events (e.g., field trips). These data were used to describe the relationships among the daily literacy activities, the classroom environment, and the overall life in the nursery school. Parents contributed information about home reading practices, beliefs about reading, details about book selection and the sources of books, children's interest in books, topics discussed during book reading, goals for children's reading and literacy development, and overall expectations of the nursery school.

Impact of the Study

From the data provided in the detailed transcripts of the language interactions among the children and teacher, Cochran-Smith derived patterns of talk "to provide a way of looking at, thinking about, and talking about early literacy that can help others see more clearly some of the issues involved in studying and making decisions about this process" (p. 253). As a result of her efforts, *The Making of a Reader* contributed three main ideas to the field.

1. *Story reading should focus on making meaning, and making meaning requires thinking.* Cochran-Smith emphasized that story reading is about mak-ing meaning and that complex mental processes are involved. These include linking information that is provided in various parts of the text, applying world knowledge, and drawing inferences. Cochran-Smith stressed that our talk with young children about stories should elicit engagement in these mental opera-tions. Moreover, an overabundance of talk, by children or adults, based on the recollection of facts or the labeling of images does not cultivate deeper compre-hension or prime the mental processes that are vital to it.

In contrast to contextualized literacy activities of the nursery school, in which the meaning of print is generated by its functions and the environment in which it occurs (e.g., a stop sign on the playground's riding track, a "snacks" label on the cabinet in which food for snack time is stored), story reading is a decontextualized experience in which the functions and uses of print are removed from the immediate environment. Comprehending in a

TABLE 9.1. Cochran-Smith's Categories of Talk and Examples

Category of talk	Example	Explanation
Readiness routines were interaction sequences focused on establishing nonverbal behavioral routines for preparing to listen to and participate in story reading. These included the listeners' seating arrangements on the rug, attention to the book and story reader, posture, concentration, and behavior that did not disrupt others' attentive behavior.	TEACHER: Dan? Dan, come on, dearie. I want you to sit next to me while we read. Here, dearie. Dan? (*Motions for Dan to come sit near her.*) TEACHER: Here, Dan. Round this side. Sit right over here (*guiding Dan to spot beside her on other side of bench*).[a]	The teacher helps Dan get ready to listen to stories through explicit verbal prompts and gestures to clarify the seating arrangement.
Life-to-text interaction sequences focused on incorporating extratextual information, such as knowledge of the physical world, people, and social interaction, narrative structure, vocabulary, cultural and literary heritage, and literary conventions (p. 173) to foster understanding of the story, including cause–effect relationships and character motivation.	TEACHER: (*reading text*) Then, they were both sound asleep when Oliver's mother flitted into the room. She had been looking for Oliver all that night. "My, what a mess," she murmured softly. "What am I going to do with that boy?" TEACHER: See, his mother is a magical person too. She's a magical person (*pointing to mother*). (*Children look over blankly.*) TEACHER: Does she look like a *real* little lady? NAT: Mmm hmm (*quietly*). TEACHER: She's kind of tiny. And what does she have on her shoulders like Oliver? (*pointing to wings*) What does she have up on her shoulders? MARK: I don't know . . . NAT: Wings! (*exclaiming*) Wings!	The teacher uses information about the world to help children draw inferences about characters, in particular to understand that a genie's mother, new to the scene, was also a genie herself. The teacher fostered this thinking by calling attention to information already presented in the book (e.g., "See, his mother is a magical person") and, when children seemed nonplussed, by modeling inferencing using evidence (e.g., she was small, didn't look like a real mother, had wings, and was all white).

(continued)

TABLE 9.1. *(continued)*

Category of talk	Example	Explanation
	TEACHER: Can you see those wings? That's right. Nat knows. Just like little Oliver has wings; and I think she doesn't have any color on her clothes, does she? ANNA: She has white on her color. TEACHER: Yes, she's all white.[b]	
Text-to-life interaction sequences focused on helping children make inferences about the text to understand larger messages of the story, universal values, and the application of information in the story to their own lives. These included using book reading to deal with feelings, gather knowledge, entertain, or cultivate the imagination.	TEACHER: *(holding book out to Dan after having pointed to each room of a character's new house)* Dan, which room would you like to live in? DAN: Na-ah *(scanning page and pointing)*. This room! TEACHER: *(tapping picture)* Oh, the pretty room with the pictures? TEACHER: How 'bout you, Clay? *(holding book out to Clay)* CLAY: I'd like to live in . . . *(Points to gym.)* TEACHER: *(nodding and pointing to picture)* That's where the athlete . . . that's like a gym. CLAY: I'd, uh, I would like in there *(pointing to a science room)*. TEACHER: *(nodding)* Oh, with all the insects and the mushroom pictures.[c]	Book reading was used to foster imagination by giving children opportunities to put themselves in new situations and to consider different perspectives, especially those experienced by characters in the stories.

Note. Adapted by permission from Cochran-Smith (1984).
[a]p. 110; [b]p. 187, Segment 11; [c]p. 245, Segment 30.

decontextualized experience requires understanding how to derive meaning from the lexical (e.g., word meaning) and syntactic (i.e., word order) features of print, as well as understanding what "taking" from a read-aloud experience means. For example, taking from decontextualized print involves understanding the different demands of texts related to diverse genres (e.g., fantasy, mystery, biography, alphabet books), which function as interpretational cues (e.g., a knowledge of the fantasy genre imbues children with a framework for understanding characters with special powers, settings with pretend scenarios, and resolutions accompanied by magic).

Whereas the purposes of contextualized print cues present in the environment are obvious, decontextualized print cues are obtained from the author's and readers' mutual assumptions about the text, and its purposes are subject to negotiation. Additionally, interpreting decontextualized print requires the use of strategies that differ from interpreting contextualized print. With decontextualized print, a child must attend to the context of the book itself (i.e., not environmental cues found on playgrounds, for example, or in nursery school furnishings readily available in the immediate surroundings) and from verbal interactions with the adult. Through these verbal interactions about the meaning of the text, the adult reader thinks aloud with children about ways to apply world knowledge to the text (e.g., see in Table 9.1 "what does she have up on her shoulders? Wings, that's right.") (Cochran-Smith, 1984, p. 187) and ways to apply the meaning of texts to their everyday experiences (e.g., reading a book about fish prior to taking a trip to an aquarium to view and purchase fish) (Cochran-Smith, 1984, p. 243). This think-aloud process models and accesses the strategies necessary for understanding decontextualized print.

Cochran-Smith understood that facility with extracting meaning from the decontextualized context of story reading is important to later independent reading, which depends solely on the readers' ability to ascertain meaning from reading text. Her examples demonstrate how teachers can support the mental processes required by children to comprehend the decontextualized language found in texts.

2. *Dialogue with adults is central to thinking.* Oral language interactions with adults are paramount to children's thinking. When adults and children engage in conversation about the story, adults scaffold exchanges that enable children to interpret their and others' thinking. Life-to-text connections help children interpret text information. Text-to-life associations help children consider broader messages and the application of stories to their lives (see Table 9.1). A teacher's talk should model the integration of multiple types of knowledge needed to make sense of the story: world knowledge; literary conventions (e.g., books of a certain genre "work" a certain way); and narrative structure to help foster inferencing about characters and story events, as well as ways of interpreting stories. Conveyed by extratextual comments, these conversations help children understand and use oral language and grant access to the meaning.

The interactional exchanges in Table 9.2 show how the teacher's prompts can help children use different types of knowledge to understand the text and to promote thinking. The exchange shows support for applying world

TABLE 9.2. Example of Using Different Types of Knowledge to Understand Text

TEACHER: What's that he's got, Ben? *(Pointing to pictures of boy adding round, orange object to form snowman's nose; taps round object in circular motion.)*

ANNA, JODY: Carrot!

?: Carrot!

TEACHER: That's no carrot!

MARK: Meatballs! Meatballs! *(calling out excitedly)*

BOBBY: Meatball! Meatball! Meatball!

ANNA: _____

KRIS: Oranges!

TEACHER: *(Laughs.)* Yes, Kris, I think you . . . that's right!

?: Meatballs, meatballs, meatballs!

ANNA: They're oranges!

JODY: Oranges!

?: Tangerine?

TEACHER: Well, it's kind of oval like a tangerine *(making oval shape with hands).*

?: Oranges.

MARK: Meatball!

?: Tangeriiiiiine!

TEACHER: Does it look more like a tangerine? I don't know; it doesn't tell me. *(Turns book to herself for a closer look.)*

BRAD: Hey *(excited)* know what? Maybe it's a egg *(playful).*

TEACHER: *(Chuckles.)* But it's not white.

BRAD: Maybe it's a Easter egg . . . !

TEACHER: *(Chuckles.)*

?: Orange

BRAD: that they saved from Easter! *(Laughs.)*

Note. Adapted by permission from Cochran-Smith (1984, p. 185), Segment 10, *The Snowman* (Briggs).

knowledge (e.g., "What's he got? . . . That's no carrot.") and literary conventions (e.g., "I don't know. It doesn't tell me.") to help children draw inferences about the text. Moreover, the structure of the teacher's language nurtures children's higher-level thinking by evoking comparative reasoning about similarities and contrasts (e.g., "It's kind of oval like a tangerine. Does it look more like a tangerine?"), which is a more sophisticated analysis than a mere labeling of objects.

3. *Teachers must have the skills and knowledge to support story discussion.* This facility includes adapting oral language interactions to be responsive to children's comments and questions, and to their responses to the teacher's queries. It also requires the understanding that negotiation is involved in deriving meaning of decontextualized language found in storybooks. In texts written in the essayist literacy tradition, the author lacks an awareness of the reader's knowledge and assumes primary responsibility for conveying meaning so as to allow little room for individual interpretation. For the young child, this requires that the adult reader recognize the need for negotiated sense-making as well as adult-delivered meaning.

Table 9.3 provides an example of the skills and knowledge needed for fostering meaning (Cochran-Smith, 1984, p. 181). In this segment, Cochran-Smith describes how the teacher made explicit several implied understandings set forth in the text and the illustrations, and demonstrated how the two were integrated. For example, by pointing to a speech bubble that depicted a song playing on the radio, she called attention to the music notes surrounding the words in the bubble, which indicate that a song, not typical speech, was being emitted. She also noted the position of the radio in relation to the character (Santa) to demonstrate that Santa was listening to the song. She commented about the words of the song to indicate that the time period must be near a holiday because it was a familiar holiday song. The teacher's mediation required her knowledge of the author's assumptions about intended listeners, the teacher's skillfulness in making this knowledge explicit (e.g., pointing to pictures, describing illustrations, and modeling inferencing and the use of background knowledge) for the actual listeners, and the teacher's awareness of her role as a broker of meaning.

These three important ideas are embodied in the following statement from Cochran-Smith (1984).

The preschoolers in this setting were coming to know so many things about print because of their continual participation with adults in literacy events. In these events adults acted as intermediaries between children and contextualized print by taking on whatever parts of the events that the children could not perform themselves. Gradually, children took on more and more

TABLE 9.3. Example of Skills and Knowledge Needed to Support Meaning

Description of illustration: The page is divided into a series of 11 small frames like a comic strip: (1) Santa holds coat up to fire; (2) puts on slippers; (3) makes tea; (4) stuffs turkey; (5) carries turkey in a pan to stove; (6) makes pudding; (7) walks by presents inside door; (8) puts bubbles in hot bath; (9) in tub, singing; (10) showers, sings; (11) dries off.

TEACHER: And here's the song. Gee, this must be Christmas Day.

I hear "Hark the Herald Angels Sing." *(Points to picture in #4; in background of kitchen is radio with musical notes and words, "Hark," etc.)*

(Sings.)

Note. Adapted by permission from Cochran-Smith (1984, p. 181), Segment 9, *Father Christmas* (Briggs).

of the roles in literacy events, with uses of print preceding skills. The children were learning how to make sense of decontextualized print, because they were daily *[sic]* involved in mediated story reading sessions [in which] the storyreader essentially instructed them in how to use their knowledge to make appropriate inferences, evaluations, and responses to texts and how to take the knowledge they found in books, and apply, use, or relate it to their lives. (p. 254)

Lessons from the Study

Every author contends with the extent to which his or her recommendations or ideas are understood and applied by readers as the author had intended. The degree to which Cochran-Smith's ideas were adopted and applied in practice to teaching or expanded upon in research, however, is worth discussing.

Cochran-Smith's work accomplished its major aim of suggesting a way to look at, talk about, and think about reading to children in ways that might influence how others might study story reading practice. Her aim was carried forward in future research, as noted explicitly in the research of Dickinson and Smith (1994) and others. In its social-constructivist framing, Cochran-Smith's work also advocated that adults and children engage in verbal interactional exchanges to derive meaning. Her aims were also reflected in later research that validated the contribution of storybook reading to decontextualized language skills (Dickinson & Smith, 1994; Dickinson & Snow, 1987; Dickinson & Tabors, 1991).

Yet, not all of Cochran-Smith's ideas were heeded in later story reading research or practice. For example, the importance of fostering thinking based on storybook reading experiences, a critical component of her case study and its empirical examples, was eclipsed in some later research in which teachers were encouraged to increase oral language skills by allowing children to talk at length about experiences or topics that had little connection to the story's meaning. The priority of some later research was to foster an *interactive* experience.

The dialogic nature of Cochran-Smith's talk lay in using oral language to foster *thinking*; however, the dialogic kernel embraced in later research (Whitehurst, Zevenbergen, Crone, Schultz, Velting, & Fischel, 1999) and in some practical applications emphasized eliciting child talk. Of course, practitioners and researchers might have thought that Cochran-Smith's recommendation for how an adult might best negotiate meaning was: "Compromise with children about story meaning and let their ideas, however faulty, stand."

Cochran-Smith's support for her three central ideas for the field—that storybook reading should (1) cultivate thinking (2) through dialogue with adults (3) who are knowledgeable and skilled—is provided in examples of life-to-text and text-to-life interaction sequences; however, there is limited evidence that inference-making and complex thinking have been applied to pedagogical practices in others' subsequent research or in pedagogical guidance. This limited use of her study might have been influenced by the lack of explicit guidance for readers in her book as well as readers' difficulty in reflecting upon the examples Cochran-Smith provided and in extrapolating these to their own teaching.

Whitehurst et al. (1988): *Accelerating Language Development through Picture Book Reading*

In 1988, Whitehurst, Falco, Lonigan, Fischel, DeBaryshe, Valdez-Menchaca, and Caulfield identified the causal relationships between adult talk during picture book reading and children's language skills. Their findings provided evidence that adult talk can influence children's expressive language.

Historical Context

Whitehurst et al.'s (1988) inquiry was timely and needed, as assumptions that storybook reading led to language growth and later reading (Chomsky, 1972; Snow, 1983) lacked support from experimental evidence. Previous work in storybook reading with parents, particularly mothers, had focused on the ways in which they used story reading at home to support children's language acquisition. These case studies, along with a few descriptive studies, revealed intentionally instructive behaviors during storybook reading, including the mother's labeling of objects and providing corrective feedback for a child's labeling efforts (Moerck & Moerck, 1979; Ninio & Bruner, 1978; Snow & Goldfield, 1983), as well as making adjustments to instructional prompts to match children's increasing language skill (e.g., asking questions that probe for information that goes beyond what is explicitly stated in the story; Wheeler, 1983).

Other research documented variation between the talk of lower and higher socioeconomic status (SES) mothers to children. Specifically, mothers with lower SES were found to provide less instructive feedback to children than mothers from higher SES backgrounds (Ninio, 1980). Wells (1985b) found a correlation between the frequency of a child's listening to stories at home between the ages of 1 and 3 and children's language and reading comprehension skills at ages 5 and 7, respectively. A problem with existing research, however, was that it did not provide evidence that the frequency of home reading and children's literacy skills were causally related. Moreover, relationships between children's literacy skills and variables such as parent education and storybook reading were often obfuscated (Wells, 1985b). The paucity of causal evidence left the field uncertain about the role played by early read-aloud experiences in developing children's language skills.

To illuminate the direct and immediate impacts of storybook reading on children's language skills, Whitehurst et al. designed an intervention to test the effects of teaching parents desirable patterns of interaction and compared the intervention children's skills to the skills of children in an untrained control group. Positive findings would lay the groundwork for examining the influence of mediating variables (e.g., initial language level) and determining long-term effects, such as the persistence of gains. Follow-up studies could, for example, test the impact of particular behaviors and their effects on specific language skills and their rates of change.

Description of the Study

Twenty-nine parent–child dyads (14 in the experimental group and 15 controls) participated in the study. Children were typically developing 2½-year-olds from middle-income families. In an initial session, researchers interviewed parents to obtain family information (e.g., mother's education, frequency of book reading at home, number of siblings), and pretested children's language. Parents brought a sampling of books they read to children. From the collection of books that parents were asked to bring to the interview, researchers indicated those books with features that were most likely to reinforce the type of books to read. Parents were asked to audiotape readings with their children three to four times per week, were given weekly reminders by phone, and were asked to mark both taped and nontaped readings on a weekly checklist. All parents were told that the purpose of the study was to show the value of picture book reading to children's language development; however, parents in the control group were not instructed to modify any of their reading practices.

Parents in the experimental group participated in one 25–30-minute training session prior to implementing each of two 2-week read-aloud assignments. Aware of the variation in ways that parents engage during reading, Whitehurst et al. (1988) trained them to use a set of behaviors identified in prior research as probably helpful to children's language. These behaviors included: (1) evocative techniques (i.e., prompts to talk, as evident in *what* vs. *yes/no* questions; Wells, 1985b); (2) feedback that is *maximally informative* (p. 553) and employs expansions of children's utterances, corrective modeling, and other recommendations that serve to compare the child's incorrect response to more accurate answers (Scherer & Olswang, 1984); and (3) expectations that the parent's talk should reflect increasing challenges commensurate with children's developing abilities (i.e., responsive to a child's language capabilities, including fostering higher levels than currently employed by a child; Moerck, 1985; Wheeler, 1983).

The training involved having parents listen to a verbal explanation of the three strategies, watch the researcher model the strategies with an assistant researcher, and participate briefly in role playing, with the assistant researcher in the role of the child. Each parent received feedback during the role-playing from the researcher on techniques. Parents received a handout to remind them of the techniques and of the need to complete their read-aloud assignment.

After 4 weeks, all families returned for their children's posttesting on three measures: the Peabody Picture Vocabulary Test—Revised (PPVT-R) (Dunn & Dunn, 1981), which is a receptive vocabulary test that requires children to point to one of four pictures that corresponds to the test word pronounced by the tester; the Expressive One-Word Picture Vocabulary Test (EOWPVT) (Gardner, 1981), which requires children to provide a single label for a pictured object; and an expressive subscale of the Illinois Test of Psycholinguistic Abilities (ITPA) (Kirk, McCarthy, & Kirk, 1968), which requires the children to tell about real objects the tester shows them (e.g., a cup), one at a time. The researchers transcribed and coded audiotapes of two home-reading sessions for each dyad. Children's mean number of words/utterance (MLU) and parents' and children's language behaviors from one story at the end of the second and fourth weeks were analyzed to determine the effects of training on language interactions at home. In addition to providing data to analyze, these transcripts also served as a check of the experimental group's fidelity to training. After each 10-second interval of the audiotapes was coded, coders identified 14 categories of parental behavior (e.g., open-ended questions, reading-not-requiring-a-response, function/attribute questions, repetition, imitative directives, praise/confirmation, yes/no questions, criticism/correction, simple what questions, labeling, directives, expansion of utterances, pointing request, and other talk not directed to child). Coders also identified three categories of child language behaviors (e.g., child word utterances, child phrase utterances, and child non-word utterances). Twenty-two children (i.e., 10 from the experimental group; 12 from the control group) returned 9 months later for delayed testing to determine the persistence of intervention effects.

The data indicated that parents in the experimental group provided significantly more praise, expansions, and repetitions of children's utterances, and more open-ended questions, than parents in the control group. The parents in the experimental group also showed lower levels of less-evocative behaviors, such as yes/no questions, reading behaviors (i.e., not requiring a response), and directives. Children in the experimental group had more child phrases and significantly higher child MLU scores and expressive language scores than children in the control group. Although scores on the receptive vocabulary test trended higher for children in the experimental group, scores were not significantly different from the control group's scores which suggest that the intervention was more efficacious for improving children's expressive language skill than their receptive skill. Results from the delayed posttest showed that between-group differences on all expressive language measures were equivalent to or greater than immediate posttest results, though not statistically significant due to attrition in the sample. Differences between group means on receptive vocabulary at posttest had faded after 9 months.

Impact of the Study

The Whitehurst et al. (1988) study contributed both practically and theoretically to the field. As the first experimental study to examine the impact of storybook reading on children's language, it demonstrated that how parents talk with children during storybook reading affects children's language skills, particularly expressive language. Second, it showed that training parents to use specific language behaviors has potential for sustained improvement. Third, it demonstrated that training parents to foster children's opportunities to talk, by asking *wh-* or *open-ended* questions, expanding and recasting children's utterances, and praising and providing corrective feedback to children, can increase a child's level of responding. On a theoretical level, the findings underscored the difficulty of increasing children's receptive vocabulary on standard measures.

The study also made a practical contribution to professional development. Ways of talking with children are teachable, even with limited amounts of training. Educators and administrators could take heart. The study may have identified a model of adult training, in which components that include explanation, demonstration, role play, a handout tip sheet, and reminders halfway through the intervention yield successful outcomes.

These findings add empirical support to the previously assumed but untested connections between adult language interactions and children's language development proffered in previous observational and descriptive studies. The authors note that the effects were demonstrated when parents were taught a broad set of strategies that honed in on increasing a child's rate of responding and suggest that the usefulness of individual strategies should be tested in future research.

Whitehurst et al.'s (1988) research has been extraordinarily important to the field, as it was the first to exhibit causal evidence that *how we talk to children matters* to their language skills. The effects of research on practice are filtered through the interpretive lens of the authors, as well as by the extent to which stakeholders interpret findings as they apply to instruction and policy or further research inquiry.

Lessons from the Study

1. *Some recommendations from the study should have been questioned before moving forward.* Whitehurst et al. (1988) suggested that the requirement for children to respond actively (i.e., to talk) during story reading may be more beneficial to children than simply listening to parents read when they prioritized child production and strategies that elicit and reward children's involvement in talk over listening to parents read text in the study's design. This guidance may have led practitioners to believe that the primary goal of story reading is to increase child talk, not support children's story comprehension, or other language skills. In turn, this may have led some practitioners to focus little on the content of children's talk during story reading.

Other factors communicated the message that child talk was paramount. Whitehurst et al. examined the functions of talk rather than the content of talk or the level of thinking it modeled or elicited. The researchers did not attempt to assess story understanding, and they found no significant effects of the feedback strategies taught to parents on the general measures of children's receptive vocabulary. Additionally, the authors' explanation of factors accounting for children's performance focused on children's production. For example, they explained that the effectiveness of the strategies might have been due to the child's practice in fluent speaking, from answering *why* and *open-ended* questions, and hearing differences in syntax contrasts offered in the parents' recasting and expanding. Both of these explanations called attention to child talk and correct language form. Subsequent research had similar protocols and priorities (Whitehurst, Arnold, Epstein, Angell, Smith, & Fischel, 1994; Whitehurst, Epstein, Angell, Payne, Crone, & Fischel, 1994). Indeed, in the decades that followed, studies that focused on interventions designed to foster child talk (Reese, Cox, Harte, & McAnally, 2003), as well as storybook reading's impact on children's expressive language skills, were prevalent (Trivette, Simkus, Dunst, & Hamby, 2012).

Other research began to yield evidence that some adult–child talk might not support the skills that foster thinking and story understanding. For example, in some studies that contrasted adult commenting and questioning on children's responding and story understanding, commenting was correlated with greater variety in children's responses and adult responses that included more information. Questioning obligated a child to respond but limited their responses to specific information (Hockenberger, Goldstein, & Haas, 1999). In another study, adult commenting was associated with child utterances that were more related to story meaning, while adult questioning was associated with child utterances that focused on story structure or print (Kertoy, 1994). Research on storyreading approaches has also identified benefits of commenting to language comprehension skills. In an experimental study with preschoolers, Lonigan, Anthony, Bloomfield, Dyer, and Samwel (1999) contrasted two read-aloud approaches: *dialogic reading,* in which the child takes on the role of storyteller and the adult assumes the role of listener, and *shared reading,* in which the adult reads the story, makes comments, and answers children's questions. Findings showed significant positive effects of shared reading over dialogic reading for language comprehension. Commenting has been found to be effective for teaching vocabulary (Barnes & Dickinson, 2016) and may even be more effective than the use of questioning (Ard & Beverly, 2001).

Beck and McKeown (2001) noted that a common strategy to prompt responding during story reading involves asking children to clarify or reaffirm something just read (e.g., "What is she holding in her hand?"), but that such literal fact-finding and confirmation does not require larger inferences that contribute to better story understanding. Moreover, used repeatedly, literal queries may limit how children learn to think about text. Beck and McKeown also discuss potential pitfalls in turning talk over to children. For example, children often report personal experiences, because these are easy to access. But doing this can divert children's attention from a story's meaning. If children's offerings veer too far from the story, incorrect associations between their offerings and the story may result. Other reading researchers have also noted that allowing students to expound upon ideas and experiences that are only tangentially related to the text can affect comprehension negatively (Trabasso & Suh, 1993).

Prior to the work of Whitehurst et al. and other researchers described above, Petrosky (1980) noted that meaning evolves slowly (p. 155) and advised that children's attempts at sense-making benefit from adult mediation. This mediation involves support to engage in higher-level thinking to explore confusions about the text.

2. *Other lessons could have aided instruction but were not taken up.* Whitehurst et al.'s (1988) principles called for adult feedback that was *maximally informative* (p. 553) but was focused on *language form* (i.e., syntax or grammar). Pedagogical practices maximized input about form, as found in expansions (e.g., creating a grammatically correct form from a child's incorrect form) and corrective modeling that help the child to compare his or her errant grammar to a standard. The recommendation to provide maximally informative feedback would have held potential for fostering language comprehension if it had focused on *language meaning,* but no such emphasis sprang forth in

research or practice. Only recently has providing informative feedback related to story understanding received attention, as reading research has identified variables beyond decoding and vocabulary skills, such as inferential thinking, that are helpful to comprehension (Oakhill & Caine, 2012; Lepola, Lynch, Kiuru, Laakkonen, & Niemi, 2016).

Dickinson and Smith (1994): *Long-Term Effects of Preschool Teachers' Book Readings on Low-Income Children's Vocabulary and Story Comprehension*

Dickinson and Smith's (1994) inquiry sought to examine the cognitive demand of teachers' talk on preschoolers' vocabulary and comprehension skills in preschool and 1 year later. They found significant relationships between analytical talk and children's vocabulary and comprehension. Their findings confirmed relationships between the quality of adult talk and children's language comprehension and fortified the belief that what we ask children to think and talk about is related to immediate and longer-term vocabulary and comprehension.

Historical Context

Dickinson and Smith's (1994) research questions were influenced by the findings of previous language, literacy, and book-reading research using case-study and naturalistic observation methods. Findings provided information about the importance of specific skills to children's later success in reading and of developing these skills well before school entry. Print skills fostered at home were among these findings (Ferrreiro & Teberosky, 1982; Sulzby & Teale, 1991), as were oral language skills (Pappas & Brown, 1987; Scollon & Scollon, 1981; Snow & Dickinson, 1991). Dickinson and Smith noted that exposure to print in many everyday experiences made it impossible to identify the specific influence of any one experience on children's literacy skills. Studies of book reading at home, however, were an exception (Heath, 1982; Wells, 1985a), and Dickinson and Smith decided to examine the effects of early experiences of reading to preschoolers.

Central to their inquiry was the work of Snow, Cancino, Gonzalez, and Schriberg (1989), Snow and Dickinson (1991), and Wells (1985). These researchers had articulated the clustering of two types of oral language skills: *contextualized skills,* in which interlocutors rely on common, unstated background knowledge and nonverbal behaviors (e.g., pointing and intonation), and *decontextualized skills,* that require the understanding and use of complex syntax, lexical knowledge, and sophisticated discourse patterns to relay information about events, and allow analyses, and the offering of criticism about ideas without reliance on clues from the immediate physical environment. Research had indicated that decontextualized skills were related to elementary students' reading comprehension because reading requires constructing meaning from the written word. The construction of meaning by young children through verbal discourse during stories read to young children is a similar process because, it too, requires relying primarily upon language to communicate ideas and opinions, select details, recreate events, and explain experiences (Dickinson & Smith, 1994). Neither Dickinson nor others had conducted subsequent studies to examine the extent to which these skills begin to cluster in younger children; however, earlier work by Dickinson and colleagues had also found some relationships between kindergarten children's decontextualized oral language abilities and their later academic skills.

Vocabulary was a prime focus in Dickinson and Smith's study because vocabulary deficits had emerged in studies of reading comprehension. Story understanding was also an area of interest for Dickinson and Smith because of its relationship to decontextualized language skill and its hypothesized contribution to later reading comprehension. Dickinson and Smith became aware of the relationship between cognitively challenging talk by 4-year-olds and their literacy skills at the end of kindergarten from a study by Beals and DeTemple (1993) that utilized language data collected in homes during mealtimes. Given that book reading was already known to buttress young children's vocabulary learning, and discussion of stories before, during, and after reading was known to foster story understanding and language skill, Dickinson and Smith saw the potential of book reading for exploring causal connections between adult talk and children's vocabulary and story comprehension.

Prior to Dickinson and Smith's study, book reading research had used descriptive methods to characterize reading styles or to look at the frequency of interactional patterns. Although other researchers' interventions examined the effects of children's participation in conversations (i.e., talking) during story reading on their language outcomes, no one used utterance-level data to analyze relationships between types of language interactions and child outcomes. Moreover, studies that had found relationships between types of parent talk during story reading and children's vocabulary were home-based. School-based approaches to utterance-level talk had examined only teachers' utterances. The potential of book reading to foster cognitively challenging talk motivated Dickinson and Smith's investigation.

Dickinson and Smith set out to identify (1) specific book-related interactional patterns and the content of utterance-level talk between teachers and preschoolers and (2) their relationship to children's vocabulary and story comprehension 1 year later. To facilitate this inquiry, the researchers used data from the Home School (HS) study, a longitudinal investigation in which 84 children were followed from preschool through fourth grade to examine the language and literacy practices they experienced in home and at school,

particularly practices involving extended discourse and oral language development. From observations of teacher–child talk in preschool classrooms within
the HS study, Dickinson and Smith derived types of utterance-level talk and
examined relationships between these types and children's vocabulary and
story comprehension.

Description of the Study

Participants were the teachers and 4-year-olds in 25 preschool classrooms from
Head Start and other programs serving families with low incomes. Two-thirds
of the children were white; almost one-third were black; and 4% were Hispanic.
Forty percent of the children were female. Teachers reported that the children
were proficient in English.

In a yearly visit to collect information about school experiences, researchers videotaped a book-reading session (primary data) and gathered information
about children's language environments (secondary data) through classroom
observations, teacher interviews, and children's spontaneous language use, all
of which were later analyzed along with children's scores on the PPVT-R and a
story comprehension measure 1 year later. The physical space, daily schedule,
and activities of the classrooms were similar and included reading books chosen by the teacher as a large-group experience.

All verbal behavior that occurred during book-reading sessions was transcribed and coded with conventions specified in the Codes for Human Analysis
of Transcripts (CHAT) using the Child Language Analyses (CLAN) software
of the Child Language Data Exchange System (CHILDES) (MacWhinney,
1991). Teachers' and children's extratextual utterances (i.e., talk that was not
the reading of the text from the book) were coded for (1) time of occurrence
(e.g., before, during, or after the reading); (2) type of utterance (e.g., requests
for information, responses to queries, spontaneous offerings of information);
and (3) content, including cognitively-challenging talk (e.g., analyses of characters or events, evaluative comments, vocabulary discussion), lower-demand
talk (e.g., chiming in, recall, direct labeling), and behavior management talk.
Dickinson and Smith created composite scores of related variables for analyses (e.g., prompted and responsive analysis, prediction, and vocabulary utterances by teachers and children; prompted and responsive labeling utterances
by teachers and children, etc.).

A cluster analysis revealed three significantly different interactional patterns of teacher–child behaviors. A *coconstructive* approach was characterized
by lots of teacher and child talk throughout the reading, including analytical talk initiated by the teacher. Very little talk occurred before or after the
reading. This interactional pattern was found in five classrooms. Interactional
patterns in 10 classrooms were characterized as *didactic–interactional* (DI). In

these classrooms, talk was very limited throughout story reading, and when it occurred, was dominated by organizational/child management talk and by children's chiming in on or recalling text information. Ten classrooms were also characterized as having a *performance-oriented* (PO) approach, in which extratextual talk, most of which was analytical, occurred primarily before and after the reading, with vocabulary, character motivation, or prediction and personal connection dominating the content.

An examination of the relationship between a classroom's interactional style of talk during story reading and children's vocabulary and story comprehension outcomes 1 year later found significantly higher PPVT-R scores for children in *PO* classrooms compared to scores of children in *DI* classrooms. No group relationships for story comprehension were found. *Teachers* and *children's analytical talk during* the reading (TCANAD), defined as utterances that elicited responsive analysis of events, predictions, and vocabulary talk during the reading, accounted for 50% of the variation in PPVT-R scores and continued to contribute after other classroom factors (e.g., the teacher's support for writing and time spent reading to children alone or in small groups), were considered. Additionally, TCANAD made significant contributions to children's comprehension of stories.

Impact of the Study

Dickinson and Smith's (1994) research made several unique contributions to the field. First, their inclusion of story comprehension as a variable brought to the field's attention that read-alouds should stress the goal of helping children understand stories. Second, their study underscored the important role of adults in fostering children's thinking.

Third, their study characterized book reading in ways that indicated *how* teachers' discussions of books with preschoolers in a whole-group context is strongly associated with longer-term language abilities. That is, Dickinson and Smith's interactional patterns and style-based analysis revealed that children whose teachers used a PO approach scored significantly higher on the PPVT-R, 1 year later, than children whose teachers used a DI style. This finding has two important implications for instruction. First, given that the PO approach used minimal talk during the reading, teachers need not stop repeatedly during a reading to discuss books at length. Teachers can, instead, use follow-up discussion to support comprehension. Before- and after-talk is nearly as significant. Second, although findings are most likely attributable to differences in the types of talk in which teachers engage children, the book might also matter. Teachers in classrooms where DI approaches dominated often read books whose features (e.g., predictable text, simple vocabulary, limited story line) encourage children to chime in to recite the text. Dickinson and Smith suggested that a steady diet of books with these features have limited potential for developing children's language and thinking. This finding has encouraged some practitioners to select books that have greater potential to support language and thinking in preschoolers (McGee & Schickedanz, 2007; Schickedanz & Collins, 2013; Hoffman, Teale, & Yokota, 2015) and elementary grade students (Hiebert & Cervetti, 2011).

The utterance-based approach revealed more robust relationships between talk interactions and children's vocabulary and comprehension than analysis of holistic, style-related approaches and children's skills. An implication for researchers is that pinpointing what matters to children's skills requires finer-grained analyses of teacher–child talk than those available in the analyses of styles.

Dickinson and Smith's (1994) utterance-level analyses identified the nature of talk interaction that contributes to vocabulary and comprehension 1 year later and shed light on assumptions for practitioners, including about when talk should occur, by whom, and, most importantly, what talk should be about. For example, talk was especially helpful when it occurred during and after the reading and when it included the teacher and children. Most crucially, however, talk should be analytical and draw from cognitively stimulating ways of reflecting about the story, such as making predictions, discussing vocabulary, and analyzing events. Analytical discussions prompt reflection about a story's plot and the text's language; focuses on evidence that reveals characters' states of mind, including their goals and motivation; enables children to explore their own reasoning; and supports the creation of stronger conceptual bases for word learning because a teacher–child focus on getting to the meaning of the written text includes discussions of vocabulary that expose children to a word multiples times as its meaning is clarified.

Lessons from the Study

First, in addition to contributing evidence that adult talk during story reading with preschoolers is causally related to children's language development, Dickinson and Smith identified the content and type of talk that is related to children's vocabulary and story comprehension. Their examination of utterance-level talk also provided much-needed evidence that educators must attend to the details of what they say to children and how this talk prompts children to engage in reasoning and analytical thinking. This message should have prompted practitioners to engage in higher-level types of talk, especially analytical discourse, and should have prompted researchers to develop and test interventions to identify how best to teach educators to proceed with instruction. At the very least, the study should have prompted more reflection about the ways of talking with young children in the story-reading context that model and prompt their thinking.

Dickinson and Smith's findings motivated a broader conversation about extant reading theory and future instruction because they called for a shift from a mostly all-encompassing focus on print-related knowledge (e.g., pho-nological awareness, letter–name knowledge, and spelling conventions) in theories of reading comprehension to a focus whose foundation rests on oral language and reasoning skill. Print skills are better understood by research-ers, and easier to measure, than comprehension-related foundations, but an overemphasis on print skills may undermine language competencies which are critical to later reading achievement. The Dickinson and Smith study should have caused a shift in focus during storyreading to the goal of fostering higher level language and comprehension abilities that involve drawing inferences, not just literal level talk.

But these messages remained largely unheeded in practice and research. A great deal of subsequent research on story reading to young children reveal that parents and teachers still engage in mostly literal talk—the naming of items pictured or the recall of basic facts (e.g., *Who, what, where?*)—not on reason-ing and causal inferencing (e.g., *Why? How? What might have . . . ?*) (Danis, Bernard, & Leproux, 2000; Price, van Kleeck, & Huberty, 2009). Although some experimental studies that followed Dickinson and Smith's study exam-ined story comprehension (Collins, 2016b; Paris & Paris, 2007; Reese & Cox, 1999; van Kleeck, Vander Woude, & Hammett, 2006; van Kleeck, 2008), much of the storybook reading research and the guidance provided for teachers has continued to focus primarily on receptive and expressive vocabulary and print skill outcomes (Blewitt, Rump, Shealy, & Cook, 2009; Ewers & Brown-son, 1999; Justice & Ezell, 2002; Justice, Kadaravek, Fan, Sofka, & Hunt, 2009; Justice, Weber, Ezell, & Bakeman, 2002; Sénéchal, 1997; Whitehurst et al., 1999; Zevenbergen, Whitehurst, & Zevenbergen, 2003). In their article, "Speaking Out for Language: Why Language is Central to Reading Devel-opment," Dickinson, Golinkoff, and Hirsh-Pasek (2010) criticize the National Early Literacy Panel's (NELP) treatment of the role of language to reading development (NELP, 2008). Chief among their complaints was that the NELP had prioritized skills with the greatest *direct* effects on reading and had ignored skills with indirect effects. Additionally, the report of the NELP examined skills during a span of only a few years—essentially a cross-section of develop-ment—which was too limited to reveal the longer-term influences of language, and had stressed the importance of developing code-related skills needed for word recognition, while understating the importance of oral language skill and background knowledge to later reading success.

Within the last decade, some research has focused on meaning, rather than code-related literacy skills, in the talk of parents and teachers during read-alouds (Hindman, Connor, Jewkes, & Morrison, 2008) and on the relationship between inferential talk and preschoolers' story comprehension (Tompkins, Guo, & Justice, 2013). Other research, using new interventions, shows promise for changing teachers' talk (Collins et al., 2017) and children's thinking (Col-lins, 2016b).

SYNTHESIS AND CHANGE:
THE MAP WE HAVE AND THE ROAD AHEAD

Looking Back

The pivotal research discussed here mapped a direction for the field in the decades that have followed by demonstrating that *the way we talk matters to children's language skills* (see Figure 9.1). All of them highlighted the importance of the children's interactions with books during the *preschool years* (i.e., prior to formal schooling). These studies also expanded the context in which story reading was investigated to large-group sessions in early education settings and also expanded home-based studies to include interventions designed to influence parental behaviors. These studies illuminated the dire need to focus attention on early behaviors and interactions long before difficulties develop when children are learning to read.

Storybook reading has enormous potential for nourishing children's early language and thinking skills, but it remains underutilized because attention to children's comprehension and thinking is still frequently missing in many classrooms. Instead, there is an almost relentless acceptance of children's talk, no matter its content, to the near exclusion of teacher guidance that would engage children in analytical thinking to foster discourse that would deepen story understanding. Teachers have often continued to focus on singular outcomes

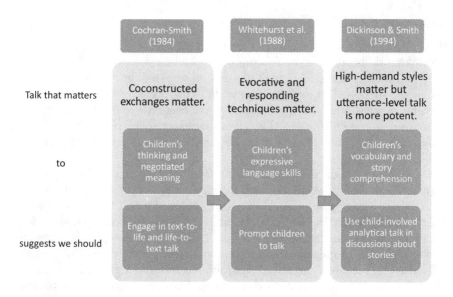

FIGURE 9.1. The way we talk to children matters: The evolution of this message across pivotal research.

(e.g., expressive language or vocabulary) rather than on multiple outcomes since these pivotal studies were conducted. In the sections that follow, I suggest a different priority for storybook reading and provide a few guiding principles that I have drawn from the pivotal works and from more current research on language and storybook reading, including empirical evidence from my work with preschool educators and researchers.

Looking Ahead: A Bold Idea and Its Guiding Principles

I think the primary goal of storybook reading should be to *foster comprehension of stories and higher-level thinking about text*. As Cochran-Smith states, early literacy is much more than readying oneself for "breaking the code" (p. 257). Reading aloud can and should do more by fostering sense-making and by helping children integrate world knowledge with textual information and draw inferences about both written text and illustration. Of course, thinking is also facilitated by oral language skills (e.g., vocabulary, syntax), but these language skills are most relevant when employed in the service of fostering story understanding and reasoning. Dickinson and Smith advocated practices and future research that de-emphasized focus on phonological awareness, alphabet knowledge, and print skills, embracing instead, the support of oral language and listening comprehension.

Foster Inferential Thinking

A focus on the understanding of text and the development of higher-level thinking skills during story reading requires adult discourse that both models and elicits/scaffolds children's higher-level thinking. In particular, children must be supported in *thinking inferentially*. This cognitive skill involves analyzing, synthesizing, and drawing causal connections from information in a book's text and illustrations. The more that experience of this kind occur in the early years, the greater the benefit to later reading comprehension (van Kleeck, 2006).

Recent research also clarified that inferential thinking develops separately from vocabulary (Oakhill & Cain, 2012), makes independent contributions to narrative comprehension (Florit, Roch, & Levarato, 2011; Lepola, Lynch, Laakkonen, Silvén, & Niemi, 2012), and contributes to listening comprehension (Kendeou, van den Broek, White, & Lynch, 2009). Listening comprehension is essential to reading comprehension beyond other oral language skills, such as oral vocabulary and word recognition (Oakhill & Cain, 2012). Longitudinal research on the role of specific early oral language skills, such as vocabulary and inferential thinking, to later reading comprehension is needed, along with translations of findings to pedagogy.

In recent decades, a few researchers have examined young children's inferential thinking using experimental methodologies (Collins, 2016a, 2016b; Paris & Paris, 2007; van Kleeck et al., 2006). Findings from this research reveal that a focus on inferential talk impacts children's story comprehension and higher-level thinking skills. For example, Collins (2016b) found benefits of high-demand discussion to inferential knowledge about the story and equivalence of low-demand discussion and no discussion for literal knowledge acquisition (i.e., hearing the story read aloud was sufficient for acquiring literal information). All children benefitted from high-demand talk, which suggests there is no need to wait for a high level of oral language before engaging children in cognitively challenging talk (Collins, 2016b). More information is needed, however, about effective protocols for training teachers to increase their inferential talk during reading alouds and about courses of change in teachers' behavior and new methods of analysis that capture interaction and directional influences of inferential talk. Finally, we need to know more about how developing children's early facility in inferential thinking interacts with vocabulary and background knowledge to influence later reading comprehension.

Attend to Utterance-Level Talk

As Dickinson and Smith demonstrated, we must attend to the *utterance-level of talk* in research and to its translation into practice. Storybook reading styles or theoretical statements about teaching and learning are too broad to yield practice-based strategies. We need to craft examples of story reading language that models and elicits reasoning and analytical thinking to better ensure its use by teachers. Few studies since the pivotal research have defined and examined talk at the utterance level, with the exception of some researchers (e.g., Collins, Paris, van Kleeck, and colleagues) who have examined utterance-level talk and have provided nuanced definitions of high-demand talk that distinguish among literal utterances, support for vocabulary, inferencing, and social and personal attributes.

Support Multiple Skills

In research and in practice, multiple skills (e.g., language and thinking), rather than a singular capability, should be examined and supported. Read-aloud pedagogy in many classrooms has changed for the better because more educators support children's vocabulary learning by explaining new words and exposing children to words multiple times over multiple readings. Nevertheless, support for vocabulary is still quite often the only goal, with fostering story understanding and complex thinking skills ignored. A focus on just one skill, no matter its importance to later reading, communicates wrong messages to children about the purposes of reading. As Cochran-Smith (1984) noted, our routines and practices of talking with children teach them what to value in this context. If we teach in a way that suggests to children that only words are worth attention, then children may not attend to sense-making, engage in talk that cultivates reasoning, or develop requisite thinking for comprehending in listening contexts now and when reading independently later.

Dickinson and Smith hypothesized that vocabulary can be fostered by the same talk that supports story comprehension. Indeed, this stance is warranted because they found that child-involved analytical talk benefitted both vocabulary and story comprehension. We now know that vocabulary and inferential thinking develop somewhat separately and that vocabulary is not an adequate proxy for later reading comprehension (Lepola, Lynch, Kiuru, Laakkonen, & Niemi, 2016; Oakhill & Cain, 2012); therefore, instructional strategies must be tailored to support both vocabulary and inferential thinking.

Respond Strategically to Children's Comprehension Needs

Our *responsivity to children* also needs revamping. Prior research, including studies conducted by the pivotal researchers might have implied that responsivity involves (1) acknowledging all of the children's comments and questions throughout a read-aloud; (2) permitting extended adult/child exchanges as long as they elicit child talk; and (3) following a child's conversational lead as if "active responding" is only a matter of speech production. From my observation, it seems that some practitioners have been led to believe that anything the child offers, even if inaccurate, irrelevant, and sorely lacking in coherence, counts as worthy "interaction." Moreover, some teachers enlist children in round-robin turn-taking to elicit additional ideas after a correct answer has been offered. This kind of "what-do-YOU-think" approach undermines the development of critical thinking, including reasoning (i.e., hearing from everyone after a sensible and evidence-based answer has been given suggests that no line of thinking is necessary), and creates talk fests of opportunity for all to share, not discussion that is pedagogically valuable. Teachers seem reluctant to tell children *no* or to indicate that their thinking has gone awry in this context, as if doing this will damage self-esteem or diminish children's willingness to share comments. Herein lies the paradox: children value information and being taught how to use it. Being informed of errant thinking, when accompanied by evidence and reasoning, is liberating, even engaging and interesting. Yet, teachers often avoid trying to lead children into realizing that their thinking did not consider certain evidence or that some background they do not yet have is required and can be supplied by the teacher. As a consequence, some preschool teachers encourage children to entertain falsehoods while also continuing to believe that preschoolers are incapable of engaging in higher level thinking if teachers provide appropriate scaffolding.

What is needed is a broader conception of responsivity that includes the modeling of reasoning by the teacher and the use of strategies that walk children through evidence in a storybook reading to draw an inference that is necessary for story understanding. This broader conception of responsivity requires good judgment about when to respond and how and when to keep reading for the time being to maintain story continuity and keep children engaged, especially in a first reading. Effective responsive teachers would also understand how to use literal facts provided in the book in the service of supporting children's more complex thinking.

Conclusion and Recommendations for Educators, Administrators, and Researchers

Here, I provide several action steps that can make the most of read-aloud experiences for children's later reading success. The suggestions proposed are followed by a note about their relevance for educators, administrators, and researchers.

Support Vocabulary and Other Language Skills

Supporting language, especially vocabulary, begins with selecting literature (Hoffman et al., 2015; Teale, Yokota, & Martinez, 2008) with rich vocabulary, some complex syntax, interesting characters, and engaging plots. Teachers then select words worth supporting in books they will read aloud to children, think about the meaning(s) of these words, and select the most appropriate instructional strateg(ies) for teaching each one during the reading (Collins, 2010, 2012). Reading each book multiple times, across a period of time, provides repeated exposures to words and a text's complex syntax (McGee & Schickedanz, 2007; Schickedanz & Collins, 2013), which aids new vocabulary learning and surely also strengthens patterns of discourse and language comprehension.

The acquisition of new vocabulary is one important goal for story reading and the process of this acquisition is multifaceted. We must consider both vocabulary breadth (i.e., the number of words to which we expose children) and vocabulary depth (i.e., multiple meanings, important morphological details, and nuances of words' pronunciation). Vocabulary depth aligns more closely with reading achievement than does vocabulary breadth and is measured by asking children to provide definitions or to explain words (National Early Literacy Panel, 2008). The ability to do this requires information about a word that goes beyond the ability to identify it (i.e., receptive vocabulary knowledge) or to use it to label a picture or object an adult presents or to use it to communicate. Nonetheless, although vocabulary is a cornerstone within an important set of oral language skills, good reading comprehension requires knowledge of syntax, facile listening comprehension, and other general language abilities. The strong association between broader language skill and reading achievement has been found in studies that span all of the school years through highschool (Foorman, Koon, Petscher, Mitchell, & Truckenmiller, 2015).

After research had identified vocabulary as an important variable for reading comprehension, vocabulary teaching became an important component of reading instruction. A consideration of fairly current research evidence prompted a leading reading educator to provide a refined message in 2016 about the role of vocabulary in reading achievement:

> Teaching vocabulary is still a good idea—vocabulary is an important part of language—but teaching language is a broader concern, and just focusing on one aspect of it is probably a big mistake. . . . That doesn't mean vocabulary teaching should fade away. It only needs to be supported with greater instructional attention to listening comprehension, syntax, and cohesion (how the ideas link to each other across a text). (p. 247)

Have Higher-Level Conversations to Support Inferential Thinking

Discussion during story reading is needed to elicit and guide children's thinking. As Cochran-Smith noted, discussion allows the mutual consideration of ideas and exposes children to oral language in the transaction of meaning. In view of the unique effects of inferencing skill to later reading comprehension, teachers should plan talk that engages children in analytical thinking about story events and character motivation and prompts thinking across sections of connected text (McKeown & Beck, 2003). Teachers can "think aloud" to model the use of explicit information to arrive at implied understandings and to demonstrate using evidence to support conclusions they have drawn in the modeling. For example, consider this excerpt of teacher–child interaction in a conversation of one part of *Henry's Happy Birthday* (Keller, 1990). The teacher wanted to support children's understanding that Henry was enduring several disappointments in his day that probably had contributed to his feeling unhappy on his birthday, which he expressed at one point in the story. To get the discussion started, she posed this question: "Was Henry having a good birthday so far?" She modeled thinking about the evidence that could be used to answer the question by flipping back a few pages to illustrations where Henry is reticent upon finding his mother baking a cake that was not his requested chocolate. The teacher then asked, "On this page, was Henry excited about the cake Mama was baking?" Some children said he was not, and the teacher said, "You're right. He wasn't. Look at his face. He doesn't seem pleased about the cake." Then, she asked, "What did he say?" After several children had responded, the teacher said, "He told his Mom, 'You said I could have chocolate,' when he saw the cake." After pausing for a moment, the teacher asked, "So, how did he feel about the cake?" and then led the children in a discussion of Henry's disappointment as well as his reluctance to be forthright about it.

In a second vignette that adds support for Henry's mood, the teacher continued the discussion by asking, "Did Henry want to wear the clothes Mama picked out?" After several children responded that he did not, she asked, "How do you know?" Children acknowledged that he put on other clothes first and that he wanted to wear his favorite T-shirt. Affirming children's responses, the teacher supported ensuing conversation about the clothes Henry picked out first, his mother's reason for his needing to change clothes, and his indictment of his appearance upon a final check in the mirror.

The teacher turned to a final set of illustrations and asked, "What did Henry think when he first saw the wrapped gifts that his friends brought?" The teacher reread the text that reminded listeners of Henry's dismay at the packages' sizes, shapes, and near-certain incongruence with what he wanted. The children and teachers discussed these details to arrive at the understanding of another disappointment for Henry. The teacher summarized, "So, with all of these things not going Henry's way, I think he might have been feeling unhappy about his birthday right now."

Integrate Vocabulary and Inferential Thinking Support

Many current professional development initiatives and preservice teacher programs tend to focus too narrowly in read-alouds on supporting vocabulary only, not a wider range of language and reasoning skills. Developing teachers' facility in supporting multiple skills is difficult and time-consuming. In a recent longitudinal intervention designed to foster skill in this area, teachers were given scripted guidance for questions to ask during a reading to foster children's engagement in higher-level thinking about the story (Collins, Nesbitt, Rivera, Toub, Hassinger-Das, & Ilgaz, 2017). Findings revealed a higher fidelity to vocabulary-support strategies than to comprehension-support strategies, indicating a potential limit to the amount of new information teachers can learn to implement at one time. Findings also suggested that vocabulary support is both more familiar to teachers and easier to learn than are strategies for supporting young children's inferential thinking. Thus, administrators would be wise to offer training that reflects sufficient duration and intensity for teachers to develop proficiency. These efforts must include not only initial group sessions, but follow-up coaching, observations of exemplary teachers, and opportunities for studying commercially available picture books and access to experts in the field. Educators also benefit when professional development (PD) activities include a focus on interactions between teachers and children and provide examples, and not only teach specific behaviors but provide conceptual and theoretical underpinnings at a level that is appropriate for each group of educators (Cunningham, Zibulsky, & Callahan, 2009; Early et al., 2007; Teale, 2003).

Respond Strategically to Children

Fostering thinking requires responding to children's sense-making during interactions that adults orchestrate and when children comment spontaneously and ask a question. If teachers respond in an untimely or minimal way, or do not respond to a child's error, opportunities are lost for nurturing the child's thinking (Collins & Schickedanz, 2015; Schickedanz, 2014). Teachers need PD focused on what comprises high-quality responses to children's comments and questions during read-alouds, including discussions about when a teacher's response is not necessary at the moment and would likely derail story understanding or trains of thought of other children in the group. It takes some experience with story reading for children to learn that many questions that pop into their minds, early in a story, are answered as events unfold to provide more literal facts. Teachers can be advised to become familiar with stories they plan to read, which helps them know when it is wise to respond by saying, "I think we'll learn more about that on the next few pages. Let me read on for a while." Skill in responding also requires knowledge about how children think, the common sources of children's confusion in stories, and features of high-level responding and why (see Figure 9.2). This new terrain is a critical ground for educators, researchers, and administrators.

The Legacy of the Pivotal Studies

The pivotal studies revealed that how we talk with young children matters to their language abilities, and more importantly, to their thinking capacities. This message should have been the map to guide our course for story reading research and practice in the decades that followed. But, we got off track. As a synthesis of the pivotal works shows, advice to model decontextualized language to foster thinking was ignored (i.e., a road not taken); research and practice prioritized language production more than language comprehension (i.e., detours were taken); and insights about cognitively challenging utterances were not adopted (i.e., righting our course was thwarted). The priority for adult–child interactions during story reading should have been on fostering meaning and thinking. Are we poised for a course correction?

Research within the last decade suggests that we might be heading in the right direction. Recent longitudinal studies of young children have identified unique contributions of individual oral language skills and inferential thinking to listening comprehension (Florit et al., 2011; Lepola et al., 2012, 2016) and later reading comprehension (Oakhill & Caine, 2012; Kendeou et al., 2009). These findings have yielded deeper understandings of the independent roles of multiple skills to reading achievement, and of the need to cultivate higher-level thinking abilities, not just vocabulary, in the early years. Moreover, some recent experimental interventions have prioritized comprehension and have

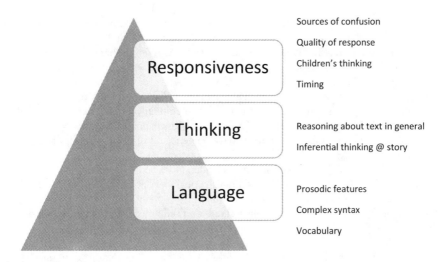

FIGURE 9.2. Making the most of storybook reading: What teachers need to support.

found effects of high-demand talk between adults and children on children's inferencing abilities (Collins, 2016b; van Kleeck, 2006, 2008). These lines of research carry forward the message of the pivotal studies.

Twists and turns are part and parcel of scientific inquiry; some routes are fruitful and some are not. The legacy of the pivotal studies lies in making the most of the fruitful routes and recognizing those that are not. Engaging young children in the complex thinking processes needed for comprehending stories in preschool today and apprehending the meaning of texts in later grades makes the most of reading aloud. It is the legacy of the pivotal studies and is ours for the taking. Let's not waste children's time with anything less.

REFERENCES

Ard, L. M., & Beverly, B. L. (2001). Preschool word learning: During joint book reading: Effects of adult questions and comments. *Communication Disorders Quarterly, 26*(1), 17–28.

Barnes, E., & Dickinson, D. K. (2016). The impact of teacher's commenting strategies on children's vocabulary growth. *Exceptionality, 25*(3), 186–206.

Beals, D., & DeTemple, J. (1993). Home contributions to early language literacy development. In D. Leu & C. Kinzer (Eds.), *Forty-second yearbook of the National Reading Conference* (pp. 207–216). Chicago: National Reading Conference.

Beck, I. L., & McKeown, M. G. (2001). Text talk: Capturing the benefits of read-aloud experiences for young children. *The Reading Teacher, 55*(1), 10–20.

Biemiller, A., & Boote, C. (2006). An effective method for building meaning vocabulary in primary grades. *Journal of Educational Psychology, 98*(1), 44–57.

Blewitt, P., Rump, K. M., Shealy, S. E., & Cook, S. A. (2009). Shared book reading: When and how questions affect young children's word learning. *Journal of Educational Psychology, 101*(2), 294–304.

Bus, A. G., van IJzendoorn, M. H., & Pellegrini, A. (1995). Joint book reading makes sense for success in learning to read: A meta-analysis on intergenerational transmission of literacy. *Review of Educational Research, 65*(1), 1–21.

Chomsky, C. (1972). Stages in language development and reading exposure. *Harvard Educational Review, 42*, 1–43.

Cochran-Smith, M. (1984). *The making of a reader.* Norwood, NJ: Ablex.

Collins, M. F. (2010). ELL preschoolers' English vocabulary acquisition from storybook reading. *Early Childhood Research Quarterly, 25*(1), 84–97.

Collins, M. F. (2012). Sagacious, sophisticated, and sedulous: The importance of discussing 50-cent words with preschoolers. *Young Children, 67*(5), 66–71.

Collins, M. F. (2016a). Increasing children's and teachers' abilities to engage in inferential talk in preschool. In M. McKeown (Chair), *Talk that supports language across grades.* Paper presented at the annual meeting of the American Education Research Association, Washington, DC.

Collins, M. F. (2016b). Supporting inferential thinking in preschoolers: Effects of discussion on children's story comprehension. *Early Education and Development, 27*(7), 932–956.

Collins, M. F., Nesbitt, K. T., Rivera, B. L., Toub, T. S., Hassinger-Das, B., & Ilgaz, H. (2017). Effects of a book reading and play intervention on children's story comprehension. In D. K. Dickinson (Chair), *Fostering teachers' skill in supporting inferential thinking in preschool.* Paper presented at the biennial meeting of the Society for Research in Child Development, Austin, TX.

Collins, M. F., & Schickedanz, J. A. (2015, July). *Knowledge teachers need to provide high quality feedback for children's story misunderstandings.* Paper presented at the annual meeting of the International Literacy Association, St. Louis, MO.

Crago, H., & Crago, M., (1976). The untrained eye?: A preschool child explores Felix Hoffman's 'Rapunzel.' *Children's Literature in Education, 22*, 133–151.

Cunningham, A. E., Zibulsky, J., & Callahan, M. D. (2009). Starting small: Building preschool teacher knowledge that supports early literacy development. *Reading and Writing, 22*(4), 487–510.

Danis, A., Bernard, J., & Leproux, C. (2000). Shared picture-book reading: A sequential analysis adult-child verbal interactions. *British Journal of Developmental Psychology, 18*, 369–388.

Dickinson, D. K., Golinkoff, R., & Hirsh-Pasek, K. (2010). Speaking out for language: Why language is central to reading development. *Educational Researcher, 39*(4), 305–310.

Dickinson, D. K., & Neuman, S. B. (Eds.). (2011). *Handbook of early literacy research* (Vol. 3). New York: Guilford Press.

Dickinson, D. K., & Smith, M. W. (1994). Long-term effects of preschool teachers' book readings on low-income children's vocabulary and story comprehension. *Reading Research Quarterly, 29*(2), 104–122.

Dickinson, D. K., & Snow, C. E. (1987). Interrelationships among prereading and oral language skills in kindergartners from two social classes. *Early Childhood Research Quarterly, 2,* 1–26.

Dickinson, D. K., & Tabors, P. O. (1991). Early literacy: Linkages between home, school, and literacy achievement at age five. *Journal of Research in Childhood Education, 6,* 30–46.

Dodge, D. T., Colker, L. J., & Heroman, C. (2010). *The creative curriculum for preschool* (5th ed.). Bethesda, MD: Teaching Strategies.

Dunn, L. M., & Dunn, L. M. (1981). *Peabody Picture Vocabulary Test—Revised.* Circle Pines, MN: American Guidance Service.

Early, D. M., Maxwell, K., Burchinal, M., Alva, S., Bender, R. H., Bryant, D., . . . Zill, N. (2007). Teachers' education, classroom quality, and young children's academic skills: Results from seven studies of preschool programs. *Child Development, 78*(2), 558–580.

Ewers, C. A., & Brownson, S. M. (1999). Kindergarteners' vocabulary as a function of active vs. passive storybook reading, prior vocabulary, and working memory. *Journal of Reading Psychology, 20,* 11–20.

Ferreiro, E., & Teberosky, A. (1982). *Literacy before schooling.* Portsmouth, NH: Heinemann.

Florit, E., Roch, M., & Leverato, M. (2011). Listening text comprehension of explicit and implicit information in preschoolers: The role of verbal and inferential skills. *Discourse Processes, 48*(2), 119–138.

Foorman, B. R., Koon, S., Petscher, Y., Mitchell, A., & Truckenmiller, A. (2015). Examining general and specific factors in the dimensionality of oral language and reading in 4th–10th grades. *Journal of Educational Psychology, 107*(3), 884–889.

Gardner, H. (1981). *Expressive one-word picture vocabulary test.* Novato, CA: Academic Therapy Publications.

Heath, S. B. (1982). What no bedtime story means: Narrative skills at home and school. *Language in Society, 11,* 49–76.

Heath, S. B. (1983). *Ways with words: Language, life, and work in communities and classrooms.* New York: Cambridge University Press.

Hiebert, E. F., & Cevetti, G. N. (2011). *What differences in narrative and informational texts mean for the learning and instruction of vocabulary* (Reading Research Report 11.01). San Francisco: Text Project.

Hindman, A. H., Connor, C. M., Jewkes, A. M., & Morrison, F. J. (2008). Untangling the effects of shared book reading: Multiple factors and their associations with preschool literacy outcomes. *Early Childhood Research Quarterly, 23,* 330–350.

Hockenbarger, E. H., Goldstein, H., & Haas, L. S. (1999). Effects of commenting during joint book reading by mothers with low SES. *Topics in Early Childhood Special Education, 19*(1), 15–27.

Hoffman, J. L., Teale, W. H., & Yokota, J. (2015). The book matters!: Choosing complex narrative texts to support literary discussion. *Young Children, 70*(4), 8–15.

Jumpstart for Young Children, Inc. (2018). *Jumpstart children first curriculum.* Boston: Jumpstart.

Justice, L. M., & Ezell, H. K. (2002). Use of storybook reading to increase print awareness in at-risk children. *American Journal of Speech–Language Pathology, 11,* 17–29.

Justice, L. M., Kadaraek, J., Fan, X., Sofka, A., & Hunt, A. (2009). Accelerating preschoolers' early literacy development through classroom-based teacher–child storybook reading and print referencing. *Language, Speech, and Hearing Services in Schools, 40,* 67–85.

Justice, L. M., Weber, S. E., Ezell, H. K., & Bakeman, R. (2002). A sequential analysis of children's responsiveness to parental print references during shared book-reading interactions. *American Journal of Speech–Language Pathology, 11,* 30–40.

Keller, H. (1990). *Henry's happy birthday.* New York: Greenwillow.

Kendeou, P., van den Broek, P., White, M. J., & Lynch, J. S. (2009). Predicting reading comprehension in early elementary school: The independent contributions of oral language and decoding skills. *Journal of Educational Psychology, 101*(4), 765–778.

Kertoy, M. (1994). Adult interactive strategies and the spontaneous comments of preschoolers during joint storybook readings. *Journal of Research in Childhood Education, 9,* 58–67.

Kirk, S. A., McCarthy, J. J., & Kirk, W. D. (1968). *Illinois Test of Psycholinguistic Abilities.* Urbana: University of Illinois Press.

Lepola, J., Lynch, J., Kiuru, N., Laakkonen, E., & Niemi, P. (2016). Early oral language comprehension, task orientation, and foundational reading skills as predictors of grade 3 reading comprehension. *Reading Research Quarterly, 51*(4), 373–390.

Lepola, J., Lynch, J., Laakkonen, E., Silvén, M., & Niemi, P. (2012). The role of inference making and other language skills in the development of narrative listening comprehension in 4–6-year-old children. *Reading Research Quarterly, 47*(3), 259–282.

Lonigan, C. J., Anthony, J. L., Bloomfield, B. G., Dyer, S. M., & Samwel, C S. (1999). Effects of two shared-reading interventions on the emergent literacy skills of at-risk preschoolers. *Journal of Early Intervention, 22*(4), 306–322.

MacWhinney, B. (1991). *The CHILDES Project: Tools for analyzing talk* (2nd ed.). Mahwah, NJ: Erlbaum.

Marilus, L. M., & Neuman, S. B. (2013). How vocabulary interventions affect young children at risk: A meta-analytic review. *Journal of Research on Educational Effectiveness, 6,* 223–262.

McGee, L. M., & Schickedanz, J. A. (2007). Repeated interactive read-alouds in preschool and kindergarten. *The Reading Teacher, 60*(8), 742–751.

McKeown, M., & Beck, I. (2003) Taking advantage of read-alouds to help children make sense of decontextualized language. In A. van Kleeck, S. A. Stahl, & E. Bauer (Eds.), *On reading to children: Parents and teachers* (pp. 159–176). Mahwah, NJ: Erlbaum.

Moerk, E. L. (1985). Picture book reading by mothers and young children and its impact upon language development. *Journal of Pragmatics, 9,* 547–566.

Moerk, E. L., & Moerck, C. (1979. Quotations, imitations, and generalizations: Factual and methodological analyses. *International Journal of Behavioural Development, 2,* 43–72.

National Early Literacy Panel. (2008). *Developing early literacy: Report of the National Early Literacy Panel.* Washington, DC: National Institute for Literacy. Available at *https://lincs.ed.gov/earlychildhood/NELP/NELPreport.html.*

National Governors Association Center for Best Practices & Council of Chief State School Officers. (2010). *Common Core State Standards for English language arts and literacy in history/social studies, science, and technical subjects.* Washington, DC: Authors.

National Reading Panel. (2000). *Report of the national reading panel: Teaching children to read: An evidence-based assessment of the scientific research literature on reading and its implications for reading instruction.* Washington, DC: National Institute for Child Health and Human Development and the National Institutes of Health.

Neuman, S. B., & Dwyer, J. (2009). Missing in action: Vocabulary instruction in pre-K. *The Reading Teacher, 62,* 384–392.

Neuman, S. B., Snow, C. E., & Canizares, S. (2010). *Building language for literacy.* New York: Scholastic.

Ninio, A. (1980). Picture book reading in mother–infant dyads belonging to two subgroups in Israel. *Child Development, 51,* 587–590.

Ninio, A., & Bruner, J. S. (1978). The achievement and antecedents of labeling. *Journal of Child Language, 5,* 1–15.

Oakhill, J., & Cain, K. (2012). The precursors of reading ability in young readers: Evidence from a four-year longitudinal study. *Scientific Studies of Reading, 16*(2), 91–121.

Pappas, C. C., & Brown, E. (1987). Young children learning story discourse: Three case studies. *Elementary School Journal, 4,* 455–466.

Paris, A. H., & Paris, S. G. (2003). Assessing narrative comprehension in young children. *Reading Research Quarterly, 38*(1), 36–76.

Paris, A. H., & Paris, S. G. (2007). Teaching narrative comprehension strategies to first graders. *Cognition and Instruction, 25*(1), 1–44.

Petrosky, A. R. (1990). The inferences we make: Children and literature. *Language Arts, 57*(2), 149–156.

Price, L., van Kleeck, A., & Huberty, C. (2009). Talk during book sharing between parents and preschool children: A comparison between storybook and expository book conditions. *Reading Research Quarterly, 44*(2), 171–194.

Reese, E., & Cox, A. (1999). Quality of adult book reading affects children's emergent literacy. *Developmental Psychology, 35*(1), 20–28.

Reese, E., Cox, A., Hart, D., & McAnally, H. (2003). Diversity in adult's styles of reading books to children. In A. van Kleeck, S. Stahl, & E. Bauer (Eds.), *On reading books to children* (pp. 37–57). Mahwah, NJ: Erlbaum.

Scherer, N. J., & Olswang. L. B. (1984). Role of mother's expansions in stimulating children's language production. *Journal of Speech and Hearing Research, 27*(3), 387–396.

Schickedanz, J. A., & Collins, M. F., (2013). *So much more than the ABCs: The early phases of reading and writing.* Washington, DC: National Association for the Education of Young Children.

Schickedanz, J. S. (2014). *Accounting for variations in the quality of teachers' explanations in feedback to preschoolers' story time misunderstandings.* Paper presented at the annual meeting of the Literacy Research Association, Marco Island, FL.

Schickedanz, J. S., & Dickinson, D. K. (2004). *Opening the world of learning.* New York: Pearson.

Scollon, R., & Scollon, S., (1981). *Narrative, literacy, and race in interethnic communication.* Norwood, NJ: Ablex.

Sénéchal, M. (1997). The differential effect of storybook reading on preschoolers' acquisition of expressive and receptive vocabulary. *Journal of Child Language, 24*(1), 123–138.

Shanahan, T. (2016). Thinking with research: Research changes its mind (again). *The Reading Teacher, 70*(2), 245–248.

Snow. C. E. (1983). Literacy and language: Relationships during the preschool years. *Harvard Educational Review, 53,* 165–189.

Snow, C. E., Cancino, H., Gonzalez, P., & Shriberg, E. (1989). Giving formal definitions: An oral language correlate of school literacy. In D. Bloome (Ed.), *Classrooms and literacy* (pp. 233–249). Hillsdale, NJ: Ablex.

Snow, C. E., & Dickinson, D. K. (1991). Skills that aren't basic in a new conception of literacy. In A. Purves & L. Jennings (Eds.), *New conceptions of literacy.* Albany: State University of New York Press.

Snow, C. E., & Goldfield. B. A. (1983). Turn the page please: Situation-specific language acquisition. *Journal of Child Language, 10,* 551–569.

Sulzby, E., & Teale, W. (1991). Emergent literacy. In R. Barr, M. L. Kamil, P. B. Mosenthal, & P. D. Pearson (Eds.), *Handbook of reading research* (Vol. 2, pp. 727–758). New York: Longman.

Teale, W. H. (1981). Parents reading to their children: What we know and need to know. *Language Arts, 58*(8), 902–912.

Teale, W. H. (2003). Reading aloud to young children as a classroom instructional activity: Insights from research and practice. In A. van Kleeck, S. A. Stahl, & E. Bauer (Eds.), *On reading books to children: Parents and teachers* (pp. 159–176). Mahwah, NJ: Erlbaum.

Teale, W. H., Yokota, J., & Martinez, M. (2008). The book matters: Evaluating and selecting what to read aloud to young children. In A. Debruin-Parecki (Ed.), *Effective early literacy practice: Here's how, here's why* (pp. 101–121). Baltimore: Brookes.

Tompkins, V., Guo, Y., & Justice, L. (2013). Inference generation, story comprehension, and language skills in preschool years. *Reading and Writing, 26,* 403–429.

Trabasso, T., & Suh, S. (1993). Understanding text: Achieving explanatory coherence through on-line inferences and mental operations in working memory. *Discourse Processes, 16,* 3–34.

Trivette, C. M., Simkus, A., Dunst, C. J., & Hamby, D. W. (2012). Repeated book reading and preschoolers' early literacy development. *Cell Reviews, 5*(5), 1–13.

van Kleeck, A. (2006). Fostering inferential language during book sharing with prereaders: A foundation for later text comprehension strategies. In A. van Kleeck (Ed.), *Sharing books and stories to promote language and literacy* (pp. 269–317). San Diego, CA: Plural.

van Kleeck, A. (2008). Providing preschool foundations for later reading comprehension: The importance of and ideas for targeting inferencing in storybook-sharing interventions. *Psychology in the Schools, 45*(7), 627–643.

van Kleeck, A., Vander Woude, J., & Hammett, L. (2006). Fostering literal and inferential language skills in Head Start preschoolers with language impairment using scripted book-sharing discussions. *American Journal of Speech–Language Pathology, 15,* 85–95.

Wells, G. (1985a). *Learning, language, and education.* Philadelphia: NFER-Nelson.

Wells, G. (1985b). Preschool literacy-related activities and success in school. In D. R. Olson, N. Torrance, & A. Hildyard (Eds.), *Literacy, language, and learning:*

The nature and consequences of reading and writing (pp. 229–255). New York: Cambridge University Press.

Wheeler, P. (1983). Context-related age characteristics in mothers' speech: Joint book reading. *Journal of Child Language, 10,* 259–263.

Whitehurst, G. J., Arnold, D. H., Epstein, J. N., Angell, A. L., Smith, M., & Fischel, J. E. (1994). A picture book reading intervention in daycare and home for children from low-income families. *Developmental Psychology, 30,* 679–689.

Whitehurst, G. J., Epstein, J., Angell, A., Payne, A., Crone, D., & Fischel, J. (1994) Outcomes of an emergent literacy intervention in Head Start. *Journal of Educational Psychology, 86,* 542–555.

Whitehurst, G. J., Falco, F. L., Lonigan, C. J., Fischel, J. E., DeBaryshe, B. D., Valdez-Menchaca, M. C., & Caulfield, M. (1988). Accelerating language development through picture book reading. *Developmental Psychology, 24*(4), 552–559.

Whitehurst, G. J., Zevenbergen, A. A., Crone, D., Schultz, M. D., Velting, O. N., & Fischel, J. E. (1999). Outcomes of an emergent literacy intervention from Head Start through second grade. *Journal of Educational Psychology, 91,* 261–272.

Zevenbergen, A. A., Whitehurst, G. J. & Zevenbergen, J. A. (2003). Effects of a shared-reading intervention on the inclusion of evaluative devices in narratives of children from low-income families. *Journal of Applied Developmental Psychology, 24,* 1–15.

Zucker, T. A., Justice, L. M., Piasta, S. B., & Kaderavek. J. N. (2010). Preschool teachers' literal and inferential questions and children's responses during whole-class shared reading. *Early Childhood Research Quarterly, 25*(1), 65–83.

CHAPTER 10

The Impact of Pivotal Research on the Role of Play in Early Literacy Development

Muriel K. Rand and Lesley Mandel Morrow

Play is the highest form of research.
—ALBERT EINSTEIN

In Ms. Jensen's preschool class, the children are pretending to work in a hospital. In the dramatic play area, one child is seeing patients and writing down prescriptions. The children in the waiting room are reading books. In the block area, the children are pretending that a large box is the ambulance. They have put a sign on it using scribble writing, and they are looking at a children's book that shows them how to help someone who's injured. Two children in the science center are pretending to work in the hospital laboratory and are copying from a large book that has pictures of x-rays. On a table they are drawing and writing what they see in a journal. In the art area, other children are creating a large poster with the hospital's name on it to hang in the front of the room.

In Ms. Jones' preschool class, several children are using play doh to form the letters of their first names, which are written on cards for them to copy. Another group of children is putting together two-piece puzzles that require matching upper- and lowercase letters. Two other children are using Legos with one letter written on each piece to build "name towers" beginning with their own name and then the names of classmates, which they recreate from name tags that include children's photos. A final group is playing a game that involves tossing beanbags onto a Twister game that has been modified to incorporate letters.

In both of the scenarios above, an observer could argue that some form of play is involved. In the second scenario children are engaged in playful activities that offer opportunities to practice skills related to learning the "code" of written English, which are necessary in learning to read and write in the lower elementary grades. The first scenario displays the kind of play that is the focus of this chapter—sociodramatic play that develops decontextualized language, incorporates literate behaviors, and allows children to enact the use of reading and writing in everyday life.

While few would argue that play does not have a useful role in early literacy development and in preschool classrooms, there has been an ongoing tension between the kinds of play depicted in these two scenarios. Currently, the use of play-based tasks to practice discrete literacy skills (e.g., making play doh letters) is a hallmark of early childhood and kindergarten classrooms. In contrast, the kind of play described in the first scenario may be underutilized in these settings. We believe that the preference for certain types of play is rooted in the perception that some activities are more academic (those in scenario 2) while some are more socially and emotionally focused (those in scenario 1). However, this perception is unfounded; sociodramatic play has been shown to be an important context for the development of academic skills.

In this chapter, we discuss the potential of sociodramatic play for early literacy development. We examine three pivotal studies—each published between 1985 and 1991—that led us to the understanding that planned, purposeful play experiences play critical roles in early literacy development and should be incorporated within early childhood classroom settings. We explain what this pivotal research revealed about the kinds of play that are most beneficial and how early childhood educators can intentionally harness children's play to support literacy learning. Finally we offer a vision for ending the tension between sociodramatic and more academically oriented play and describe an approach that offers a balance.

BACKGROUND ON PLAY AND EARLY LITERACY DEVELOPMENT

Throughout the 20th century, theorists have addressed early childhood learning from child-centered theoretical perspectives. Child-centered approaches posit that it is best to furnish children with motivating opportunities that stimulate exploration in playful environments. Rousseau (1712–1778) believed that children's learning evolved naturally as a result of their innate curiosity. Pestalozzi (1746–1827) also believed in natural learning, but thought that children needed adult facilitation to enhance their development. Froebel (1782–1852) emphasized the importance of play as a vehicle for learning, and coined the term *kindergarten*, which literally means "children's garden." Piaget postulated that children acquire knowledge by interacting with objects and other people's ideas; subsequently, their knowledge changes and is reorganized in response to those objects and experiences (Piaget & Inhelder, 1969). Dewey's (1916) philosophy of early childhood education led to the concept of a child-centered curriculum built around the interests of children and a problem-based learning approach.

Vygotsky (1978, 1986) recognized that children learn as a result of their social interactions with others. He particularly emphasized that children learn from interacting with others who are more developed than they are linguistically, cognitively, socially, and emotionally. The importance of sociodramatic play for Vygotsky is that it allows young children to inhabit their zone of proximal development: "In play a child is always above his average age, above his daily behavior; in play it is as though he were a head taller than himself . . . in play it is as though the child were trying to jump above the level of his normal behavior" (Vygotsky, 1978, p. 96). This theoretical orientation not only provides support for play-based learning, it also emphasizes the supportive role that adults play in scaffolding interactions during play.

These theories of development and learning affected the policies and curriculum adopted in preschools in the United States. In 1965, President Johnson created the Head Start program, the first federal initiative directed at preschool education. The goal of Head Start was to prepare low-income children to become ready for kindergarten by focusing on health, social and emotional development, and the dignity and self-worth of the child and family. The program established the first requirements or mandates for public preschools, and as government-sponsored research proliferated, the role of academic learning in preschool became a focus for investigation (Hodges & Cooper, 1981). Major research studies examined variations in curricula that were grouped into preacademic programs that taught academic skills directly, cognitive discovery programs that promoted academic learning through play experiences, and discovery programs that aimed to foster development in social, emotional, physical, and cognitive domains (Bissell, 1972). These studies are now seen as controversial due to methodological issues; however, they began the trend toward distinguishing between different types of preschool programs based on which academic learning skills were emphasized.

The pivotal research studies on literacy and play that are the focus of this chapter occurred within this educational and political context, in part as a response to the increased attention paid to academic learning and skills-based instruction in preschool education. Skills-based instructional models, such as DISTAR, involve the systematic explicit teaching of literacy skills (Bereiter & Engelmann, 1966). Skills-based instruction has its roots in behaviorist theories of learning, which suggest that complex cognitive activities, such as reading and writing, can be broken down into a series of composite skills that are taught one at a time (see Morrow & Tracey, 2006). Skills-based curricula were often scripted for the teacher, who provided fast-paced drills on isolated literacy skills in small groups.

Over time, direct instruction was criticized by theorists who advocated a more play-based, child-initiated curriculum. During the 1980s, a new lens for interpreting literacy learning during the preschool years was introduced and became influential. The term *emergent literacy* (Teale & Sulzby, 1986) was used to describe the period in a child's life between birth and the time when the child can read and write conventionally, usually at about the third grade. From this perspective, literacy is viewed as beginning at birth and growing through authentic learning experiences at home and in school. Emergent literacy theory is based on the beliefs that children's development in the areas of listening, speaking, reading, and writing are all interrelated, and that strengthening of any one of these four areas will have positive effects on the others (see Teale et al., Chapter 8, this volume).

This focus on emergent literacy competed with an emphasis on reading readiness, a direct-instruction approach that taught isolated skills, such as alphabet knowledge, small-motor coordination for writing, and rhyming. Over the next decade, much literacy research was directed toward establishing the value of play-based literacy approaches in reaction to the prevalent reading-readiness curricula found in basal reading series. For example, in 1986, Winograd and Greenlee published an article in *Educational Leadership* condemning the hierarchy of skills approach in reading programs and advocated for "combining the skill and will of reading" by focusing on motivation, interest, and intentionality (p. 20).

THREE PIVOTAL STUDIES ON LITERACY AND PLAY

Given the conflict between play-based approaches to early literacy and academic skills-based curricula, we will look closely at three pivotal studies that had a significant impact on literacy research and practice at that time, examine why they were influential, and discuss the effects of these pivotal studies on the field of early literacy today.

Pellegrini (1985): *The Relations between Symbolic Play and Literate Behavior*

Pellegrini's pivotal review of research established a basis for future research and offered a thorough, detailed critique of the research on the connections between play and literate behavior until that time. Focusing particularly on symbolic play, which is most prevalent in the preschool and primary period, Pellegrini examined the ways in which the elements of play corresponded to the cognitive learning needed for literacy in school. See Table 10.1 for a summary of the themes found within the studies reviewed.

One area he examined was the research that showed that children use decontextualized language during play. For example, when children are pretending to play house, they let others know who they are, and what props they are using through language that refers to objects and events that are not in their immediate surroundings rather than pointing or referring to the environment they can see: "I'll be the mommy, and you're the hungry baby. This is your

TABLE 10.1. Summary of Themes within the Research Reviewed by Pellegrini

Term	Description	Examples
Literate behavior	The production and comprehension of decontextualized language and the development of narrative competence.	Children use decontextualized language when they describe the roles they are playing and the props they are using. They develop story elements in their play themes, such as settings, roles, episodes, and conclusions.
Symbolic play and the generation of decontextualized language	Adult-tutored fantasy play was found to be effective for primary-grade children's generation of cohesive story retellings.	Adults guide children in acting out well-known stories such as "The Three Little Pigs" and then test their use of decontextualized language when they retell the story.
Symbolic play and narrative competence	In social-symbolic play children practice generating role-appropriate behavior and language. Through the use of symbolic role play, their concepts of these roles and narrative events become generalized.	Children use different language and actions depending on the role they are playing. Babies speak differently than mothers; villains act differently than heroes. This helps children learn about characters and roles in narrative texts.
Symbolic play and story production and comprehension	Experimental research focused on the effects of play-training studies on story production and comprehension.	Children act out stories, either with or without help from the teacher. Other groups discuss or draw pictures of the story after it is read. Children are then tested on their ability to recall the story elements.

bottle (handing the child a round block)." Since decontextualized language is necessary for school learning and reading texts, young children need to learn to both utilize and understand it.

Pellegrini also reviewed research that addressed the connection between play and narrative competence. He found that the research showed that when children engage in thematic fantasy play, they include the elements of story structure. For example, the children develop a setting (doctor's office) and characters' roles (doctor, patient), and plot episodes (the patient is sick and needs a shot). These enactments enhance the child's ability to understand and generate narrative structures that are later needed for reading and writing narrative texts.

Pellegrini further examined the research elements of thematic fantasy play, distinguishing among the effects in experimental studies of fantasy enactment, reconstructing stories, and conceptual conflict. One group of children reenacted a story through play with adult guidance. This condition included all elements: fantasy reenactment, story reconstruction, and conceptual conflict. Another group discussed the story in a manner that included story reconstruction and conceptual conflict but no fantasy play. The control group drew pictures of the story. The fantasy-enactment group and discussion group performed better than the control on measures of story comprehension. There was no difference between the play and discussion groups, leading Pelligrini to conclude that the story reconstruction and conceptual conflict were the most important elements in improving comprehension. When tested a week later, there were no lasting effects of the play or discussion treatments.

Pellegrini summarizes this extensive review of the literature by noting that that decontextualized language and narrative skills are involved in both symbolic play and school-based literacy events. Experimental results gave strong evidence for a causal relationship between reconstructing stories, conceptual conflict, and narrative competence. The fantasy element in play was not found to increase comprehension; however, Pellegrini called for more research in this area to make stronger conclusions. Overall, the body of research reviewed in this article provided a solid foundation that supported the value of play in early literacy development and that researchers could build on over the next decade.

Following Pellegrini's extensive review, other researchers, including Neuman and Roskos (1990) and the two of us, who are the authors of the third pivotal study selected for this chapter, began to investigate the more practical implications of the connection between literate behavior and play behavior. At this point, less time and emphasis was being given to child-initiated play in preschool and kindergarten. In 1987, NAEYC released the first of its influential position papers on developmentally appropriate practice (Copple & Bredekamp, 1987). This position paper arose, in part, out of the perceived need to counteract the trend toward a "push-down curriculum," in which academic skills that were once commonly taught in first grade were now being introduced in kindergarten and preschool classrooms.

Neuman and Roskos (1990): *Play, Print, and Purpose: Enriching Play Environments for Literacy Development*

It was within this historical context that the pivotal research of Neuman and Roskos (1990) elaborated on the connections between literate behaviors and play that Pellegrini reviewed and extended his work with a focus on the role of print in play environments in promoting reading and writing behaviors. In earlier work, Neuman and Roskos showed that children use five functional domains of literacy in classroom play: exploring the environment, interacting with others, expressing themselves, authenticating events, and transacting with a text. Keeping these functions in mind, they studied the effects of offering age-appropriate, authentic, and useful props in preschool classrooms.

Description of the Study

Neuman and Roskos redesigned the play areas in two preschools serving 37 children in four ways.

- They improved the spatial definition of each play center using cupboards, screens, and tables, and hung mobiles at eye level with the name of the center on them.
- They increased labeling and environmental print so that all key items and objects were identified with a printed label or symbol.
- They enriched four centers—office, kitchen, post office, and library—that represented real-life contexts with literacy materials.
- They clustered literacy-rich centers together in a quieter area.

In comparing the children's behavior before and after the play areas were redesigned, the authors found that children's literacy behaviors became more purposeful and extended (pp. 218–219), as shown in Figure 10.1.

The change in environment also led to a more thematic use of materials. For example, the theme-related props used within explicit settings, such as a post office or library, gave children clearer cues for how to engage in reading and writing in purposeful ways. In addition, literacy activities in play became more connected and more interactive. The use of themes furthered a connection among literacy activities, which became sustained over time and more collaborative, as seen in Figure 10.2.

Finally, the study revealed that children took on more roles that used literacy-related behaviors even though there was no evidence of this kind of role-related literacy play before the intervention. To summarize, Neuman and

Michael and Scott are playing "sign-up," a popular pretend play theme for these children. In this instance, they want people to "sign up" for the homeless. Scott has a small clipboard and pencil. He circulates throughout the classroom, asking different teachers and children to sign their names on his clipboard. Michael remains in the office "writing" at the desk. Periodically, he looks up and directs Scott to ask someone else. "All these people . . . all these people." Finally, Scott returns with a list of signatures. Both boys pretend to "enter" the list of names into the computer. Scott points to names on the list, and Michael types them. When they are done, Scott removes the paper from the clipboard and is sent out again to gather more names.

FIGURE 10.1. Writing for authentic purposes during pretend play.

Roskos found that creating a carefully designed play environment resulted in children using reading and writing in more purposeful and complex ways. "Reading and writing were tools to manipulate and to work with for some larger purpose in play experiences" (p. 221).

Hilary and Sara are sitting at the table in the post office play center. They are writing letters, then inserting them in the "mailbox" at the corner of the table. They are mailing letters, retrieving them, and pretending to read the messages. Hilary grabs a marker and a clipboard. Sara begins to guide her in what to write. She is pointing at Hilary's paper and talking softly. They seem to be trying to spell a word, and both refer to the hanging mobile over the play center for help with spelling or letter formation. Hilary begins to scribble rapidly on her paper. She shows Sara her scribbles, and Sara says, "Baby, you're bad!" They both giggle and continue making and sending letters to one another.

FIGURE 10.2. Reading and writing letters during pretend play.

Morrow and Rand (1991): *Promoting Literacy during Play by Designing Early Childhood Classroom Environments*

During this same time period, we extended Pellegrini's work by honing in on the role of the adult during play, and complemented Neumann and Roskos' work by experimenting with changes to the physical environment of the room. In planning the research, we were aware of the need to bridge the research–practice gap and to promote play-based literacy practices. As the idea of developmentally appropriate practice (DAP), which described play as a significant contributor to children's development, gained hold, our research was positioned to offer a balanced approach that included adult planning and guidance within child-directed play (Morrow & Rand, 1991).

Description of the Study

In our study, 170 children from 13 preschool and kindergarten classes were randomly assigned to one of four groups.

1. *Paper, pencil, and books with adult guidance.* These literacy materials were added to centers, and teachers modeled how to use them.
2. *Thematic materials with adult guidance.* The dramatic play area of the classroom was converted into a veterinarian's office. It was furnished with literacy materials, such as prescription pads, magazines, books, posters, brochures about pet care, pens, pencils, address books, appointment cards. The teacher modeled, and then guided children, in how to use these materials during play.
3. *Thematic materials without adult guidance.* These classrooms had the same thematic materials; however, the teacher mentioned the materials at the beginning of the play period but did not model how the materials were to be used, nor guide the children.
4. *Traditional curriculum control.* Classrooms had dramatic play areas set up as kitchens; however, no changes were made.

Play periods were held for at least 30 minutes per day. We then tracked the behaviors of the children in the different groups, looking specifically for *reading* (browsing, pretend reading, book handling, reading silently), *writing* (drawing, scribbling, tracing, copying, dictating, writing using invented forms, etc.), and *paper handling* (sorting, shuffling, and scanning).

The results showed that children in the first paper, pencil, and books with adult guidance group and the children in the second thematic play with adult guidance group both demonstrated more literacy behaviors than the other two groups. The first group engaged in the most writing activities, and the second group engaged in the most reading activities. The rich context that the thematic materials and adult guidance groups offered can be seen in the following examples (p. 400).

- Jessica was waiting to see the doctor. She told her stuffed dog not to worry and that the doctor wouldn't hurt him. The teacher handed her a book, and asked if her dog would like to hear a story while she waited. Jessica pretended to read *Are You My Mother?* to her pet and showed him the pictures as she read.
- Jennie ran into the doctor's office shouting, "My dog got runned over by a car." The child acting as the doctor bandaged the dog's leg, and then the teacher suggested that the incident must be reported to the police. With the teacher's guidance, the children got out the telephone book and turned to a map to find the spot where the dog had been hit. Then they called the police on the toy phone to report the incident.

- Preston examined a pet teddy bear. He took the bear's temperature and blood pressure and recorded the numbers. Then he gave the bear a shot and said, "I'm sorry. I hope I didn't hurt you." The teacher asked him if he needed to write a prescription for the bear. He said, "Yes!" and then wrote out a prescription in scribble writing. He then read it to the bear and its owner. As he pointed to the paper, he said, "Now, this says that you make sure you take 100 of these pills every hour until you're better."
- Joshua had just examined a dog. The teacher handed him a file folder and asked if he needed the patient's chart. Joshua nodded and, as he was going to write in the patient's folder, he said, "You know what? I'm going to write his name in dog language. How do you spell *RUFF?*" The teacher helped him spell the word.

The Morrow and Read study demonstrated that the classroom environment can be altered to promote literacy during play, but that the active participation of an adult is necessary to mediate play. With the aim of bridging research and practice now achieved, our article concluded with a list of possible themes and literacy materials that could be added to preschool and kindergarten classrooms. In our suggestions we emphasized play activities that incorporated familiar situations and events.

Impact of the Studies

Research into the practical relationship between play and literacy, as exemplified by the Morrow and Rand and Neuman and Roskos studies, and those reviewed by Pellegrini, established very clearly that *intentional, planned enhancement of sociodramatic play environments and experiences significantly increased preschool, kindergarten, and primary children's engagement in literacy activities.* Embedded within these studies was also the central role of the adult in literacy engagement.

In this section, we review subsequent studies that examined the role of the adult within sociodramatic play directly and systematically. This research established a link between adult guidance and student engagement in literacy activities during dramatic play.

Fifteen years after the last of the three studies described in this chapter, Morrow and Schickedanz (2006) revisited the literature and showed that research conducted after 1991 clearly described the relationship between play, environmental supports, and literacy development studies to that point did not offer evidence of causal relationships between play and literacy development. Their 2006 literature review summarized research up to that time.

- Studies of literacy behavior exhibited by preschoolers during spontaneous dramatic play.
- Studies of the effects of literacy-enriched environments on children's literacy development.

- Studies of the variety of roles assumed by adults during children's play.
- Studies of the added benefit to children's engagement provided by the literacy-related behavior of teacher mediation and support of play.
- Studies of the benefits of conversations between teachers and children during play.

Since the 2006 review, the breadth and depth of the research base on literacy and play has only expanded. For example, there has been an extension of play and literacy research to English language learners (see Banerjee, Alsalman, & Algafar, 2016; Moon & Reifel, 2008). The connection between play and literacy in school-age children in grades K–6 (Fadool, 2009) has also been explored. By extending the thematic play context to school-age children in aftercare programs, Fadool found that children's writing competence, motivation, and confidence improved. Similar to the research with younger children, materials and peer interaction were important variables for success.

Researchers have also focused on teachers' understandings and perspectives about the role of play in literacy learning. For example, in a case study of one teacher, Moon and Reifel (2008) found her that implicit beliefs and understanding affected how she planned play experiences for diverse students. She understood play activities to be concrete, manipulative, enjoyable, hands-on, and creative. This broad definition of play led her to include both sociodramatic play experiences known to increase literacy learning, as well as activities not aligned with DAP or even her own expressed beliefs. In particular, "Ms. Joyce used play in the form of games or 'tricks' in her classroom to encourage children to concentrate on their learning in a fun way" (p. 62). It may be the case that this teacher, like others we have observed, felt that including literacy activities in the preschool curriculum would only be developmentally appropriate if the activities were fun and playful. This line of research has implications for teacher training in understanding the play–literacy connection.

The original research on play has been extended as the play context has been examined through new ideological lenses. For example, Wohlwend (2008) viewed kindergarten as a nexus (or series of connections) of practice and used a sociocultural perspective to analyze classroom activities. He examined how play activities, classroom design, reading, and writing practices expand and/or restrict opportunities for diverse learners to mediate materials and meanings and to participate more fully in peer and school cultures. According to Wohlwend, "Expanded definitions of literacy, such as the nexuses described here, challenge current trends toward scripted, reductive curricula and the related erosion of play periods in early childhood classrooms. This reconceptualization of classrooms as nexuses of practice supports integrated curricula that blend literacy and play practices as interconnected and interdependent ways of interpreting and producing texts, images, artifacts, and social spaces that enrich meaning making and expand opportunities for diverse ways of participating at school" (2008, p. 332).

We find it notable that research interest in play and learning has expanded beyond psychological and educational realms, and that sociological theories and research methods are now being used to understand literacy learning and activities during play.

Another area of research that has been given impetus by these pivotal studies is the association between literacy, play, and technology. Two decades ago, Liang and Johnson (1999) provided insightful reflections about the issues surrounding literacy, young children, technology, and play. While they concluded that "technology can and does mix well with play and emergent literacy" (p. 59), there are valid concerns about what might be displaced in the classroom. Computer enhancement is motivating to young children, and technology may enable children to engage in some literacy behaviors, such as writing, more successfully at earlier ages (e.g., before their fine motor skills are well developed enough for the use of traditional writing tools). Curricula can be enhanced through the use of websites and electronic communication, and play can be enriched with digital cameras and scanners. For example, in one preschool, children were acting out a television interview that the teacher recorded on her cell phone. The children were able to watch their dramatic play sequence and reflect on it. Liang and Johnson conclude that it is important for technology, play, and literacy to be closely tied together and integrated into general program and curriculum plans. Certainly, the use of technology opens another important area for future research that continues to advance pivotal studies in literacy and play.

Influence of the Studies on Policy and Practice

Around 2000, both state and national education standards were adopted, and they eventually led to the later development of the Common Core State Standards (CCSS), which has introduced more rigorous formal instruction in the English language arts curriculum. As we saw in the 1980s, when there was a shift toward more teacher-centered academic learning in early childhood, the role of play in the early childhood curriculum has been questioned again, despite the body of research showing the links between play and learning. We believe this misconception stems from a misunderstanding of the role of standards in contrast to the role of instructional practices. When using a play-based framework for understanding early instruction, one can see that the Common Core State Standards do not rule out play as an instructional tool. Here are two examples that show how literacy standards can be achieved in a play-based environment:

- The kindergarten reading indicator "CCSS.ELA-LITERACY.RL.K.2 With prompting and support, retell familiar stories, including key details" can be satisfied through sociodramatic play in reenacting familiar stories.
- Play contexts can help children learn the phonics skills in the reading foundational skills standard "CCSS.ELA-LITERACY.RF.K.3.A. Demonstrate basic knowledge of one-to-one letter–sound correspondences by producing the primary sound or many of the most frequent sounds for each consonant." Examples of these skills include the way children use invented spelling to write prescriptions when pretending to be a doctor, create signs for their block creations, or compile shopping lists for their play store.

This concern that the standards movement would deter teachers from using play as an instructional method was strong enough that in 2014, the National Association for the Education of Young Children (NAEYC) included a chapter on the relationship between DAP and the Common Core State Standards in their book on developmentally appropriate practice in kindergarten (Biggam & Hyson, 2014). This chapter challenges the myths that play is not compatible with academic rigor, and offers many suggestions for using DAP in conjunction with standards. In 2015, NAEYC released a white paper related to the Common Core State Standards and developmentally appropriate practice. It was designed to help teachers and policymakers better understand the research and issues surrounding standards and DAP.

During the last decade, there has also been an increase in universal preschool programs, which are publicly funded to ensure access for all children. Interestingly, expanded preschool has encouraged curriculum models that were included in the original Head Start research to continue to flourish. The expansion has also allowed for the creation of new curriculum models. For example, High Scope, Creative Curriculum, Curiosity Corner, and the newly developed Tools of the Mind, which are all based on early theoretical frameworks, such as those of Piaget and Vygotsky and rely heavily on research showing the connection between play and early literacy, are commonly used in preschool classrooms today.

The continuing emphasis on play within currently used curricula is evident, for example, in the Tools of the Mind curriculum, which has a pronounced emphasis on learning literacy through theme-based play centers (Barnett, Jung, Yarosa, Thomas, Hornbeck, Stechuk, & Bruns, 2008). In this curriculum, created by Bodrova and Leong (1996), children play in thematic centers, and literacy learning is embedded in play. Extrapolating from Vygotsky's theoretical perspective, Bodrova (2008) sees play as the leading source of development in preschool years because of its potential for enabling children to engage within the zone of proximal development. Dramatic play in *Tools of the Mind* classrooms is very specifically defined as the creation of imaginary scenarios in which children take on and act out roles and follow a set of rules determined by specific roles. This play context develops abstract, symbolic thinking. The curriculum is structured to allow children to engage in "mature play," which is proposed as necessary for optimal learning. Mature play involves object substitutions and role play within high-quality scenarios that last for several days or weeks. Role playing and following a set of rules for play are believed to develop self-regulation, which is necessary for later learning in formal instructional settings.

Bodrova (2008) also tackles head-on the pressure felt in early childhood education to start teaching academic skills at younger and younger ages instead of encouraging play. She shares concerns that much of today's play in early childhood classrooms is not mature and has declined in quality and quantity. Play offers an important context for the development of self-regulation and the neurological aspects of learning. Make-believe play enhances academic learning, rather than competing with it, in the following areas.

- Oral language development—the use of decontextualized language to establish play contexts.
- Metalinguistic awareness—understanding the relationship between words and objects.
- Imagination—using images for text comprehension (Duke & Pearson, 2002).
- Understanding authentic purposes for reading and writing.

The research of Bodrova, Leong, and others now continues the tradition of formal inquiry into play and early literacy represented by Pellegrini, Morrow, and Rand, and Neumann and Roskos (see, for example, Bodrova, 2008; Bodrova & Leong, 2003, 2015).

Take-Aways from the Studies That Support Practice and Reflection

Reflecting on the body of research related to play and early literacy is critical now that pressure from the standards movement is leading to more formalized instruction of literacy skills. Along with a growing number of publicly funded preschools, this tilt toward formal instruction brings serious challenges and opportunities. We must try to reconcile the need for formal instruction with the potential that play settings generate in children's early learning. The follow section provides an overview of three important take-aways from this research literature, starting from the pivotal studies discussed in this chapter and including recent studies that expanded upon them.

1. *Intentional/planned environments in early childhood literacy development should be encouraged.* The first take-away from research on play and literacy is

that the classroom environment increases the likelihood that literacy behaviors will occur during play and that there will be high-quality learning. In particular, thematic play materials should be included in centers that provide children with a choice of rich materials for language use and opportunities for manipulating and exploring books and printed materials and engaging in authentic writing. For example, a thematic play center set up like a doctor's office might include the following items:

- Doctor's coats and examination tools to encourage taking on roles (Bodrova, 2008).
- Books for patients to read while waiting to see the doctor.
- Writing materials for the doctor to use to make appointments, write prescriptions, and take notes.

In addition, reading and writing materials should be placed in all areas of the room to capitalize on the spontaneous use of these materials in the block area, art center, science center, and other locations.

Fadool's (2009) research on the literate play observed among school-age children in an aftercare setting also offers a concrete example of how literacy materials are instrumental in the success of the play. His research found that themed dramatic play areas, such as a house, kitchen, restaurant, and school supported collaborative play. The thematic props, such as menus, signs, and job applications, became accessible sources for reading and writing. When these materials were added to the centers, the children increased the number of elaborate play events and organized literacy experiences easily. Literacy play became a natural part of the day and gained popularity throughout the year.

The importance of carefully planning the environment stems from two aspects of learning: the opportunity for children to use literacy materials during sociodramatic play and the opportunity for children to playfully interact with literacy materials while doing other types of activities.

2. *The role of the teacher or adult is important in play contexts.* The second take-away from this research clearly shows that adult guidance and scaffolding during play can improve literacy learning. This assistance can take the form of directing, playing, extending, and redirecting (Morrow & Schickedanz, 2006). For example, recent work using play interventions in the Tools of the Mind program shows that adults can assist during play in the following ways (Bodrova & Leong, 2001; Bodrova, Leong, Norford, & Paynter, 2003; Barnett et al., 2008).

- Using toys and props as symbols.
- Developing consistent and extended play scenarios.
- Developing and maintaining play roles and rules.

This additional adult assistance will increase the quantity and quality of play, along with improvements in early academic skills.

The population of English language learners (ELLs) is growing and is expected to comprise more than 40% of American elementary and secondary school population by 2030 (Thomas & Collier, 2002). Addressing the particular needs of developing literacy skills in early childhood ELLs is of critical importance in the United States. An example of how strengthening adult support helps ELLs comes from Snow, Eslami, and Park (2015), who describe children's writing during literacy-enriched block play. They found that some ELLs benefit from explicit guidance and modeling from an adult in learning how writing is used in the play context. Moon and Reifel (2008) also show how assuming the role of provider, player, facilitator, helper, and monitor during children's play helped children from diverse language backgrounds develop literacy skills through play. Teachers also need to consider the tools or props used in play environments for diverse learners. For example, kitchens and housekeeping areas need items that are familiar to all children (e.g., tortilla press, chopsticks, and a variety of foods and menus) that represent the diverse backgrounds of the children. Adults' facilitation is more successful within play contexts that incorporate familiar and engaging toys and props (see Roberts, Chapter 2, this volume).

3. *Reject the idea that there is a dichotomy between academics and play.* The third take-away from the recent research is the need to promote ways to meet literacy standards within a play-based approach. One recent example can be seen in Harden (2016), who followed the journey into literacy of a 4-year-old girl named Lucy. Through experiences in dramatic play, puppetry, props, and adult-guided drama, she became an engaged and motivated writer. Themes, such as a "hotel" play frame, encouraged her and her peers to develop agency as authors. She wrote constantly and spontaneously during her play times, and as a result also developed skills in phonemic writing and sounding out words. Another example of thematic play was a veterinarian's office (similar to that described in the pivotal research of Morrow and Rand). In this context, Lucy composed the message: "Vet. I look after cocky" by sounding out "vet," then asking for help with the rest of the sentence. Signs and cards, along with books, were particularly important text forms in the classroom. By the end of the school year, she wrote poetry and drew a humorous picture of a fox with the following label: "I am a fox with chickenpox." This research demonstrates the valuable place that dramatic play can have in the exploration and consolidation process of young children's writing development.

Rejecting the dichotomy between play and formal instruction will mean allowing more time for planned, adult-supported play experiences in early childhood classrooms. The play context will be an integral part of formal instruction in which valuable literacy skills, behaviors, and attitudes will develop over time in a developmental progression. Teachers will be prepared to use intentional teaching strategies during play to encourage and guide the literacy behaviors.

CONCLUSION

In this chapter we have explored the importance of sociodramatic play for early literacy development. Three pivotal studies published between 1985 and 1991 demonstrate that there are powerful ways that play buttresses the use of decontextualized language, the development of narrative competence, and the opportunity to practice literate behaviors, such as reading and writing in authentic contexts. In addition, these research studies uncovered important pedagogical strategies, such as adult support and carefully designed play environments, for capitalizing on the potential of learning through play.

Maintaining an active role for the teacher during play is instrumental in scaffolding children's learning. Teachers should guide children through play scenarios by suggesting roles, props, and actions. When children have this encouragement, they are more likely to engage in literacy behaviors, develop the ability to create stories, and use the type of language needed for writing and reading. New teachers must be prepared to use these intentional teaching strategies during play to optimize the play context for literacy development.

Another pivotal finding from this research is the importance of planned play environments in early childhood literacy development. Thematic play centers in the classroom, such as a doctor's office, post office, or library, should feature a variety of materials, including props for role playing, well-defined play areas, printed labels, and plenty of activities to choose from. The play context, when well designed, will create authentic reading and writing areas for children to use materials related to the play theme, such as writing prescriptions or reading signs. The combination of a rich play environment and strong adult guidance ensures the greatest likelihood of literacy learning through play.

There has been a history of tension between advocates of play-based learning and those who focus on more academic skills in early childhood. The pivotal studies reviewed in this chapter demonstrate that we need to reject the dichotomy of play versus formal instruction and allow more time for planned, adult-supported play experiences. In so doing, we will have the best of both worlds—play and academic learning—while giving children the literacy experiences most critical for their success.

REFERENCES

Banerjee, R., Alsalman, A., & Algafar, S. (2016). Supporting sociodramatic play in preschools to promote language and literacy skills of English language learners. *Early Childhood Education Journal, 44,* 299–305.

Barnett, W. S., Jung, K., Yarosz, D. J., Thomas, J., Hornbeck, A., Stechuk, R., & Bruns, S. (2008). Educational effects of the Tools of the Mind curriculum: A randomized trial. *Early Childhood Research Quarterly, 23*(3), 299–313.

Bereiter, C., & Engelmann, S. (1966). *Teaching disadvantaged children in the preschool.* Englewood Cliffs, NJ: Prentice-Hall.

Biggam, S. C., & Hyson, M. C. (2014). The common core state standards and developmentally appropriate practices: Creating a relationship. In C. Copple, S. Bredekamp, D. Koralek, & K. Charner (Eds.), *Developmentally appropriate practice: Focus on kindergarteners* (pp. 95–112). Washington, DC: National Association for the Education of Young Children.

Bissell, J. S. (1972). *Planned Variation in Head Start and Follow Through.* Washington, DC: Department of Health, Education, and Welfare, Office of Child Development.

Bodrova, E. (2008). Make-believe play versus academic skills: A Vygotskian approach to today's dilemma of early childhood education. *European Early Childhood Education Research Journal, 16*(3), 357–369.

Bodrova, E., & Leong, D. J. (1996). *Tools of the mind: The Vygotskian approach to early childhood education.* Englewood Cliffs, NJ: Merrill/Prentice Hall.

Bodrova, E., & Leong, D. J. (2001). *Tools of the mind: A case study of implementing the Vygotskian approach in American early childhood and primary classrooms* (Innodata Monographs 7). Geneva: International Bureau of Education.

Bodrova, E., & Leong, D. J. (2003). Chopsticks and counting chips: Do play and foundational skills need to compete for the teacher's attention in an early childhood classroom? *Young Children, 58*(3), 10–17.

Bodrova, E., & Leong, D. J. (2015). Vygotskian and post-Vygotskian views on children's play. *American Journal of Play, 7*(3), 371–388.

Bodrova, E., Leong, D. J., Norford, J. S., & Paynter, D. E. (2003). It only looks like child's play. *Journal of Staff Development, 24*(2), 47–51.

Copple, C., & Bredekamp, S. (1987). *Developmentally appropriate practice in early childhood programs serving children from birth through age 8.* Washington, DC: National Association for the Education of Young Children.

Dewey, J. (1916). *Democracy and education.* New York: Macmillan.

Duke, N. K., & Pearson, P. D. (2002). Effective practices for developing reading comprehension. In A. F. Arstrup, S. J. Samuels, & J. Samuels (Eds.), *What research has to say about reading instruction* (3rd ed.). Newark, DE: International Reading Association.

Fadool, M. C. (2009). "We don't serve no ice cream!": Enhancing children's understanding and use of literacy through play events. *Journal of Reading Education, 34*(3), 23–29.

Harden, A. (2016). "Caterpillars and catalysts": A year of literacy learning in an early years classroom privileging dramatic pedagogies. *Australian Journal of Early Childhood, 41*(3), 20–28.

Hodges, W., & Cooper, M. (1981). Head start and follow through: Influences on intellectual development. *Journal of Special Education, 15*(2), 221–238.

Liang, P., & Johnson, J. (1999). Using technology to enhance early literacy through play. *Computers in the Schools, 15*(1), 55–64.

Moon, K., & Reifel, S. (2008). Play and literacy in a diverse language pre-kindergarten classroom. *Contemporary Issues in Early Childhood, 9*(1), 49–65.

Morrow, L., & Rand, M. (1991). Promoting literacy during play by designing early childhood classroom environments. *The Reading Teacher, 44*(6), 396–402.

Morrow, L., & Schickedanz, J. (2006). The relationship between sociodramatic play and literacy development. In D. Dickinson & S. Neuman (Eds.), *Handbook of early literacy research* (Vol. 2, pp. 269–280). New York: Guilford Press.

Morrow, L. M., & Tracey, D. H. (2006). *Lenses on reading: An introduction to theories and models.* New York: Guilford Press.

National Association for the Education of Young Children. (2015). *Developmentally appropriate practice and the Common Core State Standards: Framing the issues.* Washington, DC: Author.

Neuman, S., & Roskos, K. (1990). Play, print, and purpose: Enriching play environments for literacy development. *The Reading Teacher, 44*(3), 214–221.

Pellegrini, A. D. (1985). The relations between symbolic play and literate behavior: A review and critique of the empirical literature. *Review of Educational Research, 55*(1), 107–121.

Piaget, J., & Inhelder, B. (1969). *The psychology of the child* (H. Weaver, Trans.). New York: Basic Books.

Roskos, K., & Christie, J. (2013). Gaining ground in understanding the play-literacy relationship. *American Journal of Play, 6*(1), 82–97.

Snow, M., Eslami, Z. R., & Park, J. H. (2015). Latino English language learners' writing during literacy-enriched block play. *Reading Psychology, 36*(8), 741–784.

Teale, W. H., & Sulzby, E. (1986). *Emergent literacy: Writing and reading.* Norwood, NJ: Ablex.

Thomas, W. P., & Collier, V. P. (2002). *A national study of school effectiveness for language minority students' long-term academic achievement.* Santa Cruz, CA: Center for Research on Education, Diversity and Excellence.

Vygotsky, L. S. (1978). *Mind in society: The development of higher psychological processes.* Cambridge, MA: MIT Press.

Vygotsky, L. S. (1986). *Thought and language.* Cambridge, MA: MIT Press. (Original work published 1962)

Winograd, P., & Greenlee, M. (1986). Students need a balanced reading program. *Educational Leadership, 43*(7), 16–21.

Wohlwend, K. E. (2008). Kindergarten as nexus of practice: A mediated discourse analysis of reading, writing, play, and design in an early literacy apprenticeship. *Reading Research Quarterly, 43*(3), 332–334.

CHAPTER 11

Family Literacy

Is It Really All About Storybook Reading?

Susan M. Dougherty and Jeanne R. Paratore

> The terms *family literacy* and *parent–child book reading* have
> become conflated, leaving us with a major conundrum:
> we cannot begin to design culturally relevant early literacy
> instruction and test its effectiveness if we do not know what
> home literacy practice actually looks like for many children.
> —VICTORIA PURCELL-GATES (2017, p. 366)

Throughout the history of public education in the United States the role of parents in preparing children for school success has been a constant theme. Parents are encouraged and advised by educators, policymakers, and a great array of other commentators to play a prominent role in supporting the literacy development of their young children, and are often criticized when their home literacy practices don't match school-based practices. Throughout, the advice that parents must read to their young children has been paramount. The five pivotal studies that are the focus of this chapter, like many that preceded them and others that followed, specifically address the issue of parent–child reading and other home literacy experiences. In these studies (and others), even as researchers attempt to understand the effects of storybook reading, in particular, there is an ongoing quest to understand more deeply what constitutes "literacy-rich" home environments and a growing realization that this construct itself is as diverse as the families and children it is intended to support.

In this chapter we begin with a brief description of the history of the perceived role of parents in their children's reading development. Then, we explain what these pivotal studies taught us about parent–child storybook reading and other types of parent–child interactions with print. We describe how these studies shaped our thinking about the role of families in supporting literacy development and how these studies have been used by those who develop programs for families. We also point out that current messages about the impact of parent–child storybook reading and other family literacy interactions are often incomplete and continue to "lay blame" and do little to support families as they interact with their children at home.

PERCEIVED ROLE OF PARENTS IN CHILDREN'S READING DEVELOPMENT: A BRIEF HISTORICAL REVIEW

The perceived role of the family with regard to supporting literacy development during early childhood has changed over the years, but the idea that parents should read to their young children has remained a constant. From the time that reading and writing became necessary skills for the majority of adults in western society, reading to children has been suggested as an important way to support young children's learning and growth toward literacy. As early as 1798, when the father–daughter team of M. and R. Edgeworth published an influential book titled *Practical Education* in England, educational guides advocated that children read or be read "books that cultivate the habit of reasoning" (van Kleeck & Schuele, 2010). Prior to the Industrial Revolution and the advent of public schooling, it was widely seen as the responsibility of the family (i.e., mothers) to ensure that their children learned to read and write, primarily for the purpose of engaging with religious texts. In the United States, the task was primarily accomplished through rote memorization of letter sounds and syllables (Banton Smith, 2002).

In the 1820s and 1830s, though, as many more young children attended "infant schools," primarily due to the number of working class mothers taking jobs in factories, educators began to discourage the teaching of formal literacy skills in the home. This shift occurred in part because of the growing influence of progressive ideas, first championed by the philosopher Jean Jacques Rousseau and popularized by influential educators of the time. As explained by van Kleeck and Schuele (2010), the prohibition against "teaching" children was also convenient at a time when schools organized by grade were proliferating, as it ensured that children at school entry all "needed" instruction in the same literacy skills (e.g., recognizing letters, letter formation, letter–sound correspondence). Teaching was whole class and carefully sequenced in those times, and it was thought best if all children arrived to school with basically the same learning needs.

During this period, progressive ideas, which suggested that formal didactic instruction in the home could be harmful, were beginning to take hold. In 1907, interpreting the writings of Rousseau, Compayre explained: "Positive education will only begin for Émile after a long intellectual idleness and an equally lengthy moral inactions. Since nature tends of itself toward its ends, she should be left alone. . . . The best educator is the one who acts least, intervening only to remove obstacles which would hinder the free play of nature, or to create circumstances favorable to it" (p. 25). A few decades later, Dewey (1916) would reinforce these ideas, largely diminishing the importance of subject matter and emphasizing the learning processes and natural curiosity of children.

At the same time, however, although the formal teaching of subjects at home was not encouraged, the idea that children lay a foundation for learning in general, and literacy in particular, through "natural" interactions at home was widely accepted. Huey's (1908) classic and highly influential book *The Psychology and Pedagogy of Reading* included a chapter dedicated to describing the "natural" experiences that might support later, formal reading instruction. In it, Huey recommended building with alphabet blocks, writing signs that connect to the child's play (e.g., "keep off the grass"; "out to lunch"), and connecting whole words to objects (e.g., labeling familiar objects). Huey cautioned against teaching an "analysis of words" and described the precocious child learning to read at home by questioning parents as they read aloud and asking them to point out particular words within the text. His oft-quoted claim has served as a beacon to understanding home influences on reading development: "So almost as naturally as the sun shines, in these sittings on the parent's knee he comes to feel and say the right parts of the story or rhyme as his eye and finger travel over the printed lines, and all the earlier and more certainly if illustrative pictures are placed hard by to serve as landmarks. . . . The secret of it all lies within parents' reading to and with the child" (p. 332).

Eventually, the reading-readiness view of reading acquisition, which held that a child had to be "mentally ready" to learn to read, reinforced the belief that parents and others should avoid teaching literacy skills (e.g., letter names, letter–sound relationships) to children before they started school. According to Teale (1995) the "reading readiness" view predominated from the 1920s to the 1980s and was supported by two prevailing theories about the mechanism by which children became "ready" to read. Some believed that readiness was a factor of maturation and that only time was required for a child's mental capacities to "ripen" to the point where he would be ready to be taught to read. Others believed that readiness was a matter of experience, and that frequent engagement with particular activities (e.g., visual and auditory discrimination tasks) would foster the development of the mental skills needed for reading. Regardless of the underlying assumptions about reading readiness in play, the consensus remained that children would not be ready to learn to read during the preschool or kindergarten years.

Overall then, throughout the history of early childhood education in the United States the home and also child-care settings were viewed as places for only a natural unfolding of early reading and writing skills. Parents were explicitly warned not to attempt to directly teach literacy skills but were encouraged to "enrich" their children's environment with storybooks, play activities, and materials that allowed for creative exploration. According to Van Kleeck and Schuele (2010), the general guideline that parents should not attempt to teach early literacy skills was assimilated into mainstream culture and remains influential. "We see these ideas manifested in today's practices that the vast majority of middle-class parents stop short of actually teaching their children to read. They do typically teach their children letter names and sounds in playful fashion but they are much less likely to teach them to write letters or to read or write words" (p. 344).

Many decades later, the notion of "reading readiness" and the need to "wait" for children to be mentally ready to read and write gave way to the emergent literacy view of early literacy development. In many ways, the emergent literacy view followed from the prevalent ideas about the natural unfolding of literacy, but it also extended our thinking in important and consequential ways. As researchers like Durkin (1966) and Clay (1967) examined the ways in which young children engaged in literate acts within natural contexts, they noted that the playful "writing" and "reading" of young children were important precursors to conventional forms that would be formally introduced as they entered school settings in kindergarten and first grade. Moreover, they found that when young children were immersed in these playful opportunities to read and write, they often self-initiated reading and writing activities, engaging in "scribble writing" and "readings" (e.g., imaginative or memorized) of familiar books as they developed foundational reading and writing skills. Although their work was clearly grounded in these earlier studies, Teale and Sulzby's (1986) book *Emergent Literacy* was especially influential in bringing widespread attention to these important ideas and, in particular, underscored two essential understandings about early literacy: First, that it is not a "sit and wait" process, but rather one that develops incrementally and somewhat systematically from the earliest days of a child's life; and second, that reading and writing are reciprocal processes that emerge in relationship with each other; and further, it may even be the case that writing precedes the emergence of reading.

With these historical traditions as a backdrop, we now turn to the five studies we identified as pivotal to the current understanding and practical applications related to family literacies, in general, and parent–child storybook reading, in particular.

UNDERSTANDING FAMILY AND COMMUNITY CONTEXTS FOR LITERACY LEARNING

Heath (1983): *Ways with Words: Language, Life and Work in Communities and Classrooms*

Although a number of researchers studied the home literacy environments of young children, Heath's (1983) study had an especially immediate and lasting impact. In her ethnography conducted over a period of 10 years in the Piedmont region of North Carolina, Heath set out to discover the ways that families in two communities (Trackton, a low-income black community, and Roadville, a low-income white community) used language and literacy in the course of their daily lives. Heath found that virtually all of the Trackton and Roadville families engaged children in rich and literate discourse, but they did so in ways that were substantially different from middle-class Main-town families. Children in Trackton had few experiences asking or answer-ing "school-like" questions (i.e., the types of questions for which the adult knows the answer) or otherwise displaying their knowledge through labeling and describing; they rarely recounted or retold shared experiences; and they had few experiences with storybook reading. They did, however, answer many questions related to genuine queries; they learned the names of objects and events as they were encountered during daily activities or interactions; and they learned to tell stories in collaboration with others, usually coconstructing a narrative within a process sprinkled with frequent interruptions and embel-lishments, both true and false. These differences were consequential, prevent-ing children from readily mapping their experiences and resulting predisposi-tions toward language and literacy use neatly onto what would be expected in the classroom.

In Roadville, parents engaged children in some book reading (most books of the labeling type rather than narrative, fictional texts), and, like the children of Maintown, they were often asked school-like questions, but their literacy interactions largely ended here. Unlike Maintown parents, they did not link book reading with other events in their children's lives, and for the most part, parent participation in book reading ended when their children entered school. The Roadville children at first did reasonably well in school; they learned to write letters and decode basic words. But as learning expectations advanced beyond reading and writing simple texts, they, like the children of Trackton, begin to fall behind.

The influence of Heath's work is difficult to overstate. It became (and remains) common required reading for literacy and language researchers and teachers and students in undergraduate and graduate literacy and language courses. According to Google Scholar, *Ways with Words* has been cited over 13,000 times. While the number of citations is impressive, they don't fully capture the influence of Heath's work. We believe it is fair to suggest that her description of the ways home use of language and literacy intersects with school structures and expectations for literacy learning remains the most often discussed work of this type; it seems to us that no discussion of literacy and home environments is complete without reference to her ethnography and the research that followed it. Perhaps most often cited was the phrase "what no bedtime story means" (Heath, 1982, p. 49), the title of an article in which she analyzed "the community patterns and the paths to development" (p. 51) taken by children raised with different linguistic and literacy traditions. Heath's statement concluding this analysis foreshadowed the influence her work would have on this area of study over the next several years.

> In conclusion, if we want to understand the place of literacy in human societies and ways children acquire the key literacy orientations of their communities, we must recognize two postulates of literacy and language development. (1) Strict dichotomization between oral and literate traditions is a construct of researchers, not an accurate portrayal of reality across cultures. (2) A unilinear model of development in the acquisition of language structures and uses cannot adequately account for culturally diverse ways of acquiring knowledge or developing cognitive styles. (p. 73)

Purcell-Gates (1996): *Stories, Coupons, and the "TV Guide": Relationships between Home Literacy Experiences and Emergent Literacy Knowledge*

Over a decade later, educators' interest in understanding more deeply how children's home literacy experiences contribute to early literacy learning remained strong, and Purcell-Gates's (1996) investigation of the experiences young children have at home with written materials and the relationship between children's interaction with written materials and writing instruction at school age was an apt response. Purcell-Gates conducted her descriptive study in the homes of 20 low-income, English-speaking families: black (10), white (7), Hispanic (2), and Asian American (1) families were included in the set. Each family had at least one child between the ages of 4 and 6. Purcell-Gates's research assistants spent many hours observing these families, with the goal of being present in the home for a cumulative week, with observations conducted each day of the week from the child's waking to bedtime, so that at the end of data collection the full range of routine family events had been observed. During the time the research assistants were in the homes they adopted the role of participant observers, engaging with the family but trying not to change the typical dynamic. They recorded all instances of the use of print that occurred in their presence, evidence of print use outside of their visits (e.g., a letter waiting to be mailed), and materials related to literacy in the home (e.g., TV guides, writing materials, printed notices). The focal children were administered a battery of written language assessments, including those that assessed children's written-register knowledge, alphabetic-principle knowledge and their understanding of the intentionality of print and concepts of writing and print.

After coding the observation reports across several domains (e.g., uses of print, complexity of print), Purcell-Gates was able to identify the types of print most frequently present in the families' homes and the contexts in which print was most commonly used. First, she found that print was mostly commonly involved in activities related to entertainment (e.g., TV watching, playing board or card games) and daily living routines (e.g., writing grocery lists, consulting recipes). Purcell-Gates also found that the type of print read and written was most commonly at the word and clausal–phrasal level. That is, families most often read and wrote short segments of text (a few words on a coupon, a name of a movie, single words on a grocery list). The second most common text type utilized in the homes was at the highest level of complexity, which includes adult books, documents, and magazines.

Purcell-Gates found some relationships between the frequency and types of print used in the homes and child literacy outcomes that were separate from the effects of schooling. Children whose families interacted with print more frequently and who interacted with their mothers around print (e.g., watched or helped write a note, were read to) scored higher on measures related to understanding the "big picture" of print (grasping the significance of print and the ways it functions in the lives of people). Second, preschoolers who experienced more at-home experiences with higher-level types of texts (which Purcell-Gates classified as more "written" compared with briefly worded text), scored higher on measures of "understanding writing as a system" and concepts of print. Additionally, preschoolers whose parents read to them scored higher on measures of knowledge of the written register. Experience with reading and writing for entertainment purposes within the home resulted in a greater understanding of the alphabetic principle (that sounds map onto specific letters and letter patterns) for all children at all grade levels (preschool to second grade) as Purcell-Gates explained:

> So simply by living and participating in home contexts that included people reading books and magazines, reading the TV Guide for program information, and reading the rules for a board game (as examples of literacy that mediate entertainment activities), young children could begin to construct knowledge about written language and how it works to signify linguistically. (p. 423)

Finally, Purcell-Gates noted that the beginning of formal schooling (e.g., entering kindergarten) corresponded with parent involvement in their children's learning. Parents across the sample began to intentionally interact with their children around print with much greater frequency once they entered school, reading to them, playing letter games, and helping them to write.

Especially influential in this study was Purcell-Gates's concluding statement that quite clearly urged educators to shift their focus from mediating or changing what parents do at home to instead developing ways to learn from parents and children about their day-to-day literacy routines and then figure out ways to integrate family literacies with school-based practices.

> I believe that we can conclude from the descriptions that result from this study that children from low-SES homes, despite their relatively low showing on reading/writing achievement measures as they progress through school, *are learners and do learn* about the ways in which written language functions

to the degree to which they experience it in their lives. To the degree to which they experience others reading and writing text for different purposes and at complex, as well as simple, levels of complexity, and to the degree to which they are personally focused upon and involved with print and the reading and writing of it, young children from low-SES homes will acquire critical emergent literacy knowledges and build firm foundations for future literacy development. The issue is not, thus, getting them ready to learn, but rather creating literacy environments within which the learning that they already do on an ongoing basis includes the different emergent literacy concepts needed for school success. (p. 427)

To summarize, Purcell-Gates's (1996) study revealed a number of important insights about the role of the home environment in the literacy learning of young children from low-income families. As the title of the article suggests, children were exposed to print in most homes in the sample, and this exposure enabled children to grasp the "big picture" of the written register. Through watching their parents cut coupons, write notes, or consult a guide to TV shows the children learned that print carries meaning. Purcell-Gates also found that interaction with and exposure to more complex forms of written text (e.g., watching adults read magazines or documents, being read storybooks), was associated with learning the alphabetic principle, an important foundational skill for success in early reading and writing.

EXAMINING AND REEXAMINING
THE IMPORTANCE OF PARENT–CHILD BOOK READING

Within the framework of the home as a source of "natural" events that would promote the development of dispositions and foundational understandings key to formal literacy instruction, and with studies like those of Heath and Purcell-Gates as a backdrop, a number of other influential studies (e.g., Cochran-Smith, 1984; Mason & Allen, 1986, Taylor & Dorsey-Gaines, 1988; Teale, 1986) examined and documented the diversity in children's family and community literacy experiences. Consistently, these researchers reached a conclusion that family literacies are broad and divergent, varying in significant ways in relation to an array of factors, including culture, race, language, parent education, and socioeconomic status (SES). Yet, even as understandings about the diversity of family literacies were evolving and expanding, the positioning of parent–child storybook reading as a central component in school success remained at the forefront. In 1985, the widely influential federal report *Becoming a Nation of Readers: The Report of the Commission on Reading* by Anderson, Hiebert, Scott, and Wilkinson further emphasized its importance with this single, straightforward claim: "The single most important activity for building the knowledge needed for eventual success in reading is reading aloud to children" (p. 23). Later in the report, the authors elaborated: "Parents play roles of inestimable importance in laying the foundation for learning to read. Parents should informally teach preschool children about reading and writing by reading aloud to them, discussing stories and events, encouraging them to learn letters and words and teaching them about the world around them. These practices help prepare children for success in reading" (p. 57). Perhaps in direct response, a number of studies were conducted related to the effect of parent–child reading, and we address these works next.

Scarborough and Dobrich (1994): *On the Efficacy of Reading to Preschoolers*

Although popular consensus continued to call for parent–child read-alouds as essential foundational activities, the results of studies in the early 1990s challenged this conclusion. In 1994, Scarborough and Dobrich conducted a review of the existing studies on parent–child reading, with the aim of consolidating the evidence gathered across a range of research studies and addressing the question of "how much" parent–child read-alouds matter in early literacy development. They grouped the studies under five categories, each representing a reasonable hypothesis about how these read-alouds might be connected to early literacy development.

First, they examined nine studies that looked for associations between the frequency of parent–child read-alouds and literacy achievement during the school years. While overall they reported a modest relationship, they also cautioned that the frequency of parent–child read-alouds was one of the less-potent variables in these studies. That is, factors such as SES and child language ability had a stronger relationship with literacy achievement in school.

Scarborough and Dobrich next investigated eight studies that sought associations between the frequency of parent–preschooler read-alouds and emergent literacy skills, hypothesizing that home literacy activities might have a greater effect on skills developed before formal schooling would have an influence on a child's development. As was the case with the previous analysis, they found a modest relationship between the frequency of read-alouds and the development of emergent literacy skills, noting that other variables (e.g. parent encouragement for literacy skill development, child interests) were more closely aligned with skills development.

The next set of nine studies gathered by Scarborough and Dobrich (1994) examined the relationship between the frequency of parent–preschooler read-alouds and preschool oral-language skills. They explained that parent–child reading may influence literacy development through oral language, particularly because parents rarely point out print features as they share books with young children. Instead, parents are more likely to focus on the semantic content, offering opportunities to hear new vocabulary and elaborated language. After examining the identified nine studies, the authors found a moderate relationship between oral language development and at-home read-alouds, but, contrary to what might be expected, they reported that the relationship was not any stronger than that found for print-related skills.

Scarborough and Dobrich also examined studies that sought associations between the quality of parent–child reading and either emergent literacy skills or oral language abilities. These studies attempted to identify features of parent language during reading that might offer more support for literacy and language learning. For example, some studies looked for the presence of extra-textual talk (e.g., comments about the story) or decontextualized language use (e.g., talk about things outside of the book-reading context, such as a past event experienced by the child). Again, these studies found only small correlations between the variables under investigation and the outcome measures, leading the authors to state, "the qualitative nature of parental behavior during shared reading sessions has not generally been a better predictor of language and literacy outcomes" (p. 277).

The final set of studies reviewed by Scarborough and Dobrich (1994) were intervention studies, in which an attempt was made to modify the read-aloud frequency or behaviors of parents in an experimental group and then compare their children's outcomes with the outcomes of children of parents in a control group, who presumably continued to read aloud in similar ways prior to their involvement in the study. Although the authors found little evidence for an effect on emergent literacy skills, they determined that the nine studies that tested oral-language outcomes offered evidence of modest effects and potentially long-lasting effects.

In summary, Scarborough and Dobrich's (1994) analysis led them to conclude that the association between parent–child reading and children's literacy development existed, but it was more modest than previously thought, accounting for "no more than 8% of the variance" in present or later literacy knowledge. Notably, among their conclusions was not that parent–child reading is unimportant, but rather that it may be "more complex or interactive" than generally assumed. They argued quite strongly that claiming that parent–child shared reading is an important factor in developing child literacy without stressing the complexity involved may be an overstatement and misleading. We find the closing words of their article relevant to the current discussion.

> Can it be said that reading aloud to young children "is the single most important activity for building the knowledge required for eventual success in reading" (Commission on Reading, National Academy of Education, 1985, p. 23)? If so (and we leave it to each reader to make such a determination), then future research should be focused on pinning down the aspects

of shared reading that are most beneficial. If it is not, then perhaps more attention should be directed to identifying and promoting other ways of enhancing children's preparedness for literacy acquisition. (pp. 296–297)

Bus, van IJzendoorn, and Pellegrini (1995): *Joint Book Reading Makes for Success in Learning to Read: A Meta-Analysis on Intergenerational Transmission of Literacy*

Shortly after the Scarborough and Dobrich study, Bus, van IJzendoorn, and Pellegrini (1995) conducted a meta-analysis (33 samples, including $N = 3,410$ participants) that examined the relationship between frequency of parent-to-preschooler book reading and literacy outcome measures, including language growth, emergent literacy skills, and reading achievement among school-age children. The analyses yielded effect sizes of $d = 0.67$ for language skills, $d = 0.55$ for reading skills, and $d = 0.58$ for emergent literacy. Thus, while Scarborough and Dobrich stated that there was, at most, evidence that 8% of the variance in reading achievement at school age could be explained by the frequency of parent–preschooler book reading and that the evidence for effects on emergent literacy and oral language skills was even less, Bus and colleagues calculated significant effect sizes for emergent literacy and oral language skills in addition to reading achievement. Bus and colleagues argued that their outcomes differed from those of Scarborough and Dobrich because a more extensive collection of studies was included and because their meta-analysis had methodological advantages. They concluded unequivocally that the emphasis that had been placed on the importance of parent–child reading had not been misplaced, but they also noted the need for a more fine-grained analysis of the precise behaviors and interactions that make a difference in children's literacy and language development.

> Our quantitative results give straightforward support for family literacy programs and the need to further explore the aspects of shared reading that are most beneficial. The results of the current meta-analysis support the hypothesis that parent-preschooler book reading is related to outcome measures such as language growth, emergent literacy, and reading achievement. (p. 15)

More important, these two research teams had vastly different perspectives on the implications of their findings. Bus and colleagues claimed that family literacy programs that promote parent–child book reading are wholly justified in their focus on book reading. Scarborough and Dobrich, on the other hand, suggested that such an emphasis may be unjustified and argued that it would be wise to uncover and address other factors that influence early literacy development.

At this point, we imagine that our readers might be questioning the selection of these two studies as "pivotal," given that they presented such opposing views of the role of parent–child storybook reading. We asked the same question, and our answer reflects the fact that both studies illustrate, for us, the debate about parent–child book reading that has continued for more than 20 years and continues to be part of the continuing discussion about whether book reading alone is sufficient or whether other factors are part of the solution.

Sénéchal, Lefevre, Thomas, and Daley (1998): *Differential Effects of Home Literacy Experiences on the Development of Oral and Written Language*

In our final pivotal study, Sénéchal, Lefevre, Thomas, and Daley (1998) investigated the effects of two types of home literacy experiences—storybook reading and parent teaching of literacy skills—on children's acquisition of oral language and print knowledge. They hypothesized that these two home literacy activities may affect young children's literacy development in different ways, with one activity (shared reading) fostering oral-language knowledge while the other (direct teaching of literacy skills) might foster written-language development (i.e., phonemic awareness, letter–name and letter–sound knowledge). The study was designed to tease out and account for potentially important relationships, for example, if parents who engage in frequent shared book reading also engage in direct teaching of literacy skills, essentially the two activities are conflated as one. Moreover, they sought to determine if children's early literacy experiences at home have lasting consequences for their reading achievement.

The sample included families of 110 kindergartens (a mix of 4- and 5-year-olds) and 58 first-grade students living in Ottawa, Canada. All families were middle class and English speaking and most were white. In the fall, the researchers gathered data that allowed them to quantify aspects of the home literacy environment. Parent teaching was measured through the use of checklists in which parents reported how often they taught specific literacy skills, such as saying or writing letter names. Storybook exposure was evaluated using title and author recognition checklists, a method established as more reliable than self-report measures in previous research (e.g., Stanovich & Cunningham, 1992). The children were administered several oral language (vocabulary, listening comprehension, and phonological awareness) and written language assessments (print concepts, alphabet knowledge, invented spelling, decoding). First graders were also administered a reading achievement measure.

The data analyses indicated no relationship between storybook reading and parent teaching; that is, parents who reported frequent storybook reading did not necessarily report direct teaching of literacy skills and vice versa. Regression analyses indicated that parent storybook reading and parent teaching affected different types of knowledge. Storybook reading was a significant factor in the development of oral-language knowledge (explaining 2% of the variance), while parent teaching was a significant factor in the development of written-language knowledge (explaining 7% of the variance). Among the most interesting findings were the following.

> The results of the regression analyses are consistent with the hypothesis that the impact of home literacy experiences on children's reading at the end of Grade 1 was mediated through oral- and written-language skills. Parent teaching did not account for any additional variance in word reading once oral- and written-language skills were entered in the model. Storybook exposure, however, accounted for an additional 2% of the variance, which corresponds to a small effect size (.29). Although this result was not statistically significant, it raises the possibility that storybook exposure (measured in the fall of Grade 1) has a small direct association with children's reading at the end of Grade 1. (p. 110)

As such, like Scarborough and Dobrich (1994), this study confirmed a smaller effect on shared storybook reading than reported by Bus and colleagues (1995). Of particular importance is the conclusion reached by Sénéchal and colleagues in which they caution that educators pay attention to the nonunitary nature of the effect of the different home literacy interactions and literacy development.

> The results of the present research provide support for a distinction between two different aspects of home literacy experiences with respect to the role such experiences might have in the development of oral and written language. In this middle-class sample, parents' knowledge of children's literature was related to children's oral-language skills, whereas the amount of teaching about reading and writing reported by parents was related to children's acquisition of written-language skills. One important implication of these findings is that home literacy experiences should not be considered a unitary construct. Rather, storybook reading and parent teaching may be independent experiences, with different links to early skills and, ultimately, to reading acquisition. (p. 111)

Both concurrent with and subsequent to these selected pivotal studies related to the effects of parent–child storybook reading, other research examined the outcomes of particular types of parent–child interactions during shared reading. For example, some studies have investigated the effects of various read-aloud conditions on children's language knowledge. These conditions included single and repeated readings that were interactive and noninteractive. Single reading of a storybook increased children's receptive, but not expressive, vocabulary (Sénéchal & Cornell, 1993), while repeated readings and questions were more likely to increase receptive vocabulary than a single reading did (Sénéchal, 1997). Answering questions during (three) repeated readings resulted in greater word learning than a single reading or rereadings without questioning (Sénéchal, 1997). Other studies indicated that when children take an active role in shared reading and parents offer feedback through expanded talk, modeling, corrections and praise, they learn substantially more words (e.g., Arnold & Whitehurst, 1994; Valdez-Menchaca & Whitehurst, 1992; Whitehurst et al., 1994). These results were consistent across groups of children of different SES and with children who scored below average on language measures.

Effects related to particular characteristics of the talk surrounding book reading were also found. Weizman and Snow (2001), for example, found that parent utterances, characterized as instructive or helpful, were as important to child vocabulary development as the number of sophisticated words spoken. Word understanding is less likely to occur from passive encounters, and word knowledge is likely to increase from opportunities to connect and link new words to other words and concepts (Nagy & Scott, 2000). Questioning and elaboration during repeated readings very likely foster increasingly deeper understanding of word meanings, helping children go beyond their initial, superficial, "fast mapping" knowledge (Carey, 1978).

Adding to the complexity of appreciating the effects of parent–child shared reading on children's literacy learning is evidence that outcomes are mediated by children's initial vocabulary knowledge. While some studies (e.g., Haden, Reese, & Fivush, 1996) have found that children whose mothers emphasized understanding the story had higher vocabulary scores than children whose mothers emphasized describing and labeling objects and ideas, other studies (Reese, Cox, Harte, & McAnally, 2003) have found a more complex relationship. Specifically, children with smaller initial vocabularies showed the greatest vocabulary gains when mothers described and labeled objects, while children with larger initial vocabularies benefited most from a style emphasizing overall story comprehension. Thus, for children with larger vocabularies, conversations need not be related to the word itself, but can be more broadly related to the context in which the word appears (DeTemple & Snow, 2003), while children with smaller vocabularies need more intentional support in learning new words.

Quite evidently, these studies confirm Scarborough and Dobrich's (1994) argument that parent–child book reading is a multilayered process that demands careful and systematic study to fully understand the parental actions necessary to realize beneficial outcomes.

SUMMARY OF MAJOR FINDINGS OF PIVOTAL RESEARCH

Taken together, these five pivotal studies provide solid evidence that home language and literacy practices influence young children's language and literacy development and also their disposition toward school-based literacy learning activities. They also support a finding that the particular nature of the influence depends on the type of activity and interaction. In this section we first present the overall findings of the five studies.

1. *Home literacy practices support children's literacy development in a variety of ways.* We know from the research of Heath and Purcell-Gates, along with numerous other studies that were published either concurrently or later (e.g., Compton-Lilly, 2003; Delgado-Gaitan, 1996; Taylor & Dorsey-Gaines, 1988; Valdés, 1996) that within home and community settings, young children are routinely encouraged to write and read in myriad ways. They read grocery lists, coupons, recipes, notes, logos, and words on food packaging and games, and they read books, including children's books and religious texts. They create notes, lists, drawings, letters to family members, and labels of various types. They listen to, learn, and memorize stories, songs, prayers, riddles, and rhymes, and they recite them for themselves, family, and friends. In some families, they are taught letters of the alphabet and words, and they see family and community members reading and writing. Overall, prior to school entry, most children have had some experience with varied forms of literacy, and as such, have had opportunities to develop both language and concept knowledge and also emerging identities as readers and writers. Succinctly stated by Anderson, Streelasky, and Anderson (2007) in their review of related research: " . . . many educators now accept the notion that literacy is a part of daily life in most families and communities in Western societies" (p. 144).

2. *Storybook reading is not a universal practice.* Notwithstanding the evidence that families studied by both Heath and Purcell-Gates were rich in many kinds of literacy activities, the practice of parent–child storybook reading did not play a large role in all young children's home literacy experiences. Instead, as noted by Purcell-Gates (2017), parent–child book reading is itself "a cultural practice and does not reflect the worlds of many young children" (p. 366). There remains little evidence, however, that teachers have responded to this observation by rethinking the ways they might learn more about the literacy experiences their students do have, and consider ways to build on and connect these out-of-school experiences to in-school literacy instruction. Instead, the claim that parent–child reading is at the heart of early reading success has persisted, and it has prompted other researchers to study more closely its relationship to early reading success. We summarize the results of this line of research in the next section.

3. *Parent–child book reading exerts a limited influence on early reading skills (e.g., phonemic awareness, letter–sound knowledge), but has a greater influence on*

language knowledge (e.g., vocabulary). As noted previously, the studies of Scarborough and Dobrich (1994), Bus et al. (1995), and Sénéchal et al. (1998) were especially instructive in unpacking the effects of parent–child reading on children's early reading development; and although the overall findings prompted some to diminish the importance of parent–child storybook reading, it caused others to argue the opposite. That is, given the persistence of the achievement gap between children in high- and low-income schools—even after an all-out and largely successful effort has been made to develop knowledge of discrete reading skills (Herlihy, Kemple, Bloom, Zhu, & Berlin, 2009)—a broadly held consensus has emerged in which a knowledge gap, rather than a skills gap, is targeted as the culprit (e.g., Neuman, 2006). Alongside this, there is a growing awareness (e.g., Juel, 2006; Sénéchal, 2011) of decades-old evidence that vocabulary knowledge measured in kindergarten predicts reading performance starting at the end of grade 3 and beyond (Sénéchal, Ouelette, & Rodney, 2006; Whitehurst & Lonigan, 2002). Moreover, there is evidence that a vocabulary gap that starts to form in children's early years is very difficult to mediate (Whitehurst & Lonigan, 2002). These findings make it unwise to emphasize (and at times, even mandate) instruction of children's skill knowledge (e.g., phonemic awareness, letter names) at the expense of language and world knowledge.

While it might be tempting to emphasize home-based skills instruction over parent–child storybook reading, in the longer term, the affordances of book reading are especially consequential. But because these studies, and even those that came later (e.g., Sénéchal & Young, 2008) persisted in comparing school-like literacy events (e.g., shared book reading, teaching specific skills, listening to children read books) as sources of early literacy foundational skills, they have done little to contextualize parent–child book reading within a broader and more representative "collection" of literacy events that, if recognized and promoted by parents and teachers, would likely provide a rich foundation for literacy learning.

4. *How books are read makes more of a difference than how often books are read.* Scarborough and Dobrich (1994) included a group of studies that examined the "quality" of parent–child read-alouds in an attempt to understand whether the ways in which parents and children interact with books makes a difference in what they learn about language and literacy. This line of research has been extended over the past quarter century. Subsequent studies (e.g., Hammett, van Kleeck, & Huberty, 2003; Melzi & Caspe, 2005; Neuman, 1996; van Kleeck, Gillam, Hamilton, & McGrath, 1997) have uncovered a wide variety of ways in which parents and their children interact with books, and that these differences do influence what is absorbed from the read-aloud experience.

HAVE THE FINDINGS INFLUENCED PRACTICE?

Within each of the pivotal studies, the authors suggest that their work will have implications for intervention programs or for educators or others working with families. They suggest that understanding how various types of experiences in the home contribute to the development of language and literacy skills can guide the development of programs that could make a difference in the academic trajectory of young children. Programs that support the literacy development of young children were already in existence at the time the pivotal studies discussed here were published. Among the largest and most widespread model was Even Start, a federally funded education program that targeted parents with low literacy skills or with limited English proficiency and their children, with a focus on children younger than 7. Based on a model that included parent education, early childhood education, and parent–child activity time, Even Start funded projects were studied extensively, in three large-scale national evaluations, and each time the studies yielded findings that showed no significant differences between Even Start and other programs that served as statistical controls. According to quality of instruction indicators, in the early childhood classrooms "there was not sufficient emphasis on language acquisition and reasoning" (St. Pierre, Ricciuti, Tao, Creps, Swartz, Lee, & Parsad, 2003, p. 7) to enable Even Start youngsters to outperform their peers in the control group or in other early childhood programs. Regarding the overall efficacy of Even Start, St. Pierre, Ricciuti, and Rimdzius (2005) concluded:

> The fact that two experimental studies of Even Start show similar results, even though they were done at different times, one in the early 1990s at the very beginning of the program (St. Pierre, Swartz, Gamse, Murray, Deck, & Nickel, 1995) and a second after a decade of program implementation and many amendments to the program (St. Pierre et al., 2003), lead us to question the theoretical model underlying Even Start and most other family literacy programs. (p. 965)

Critics of the Even Start model argued that its biggest downfall (and that of many similar family literacy programs) is the tendency to design programs in which families are simply encouraged to mimic mainstream ways of interacting with books. The educators that deliver these programs are likely to perceive their role as *teaching* families how to read books to their children. Unfortunately, this attitude often reflects a deficit view of families and fails to recognize the ways in which literacy is already enacted in their lives. It suggests a "one-way street" in which educators, who often are members of the dominant culture, endeavor to transmit cultural ways of being. Anderson and colleagues (2007), in their review of family literacy programs on the World Wide Web, noted.

As we examined and read through this corpus of material, we were struck by the continuing presence of deficit language. It is disconcerting to encounter the cherubic images of contented families sharing storybooks juxtaposed on the same page with allusions to "social assistance," "poor parents," "low literate families," and the like. In addition to being inaccurate in that many families living in poverty value literacy and engage in literacy practices (Taylor & Dorsey-Gaines, 1988), such messages are also paternalistic and disturbing. Auerbach (1995) a decade ago warned that although most family literacy programs purported to operate from a perspective of building on the strengths of families and communities, deficit assumptions still underpinned many of them. Unfortunately, this still seems to hold in some cases. (p. 153)

What we need, instead, are programs that recognize the rich ways that literacy plays out in families, regardless of whether storybook reading is a naturally occurring event. We need programs that build upon cultural practices and demonstrate to families how particular parent–child interactions map onto classroom expectations of children's literacy development. Ideally, we need programs that allow educators to recognize the types of literacy activities that are part of the everyday lives of the families that they encounter. We are not suggesting that as we work with families we pretend that storybook reading accompanied by particular types of parent–child interactions is not a good foundation for the development of important language and literacy skills. But we do suggest that administrators and teachers enter into a genuine partnership with parents and community members that is based on an *exchange* of information, such that administrators and teachers acquaint themselves with family literacy interactions that are part of the family's daily and weekly routines; and that those types of interactions become solidly integrated into classroom-based literacy events. The other part of the partnership involves administrators and teachers introducing parents to some of the school-based literacy routines, including parent–child reading, in ways (e.g., through repeated readings, parent elaborations, and use of questions) that will support the positive outcomes realized in some of the studies.

CONCLUSION

An important message that remains muted in discussions of family literacy is the broad array of literacy events and activities that support children's understanding of print and its purpose within everyday life. The ongoing emphasis on parental attention to shared book reading and reading skills as the major sources of early literacy development dismisses compelling and consistent evidence uncovered by Compton-Lilly (2003), Heath (1984), Purcell-Gates (1996), Taylor and Dorsey-Gaines (1988), and many others that documents both the presence and diversity of family literacy interactions. Purcell-Gates (2017) underscored the negative consequence of dismissing this evidence: "The terms *family literacy* and *parent–child book reading* have become conflated leaving us with a major conundrum: we cannot begin to design culturally relevant early literacy instruction and test its effectiveness if we do not know what home literacy practice actually looks like for many children" (p. 366).

A failure to recognize and acknowledge literacy practices that differ from those codified as important so many years ago carries with it damaging consequences. It prompts the persistence of the deficit view of families who do not match idealized conceptions, and this, in turn, interferes with young children's ability to develop positive literate identities of themselves and their families. As noted by Paratore, Edwards, and O'Brien (in press), some teachers are so convinced that their children's parents lack interest in and the ability to support their children's academic learning, that they fail to reach out to them altogether.

Finally, we offer some recommendations for educators—both those who interact with families in their roles as classroom teachers and those who work within "family literacy" programs. We believe that attention to the following points will result in far more beneficial outcomes for young children.

- Recognize that families care.
- Recognize that all kinds of interactions with print offer value.
- Recognize that access to books is important.
- Recognize that storybook reading is a cultural phenomenon, and it is challenging to integrate new cultural practices into everyday life.
- Recognize that finding culturally relevant ways for families to engage in book reading and other literacy experiences are possible and powerful.

REFERENCES

Anderson, J., Streelasky, J., & Anderson, T. (2007). Promoting and representing family literacy on the World Wide Web. *Alberta Journal of Educational Research, 53*(2) 143–156.

Anderson, R. C., Hiebert, E. H., Scott, J. A., & Wilkinson, I. A. G. (1985). *Becoming a nation of readers: The report of the commission on reading.* Washington, DC: National Institute of Education.

Arnold, D. S., & Whitehurst, G. J. (1994). Accelerating language development through picture book reading: A summary of dialogic reading and its effects. In D. K. Dickinson (Ed.), *Bridges to literacy: Children, families, and school* (pp. 103–128). Cambridge, UK: Blackwell.

Auerbach, E. (1995). Deconstructing the discourse of strengths in family literacy. *Journal of Reading Behavior, 27*(4), 643–661.

Banton Smith, N. (2002). *American reading instruction, special edition.* Newark, DE: International Reading Association.

Bus, A. G., van IJzendoorn, M. H., & Pellegrini, A. D. (1995). Joint book reading makes for success in learning to read: A meta-analysis on intergenerational transmission of literacy. *Review of Educational Research, 65*(1), 1–21.

Carey, S. (1978). The child as word learner. In J. Bresnan, G. Miller, & M. Halle (Eds.), *Linguistic theory and psychological reality* (pp. 264–293). Cambridge, MA: MIT Press.

Clay, M. (1967). The reading behaviour of five year old children: A research report. *New Zealand Journal of Educational Studies, 2*(1), 11–31.

Cochran-Smith, N. (1984). *The making of a reader: Language and learning for human service professions monograph series.* Norwood, NJ: Ablex.

Compayre, G. (1907). *Herbart, and education by instruction.* (M. E. Findlay, Trans.). New York: Crowell.

Compton-Lilly, C. (2003). *Reading families: The literate lives of urban children.* New York: Teachers College Press.

Delgado-Gaitan, C. (1996). *Protean literacy: Extending the discourse on empowerment.* Bristol, PA: Falmer Press.

DeTemple, J., & Snow, C. E. (2003). Learning words from books. In A. van Kleeck, S. A. Stahl, & E. B. Bauer (Eds.), *On reading books to children: Parents and teachers* (pp. 16–36). Mahwah, NJ: Erlbaum.

Dewey, J. (1916). *Democracy and education.* New York: Simon and Schuster.

Durkin, D. (1966). *Children who read early.* New York: Teachers College Press.

Edgeworth, M., & Edgeworth, R. L. (1798). *Practical education.* London: Johnson.

Haden, C. A., Reese, E., & Fivush, R. (1996). Mother's extratextual comments during storybook reading: Stylistic differences over time and across texts. *Discourse Processes, 21,* 135–169.

Hammett, L. A., van Kleeck, A., & Huberty, C. J. (2003). Patterns of parents' extratextual interactions during book sharing with preschool children: A cluster analysis study. *Reading Research Quarterly, 38*(4), 442–468.

Heath, S. B. (1982). What no bedtime story means: Narrative skills at home and school. *Language in Society, 11*(1), 49–76.

Heath, S. B. (1983). *Ways with words: Language, life, and work in communities and classrooms.* Cambridge, UK: Cambridge University Press.

Herlihy, C., Kemple, J., Bloom, H., Zhu, P., & Berlin, G. (2009). *Understanding reading first: What we know, what we don't, and what's next.* New York: MDRC.

Huey, E. B. (1908) *The psychology and pedagogy of reading.* New York: MacMillan.

Juel, C. (2006). The impact of early school experiences on initial reading. In D. K. Dickinson & S. B. Neuman (Eds.), *Handbook of early literacy research* (Vol. 2., pp. 410–426). New York: Guilford Press.

Mason, J., & Allen, J. B. (1986). A review of emergent literacy with implications for research and practice in reading. *Review of Research in Education, 13*(1), 3–47.

Melzi, G., & Caspe, M. (2005). Variations in maternal narrative styles during book reading interactions. *Narrative Inquiry, 15*(1), 101–125.

Nagy, W. E., & Scott, J. A. (2000). Vocabulary processes. In M. L. Kamil, P. B. Mosenthal, P. D. Pearson, & R. Barr (Eds.), *Handbook of reading research* (Vol. 2, pp. 269–284). Mahwah, NJ: Erlbaum.

Neuman, S. B. (1996). Children engaging in storybook reading: The influence of access to print resources, opportunity, and parental interaction. *Early Childhood Research Quarterly, 11,* 495–513.

Neuman, S. B. (2006). The knowledge gap: Implications for early education. In D. K. Dickinson & S. B. Neuman (Eds.), *Handbook of early literacy research* (Vol. 2, pp. 29–40). New York: Guilford Press.

Paratore, J. R., Edwards, P. A., & O'Brien, L. (in press). Building strong home, school, and community partnerships through culturally relevant teaching. In L. M. Morrow & L. Gambrell (Eds.), *Best practices in literacy instruction* (6th ed.). New York: Guilford Press.

Purcell-Gates, V. (1996). Stories, coupons, and the "TV Guide": Relationships between home literacy experiences and emergent literacy knowledge. *Reading Research Quarterly, 31*(4), 406–428.

Purcell-Gates, V. (2017). Breaking the barrier of blame: Parents as literacy brokers. In N. Kucirkova, C. E. Snow, V. Grover, & C. McBride (Eds.), *The Routledge international handbook of early literacy education: A contemporary guide to literacy teaching and interventions in a global context* (pp. 362–372). New York: Routledge.

Reese, E., Cox, A., Harte, D., & McAnally, H. (2003). Diversity in adults' styles of reading books to children. In A. van Kleek, S. A. Stahl, & E. B. Bauer (Eds.), *On reading books to children: Parents and teachers* (pp. 37–57). Mahwah, NJ: Erlbaum.

Scarborough, H. S., & Dobrich, W. (1994). On the efficacy of reading to preschoolers. *Developmental Review, 14*(3), 245–302.

Sénéchal, M. (1997). The differential effect of storybook reading on preschoolers' acquisition of expressive and receptive vocabulary. *Journal of Child Language, 24*(1), 123–138.

Sénéchal, M. (2011). A model of concurrent and longitudinal relations between home literacy and child outcomes. In D. K. Dickinson & S. Neuman (Eds.), *Handbook of early literacy research* (Vol. 3, pp. 175–188). New York: Guilford Press.

Sénéchal, M., & Cornell, E. H. (1993). Vocabulary acquisition through shared reading experiences. *Reading Research Quarterly, 28*, 360–374.

Sénéchal, M., Lefevre, J., Thomas, M. E., & Daley, K. E. (1998). Differential effects of home literacy experiences on the development of oral and written language. *Reading Research Quarterly, 33*(1), 96–116.

Sénéchal, M., Ouellette, G., & Rodney, D. (2006). The misunderstood giant: On the predictive role of vocabulary to reading. In S. B. Neuman & D. Dickinson (Eds.), *Handbook of early literacy* (Vol. 2, pp. 173–182). New York: Guilford Press.

Sénéchal, M., & Young, L. (2008). The effect of family literacy interventions on children's acquisition of reading from kindergarten to grade 3: A meta-analytic review. *Review of Educational Research, 78*, 880–907.

St. Pierre, R. G., Ricciuti, A. E., & Rimdzius, T. A. (2005). Effects of a family literacy program on low-literate children and their parents: Findings from an evaluation of the even start family literacy program. *Developmental Psychology, 41*(6), 953–970.

St. Pierre, R., Ricciuti, A., Tao, F., Creps, C., Swartz, J., Lee, W., & Parsad, A. (2003). *Third National Even Start evaluation: Program impacts and implications for improvement.* Washington, DC: U.S. Department of Education.

St. Pierre, R. G., Swartz, J. P., Gamse, B., Murray, S., Deck, D., & Nickel, P. (1995). *National evaluation of the even start family literacy program: Final report.* Cambridge, MA: Abt Associates.

Stanovich, K. E., & Cunningham A. E. (1992). Studying the consequences of literacy within a literate society: The cognitive correlates of print exposure. *Memory and Cognition, 20*(1), 51–68.

Taylor, D., & Dorsey-Gaines, C. (1988). *Growing up literate: Learning from inner-city families.* Portsmouth, NH: Heinemann.

Teale, W. H. (1986). Home background and young children's literacy development. In W. H. Teale & E. Sulzby (Eds.), *Emergent literacy: Writing and reading* (pp. 173–205). Norwood, NJ: Ablex.

Teale, W. H. (1995). Young children and reading: Trends across the 20th century. *Journal of Education, 177*(3), 95–127.

Teale, W. H., & Sulzby, E. (Eds.). (1986). *Emergent literacy: Writing and reading.* Norwood, NJ: Ablex.

Valdés, G. (1996). *Con respeto: Bridging the distances between culturally diverse families and schools: An ethnographic portrait.* New York: Teachers College Press.

Valdez-Menchaca, M. C., & Whitehurst, G. J. (1992). Accelerating language development through picture book reading: A systematic extension to Mexican day care. *Developmental Psychology, 28,* 1106–1114.

van Kleeck, A., Gillam, R. B., Hamilton, L., & McGrath, C. (1997). The relationship between middle-class parents' book sharing discussion and their preschoolers' abstract language development. *Journal of Speech, Language, and Hearing Research, 40,* 1261–1271.

van Kleeck, A., & Schuele, M. C. (2010). Historical perspectives on literacy in early childhood. *American Journal of Speech–Language Pathology, 19*(4), 341–355.

Weizman, Z. O., & Snow, C. E. (2001). Lexical output as related to children's vocabulary acquisition: Effects of sophisticated exposure and support for meaning. *Developmental Psychology, 37*(2), 265–279.

Whitehouse, M., & Colvin, C. (2001). "Reading" families: Deficit discourse and family literacy. *Theory Into Practice, 40*(30), 212–219.

Whitehurst, G. J., Arnold, D. S., Epstein, J. N., Angell, A. L., Smith, M., & Fischel, J. E. (1994) A picture book reading intervention in day care and home for children from low-income families. *Developmental Psychology, 30,* 679–689.

Whitehurst, G. J., & Lonigan, C. J. (2002). Emergent literacy: Development from prereaders to readers. In S. B. Neuman & D. K. Dickinson (Eds.), *Handbook of early literacy research* (pp. 11–29). New York: Guilford Press.

CHAPTER 12

Enhancing Children's Access to Print

Susan B. Neuman and Donna Celano

All children can learn what we teach, if provided with the prior and current conditions of learning.
—BENJAMIN BLOOM

Children's early literacy development begins long before formal instruction in reading and writing. From the very beginnings of life, children are absorbing the sounds and rhythms of meaning as caregivers cuddle and respond to their infants' coos and cries. Child development specialists suggest that infants are far from passive. Indeed, they are active participants in their world (Fernald & Weisleder, 2011). Within the first year, children will begin to imitate sounds, recognize familiar voices, and engage in shared communication with their first books. Satisfying and interpersonal experiences with stories and pictures may captivate their interest and imagination and become woven into the tapestries of their inner representations. These are the roots of early literacy development.

PIVOTAL RESEARCH ON CHILDREN'S ACCESS TO PRINT

Children who are early readers come from families that have books in the home and that read to their children often. There is now overwhelming evidence that stimulating experiences with books have facilitative consequences for literacy development (Bus, van IJzendoorn, & Pellegrini, 1995). Studies have shown that children learn new words from direct references in stories (Biemiller & Boote, 2006). They gain new vocabulary after hearing a story read, especially when the words are repeated in the text. However, they also learn from informal encounters with words in story conversations with caregivers (Mol, Bus, & deJong, 2009). Whitehurst, Arnold, Epstein, Angell, Smith, and Fischel (1994), for example, provide a persuasive case for dialogic reading, indicating that problem-solving discussions during storybook reading have a significant and powerful influence on children's developing expressive and receptive language.

Children learn a wide array of language competencies related to literacy development through books. For example, Snow, Tabors, Nicholson, and Kurland (1995) differentiate between contextualized and decontextualized language skills. In face-to-face conversations, children and adults learn to draw on their shared knowledge, negotiate meaning, and respond to feedback from one another. Decontextualized language skills are developed as children explain ideas in texts, tell their own stories, use language to create fantasy worlds, and convey information to others. Snow and her associates suggest that children's skills with decontextualized language not only relate to their developing narrative competence, but also to their long-term comprehension abilities in the middle grades (Lawrence, Crosson, Pare-Blagoev, & Snow, 2015).

There is also increasing evidence that the type of book or genre influences children's conceptual knowledge and understanding (Neuman & Kaefer, 2018). Different kinds of children's books encourage different type of interactions. Predictable books, for example, facilitate rhyming, chiming, and coparticipation between adults and children. Similarly, characteristic features of informational books, such as the use of technical language and comparisons and contrasts, lead to questions that link content to children's past experiences and acquired knowledge (Pappas, 1991). In addition to adult guidance, text styles and genres act as scaffolds for helping children develop important cognitive skills like making predictions and drawing inferences. Consequently, research indicates that the amount, type, and quality of storybook reading experiences are consistently associated with an array of reading proficiency indicators and topical knowledge.

Today, however, there are wide disparities in children's access to books, and many children are *not* the beneficiaries of these early reading experiences. In this chapter, we first examine our research (which our editors have so graciously described as "pivotal"). We then discuss recent sociocultural shifts in the concentration of poverty and its consequences on book access. Taken together, this research raises the critical question: How are children to learn to read without access to books?

Neuman and Celano (2001): *Access to Print in Low-Income and Middle-Income Communities: An Ecological Study of Four Neighborhoods*

Our pivotal study (Neuman & Celano, 2001) was designed to challenge a prevailing assumption: That books and other literacy-related resources are easily and equally accessible to all families and their children. Previously, it was assumed that all communities and neighborhoods afforded such opportunities because children's books, newspapers, and magazines were easily available for purchase. It was also thought that low-income families with limited funds could easily visit the local library, their child-care programs, or early elementary school libraries to borrow books.

These assumptions, however, had never been tested. In fact, little information was known about the potential magnitude of differences in access to literacy materials and resources. Therefore, our study was designed to examine the potential disparities in print environments for thousands of children from four local neighborhoods in a large urban city in the United States. It set out to carefully document the availability of print in these communities, focusing on the resources considered to be influential in a child's development as a reader. In so doing, we attempted to build an empirical case for examining these underlying resources and potential constraints that might enhance or inhibit children's early literacy development.

We engaged a multicultural team of urban anthropology doctoral students in ethnographic data collection that was both rigorous and thorough. Together, we explored neighborhoods street-by-street, counting the number of books and other printed materials we could find. We examined the signage, number of logographic signs, and public places (spaces) where we might find print available to customers (e.g., laundromats, bus stations, fast-food joints, and diners). We visited local child-care centers and school and public libraries and counted the numbers of books and other materials that might be available to young children.

We found minor differences in access to print between neighborhoods of similar incomes (see Table 12.1). Both the middle-class community and the blue-collar community seemed to have print resources available to children, although the well-to-do neighborhood (Chestnut Hill) clearly afforded more opportunity than the blue-collar neighborhood (Roxborough). On the other hand, however, we found stark and triangulated differences in access to print for those children living in low-income neighborhoods compared to their middle-class peers. Children in middle-income neighborhoods had multiple opportunities to observe, use, and purchase books (approximately 13 titles per child). In contrast, few opportunities were available for low-income children who had approximately one title per 300 children. Other avenues of access to print, as well, were unavailable. School libraries in poor communities were often closed, unlike thriving libraries in middle-class schools, which featured 12 titles per child. Public libraries were open only for a few hours each day in low-income neighborhoods, compared with the number of hours in middle-income neighborhoods. Additionally, while middle-class child-care centers featured many quality books for the children in their care, in low-income neighborhoods, fewer than one to two books were available per child. And of those books, the majority were mediocre or of poor quality.

This pool of data highlighted how differences in economic circumstances seemed to translate into extraordinary differences in the availability of print resources for children who lived in low- or middle-income communities. Inequity was reported in the number of resources, the choice and quality of materials available, public spaces and other places for reading, the amount and quality of literacy materials in child-care centers, and the number of school and local public libraries in these communities. Long before formal schooling begins, considerable variations in patterns of early literacy were likely to be evident owing to the resources available to a young child in these communities.

BOOK DESERTS

One could argue, however, that the problem has become even more complicated in the last decade. *Income segregation,* or socioeconomic residential sorting reflects the extent to which families of different incomes live in different neighborhoods, consolidating those who live in wealthier, as well as

TABLE 12.1. Number of Stores That Include Access to Print

Stores	Poor community	Middle-class community
Children's resources		
Bookstores	0	3
Drugstores	0	2
Grocery stores	0	1
Discount stores	1	0
Corner stores	1	0
Other stores	2	1
Children's stores	0	4
Total	4	11
Young adult resources		
Bookstores	0	1
Drugstores	0	0
Grocery stores	0	0
Discount stores	0	0
Corner stores	0	0
Other stores	0	0
Total	0	1
Total number of stores	4	12
Total number of titles	33	16,453

those who live in poorer communities (Bischoff & Reardon, 2014). In essence, today, the wealthy individual is likely to associate strictly with those who are equally wealthy, while the poor individual, ever more isolated, is likely to interact solely with others who are poor. This rapid rise of income segregation has consequences for young children and their development. Because most young children spend a great deal of time in their own neighborhoods, they have the potential to further accentuate the economic advantages of high-income families and exacerbate the economic disadvantages of low-income children (Massey, 2007). Furthermore, poorer children are likely to attend poorer schools in their neighborhoods.

Consequently, given the changes in the demographic landscape we chose to examine how these changes might affect children's access to print. To achieve a more national perspective, we focused our analysis on the resources available in six neighborhoods in three cities along the east coast (Anacostia and Capitol Hill in Washington, D.C.), the Midwest (Hamtramck and University City in Detroit), and the west coast (Vermont Square and Culver City in Los Angeles) (Neuman & Moland, 2016). In this study, we focused on the summer months when schools were closed, and when many preschools and child-care programs were in summer recess. It has been shown that these are the critical months when poor children experience fewer options for learning outside of school and therefore might represent the most crucial time for book reading. Entwisle, Alexander, and Olson (2014) have proposed the "faucet theory" in describing the differences in the learning trajectories for poor and middle-class children. When schools are open, all children are learning, but when schools are closed, children in poor communities are too often left behind without the resources to learn. The *summer slide* has become the term of art for this phenomenon: Without resources, school readiness skills accumulated throughout the year are likely to drop precipitously during summer, whereas, for middle-class children, they are likely to be stable or even grow (Quinn, Cooc, McIntyre, & Gomez, 2016). In this scenario, therefore, limited access to books in the home may have serious consequences for children's continuing growth in reading and skill development (see Table 12.2).

Once again, our results revealed the disparities in access to print for children who lived in high-poverty neighborhoods. None of the communities appeared to have an abundance of reading resources or an adequate choice of books for children, especially for those in the early years. According to our calculations, for example, 830 young children in Anacostia, D.C., would have to share one book during the summer months. Furthermore, the only book title we found throughout this community (e.g., literally in the President's backyard) was a Spanish dictionary.

In theorizing about these resource inequalities, we use the term *book deserts* and argue that, like the food desert construct, these shortages in neighborhoods have significant consequences for the well-being of families. This term

TABLE 12.2. Number of Children Who Would Have to Share One Book

Neighborhood	Children 0–5 per preschool book	Children 0–18 per all children's books
Anacostia, D.C.	N/A (no preschool books; 1,411 children <5)	830
Capitol Hill, D.C.	2.5	2
Hamtramck, Detroit	37	42
University District, Detroit	5	11
Vermont Square, Los Angeles	12	13
Culver City, Los Angeles	1.4 books per child	1

helps us draw attention to the *structural inequalities*—rather than the individual or family characteristics—that result in academic gaps between communities. In essence, it describes one of the critical barriers to children's achievement and further aspirations to succeed in school.

LOOKING FOR SOLUTIONS: A THEORY OF PHYSICAL AND PSYCHOLOGICAL PROXIMITY

How do we begin to solve this problem? How do we develop viable interventions that improve children's access to print? Recognizing that it is critical for children to be immersed in a book culture early on, what can we do to change the odds for children who live in book deserts? Although libraries are critically important, studies suggest that the very presence of books in children's homes is related to reading achievement (Mullis, Martin, Foy, & Drucker, 2012).

From our work in communities, we developed a theory of action. In this model, we posit that children need both *physical* access and *psychological* proximity to books to enhance their early literacy skills (Neuman & Carta, 2011). Research in ecological psychology demonstrates that the physical environment has a coercive effect; that over time, individual behavior tends to be consistent with the situational demands of a setting. For example, close physical access to books creates an "environmental press" (Gump, 1975) a tendency to enact an activity associated with print. In short, the physical setting, including the resources within it and the opportunities that it affords, has behavioral consequences.

This model suggests a number of interesting possibilities. For example, there are a now a fairly sizable number of studies showing that it can be used to our advantage (Neuman & Roskos, 1992; Vukelich, 1994). In one of the first intervention studies of its type, Morrow and Weinstein (1986) examined the influence of creating library corners in early childhood settings. These library corners were specially constructed to include a specific location with well-defined borders; comfortable seating and cozy spots for privacy; and accessible, organized book materials and related book activities. The researchers found that the frequency of use rose significantly when these library corners were made more physically accessible and attractive. Similarly, in our large-scale study in 500 child-care settings (Neuman, 1999), library corners were created to "put books in children's hands" (p. 286). Observations indicated that children spent significantly more time interacting with books when they were placed in close proximity to children's play activities.

However, positive environments not only include physical settings, but also the psychological dimension of literacy learning as well (Tharp & Gallimore, 1988). Children are influenced by the presence of other participants and their background experiences and values; it is the integration of place, people, and occasion that supports opportunities for learning. These individuals are in effect social and psychological resources that provide information and feedback. From a Vygotskian perspective (Vygotsky, 1978), the participants in these early learning settings have the potential to help children perform at a higher level than they would be able to by interacting with their physical environment alone. For example, there is strong evidence that the amount of verbal input that children receive enhances their language development (Hart & Risley, 1995; Hoff, 2006), and that children whose parents and teachers engage them in rich dialogues around books have higher scores on tests of both verbal and general ability (Mol & Neuman, 2014).

Therefore, the second part of our model argues for greater psychological proximity to other adults or peers to support children's access to print. Young children especially need an adult or more capable peer to read to them and to convey the sheer pleasures of reading together. Consequently, our next step in developing our intervention was to establish a book distribution program that might address these critical features. To do so, we turned to the corporate responsibility office of JetBlue Airways, a company that was already involved in book distribution programs. Our collaboration allowed us to examine our theory-driven assumptions regarding access to print.

Reaching Families Where They Are

Recognizing the seasonal variations (e.g., summer learning slide) and the limited opportunities for access to low-income children, we planned our book distribution program for the summer months. We realized that it was imperative to "reach people where they are" (Neuman & Knapcyzk, in press), to enhance the physical access to books in places where people were most likely to congregate within the neighborhoods. Our working hypothesis was that close physical proximity might create a demand to access books and to use them.

Working with their creative partners, JetBlue came up with an innovative idea—to place carefully wrapped books in a vending machine that could both dispense and track book use. In these machines, which were located throughout the city (in this case, Detroit), children's books, generously provided by Random House, were placed in slots by age ranges (birth through teen). All books were available free of charge. The machines worked like a snack machine, in that an individual could review the selections, press a button for the desired title, and receive the product, in this case, a book. See Figure 12.1 for an example of a typical machine.

The collaborative team at Random House selected book titles that represented a variety of genres, including fiction and nonfiction with multicultural

FIGURE 12.1. A vending machine for books.

themes, and authors. Selections were to be changed every 2 weeks to encourage people to return books in a timely manner.

Our research team used a number of methods to examine book access (Neuman & Knapczyk, in press). For example, we conducted brief interviews with participants who used the machines and observed traffic patterns. We reviewed the particular book selections made throughout the summer. At the same time, we noticed that in two of the locations located close by their homes, parents and their children would regularly visit the machines, whereas for two of the other locations, one would need a car in order to visit more regularly. Furthermore, in one of the nearby locations, children in the child-care center would also visit the machines on a regular basis. Based on how the vending machines were used, we were able to create a four-cell chart, taking advantage of the natural variations in both child-care centers' use of the machine (e.g., weekly visits or not), and parents' use of the machine (e.g., whether they accessed books or not). For example, children who visited the vending machines in child care and independently visited with their parents or grandparents were identified as receiving high adult support; those that neither visited when they were in child care nor with their parent or guardian were identified as low adult support. The two groups in between represented either one or the other type of support.

Taking advantage of this natural experiment, we created measures of the Title Recognition Test, based on West and Stanovich's model (West, Stanovich, & Mitchell, 1993), to determine if the presence and use of the machines might enhance adult and child's exposure to print (see Figure 12.2).

True to our prediction, children who had the highest adult support were able to recognize more book titles than the other three groups. This group

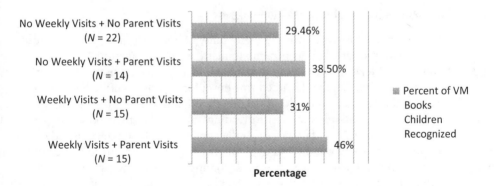

FIGURE 12.2. Percentage of vending machine books recognized by children (using the Title Recognition Test).

recognized almost half of the book titles in contrast to those children who received the lowest adult support, who identified approximately a quarter of the titles. Children who had at least one type of support (either from the center or home) were able to identify more books than those who had none.

Considering the possible trajectory of reading skill development, it suggests that greater exposure to print might create a "thirst" for reading that is later tied to reading proficiency. Mol and Bus (2011), for example, in a meta-analysis of 99 studies of print exposure, argue for a spiral of causality: Because of their continual exposure to print, children read more and comprehend better and improve more with each year of education. In their analysis, print exposure for preschool and kindergarten children accounted for 12% of the variance in oral-language skills, reaching as high as 34% for students at college age.

Children become exposed to print, therefore, not merely through its physical proximity, which has been and remains an important limitation of many book distribution programs (Neuman, 2017). People matter, and it is the social bond that connects the two and makes reading meaningful to young children. These adults act as models, demonstrating to children through their actions that reading is important (Price, van Kleeck, & Huberty, 2009). Our results indicated that those children who had the support of both parents and teachers seemed to thrive and slightly gain throughout the summer; those who did not, or who had less support, had fewer opportunities to make gains. In this respect, our work has highlighted both the strengths and the limitations of our theoretical model. It suggests that the provision of one side of the equation only is insufficient; rather, both are necessary. Without access to books, one cannot read to children; absent an adult presence, children cannot be read to. Together, physical and psychological supports are critical to enhance children's opportunities to learn to read.

Implications for Greater Access to Books

As our interviews revealed, the close proximity of books to where people were likely to gather clearly had its benefits to many in these communities. In only 8 weeks, over 64,000 books were distributed, many to repeat users. Based on our conversations, families regarded this novel form of distributing books as a welcome contribution to the local neighborhood and a necessary resource to help spark their children's interest in reading and develop their skills. At the same time, while 60% of families generally appreciated these books (based on our interviews), there was a substantial number of people (40%) who chose not to access books. Their primary reason, according to our interviews, was a lack of interest in reading. In other words, the physical proximity of books did not convert nonreaders into readers, suggesting that changes in the ecological environment alone may be insufficient to motivate those who do not like to read.

This raises questions for further consideration and analysis. Key among them is: How do we create a reading culture in neighborhood contexts that have been bereft of books? And possibly because of these structural inequities, how do we support communities in which many members have a limited exposure to print? Given that a family's provisions for reading, manifested by a large home library as shown in a study of 27 nations (Evans, Kelley, Sikora, & Treiman, 2010), seems to have a profound influence on children's educational attainment, how do we generate greater interest among those children and families who show little interest in reading?

Our analysis of the book selections among those who did use the vending machines may provide some initial clues (see top choices in Table 12.3). People selected books on topics that were familiar, largely through screen-based media. Characters and themes in these books were predictable, easier to access, and likely to be more entertaining than some of the unknown titles in children's literature. Based on people's prior knowledge of these story lines, one could even imagine that they could lead to livelier interactive readings, providing an easier entry point for those who would otherwise be disinclined to read. In addition, nonfiction books that featured both modern and historical figures in African American culture were among the most popular. In brief interviews, parents and grandparents expressed a desire to celebrate their culture and important milestones in their history to their young children.

Yet books linked to screen-based media are rarely, if ever, on recommended book lists for parents to read to their children (Trelease, 2013). Rather, they are often regarded as poor imitations of original stories, lacking any literary merit or quality of language. Nevertheless, they may serve to kindle an initial interest in reading, which could later motivate individuals to engage with a broader set of topics. We have some initial evidence to support this observation. Along with these types of books, readers also selected more serious topics that focused on prideful moments in black history and prominent black historical and modern figures, key topics that they wanted to share with their children.

Traditionally, educators have curated libraries, both in schools and classrooms, on the basis of "quality" or what might be considered by librarians or curriculum leaders to be the most appropriate for children. Rarely, however, have we queried the children themselves about what interests them and what motivates them to read. By not doing so, we may have missed the opportunity to curate libraries based on the cultural milieu of the children we work with. Taking account of their interests might support a greater motivation to read and a better use of books for goal-directed activities.

Our analysis indicated that children's books were highly valued in this community. Evidence for this claim was demonstrated throughout this study in several highly visible ways: by the sheer volume of use, with more than 64,000 books selected from five machines over an 8-week period, by the lines of adults and children waiting to select their favorite books, and by the number of books selected for children at all age ranges, from birth through the teenage years.

TABLE 12.3. Type of Books Distributed

Age range (years)	Distribution (total books)
0–3	18,605
4–5	15,350
6–9	16,323
10–14	14,157
Spanish titles	1,030 (available at only one location)
Multicultural titles	21,020
Book genre	
Fiction	70.5%
Nonfiction	24.5%
Other (games, puzzles)	5.0%
Book selection	
Fiction book titles based on movies or TV	64%
Fiction book title with main character of color/minority status	24%
Most popular titles in fiction	
Maze Runner (movie)	15%
Olaf! (movie)	9%
I Love My Mami! (TV)	7%
The Spectacular Now! (movie)	5%
Diary of a Wimpy Kid (movie)	5%
Show Your Colors (movie/TV)	3%
Under the Blood-Red Sun (movie)	2%
Most popular titles in nonfiction	
Barack Obama	8%
Escape North: Harriet Tubman	6%
145th Street	6%
Jackie Robinson	6%
Taking Flight	2%
Bud, Not Buddy!	1%
Teenie	1%
Ballerina Dreams	1%

Furthermore, evidence from our surveys indicated that contrary to expectations, it was not adults' educational status that drove their interest in using the machines but their perceptions of the value of reading books to young children. These families wanted to own books and valued time spent reading to their children.

This modest intervention, therefore, begins to challenge the all-too-common ideology that low-income parents devalue activities that are associated with early school success. For example, in reporting a recent Pew Research Center (2015) survey on parenting, a journalist found that families who suffer financial instability are less likely to read to their young children (33%) than the more affluent who have graduated from college (71%), and remarked that class differences may account for such findings (Miller, 2015). Middle-class parents are more likely to engage their young children in a wide array of extracurricular activities even before formal schooling begins, far more than low-income parents do. Nevertheless, what is rarely challenged in these analyses is the opportunity to learn: If poor families had more access to these extracurricular activities and an abundance of children's books at their disposal, would this gap be narrowed?

Obviously, our research can only raise such questions not definitively answer them. However, it does suggest that despite their limitations in education, (resulting from residential segregation which has turned into de facto school segregation (Lareau & Goyette, 2014), these families were more likely to recognize children's book titles and read more frequently with their children. In fact, the vending machines became a focal point of conversation between parents and children, creating opportunities for them to discuss their favorite topics and reportedly learn more about children's interests. Similarly, children would often point out the books they preferred and ask more questions. These interactions and reading-aloud practices are strongly associated with growth in vocabulary and background knowledge (Hirsch, 2006), key essentials in early literacy development. Interestingly, the families didn't seem to treat the intervention as a novelty in which over time they would lose interest. Although it was a short-term experiment—8 weeks during the summer months—there was no evidence of a decline in activity throughout the intervention. In fact, to the contrary, as parents became more confident in using the machines, activity increased; furthermore, in August with school looming ahead, waiting lines for books began to grow.

Lessons Learned

Although it is clear that the book vending machines were somewhat novel and original, other factors seemed to distinguish this method of book distribution from other programs. First and perhaps most important, the book program was designed to *reach families where they are,* bringing books in close physical proximity to where families engaged in their daily activities. Media studies (Neuman, 1995), for example, have shown that people are likely to engage in a new activity when it is close by; a newspaper is likely to be picked up if it is placed next to a diner drinking coffee; a TV will be turned on at night if it is in the bedroom. Furthermore, these activities are likely to become routinized over time. In contrast, the typical way to access books puts the burden on families to attend special events, evening programs, or workshops to buy or purchase them (Lindsay, 2010). Second, unlike other programs, our approach to book distributions gave parents a sense of agency, providing parents and children with a wide assortment from which to choose. In our observations, we found parents spending considerable time making selections, discussing different titles and topics with their children. Third, the program gave parents and children opportunities to select age-appropriate titles from birth through the teenage years. And fourth, parents and children could select as many books as they wished. As our data show, there were many repeat customers over the course of the intervention period.

Since the results of our studies are always contextualized within our community settings, they therefore cannot easily be generalized to the larger population. However, we can say that our work provides a vivid counterpoint to the view that low-income parents are less inclined to be interested in their children's early education. Our results challenge this often accepted view, and offer an alternative scenario, recognizing that providing access to resources— reaching families where they are—may be a key enabler of parent engagement and children's early literacy development.

CONCLUSION: EVERY CHILD A READER

Children need books in order to thrive in learning to read. In the earliest years, especially, children should not be given donated books or tattered and worn titles purchased at garage sales. Rather, specific factors—having a large quantity of titles of different age levels and genres accessible—seem to ensure that books will be used to their full potential.

Features of Quality Access to Books in Early Childhood

A Large Supply

There is no current estimate of the number of books in children's homes that is ideal. However, according to the American Library Association, early childhood classrooms should include single and multiple copies of about 300 book titles for young children in every classroom. Although other estimates may be somewhat more conservative, most research suggests that at least five to eight books per child is necessary to support choice and motivation to read.

A Wide Variety

Children need exposure to a wide variety of topics and genres. Some of these books may be board books with simple concepts that emphasize letter labeling and extended use of vocabulary, and some should be more challenging. In homes and classrooms, it may be worth experimenting with a core collection and a revolving collection. A core collection could contain favorite books that parents and children might wish to return to on a regular basis. The revolving collection, on the other hand, could contain a different group of books offering fresh perspectives that children could look forward to reading every few weeks. These revolving collections can include topics of interest to children, including the changing seasons and special holidays.

Different Genres

Children also need to be exposed to a range of language topics, genres, and points of view that reflect the diverse and multicultural nature of our society. Children should have access to books in which they can see themselves and others like them in the following genres:

- *Traditional stories:* Familiar stories that are found in every culture, including fables, folk tales, myths, and legends.
- *Information books:* Books that provide accurate and authentic information.
- *Fantasy:* Stories that contain make-believe characters and settings that spark children's imaginations.
- *Concept books:* Simple picture-labeling books that feature one or two words that highlight selective concepts.
- *Alphabet books and sound books:* books that focus on individual letter names and alliterative stories that emphasize similarities in beginning sounds.
- *Predictable books:* Books with common rhymes, rhythms, and songs that are highly memorable to children.

In summary, thanks to years of research we now have a better understanding of how children become literacy learners. These studies suggest that although many activities are thought to contribute to literacy development, no single activity is as central to young children's literacy as having access to books. It is during the earliest years that children learn to construct texts and make connections between oral language, reading, and writing. However, many children currently live in book deserts with limited opportunities to learn from print. Closing the "book gap" by providing greater access to print, therefore, may represent a key factor for improving reading achievement for all children.

REFERENCES

Biemiller, A., & Boote, C. (2006). An effective method for building meaning vocabulary in primary grades. *Journal of Educational Psychology, 98*(1), 44–62.

Bischoff, K., & Reardon, S. (2014). Residential segregation by income, 1970–2009. In J.

Logan (Ed.), *Diversity and disparities: America enters a new century* (pp. 208–233). New York: Russell Sage Foundation.

Bus, A., Van IJzendoorn, M., & Pellegrini, A. (1995). Joint book reading makes for success in learning to read: A meta-analysis on intergenerational transmission of literacy. *Review of Educational Research, 65,* 1–21.

Entwisle, D., Alexander, K., & Olson, L. (2014). *The long shadow: Family background, disadvnataged urban youth, and the transition to adulthood.* New York: Russell Sage Foundation.

Evans, M., Kelley, J., Sikora, J., & Treiman, D. (2010). Family scholarly culture and educational success: Books and schooling in 27 countries. *Research in Social Stratification and Mobility, 28,* 171–197.

Fernald, A., & Weisleder, A. (2011). Early language experience is vital to developing fluency in understanding. In S. B. Neuman & D. Dickinson (Eds.), *Handbook of early literacy research* (Vol. 3, pp. 3–19). New York: Guilford Press.

Gump, G. (1975). Ecological psychology and children. In E. M. Hetherington (Ed.), *Review of child development research* (Vol. 5, pp. 75–126). Chicago: University of Chicago Press.

Hart, B., & Risley, T. (1995). *Meaningful differences.* Baltimore: Brookes.

Hirsch, E. D. (2006). *The knowledge deficit: Closing the shocking educational gap.* Boston: Houghton-Mifflin.

Hoff, E. (2006). How social contexts support and shape language development. *Developmental Review, 26,* 55–88.

Lareau, A., & Goyette, K. (Eds.). (2014). *Choosing homes, choosing schools.* New York: Russell Sage Foundation.

Lawrence, J., Crosson, A., Pare-Blagoev, E. J., & Snow, C. (2015). Word Generation randomized trial: Discussion mediates the impact of program treatment on academic word learning. *American Educational Research Journal, 52*(4), 750–786.

Lindsay, J. (2010). *Children's access to print material and education-related outcomes: Findings from a meta-analytic review.* Naperville, IL: Learning Points Associates.

Massey, D. (2007). *Categorically unequal.* New York: Russell Sage Foundation.

Miller, C. (2015, December 17). Class difference in child rearing are on the rise. *New York Times,* p. 26.

Mol, S., & Bus, A. (2011). To read or not to read: A meta-analysis of print exposure from infancy to early adulthood. *Psychological Bulletin, 137,* 267–296.

Mol, S., Bus, A., & deJong, M. (2009). Interactive book reading in early education: A tool to stimulate print knowledge as well as oral language. *Review of Educational Research, 79*(2), 979–1007.

Mol, S., & Neuman, S. B. (2014). Sharing information books with kindergartners: The role of parents' extra-textual talk and socio-economic status. *Early Childhood Research Quarterly, 29,* 399–410.

Morrow, L., & Weinstein, C. (1986). Encouraging voluntary reading: The impact of a literature program on children's use of library centers. *Reading Research Quarterly, 21,* 330–346.

Mullis, I., Martin, M., Foy, P., & Drucker, K. (2012). *PIRLS 2011 international results in reading.* Chestnut Hill, MA: TIMSS and PIRLS International Study Center.

Neuman, S. B. (1995). *Literacy in the television age.* Norwood, NJ: Ablex.

Neuman, S. B. (1999). Books make a difference: A study of access to literacy. *Reading Research Quarterly, 34,* 286–312.

Neuman, S. B. (2017). The information book flood: Is additional exposure enough to support early literacy development? *Elementary School Journal, 118,* 1–27.

Neuman, S. B., & Carta, J. (2011). Advancing the measurement of quality for early childhood programs that support early language and literacy development. In M. Zaslow, I. Martinez-Beck, K. Tout, & K. Halle (Eds.), *Quality measurement in early childhood settings* (pp. 220–255). Baltimore: Brookes.

Neuman, S. B., & Celano, D. (2001). Access to print in low-income and middle-income communities: An ecological study of four neighborhoods. *Reading Research Quarterly, 36*(1), 8–26.

Neuman, S. B., & Kaefer, T. (in press). Developing low-income children's vocabulary and content knowledge through a shared book reading program. *Contemporary Educational Psychology, 52,* 15–24.

Neuman, S. B., & Knapczyk, J. (in press). Reaching families where they are: Examining an innovative book distribution program. *Urban Education.*

Neuman, S. B., & Moland, N. (2016). Book deserts: The consequences of income segregation on children's access to books. *Urban Education, 51*(6), 1–22.

Neuman, S. B., & Roskos, K. (1992). Literacy objects as cultural tools: Effects on children's literacy behaviors in play. *Reading Research Quarterly, 27,* 202–225.

Pappas, C. (1991). Young children's strategies in learning the "book language" of information books. *Discourse Processes, 14,* 203–225.

Pew Research Center. (2015). *Parenting in America: Outlook, worries, aspirations are strongly linked to financial situation.* Washington DC: Pew Research Center.

Price, L., van Kleeck, A., & Huberty, C. (2009). Talk during book sharing between parents and preschool children: A comparison between storybook and expository book conditions. *Reading Research Quarterly, 44*(2), 171–194.

Quinn, D., Cooc, N., McIntyre, J., & Gomez, C. (2016). Seasonal dynamics of academic achievement inequality by socioeconomic status and race/ethnicity: Updating and extending past research with new national data. *Educational Researcher, 45*(8), 443–453.

Snow, C., Tabors, P., Nicholson, P., & Kurland, B. (1995). SHELL: Oral language and early literacy skills in kindergarten and first-grade children. *Journal of Research in Childhood Education, 10,* 37–48.

Tharp, R., & Gallimore, R. (1988). *Rousing minds to life.* Cambridge, UK: Cambridge University Press.

Trelease, J. (2013). *The read-aloud handbook* (7th ed.). New York: Penguin.

Vukelich, C. (1994). Effects of play interventions on young children's reading of environmental print. *Early Childhood Research Quarterly, 9,* 153–170.

Vygotsky, L. S. (1978). *Mind in society: The development of higher psychological processes* (M. Cole, V. John-Steiner, S. Scribner, & E. Souberman, Trans.). Cambridge, MA: Harvard University Press.

West, R., Stanovich, K., & Mitchell, H. (1993). Reading in the real world and its correlates. *Reading Research Quarterly, 28,* 34–50.

Whitehurst, G., Arnold, D., Epstein, J., Angell, A., Smith, M., & Fischel, J. (1994). A picture book reading intervention in day care and home for children from low-income families. *Developmental Psychology, 30,* 679–689.

Pivotal Research in Early Literacy
Lessons Learned and a Call to Action

Heidi Anne E. Mesmer
and M. M. Rose-McCully

> Those who do not remember the past are condemned to
> repeat it.
> —GEORGE SANTAYANA (1905, p. 284)

In no area is Santayana's often-cited quote truer than in the area of literacy education. Trends in literacy education have ebbed and flowed across the decades often at breakneck speed without a backward glance in the rearview mirror. Thus, the contents within this volume provide the field with an opportunity to closely inspect the impact of many different studies throughout a number of areas in early literacy education and to carry forward some of the lessons learned. In truth, the work of the pivotal theorists and researchers cited in these chapters has allowed us to identify both the patterns that have improved the lives of young children and the pitfalls that may have had less than optimal effects. By pausing and taking a "macro" view of how and why certain ideas, studies, and theories became pivotal we can understand current studies that are becoming pivotal and we can even chart a course for the types of studies that we need in the future. The purpose of this afterword will be to (1) identify the big messages in early literacy learning that emerge across studies, (2) describe the ways that studies became pivotal, and (3) identify the conditions in which pivotal research can take place in the future.

PIVOTAL DEFINED

Prior to discussing pivotal research we examine the word *pivotal* and its etymology and history as a possible way to enlighten our discussion. The first usage of the word *pivot* dates back to the early 1600s, and is an Old French noun meaning "hinge pin." In the early 1800s, *pivot* was first used in a figurative sense to indicate a "central point" around which a structure moved. By the mid-1800s, *pivot* was denominalized, and common usage included *pivot* as the verb form and *pivotal* as the adjective form of the word (Pivot, n.d.). Modern usage of the noun *pivot* is tied to its first usage: a pin or point on which something rests and turns. The verb *to pivot* means "to turn (on)," and the adjective *pivotal* means "of vital or critical importance" (Pivotal, n.d.).

Pivotal research is research of vital importance that shifts or turns the current academic conversation. Pivotal research can alter the way that we think about a whole field of study (e.g., the shift from reading readiness to emergent literacy) or can alter the way we approach one aspect within a field (e.g., academics with play not academics versus play). Pivotal research can point a field of study in a previously undiscovered direction (e.g., phonological awareness, emergent literacy) and can identify an approach that combines aspects of current and previous conversations in forming a new direction (e.g., Stanovich, 1980).

Research is a process. While "knowing" is the goal, that goal is ultimately unattainable. There is no definitive end to research. Every research study adds more data to the collective pool of knowledge, but the pool will never be full. There will always be something that is missing, an idea left to discover. What makes research pivotal is that it leaves a mark on the field, and the best research creates a "pivot," a hinge upon which many other ideas, theories, and studies rest. While time may change the way that pivotal pieces of research are viewed or interpreted, they leave an indelible imprint that pivots the conversation of the time and informs the conversations of the future.

LESSONS LEARNED ABOUT EARLY LITERACY
LEARNING AND INSTRUCTION

Clear themes about early literacy learning emerge from the broad spectrum of studies described in this volume. These themes ground what we currently know about early literacy learning and are supported by this pivotal work and other conceptual articles, monographs, and books. Many of these broad themes constitute lessons learned and carried forward, ideas that are so powerful and so well-supported by research that it is very difficult to imagine turning away from them. Thus, the purpose of this section is to, in a sense, identify the pivots, the hinge pins fashioned from studies examined here and, in so doing, identify stable structures upon which new works may rest. The four themes address the following: (1) the concept of emergent literacy; (2) the centrality of alphabetic and language knowledge; (3) the role of motivation, play, self-regulation, and other behavioral skills; and (4) the significance of the home in literacy development.

Young Children Are Emerging as Literate Humans

There are few hinge pins or pivotal concepts that have been more influential than the concept of emergent literacy. This paradigm-shifting notion revolutionized perspectives about literacy learning. During the first half of the 20th century, the dominant theory dictating a child's reading readiness emphasized a child's biological maturation, or age, to determine when a child should first be exposed to reading. The reading-readiness model emphasized postponing reading and teaching reading until a child reached kindergarten or first grade. Leading developmental psychologists influenced this idea. Gesell's Maturational theory (1925) detailed the fixed sequences in development and opposed teaching children skills ahead of their developmental schedule (e.g., crawling before walking and reading before writing). Educators Morphett and Washburne (1931) determined that the appropriate age to begin reading instruction was when the child had attained the mental age of 6 years and 6 months. These ideas remained highly influential through the mid-1960s, and led to the belief that success in reading resulted from holding back on reading instruction until the latter half of first grade, and that failure in reading was, in part, due to beginning reading instruction too early.

By the late 1960s and 1970s, researchers began to observe that student reading success was not dependent on a child's age or perceived reading readiness but on a child's exposure to and interest in reading and writing or direct literacy instruction at a younger age (e.g., Clay, 1966; Durkin, 1966; Read, 1975; Teale & Sulzby, 1986). (See Schickedanz, Chapter 3, and Teale, Hoffman, Whittingham, and Paciga, Chapter 8, this volume.) The term *emergent literacy* was coined by New Zealand researcher Marie Clay (1966) in her doctoral dissertation. Clay's well-known Reading Recovery model focused on message getting (reading) and message sending (writing) as problem-solving activities for students who had not achieved satisfactory levels of reading after their first year of instruction. While Clay's work focused on emergent literacy after the first year of schooling, Teale and Sulzby's edited work (1986) focused on emergent literacy as a process of learning from birth, with an emphasis on "becoming" literate.

As the concept of "becoming literate" gained momentum, researchers began to zero in on the broader aspects of literacy instruction that include language development, listening comprehension, invented spelling, pretend reading, literate play, and alphabet learning, rather than reading instruction (e.g., decoding and comprehending text). Research began to examine literacy instruction prior to kindergarten and first grade, with an emphasis on both preschool and at-home education.

Thus, the field now widely accepts that children start their journey toward becoming literate at birth. From birth, they absorb the world around them by listening to the vocabulary of the people speaking and observing the actions of the people they see. They acquire vocabulary, syntax, and literacy habits from the adults who surround them and strive to emulate those adults through miming and mimicking. Children seek adult help in the process of understanding the world presented to them and both absorb and elicit information about reading and writing. Note that although Blair's pivotal 2002 piece cited by Hinden in Chapter 7 uses the word *readiness*, Blair takes a much more flexible view of the role of executive skills and self-regulation than Morphett and Washburne (1931). That said, as Blair's call for attention to self-regulation became popularized, it is important that we do not fall into the trap of labeling some children "ready" for literacy instruction, as evidenced by behavioral measures, and other children "not ready."

Nonnegotiables: Alphabetic Knowledge, Phonological Awareness, and Language Development

A second pivot upon which literacy development hinges is a set of language skills that undergird acquisition. To become fluent readers who understand text, young children need to develop competencies and insights about the alphabetic code and the meaning of language in preschool and earlier (see Masek, Chapter 1; Invernizzi and Buckrop, Chapter 4; Cassano, Chapter 5; and Collins, Chapter 9, this volume). Although it seems quite obvious that alphabetic language is integral to the ability to read, proponents of whole language era raised questions about how much it was actually used within word recognition. As Adams (1990) reminded the field, automaticity with letters and sounds is essential, and the ability to name letters predicts future reading ability better than any other metric (see Invernizzi and Buckrop, Chapter 4, this volume). Share (1995) further established that learning the "code" enabled children to self-teach new words, which becomes evident when a child pieces together a word that he has never read before. In a kindergarten classroom recently, we watched this process unfold as children were asked to figure out how to read the words *in, it,* and *is.* One little boy blended *it* and *in* together but puzzled over *is.* "Ice? /i/ /s?/ (unvoiced)? *Is.* That's it. *Is,*" he said as he applied his knowledge of letters and sounds. He was using code knowledge to self-teach, illustrating precisely the self-teaching hypothesis. As Invernizzi and Buckrop detail, there were crucial findings about alphabetic knowledge including that first, children acquire this knowledge both formally and informally (e.g., Mason, 1980) and that second, they use letter names to learn letter sounds (Treiman, Tincoff,

Rodriguez, Mouzaki, & Francis, 1998), a finding demonstrated causally by Share (2004).

Possessing letter–sound knowledge is no guarantee of literacy success; it is necessary but not sufficient, and this collection of pivotal studies firmly establishes that drilling the alphabet will lead to nothing but a group of trained responses happily delivered by children hoping to please adults. Invernizzi and Buckrop liken the current benchmarks for the number of letters need for future success to a veritable Ouija board—alphabet voodoo for literacy fortune-telling. They remind us of the importance of acquiring the alphabetic principle, the understanding that the alphabet functions as a symbol system for speech sounds.

However, alphabetic knowledge can and will be inert if children are not continually encouraged to use and apply that knowledge. The entire Teale and Sulzby (1986) volume reflects the many ways that children can be shown how to use letter–sound information in authentic ways. Schickendanz in Chapter 3 examines one of the most important applications of letter–sound knowledge: writing. Early literacy instruction must include name writing, expressive writing, shared writing, and interactive writing. The Read (1975) study, more than any other, illustrates the precise ways that children gradually acquire and use the various aspects of English orthography through integrating their phonemic awareness and letter–sound knowledge as they write for their own creative purposes.

In terms of acquiring literacy in an alphabetic system, the breakout finding of the 1990s was in the area of phonological awareness (PA), a voluminous body of work that Cassano in Chapter 5 boiled down to three studies that advanced the field in very specific ways: Juel (1988); Liberman, Shankweiler, Fisher, and Carter (1974); and Lundberg, Frost, and Peterson (1988). Lundberg, et al. (1988) showed that systematic PA instruction prior to traditional literacy instruction with letters and words influenced children's receptiveness to phonics instruction and future literacy achievement. Juel's landmark 1988 study indicated that an absence of phonemic awareness characterized struggling first grade readers, who had an 88% likelihood of continuing to struggle in the fourth grade. The Liberman et al. (1974) study documented the development of phonological knowledge proceeding from rhyme awareness to phoneme awareness. Together these and a host of studies that followed attested to the importance of developing children's sensitivity to phonemes through language play, picture sorts, and shared readings.

A final area in which advancements have been made is in the area of language and vocabulary development (discussed in Masek, Chapter 1, and Collins, Chapter 9, this volume). Children who become skilled comprehenders, and who are able to understand and extend ideas in books in later grades, have well-developed expressive and receptive vocabularies and language skills. The vehicle for the advancement of child language is interaction between the adult and child focusing on both the quantity and quality of words. The Hart and Risley (1995) study demonstrated the impact of high quantities of adult language on young children and their expressive vocabularies in kindergarten, and Pan, Rowe, Singer, and Snow (2005) showed that the variety or quality of the words that adults used with young children was influential. Together these studies established the importance of parents and caregivers interacting with young children frequently, supportively, and with a rich variety of words. Whitehurst, Falco, Lonigan, Fischel, DeBaryshe, Valdez-Menchaca, and Caulfield (1998), in a breakthrough study that laid the groundwork for the dialogic reading approach, experimentally demonstrated that parents who used evocative and interactive styles to read books improved their children's expressive vocabularies. In the Whitehurst et al. (1998) study, adults used praise, open-ended questions, modeling, and the elaboration of their child's utterances during storybook reading in ways that advanced language learning. Dickinson and Smith's (1994) work supported this theme because they found that a didactic–interactional style of storybook reading had the biggest impact on child language. Thus, the literature suggested that adults must simultaneously model language for children and also evoke it from them in interactive ways.

To summarize, much pivotal research supports the importance of alphabetic knowledge, PA, and language learning, and underscores the necessity of not only purposeful teaching but also highly engaging interactions that honor the child's intrinsic motivations to learn within his or her environment.

Motivation, Play, Self-Regulation, and Behavioral Skills Mediate Literacy Learning

Of late, there appears to be a pitting of academics against play in early childhood classrooms, a sort of either/or mentality suggesting that classrooms can be either responsive to children's social–emotional needs or focused on their literacy learning. In Chapter 8, Teale and colleagues describe the historical context for the view that the early childhood "play" years were distinct from the "formal learning" (or reading) years. A review of the literature documents that this is not the case. Literacy learning does not occur in a vacuum. Rand and Morrow in Chapter 10 remind us not to forget that child-centered curricula in which play is integrated actually strengthens the capacity for literacy learning. Pellegrini's (1985) pivotal literature review connected play to literacy learning by summarizing the research that showed how symbolic play improves decontextualized language and narrative skills that support later comprehension. Neuman and Roskos (1990) and Morrow and Rand (1991) both applied this crucial finding to educational environments in which they instructed teachers in *how* to incorporate play into literacy instruction. They also documented the ways that children used play in literate ways. These pivotal studies firmly showed that play is indeed children's literacy work.

Hinden further documents the ways that the nonacademic aspects of child development affect the development of literacy behaviors (Blair, 2002; Guthrie & Wigfield, 2000; Spira, Bracken, & Fischel, 2005). In a sense, motivation, self-regulation, social competency, and other behavioral skills are the mediators of literacy development that actually can affect children's development (Spira et al., 2005). Early childhood environments must help children to develop socially, emotionally, and psychologically as well as cognitively.

School Will Always Be an Influential Context for Literacy Learning

Frequently, educational research takes a compensatory perspective with respect to parents and home environments, suggesting that parents need to be coached or their lack of awareness of instructional strategies compensated for. This is especially true of low-income parents. Heath's (1983) powerful ethnography countered this assumption with detailed accounts of how parents, grandparents, and other caregivers used literacy in the communities of Roadville and Trackton. As innovative as Heath's work was, researchers, as early as 1949 (Almy) and the 1960s (Durkin, 1966; Hildreth, 1963) also recognized the power of parents as teachers. Both Durkin (1966) and Almy (1949) interviewed parents and learned that children essentially elicited knowledge from their parents about how the literate world worked. Hildreth recounted a story of a young child begging his parents to teach him how to write his name and his subversive parents defying the directions of the educational establishment in agreeing to do so. A bountiful trove of research on storybook reading reinforces the message that the nature of parents' talk influences children in powerful and long-lasting ways. In particular, parents who use a wide range of words, praise their children, elaborate and extend utterances, and ask open-ended questions contribute to their children's ultimate literacy learning (Pan et al., 2005; Whitehurst et al., 1988).

Children and families must be met "where they are," but the impact of the family as a literacy teacher must never be underestimated. This is especially true of English bilinguals, as Roberts in Chapter 2 emphasizes that a child's first language influences the development of a second language (Willig, 1985). Programs that partner with parents in respectful ways are more likely to capitalize on the positive influences of the home environment.

LESSONS LEARNED ABOUT HOW AND WHY WORKS BECOME "PIVOTAL"

As Collins in Chapter 9 aptly reminds us, pivotal research often deals with asking "the right question at the right time," and it is worth considering how the period in which the research takes place shapes questions. A volume of this sort not only offers the field the opportunity to take stock of the knowledge and findings of pivotal research, but also provides an opportunity to consider the forces acting upon the larger sociocultural context that produces pivotal studies. By examining how works became pivotal we can heed Santayana's warning and avoid patterns that negatively influenced children in the past.

Sociopolitical Events Shape the Impact of Works That Become "Pivotal"

Many authors in this volume remind us that sociopolitical events make the field more receptive to certain ideas. This is clear in Roberts, Chapter 2; Invernizzi and Buckrop, Chapter 4; Teale et al., Chapter 8; and Neuman and Celano, Chapter 12. The landmark decision in Brown vs. the Board of Education (1954) and the ensuing Civil Rights Act of 1964 had profound effects on education in the United States, as it made integrated schooling integral to fulfillment of the constitutional rights of all students. The Civil Rights movement was a veritable tipping point that led to funding mechanisms like the Elementary and Secondary Education Act (ESEA) of 1965 (commonly referred to as Title I). In terms of early literacy education, the 1965 launching of Head Start, a part of President Johnson's "War on Poverty," also had a profound influence on early childhood education.

Essentially, as state- and federally funded preschool programs popped up across the nation, teachers and researchers began to ask questions about curricula, classroom organization, and activities, thereby prompting a cascade of studies. Early on, these studies emphasized literacy development in preschoolers using exploratory, center-based approaches with less structure and teacher direction (e.g., Cochran-Smith, 1984; Morrow & Rand, 1991; Neuman & Roskos, 1990; Teale & Sulzby, 1986). Research on preschool picture book reading and on adult talk virtually exploded during this time, as evidenced by the many pivotal studies focusing on this act (Bus, van IJzendoorn, & Pellegrini, 1996; Dickinson & Smith, 1994; Pan et al., 2005; Sénéchal, Lefevre, Thomas, & Daley, 1998; Whitehurst et al., 1998).

In 2002, Early Reading First, a program created by the No Child Left Behind Act, was launched to address the academic needs of children from low-income families who were entering kindergarten without the necessary literacy skills. That same year, the National Early Literacy Panel was convened to synthesize the research base supporting high-quality practices in early childhood classrooms (Shanahan & Lonigan, 2010). As a result of this funding, early childhood programs became more academic in nature, providing instruction in letters and other preliteracy skills. Nonetheless, in 2005, McGill-Franzen's study revealed that federally funded preschool programs like Head Start were eschewing any kind of alphabet instruction at the same time that children in middle class homes and private preschools were the recipients of such instruction. Today, alphabet instruction is more prevalent in early childhood classrooms, but the field struggles to find the optimal balance between academic demands and social–emotional development.

Highly Influential Thinkers

Throughout the 20th century, a handful of educators, psychologists, and linguists have had a profound effect on the direction of education and educational research in the United States, and have influenced what became pivotal in many other fields as well. In this volume, a group of seminal thinkers have been consistently cited: Chomsky (1968) Morphett and Washborn (1931), Piaget (1936) and Vygotsky (1962). Chomsky (1965) theorized that humans had an innate language acquisition device that predisposed them to language in ways that differentiated them from others in the animal kingdom. The reverberations of this thinking were felt in the many education studies in the 1960s and 1970s that pointed to naturalistic explanations in education. The theme can be seen in the works of Mason (1980), Cochran-Smith (1984), Heath (1983), and Krashen (1982). Gesell's (1925) maturation theory in a sense fueled Morphett and Washborne's (1931) far-reaching (and detrimental) theory regarding the developmentally appropriate age to start teaching reading (6 years, 6 months). Fortunately a number of works, including Almy (1949), Hildreth (1936), and most obviously Durkin (1966), overturned this theory.

Piaget (1957) introduced the concept of constructivism, which shifted educational research in the direction of more child-centered approaches emphasizing the construction of knowledge at developmental junctures, a theory obvious in the work of Mason (1980) and Liberman et al. (1974). Perhaps more than any other educational research, Vygotsky (1977) and his zone of proximal development theory influenced what became pivotal in education and beyond. The Soviet-born Vygotsky suggested that learning was constructed and mediated by social interaction, and it took its first popular hold in the western world in 1978 with the publication of *Mind in Society*. Soon educators began to extract from Piaget's and Vygotsky's work simplified generalizations about children as "little scientists" capable of significantly generating their own development. As the field examines pivotal early literacy, it is important to remember that other far-reaching "pivotal" studies outside the field of education have played a role in what we consider to be influential.

Close Observations and Field Work Vertically Advance the Field

A striking characteristic of the most important and influential research in early literacy is that much of it stemmed from researchers who closely watched children and questioned the thinking of the time. Shirley Brice Heath's (1983) landmark study of the ways that families constructed literacy in working class white and black families powerfully revealed the influence of culture. Cochran-Smith's (1984) impressive 18-month observational study of storybook readings in preschools laid the foundation for understanding read-alouds as more than simply a quiet entertainment.

Often doctoral students, fresh out of the classroom or gathering some other field-based data, noticed something curious that would eventually propel their life's work. Hildreth (1936), for instance, observed that children's name writing improved substantially from ages 3 to 6 as she was conducting children's testing. She used this observation to drive her landmark study on writing. Marie Clay's careful observation and recording of children's oral reading errors and their emerging understandings about letters and words revolutionized the ways that teachers now guide beginning readers and match them to texts. Durkin's 1966 study and her careful interviews with parents helped to dismantle the reading "readiness" mantra of the day and showed that children learn to read as a consequence of being supported by others in learning the alphabetic system. Mason (1980) watched children in 4-year-old classrooms to understand how their alphabetic knowledge grew and changed. Similarly, Read's (1975) observations of children and discussions with their parents unlocked the potential that young children have in *using* alphabetic knowledge to write meaningful messages with "invented" spellings. Even Almy's (1949) little-known, but truly innovative work, was born out of field-based discussions with parents about play, social skills, and parents' perceptions about their children's reading readiness, as well as interviews with the children themselves.

Together these and other studies remind the field of two points when it comes to pivotal research. First, that it is produced by sharp, observant researchers who know classroom practices, children's behavior, and the research literature, and who follow their instincts about the nature of literacy learning. This trend reminds us all as researchers to never be too far from the field and to never cease to sit in classrooms observing children and talking to teachers. Second, this trend decidedly situates doctoral students as particularly critical to the field in unique ways. Usually these students have spent a great deal of time in the classroom before they begin to integrate that experience with what they have learned from the research literature. As they do so, they may come up with new ideas, new subjects for study, and new questions. It can be easy to dismiss the questions and opinions of a doctoral student, but many pivotal studies (and lines of research) were actually created by taking their contributions into account.

Pivotal Findings Can Be Overextended

Both Roberts (Chapter 2) and Collins (Chapter 9) point out that while pivotal studies can impact the field and turn it in important and positive ways, they can also have negative consequences. Roberts identifies two such works,

Dulay and Burt (1974) and Krashen (1982), that became overextended and had detrimental effects on emergent bilingual students. Both studies had popular, common sense ideas that were easy to apply, and suggested, in different ways, that the emerging bilingual child mostly needed to simply be surrounded by supportive English speakers in order to acquire a second language (L2). Dulay and Burt's "natural language" sequences suggested that both a receptive and an expressive L2 would develop naturally through exposure, and this approach was applied in ways that deemphasized instruction. In emphasizing strategies to ensure that bilinguals received comprehensible input, Krashen's (1982) piece was interpreted in ways that downplayed the importance of direct language instruction and overemphasized the "silent period" in language learning. Collins also points out how overextensions or simplifications of findings can have negative outcomes. For example, the Whitehurst et al. (1988) findings could be misinterpreted in classrooms to suggest that the main purpose of storybook reading is to help children use expressive language, that its purpose is not meaning making but cueing child language around a shared object (i.e., the book). The dialogic process has the biggest effects on expressive language and may not be the best vehicle for supporting language comprehension and thinking about stories. Thus, there is a danger that pivotal studies will not simply "pivot" or turn the field, but instead U-turn the field by adopting approaches or recommendations that have undue influence. The likelihood of this happening is heightened when the research intersects with popular ideas of the day and perspectives that seem common sense and easy to implement.

The Pivotal Conceptual Book or Article

One of the most interesting (and amazing) revelations for us as we read and reflected on these chapters is that several pivotal works in the field have been conceptual papers, monographs, or books rather than empirical studies, meta-analyses, or research reviews (e.g., Adams, 1990; Blair, 2002; Guthrie & Wigfield, 2000; Krashen, 1982; Share, 1995; Stanovich, 1980; Teale & Sulzby, 1986). Take for example, *Beginning to Read: Thinking and Learning about Print*, a comprehensively written book that supported, among many things, the importance of teaching children the alphabetic principle and having them use it in learning to read. This book was similar to other historical pieces that have made the field aware of research supporting phonics (i.e., Flesch, 1955; McGuinness, 1997; Seidenburg, 2017). The Teale and Sulzby (1986) edited volume firmly placed the idea of emergent literacy at the forefront of conceptual thinking about early childhood literacy development, most likely because the compelling argument for this concept was made by multiple respected authors. Understanding their take on literacy development likely solidified a powerful and important idea, from which the field will likely never return. These studies are valuable because often they interpret research in a popular way and are frequently very readable and understandable, especially to a teacher audience. The disadvantage of these books is that they were not subjected to the same rigorous testing procedures and peer-review process (and potential for rejection) that journal articles receive.

Unlike books and monographs, pivotal conceptual articles are published in peer-reviewed journals, and many of them are very widely cited. Share's (1995) self-teaching hypothesis established the way that internalization of the alphabetic system functions to propel young children into literacy, and Stanovich's interactive compensatory model helped to clarify the role of context for struggling readers. As Hinden discusses in Chapter 7, Guthrie and Wigfield's (2000) model of engagement unified the many studies of Concept Oriented Reading Instruction in their attempt to sketch out the parameters of engaged literacy instruction. Notably both of these authors published dozens of peer-review research articles prior to this conceptual piece and backed up their theories with substantial research, increasing the likelihood that their theories would stand up. As Roberts in Chapter 2 points out, Krashen's (1982) mostly conceptual paper that introduced the notion of comprehensible input shaped practices for decades and redirected the field away from language instruction and an overemphasis on the "silent period." The concept, based on several informal studies, was easy to implement and appealing, but thin on evidence.

It is difficult to imagine the field without works, whether it takes the form of monographs, edited volumes, or peer-reviewed articles, and all can rightfully be called "pivotal." The point here is to simply take note of the advantages and disadvantages of these types of works and to advise caution. Clearly, pieces that consolidate research findings are absolutely necessary, and theoretical or conceptual work advances the field in ways that meta-analyses cannot. Conceptual articles and books can consolidate more information and communicate it in a more comprehensive and reader-friendly style that is not possible within the restrictions of a research article. Research articles are narrowly focused, and authors are only permitted to discuss the implications of specific findings. The most successful work is written by scholars who have spent a great deal of time conducting rigorous research studies and are ready to consolidate their findings. The disadvantage of the conceptual article or book is that it can be unduly dependent on the conjecture or the viewpoint of one influential scholar. Furthermore, theories are not studies, and they cannot substitute for studies.

PIVOTAL RESEARCH FOR THE FUTURE

Reflecting on the very fact that there *is* a field of early literacy research tells us how far we have come. Only four decades ago it would have been difficult to imagine an edited book on pivotal works in early literacy even being written, and yet we have several dozen substantive, influential works that can be identified. Early literacy research is clearly on the map and is moving in new directions. If there are any recommendations, they are that future research must be synthesized and shared to advance our knowledge, and that it must be nuanced and sophisticated. Racehorse studies that pit one treatment against another, in short windows of time, will likely not become pivotal. As specified in the next section, the field needs more pivotal works that synthesize findings, fewer forced choices between instructional approaches, and more longitudinal studies.

More Meta-Analyses and Replications Are Needed

It is rare that any one study, book, chapter, or conceptual article could ever be more influential or impactful than works that synthesize multiple studies, such as research syntheses or meta-analyses. In the future, the field needs more meta-analyses and systematic research syntheses to guide practice because accumulated knowledge is so very valuable. In addition, a meta-analysis prevents one influential, appealing study or theory from unduly influencing the field. The meta-analysis privileges the accumulation of knowledge across studies. Both the Bus et al. (1995) and Willig (1985) studies are examples of powerful meta-analyses that moved the field forward. The Willig (1985) meta-analysis indicated that bilingual education is better for English language learners than English-only programs. The Bus et al. (1995) meta-analysis detailed how book reading with young children supported language development and later literacy achievement. Of course the production of meta-analyses is inherently limited by the pool of studies that exist; meta-analyses cannot be performed on studies that are not quantitative in nature and do not contain certain statistical information. Yet, as the field of early literacy research continues to grow, we can and should expect meta-analyses to appear in areas outside of self-regulation, motivation, and vocabulary learning, for example.

Replication is also important in the context of meta-analyses. The educational research field traditionally has not prized replication, a critical element of many other disciplines (Makel & Plucker, 2014). Replication studies are those that repeat earlier studies, sometimes exactly, to verify that the same results can be obtained a second, third, fourth, or fifth time. When results are duplicated, the specific features of an instructional strategy or learning trajectory that are responsible for the development of literacy across settings, research contexts, and teaching methods are fleshed out. Even very robust strategies such as dialogic reading, which are well known, are frequently applied without attention to the essential details of the strategy (Towson, Fetti, Fleury, & Abarca, 2017).

Resisting Popular Dichotomies and Forced Choices

Like so many other academic fields in the United States, literacy education is prone to extreme swings of the pendulum. Frequently, teachers feel that they must "choose" between authentic literacy activities and code instruction, for example, or social development and academic learning, but children do not benefit from approaches that pit formal instruction against broader developmental aims. We educate the whole child, and it is not necessary or even desired to eschew social–emotional well-being to advance literacy instruction or to drop literacy instruction to foster self-regulation or social, emotional, or psychological support and growth. The suggestion that teachers must choose between opposing perspectives as they educate children is false. Although specific pieces of pivotal research have, on occasion, fueled these extremes, on balance, the collection of pivotal pieces in this volume does not support forced choices and dichotomies. For example, a theme in today's Facebook posts, Op-ed pages, and policy articles is the concern that prekindergartens and kindergartens have become too academic to the detriment of children; while this may be true, the solution is not to remove all literacy instruction from the curriculum. In fact, Rand and Morrow in Chapter 9 remind us that two pivotal pieces, Morrow and Rand (1991) and Neuman and Roskos (1990) advocate the integration of literacy into play through classroom learning environments. Even the often-cited Spira et al. (2005) study not only found that kindergarten behavioral skills predicted later reading achievement, but so also did *literacy* skills. As Hinden points out, the "literacy" part of the equation was "old news"—we knew that, but nonetheless it is important not to forget that behavioral skills are equally important because they make possible the learning of developmentally appropriate literacy skills.

What the early literacy field needs increasingly are research endeavors that are led by multidisciplinary teams of researchers from the disciplines of literacy, psychology, sociology, medicine, law, and speech/language pathology. What would truly produce the next generation of pivotal studies are teams of researchers who collaborate in designing interventions and studies that will not parse out a child's literacy learning, psychological welfare, growth within a sociological context, biological wellness, or emotional development. Multidisciplinary studies can envision future early childhood classroom that integrates all elements of a child's development.

Beyond 1-Year Units

The United States is probably one of the few counties in the world with a high level of dual-income families that does not provide extended maternity benefits or universal preschool to all children. If we are going to educate the whole child, we need to think beyond 1-year units of education. Especially in the early years, children do not develop neatly in discrete of units of 1 year. Instead of having children attend a year of prekindergarten and a year of kindergarten, we need to think about what should happen within the first 2 years of early education. In her influential book *Cleverlands,* Crehan (2017) points out that Finland has 2 years of early education for young children prior to formal literacy instruction in its very transparent orthography.

This approach would intersect with the many pivotal longitudinal studies documenting how literacy learning in young children changes and grows both qualitatively and quantitatively in the early years (Almy, 1949; Cochran-Smith, 1984; Hart & Risley, 1995; Heath, 1983; Hildreth, 1936). Why, if children go through such astonishing changes across a period of time, must we fit schooling into arbitrary 1-year units? It may be that a child at a certain developmental juncture is likely to advance developmentally just before the end of a year of school. Similarly, the U.S. educators need to rethink long summer breaks, which do not advantage children from low-income homes.

This chapter began with the aphorism from Santayana about learning from history, and we can learn a great deal from the pivotal research of the past. As described, it has certainly established a clear set of standards for what young children need to know and be able to do to become literate, but there are also lessons to be learned about how this pivotal research earned its reputation. We can try to avoid the pitfalls of pivotal studies that promoted appealing ideas that were not well supported by research or pivotal studies that created entrenched doctrines (i.e., Morphett & Washburne, 1931). Future pivotal research must avoid forced choices and ideological battles because they do not benefit children. If early literacy work is in the hands of interdisciplinary teams of researchers, these kinds of dichotomous approaches are not likely to be studied.

REFERENCES

Adams, M. J. (1990). *Beginning to read: Learning and thinking about print.* Cambridge, MA: MIT Press.

Almy, M. C. (1949). *Children's experiences prior to first grade and success in beginning reading.* New York: Bureau of Publications, Teachers College, Columbia University.

Blair, C. (2002). School readiness: Integrating cognition and emotion in a neurobiological conceptualization of children's functioning at school entry. *American Psychologist, 57*(2), 111.

Bus, A. G., van IJzendoorn, M. H., & Pellegrini, A. D. (1995). Joint book reading makes for success in learning to read: A meta-analysis on intergenerational transmission of literacy. *Review of Educational Research, 65*(1), 1–21.

Chomsky, N. (1968). Language and mind. *Psychology Today, 1*(9), 48.

Clay, M. M. (1966). *Emergent reading behavior.* Unpublished doctoral dissertation, University of Auckland, New Zealand.

Cochran-Smith, M. (1984). *The making of a reader.* Norwood, NJ: Ablex.

Crehan, L. (2017). *Cleverlands: The secrets behind the success of the world's education superpowers.* New York: Random House.

Dickinson, D. K., & Smith, M. W. (1994). Long-term effects of preschool teachers book readings on low-income children's vocabulary and story comprehension. *Reading Research Quarterly, 29,* 104–122.

Dulay, H. C., & Burt, M. K. (1974). Errors and strategies in child second language acquisition. *TESOL Quarterly, 8,* 129–136.

Durkin, D. (1966). *Children who read early: Two longitudinal studies.* New York: Teachers College Press.

Flesch, R. (1955). *Why Johnny can't read—and what you can do about it.* New York: William Morrow.

Gesell, A. (1925). *The mental growth of the pre-school child.* New York: Macmillan.

Guthrie, J. T., & Wigfield, A. (2000). Engagement and motivation in reading. In M. L. Kamil, P. B. Mosenthal, P. D. Pearson, & R. Barr (Eds.), *Handbook of Reading Research* (Vol. 3, pp. 403–422). Mahwah, NJ: Erlbaum.

Hart, B., & Risley, T. R. (1995). *Meaningful differences in the everyday experience of young American children.* Baltimore: Brookes.

Heath, S. B. (1983). *Ways with words: Language, life and work in communities and classrooms.* New York: Cambridge University Press.

Hildreth, G. (1936). Developmental sequences in name writing. *Child Development, 7,* 291–303.

Juel, C. (1988). Learning to read and write: A longitudinal study of 54 children from first through fourth grades. *Journal of Educational Psychology, 80*(4), 437.

Krashen, S. (1982). *Principles and practice in second language acquisition.* New York: Pergamon Press.

Liberman, I. Y., Shankweiler, D., Fischer, F. W., & Carter, B. (1974). Explicit syllable and phoneme segmentation in the young child. *Journal of Experimental Child Psychology, 18,* 201–212.

Lundberg, I., Frost, J., & Petersen, O. P. (1988). Effects of an extensive program for stimulating phonological awareness in preschool children. *Reading Research Quarterly, 23,* 263–284.

Makel, M. C., & Plucker, J. A. (2014). Facts are more important than novelty: Replication in the education sciences. *Educational Researcher, 43*(6), 304–316.

Mason, J. (1980). When do children begin to read: An exploration of four year old children's letter and word reading competencies. *Reading Research Quarterly, 15*(2), 203–227.

McGill-Franzen, A. (1988). *Literacy and early schooling: Recursive questions of child development and public responsibility.* Unpublished doctoral dissertation.

McGuinness, D. (1997). *Why our children can't read, and what we can do about it: A scientific revolution in reading.* New York: Simon and Schuster.

Morphett, M. V., & Washburne, C. (1931). When are children ready to read. *Elementary School Journal, 31,* 496–503.

Morrow, L., & Rand, M. (1991). Promoting literacy during play by designing early childhood classroom environments. *The Reading Teacher, 44*(6), 396–402.

Neuman, S., & Roskos, K. (1990). Play, print, and purpose: Enriching play environments for literacy development. *The Reading Teacher, 44*(3), 214–221.

Pan, B. A., Rowe, M. L., Singer, J. D., & Snow, C. E. (2005). Maternal correlates of growth in toddler vocabulary production in low-income families. *Child Development, 76*(4), 763–782.

Pellegrini, A. D. (1985). The relations between symbolic play and literate behavior: A review and critique of the empirical literature. *Review of Educational Research, 55*(1), 107–121.

Piaget, J. (1936). *Origins of intelligence in the child.* London: Routledge & Kegan Paul.

Piaget, J. (1957). *Construction of reality in the child.* London: Routledge & Kegan Paul.

Piaget, J. (1972). *The child and reality.* London: Routledge & Kegan Paul.

Pivot. (n.d.). In *Online etymology dictionary.* Retrieved October 10, 2017, from *www.etymonline.com.*

Pivotal. (n.d.). In *Dictionary.com.* Retrieved October 10, 2017, from *www.dictionary.com/browse/pivotal.*

Read, C. (1975). *Children's categorization of speech sounds in English* (No. 17). Chicago: National Council of Teachers of English.

Santayana, G. (1905). *The life of reason: Or the phases of human progress.* New York: Scribner.

Seidenberg, M. (2017). *Language at the speed of sight: How we read, why so many can't, and what can be done about it.* New York: Basic Books.

Sénéchal, M., Lefevre, J. A., Thomas, E. M., & Daley, K. E. (1998). Differential effects of home literacy experiences on the development of oral and written language. *Reading Research Quarterly, 33*(1), 96–116.

Shanahan, T., & Lonigan, C. J. (2010). The National Early Literacy Panel: A summary of the process and the report. *Educational Researcher, 39*(4), 279–285.

Share, D. L. (1995). Phonological recoding and self-teaching: Sine qua non of reading acquisition. *Cognition, 55*(2), 151–218.

Share, D. L. (2004). Knowing letter names and learning letter sounds: A causal connection. *Journal of Experimental Child Psychology, 88*(3), 213–233.

Spira, E. G., Bracken, S. S., & Fischel, J. E. (2005). Predicting improvement after first-grade reading difficulties: The effects of oral language, emergent literacy, and behavior skills. *Developmental Psychology, 41*(1), 225–234.

Stanovich, K. E. (1980). Toward an interactive-compensatory model of individual differences in the development of reading fluency. *Reading Research Quarterly, 16*(1), 32–71.

Teale, W. H., & Sulzby, E. (Eds.). (1986). *Emergent literacy: Writing and reading.* Norwood, NJ: Ablex.

Tomasello, M., & Farrar, M. J. (1986). Joint attention and early language. *Child Development, 57*(6), 1454–1463.

Towson, J. A., Fettig, A., Fleury, V. P., & Abarca, D. L. (2017). Dialogic reading in early childhood settings: A summary of the evidence base. *Topics in Early Childhood Special Education, 37*(3), 132–146.

Treiman, R., Tincoff, R., Rodriguez, K., Mouzaki, A., & Francis, D. J. (1998). The foundations of literacy: Learning the sounds of letters. *Child Development, 69*(6), 1524–1540.

Vygotsky, L. S. (1962). *Language and thought.* Cambridge, MA: Massachusetts Institute of Technology Press.

Whitehurst, G. J., Falco, F. L., Lonigan, C. J., Fischel, J. E., DeBaryshe, B. D., Valdez-Menchaca, M. C., & Caulfield, M. (1988). Accelerating language development through picture book reading. *Developmental Psychology, 24*(4), 552–559.

Willig, A. C. (1985). A meta-analysis of selected studies on the effectiveness of bilingual education. *Review of Educational Research, 55,* 269–317.

Index

Note. *f* or *t* following a page number indicates a figure or a table.

Academic achievement, 37–38, 73, 196, 227
Access to print. *See also* Home environment; Print exposure
  community factors and, 282–284, 282t, 284t
  Neuman and Celano (2001): access to print in low-income and middle-income communities, 280–282
  overview, 279–280, 292–293
  physical access and psychological proximity to books, 284–292, 286f, 287f, 290t
Achievement gap, 37–38. *See also* Academic achievement
Acrophonic CV (consonant–vowel) names, 93, 98, 103
Adams (1990): phonics instruction, 146–151
Adaptive contingency, 19
Adult talk, 211–217, 223–224, 223f, 302. *See also* Adult–child interactions
Adult–child interactions. *See also* Conversations between parents and children; Parent–child interactions
  adult talk and, 211–217
  emergent literacy and, 193
  play and, 252, 254
  storybook reading and, 202–211, 205t–206t, 208t, 210t
Alphabet knowledge, 86, 87–91, 92–94
Alphabet learning and instruction. *See also* Instruction; Letter names; Letter sounds
  formal instruction and, 124–125
  Mason (1980): emergent readers, 88–91
  order of letter instruction, 96–100
  overview, 85–86, 100–107, 105t, 106t

teaching letter names and sounds, 91–94
  Treiman, Tincoff, Rodriguez, Mouzaki, and Francis (1998): learning the sounds of letters, 94–96
  Treiman and Broderick (1998): letter names versus letter sounds, 92–94
  when to begin instruction, 86–91
Alphabetic knowledge, 300–302
Alphabetic principle, 63, 76t–77t, 86–87
Alphabetical-order advantage, 103
Ambiguity of the letter sound, 94–95, 99. *See also* Letter sounds
Analytical talk, 217, 226
Attention-deficit/hyperactivity disorder (ADHD), 168
Authenticity, 251
Automaticity, 145, 146, 151–154, 155

B

Background knowledge, 33
Balanced instruction, 150–151. *See also* Instruction
Behavioral skills, 167–171, 302–303
Bilingual education, 40–45, 46–47
Bilingualism, 36–39
Book deserts, 282–284, 282t, 284t. *See also* Access to print
Book reading. *See* Parent–child book reading; Read-alouds
Book vending machines, 284–292, 286f, 287f, 290t
Bottom-up language processes
  overview, 143, 144–145
  simple view of reading and, 44–45

315

Bottom-up language processes (*continued*)
  Stanovich (1980): top-down and
    bottom-up strategies, 143–146
  word recognition and, 143–146
Bus, van IJzendoorn, and Pellegrini (1995):
    parent–child book reading, 267–268

C

California Preschool Curriculum Framework,
    63–64
Categorization of speech sounds, 62–
    65
Centers, writing. *See* Writing centers
Child–adult interactions. *See* Adult–child
    interactions
Child-centered approaches, 305
Child-directed play, 173, 174. *See also* Play-
    based learning
Choice, 160–161, 292–293
Chomsky, Carol, 58
Civil Rights Acts of 1957 and 1964, 31
Classroom environment. *See also*
    Environmental factors
  center time and, 73–74
  emergent literacy and, 194
  interest in print and, 67, 70–72
  lessons from pivotal studies, 303
  Morrow and Rand (1991): classroom
    environments, 245–253
  play and, 239–240, 251–252, 254
  preschool literacy education and, 182
Co-constructive interactional pattern,
    219–220
Code-related skills, 126, 128–130, 132–133,
    222
Cognates, 39
Collaborative work, 165, 173
Common Core State Standards (CCSS),
    249–251
Common underlying proficiency (CUP),
    38
Community. *See also* Environmental factors
  access to print and, 282–284, 282t,
    284t
  Heath (1983): language and literacy in
    homes and communities, 260–262
  Neuman and Celano (2001): access to
    print in low-income and middle-income
    communities, 280–282
Compensation, 146
Complexity, 13–16
Comprehensible input, 34–36

Comprehension. *See also* Listening
    comprehension; Reading
    comprehension
  Dickinson and Smith (1994): effect
    of teachers' talk on vocabulary and
    comprehension, 217–222
  lessons from pivotal studies, 301–
    302
  phonological awareness and, 128
  play and, 251
  storybook reading and, 203, 220, 222,
    224–227
  symbolic play and, 242t
Concept knowledge, 126, 132
Concept Oriented Reading Instruction
    (CORI), 165, 308
Consonant–phoneme acquisition-order
    advantage, 103
Content learning, 2
Context, 145, 164, 167–168
Context processor, 148
Context-dependent level, 89
Contextualized instruction, 100, 104–105.
    See also Instruction
Contextualized print, 207
Contextualized skills, 217–218, 280
Conversations between parents and children.
    See also Adult–child interactions;
    Discussions
  dyadic context of interactions and, 16–19
  overview, 22–23
  quality of language input within, 13–16
  socioeconomic status and, 10–13
Creative Curriculum (CC), 194
Cryptanalytic intent, 93–94
Cummins (1979): linguistic interdependence,
    36–39
Cummins (1981): primary language
    development, 36–39
Curiosity, 65–67
Curriculum, 193–194, 249–251, 310

D

Decoding
  emergent bilingual (EB) students and,
    43–45
  learning to read and write and, 118,
    119–120
  overview, 143
  phonological awareness and, 113,
    128
  self-teaching hypothesis and, 153

simple view of reading and, 43–45
word recognition and, 143
Decontextualized print, 207
Decontextualized skills
    access to print and, 280
    play and, 254
    storybook reading and, 217–218
    symbolic play and, 242t, 243
Development interdependence hypothesis
    (DIH), 36–39
Developmental processes. *See also*
    Literacy development; Oral language
    development; Reading development;
    Vocabulary development
    lessons from pivotal studies, 298–303
    maturation theory and, 305
    1-year units of education and, 310–311
    phonological awareness and, 116–117
    preschool literacy education and, 188
    Sénéchal, Lefevre, Thomas, and Daley
        (1998): home literacy experiences and
        oral and written language development,
        268–270
Developmentally appropriate practice (DAP),
    60, 64, 245, 248
Dialogic approaches, 202–211, 208t, 210t,
    216, 226–227
Dichotomies, 310
Didactic approaches, 258–259
Didactic–interactional (DI) interactional
    pattern, 219–220
Differentiated alphabet instruction, 105t. *See
    also* Alphabet learning and instruction;
    Instruction
Digital media, 196
Direct instruction, 100, 103. *See also*
    Instruction
Discussions. *See also* Conversations between
    parents and children
    inferential thinking and, 228–229
    storybook reading and, 207–209, 208t,
        226–227
DISTAR model, 240–241
Distinctive-visual-features-letter-writing
    advantage, 103
Dramatic play, 74, 250–251. *See also* Play-
    based learning; Sociodramatic play
Draw-A-Man Test, 56
Dual immersion programs, 42
Dual language learners (DLLs), 30. *See also*
    Emergent bilingual (EB) students

Duet study, 21
Dulay and Burt (1974): second language
    acquisition, 32–34
Durkin (1966): early reading, 61–62, 66–67
Durkin, Dolores, 57–58
Dyadic context of interactions, 16–19
Dynamic Indicators of Basic Early Literacy
    Skills (DIBELS), 155

E

Early childhood education in general. *See*
    Preschool literacy education
Early reading
    Durkin (1966): early reading, 61–62
    home literacy experiences and, 271–272
    instruction and, 154–156
    Mason (1980): emergent readers, 88–91
    motivation, engagement, and self-
        regulation and, 160
    overview, 57–58, 79
    phonics instruction and, 148–149
    phonological awareness and, 113–117
    preschool literacy education and, 181–
        182
    roles of interest and curiosity and, 66–67
    self-teaching hypothesis and, 151–154
    Teale and Sulzby (1986): emergent literacy,
        190–195, 192f
Early Reading First, 304–305
Effortful control, 168
Effortful engagement, 165. *See also*
    Engagement
Elementary and Secondary Education Act
    (ESEA) of 1965, 304
Emergent bilingual (EB) students
    Cummins (1979): linguistic
        interdependence, 36–39
    Cummins (1981): primary language
        development, 36–39
    Hoover and Gough (1990): simple view of
        reading, 43–45
    overview, 29–31, 45–47
    phonological awareness and, 113
    Willig (1985): effectiveness of bilingual
        education, 40–43
Emergent literacy. *See also* Literacy
    development
    behavioral and social skills and, 169
    family factors and, 260
    lessons from pivotal studies, 299–300
    Mason (1980): emergent readers, 88–91
    overview, 87–91, 195–198

Emergent literacy (*continued*)
  play and, 241
  preschool literacy education and, 181–182,
    188
  Purcell-Gates (1996): relationships
    between home literacy and emergent
    literacy, 262–264
  storybook reading and, 202–211,
    205t–206t, 208t, 210t
  Teale and Sulzby (1986): emergent literacy,
    190–195, 192f
Emergent readers, 148–149, 160. *See also*
  Prereaders
Engagement
  Guthrie and Wigfield (2000): engagement
    in literacy, 164–166
  higher-level thinking and, 231
  implications for practice and, 171–172
  overview, 160–163, 162f, 172–174, 308
  play and, 247
English language learners (ELLs). *See also*
  Emergent bilingual (EB) students;
  Language acquisition; Language
  development
  bilingual education and, 40–43
  overview, 30
  play and, 253
  sequences in language acquisition and,
    32–34
English language skills, 29
Enhanced alphabet knowledge (EAK),
  102–103
Environmental factors. *See also* Classroom
  environment; Home environment
  emergent literacy and, 190–195, 192f
  Morrow and Rand (1991): classroom
    environments, 245–253
  Neuman and Celano (2001): access to
    print in low-income and middle-income
    communities, 280–282
  Neuman and Roskos (1990): play
    environments and literacy development,
    244–245, 245f
  physical access and psychological proximity
    to books, 284–292, 286f, 287f, 290t
  play and, 239–240
  readiness and, 182–186
  role of in reading development, 259–260
Environmental print, 189
Even Start, 273
Executive function, 168

Explicit instruction, 101, 115–116, 130–134.
  See also Instruction
Exposure to print. *See* Access to print
Exposure to words, 152–154
Expressive language, 211–217
Expressive One-Word Picture Vocabulary
  Test (EOWPVT), 213
Expressive vocabulary, 128–130. *See also*
  Vocabulary development
Extant reading theory, 222

F

Family factors. *See also* Parent–child book
    reading; Parent–child interactions
  adult talk and, 218
  Bus, van IJzendoorn, and Pellegrini (1995):
    parent–child book reading, 267–268
  dyadic context of interactions and, 16–19
  Heath (1983): language and literacy in
    homes and communities, 260–262
  home literacy experiences and, 262–264
  lessons from pivotal studies, 303
  overview, 2, 23, 257–258, 270–275
  physical access and psychological proximity
    to books, 284–292, 286f, 287f, 290t
  quality of language input within, 13–16
  readiness and, 182–186
  role of in reading development, 258–260
  Sénéchal, Lefevre, Thomas, and Daley
    (1998): home literacy experiences and
    oral and written language development,
    268–270
  socioeconomic status and, 10–13
  storybook reading and, 202–211,
    205t–206t, 208t, 210t
Faucet theory, 283
Fluency, 146
Forced choice, 310
Formal instruction, 113–114. *See also*
  Instruction

G

Gesture use, 16, 18–19
Goals, 73
Guthrie and Wigfield (2000): engagement in
  literacy, 164–166

H

Hart and Risley (1995): early input, 10–13
Head Start program
  behavioral and social skills and, 169, 171
  early reading and, 61–62

overview, 304–305
play and, 240
preschool literacy education and, 187–188
self-regulation and, 168, 171
vocabulary development and, 10–11
Head Start-REDI (Research based,
    Developmentally informed), 171
Heath (1983): language and literacy in homes
    and communities, 260–262
Higher-level conversations, 228–229. *See also*
    Discussions
Higher-level thinking. *See also* Thinking skills
    inferential thinking and, 224–225
    responsivity to children and, 230
    storybook reading and, 224–227, 230–231,
        231*f*
Hildreth (1936): name-writing development,
    59–60, 65
Hildreth, Gertrude, 55–56
Home environment. *See also* Access to print;
    Environmental factors; Parent–child
    book reading
    early reading and, 57–58, 62
    Heath (1983): language and literacy in
        homes and communities, 260–262
    home literacy experiences and, 270–275
    interventions and, 273–274
    learning to read and write and, 119–120
    lessons from pivotal studies, 303
    Neuman and Celano (2001): access to
        print in low-income and middle-income
        communities, 280–282
    overview, 23
    Purcell-Gates (1996): relationships
        between home literacy and emergent
        literacy, 262–264
    quality of language input within, 13–16
    readiness and, 182–186
    Scarborough and Dobrich (1994): reading
        to preschoolers, 265–267
    Sénéchal, Lefevre, Thomas, and Daley
        (1998): home literacy experiences and
        oral and written language development,
        268–270
    vocabulary development and, 10–13
Hoover and Gough (1990): simple view of
    reading, 43–45

I
Illinois Test of Psycholinguistic Abilities
    (ITPA), 213
Imagination, 251

Immigrants, 31
Impact of pivotal studies, 4
Independent reading time, 160–161
Inferences, 145
Inferential thinking
    higher-level conversations and, 228–229
    storybook reading and, 224–225, 228–229
    vocabulary development and, 229
Instruction. *See also* Alphabet learning and
        instruction; Learning to read and write;
        Preschool literacy education
    bilingual education, 39–43
    categorization of speech sounds and, 63–64
    center time, 73–74
    comprehensible input hypothesis and,
        35–36
    early reading and, 57
    early writing and, 59–60
    emergent bilingual (EB) students and,
        46–47
    emergent literacy and, 193–194
    home literacy experiences and, 273–274
    Lundberg, Frost, and Peterson (1988):
        formal instruction, 121–126, 125*t*, 127*f*
    order of letter instruction, 96–100
    phonics instruction, 146–151
    phonological awareness and, 113–117,
        130–134
    play and, 240–241, 253
    preschool literacy education and, 188
    self-teaching hypothesis and, 153–154
    storybook reading and, 222
    teaching letter names and sounds, 91–94
    when to begin alphabet instruction, 86–91
    whole-group instruction and, 74–78,
        76*t*–77*t*
Interactive–compensatory model, 145, 146,
    154–155
Interest, 65–72, 67, 173
Interventions
    early reading and, 61–62
    home literacy experiences and, 273–274
    physical access and psychological proximity
        to books, 284–292, 286*f*, 287*f*, 290*t*
    vocabulary development and, 19–21
Invented spellings. *See also* Phonetic spellings;
        Spelling
    alphabet learning and instruction and, 91
    categorization of speech sounds and, 62–
        65
    overview, 58

Invented spellings (*continued*)
    preschool classrooms and instruction and, 70–71
    roles of interest and curiosity and, 65–66
    teaching phonological awareness and, 132–133

J

Joint attention, 16–19
Juel (1988): learning to read and write, 118–121

K

Kindergarten curriculum, 193–194
Knowledge hypothesis, 9
Krashen (1982): second language acquisition, 34–36

L

Language achievement, 29–30
Language acquisition. *See also* Developmental processes; English language learners (ELLs); Language development; Literacy development
    Dulay and Burt (1974): second language acquisition, 32–34
    emergent bilingual (EB) students and, 31, 45–47
    preschool literacy education and, 197
    sequences in, 32–34
    threshold hypothesis and developmental interdependence hypothesis and, 36–39
Language Acquisition Device, 31, 33
Language comprehension, 124, 216–217. *See also* Comprehension
Language development. *See also* Developmental processes; Language acquisition; Literacy development
    adult talk and, 211–217, 223–224, 223*f*
    home literacy experiences and, 270–275
    lessons from pivotal studies, 300–302
    storybook reading and, 217–222, 230–231, 231*f*
    when to begin alphabet instruction and, 87
Language Environment Analysis (LENA), 19–20
Language gaps, 12–13
Language input
    emergent bilingual (EB) students and, 45–46
    importance of, 21–23

quality of, 13–16, 21–24, 302
vocabulary development and, 10–13
Language skills, 225–226, 227–228
Language-knowledge, 126
Lau v. Nicholls (1974), 31
Learning context, 20–21
Learning to read and write. *See also* Instruction
    formal instruction and, 121–126, 125*t*, 127*f*
    Juel (1988): learning to read and write, 118–121
    lessons from pivotal studies, 298–303
    1-year units of education and, 310–311
    play and, 240–241
    preschool literacy education and, 188
    Teale and Sulzby (1986): emergent literacy, 189–195, 192*f*
Letter names. *See also* Alphabet learning and instruction
    alphabet learning and instruction and, 91–96
    emergent literacy and, 88–89, 90
    instruction and, 100–107, 105*t*, 106*t*
    lessons from pivotal studies, 300–301
    order of letter instruction, 96–100
    overview, 85–86
    phonics instruction and, 149
    Treiman and Broderick (1998): letter names versus letter sounds, 92–94
Letter sounds. *See also* Alphabet learning and instruction
    alphabet learning and instruction and, 91–96, 102, 103
    emergent literacy and, 89
    formal instruction and, 121, 125
    instruction and, 100–107, 105*t*, 106*t*
    lessons from pivotal studies, 300–301
    order of letter instruction, 96–100
    overview, 85–86
    phonics instruction and, 149
    Treiman, Tincoff, Rodriguez, Mouzaki, and Francis (1998): learning the sounds of letters, 94–96
    Treiman and Broderick (1998): letter names versus letter sounds, 92–94
    whole-group instruction and, 76*t*–77*t*, 78
Letter strings, 70–71
Letter writing, 89, 90
Letter-frequency advantage, 103

Letter–name structure, 94–95. *See also* Letter names

Letter-of-the-week approach, 97

Letter–shape confusability, 106*t*

Letter–sound analysis level, 89. *See also* Letter sounds

Liberman, Shankweiler, Fisher, and Carter (1974): syllable and phoneme segmentation, 113–117

Life-to-text interaction, 205*t*–206*t*

Listening comprehension. *See also* Comprehension

  Dickinson and Smith (1994): effect of teachers' talk on vocabulary and comprehension, 217–222

  emergent bilingual (EB) students and, 43–45

  emergent literacy and, 194

  learning to read and write and, 118

  storybook reading and, 222, 224–225

Literacy achievement, 29–30, 39

Literacy development. *See also* Developmental processes; Emergent literacy; Reading development; Vocabulary development

  access to print and, 279–280

  alphabet learning and instruction and, 100–107, 105*t*, 106*t*

  classroom environments and, 245–253

  engagement and motivation and, 164–166

  family factors and, 260–262

  formal instruction and, 121–126, 125*t*, 127*f*

  home literacy experiences and, 262–264, 270–275

  Juel (1988): learning to read and write, 118–121

  lessons from pivotal studies, 298–303

  Mason (1980): emergent readers, 88–91

  motivation, engagement, and self-regulation and, 160

  Neuman and Roskos (1990): play environments and literacy development, 244–245, 245*f*

  parent–child read-alouds and, 265–268

  phonological awareness and, 112–113, 116–117, 126, 128–130

  play and, 239–244, 242*t*, 245–253

  preschool literacy education and, 181–182, 304

  self-teaching hypothesis and, 151–154

Stanovich (1980): top-down and bottom-up strategies, 143–146

  teaching phonological awareness and, 130–133

  vocabulary development and, 9–10

  when to begin alphabet instruction and, 87–91

  word recognition and, 142

Literacy skills, 75–78, 76*t*–77*t*

Literate behavior

  Pellegrini (1985): relationship between symbolic play and literate behavior, 241–244, 242*t*

  play and, 247–248, 253, 254

Lowercase letters, 98–99, 106, 106*t*

Lundberg, Frost, and Peterson (1988): formal instruction, 121–126, 125*t*, 127*f*

M

Make-believe play, 251. *See also* Play-based learning

Mason (1980): emergent readers, 88–91

Matthew Effect, 146, 152

Maturation theory, 87, 117, 305

Meaning making

  adult talk and, 211–217

  overview, 143

  storybook reading and, 204, 206–210, 208*t*, 210*t*, 218, 222, 224–227

Meaning processor, 147–148

Meta-analysis, 40–43, 309

Metalinguistic awareness, 251

Morrow and Rand (1991): classroom environments, 245–253

Motivation

  access to print and, 292

  center time and, 73

  Guthrie and Wigfield (2000): engagement in literacy, 164–166

  implications for practice and, 171–172

  lessons from pivotal studies, 302–303

  overview, 160–163, 162*f*, 172–174

Motivation to Read Survey, 165–166

Murphy-Durrell Reading Readiness Analysis, 113–114

N

Name-writing development. *See also* Own-name advantage

  alphabet learning and instruction and, 104

  Hildreth (1936): name-writing development, 59–60

Name-writing development (*continued*)
   order of letter instruction and, 96–98
   overview, 56
   preschool classrooms and instruction and,
      69–72
   roles of interest and curiosity and, 65
   whole-group instruction and, 76t–77t
Narrative competence, 242t, 243, 254
National Early Literacy Panel (NELP), 222
Neuman and Celano (2001): access to print
      in low-income and middle-income
      communities, 280–282
Neuman and Roskos (1990): play
      environments and literacy development,
      244–245, 245f
Neurobiological research, 41–42, 166–168
No Child Left Behind Act, 163, 304–305
Novice readers, 101

O

Off-task behavior, 160–161
1-year units of education, 310–311
Oral language development. *See also*
      Developmental processes
   higher-level thinking and, 224
   parent–child read-alouds and, 265–266
   phonological awareness and, 112, 134
   play and, 251
   preschool literacy education and, 197
   Sénéchal, Lefevre, Thomas, and Daley
      (1998): home literacy experiences and
      oral and written language development,
      268–270
   storybook reading and, 210–211
   teaching phonological awareness and, 132
Oral proficiency, 29
Oral vocabulary knowledge, 128–130, 132,
      134. *See also* Vocabulary development
Orthographic patterns, 144, 145, 151–154
Orthographic processor, 147–148
Own-name advantage, 96–98, 102–103, 106t.
      See also Name-writing development

P

Pan, Rowe, Singer, and Snow (2005):
      parental language input, 10, 13–16
Parent–child book reading. *See also* Family
      factors; Home environment; Parent–
      child interactions; Read-alouds
   home literacy experiences and, 271–272
   lessons from pivotal studies, 303
   overview, 264–265, 274–275

Scarborough and Dobrich (1994): reading
      to preschoolers, 265–267
Sénéchal, Lefevre, Thomas, and Daley
      (1998): home literacy experiences and
      oral and written language development,
      268–270
   socioeconomic status and, 291
Parent–child interactions. *See also* Adult–
      child interactions; Conversations
      between parents and children; Family
      factors; Parent–child book reading;
      Parents
   adult talk and, 211–217
   dyadic context of interactions and, 16–19
   overview, 22–23
Parents. *See also* Parent–child interactions
   engagement and motivation and, 173–174
   role of in reading development, 258–260,
      302
PATHS program, 167, 171
Peabody Picture Vocabulary Test-Revised
      (PPVT-R), 213
Peer collaboration, 165, 173
Pellegrini (1985): relationship between
      symbolic play and literate behavior,
      241–244, 242t
Performance-oriented (PO) interactional
      pattern, 220
Phoneme segmentation, 113–117, 131
Phonemes
   formal instruction and, 122
   letter instruction and, 98–99
   Liberman, Shankweiler, Fisher, and
      Carter (1974): syllable and phoneme
      segmentation, 113–117
   phonological awareness and, 112, 301
   teaching phonological awareness and, 131
   word recognition and, 145
Phonetic spellings, 101. *See also* Invented
      spellings; Spelling
Phonics
   Adams (1990): phonics instruction,
      146–151
   alphabet learning and instruction and, 101
   categorization of speech sounds and, 63
   instruction and, 146–151, 155
Phonological awareness (PA)
   alphabet learning and instruction and,
      106–107
   categorization of speech sounds and, 63
   emergent literacy and, 88–89, 194

instruction and, 130–133
Juel (1988): learning to read and write, 118–121
lessons from pivotal studies, 300–302
letter instruction and, 99
Liberman, Shankweiler, Fisher, and Carter (1974): syllable and phoneme segmentation, 113–117
Lundberg, Frost, and Peterson (1988): formal instruction, 121–126, 125t, 127f
overview, 111–113, 133–134
reading development and, 126, 128–130
self-teaching hypothesis and, 152–153
struggling readers and, 120–121
whole-group instruction and, 76t–77t, 78
word recognition and, 156
Phonological confusability, 98–99
Phonological processor, 147–148
Picture book reading, 211–217, 304. *See also* Storybook reading
Pivotal studies. *See also individual studies*
in the future, 308–311
lessons learned from, 298–303
overview, 1, 2–4, 297–298, 303–308
Play-based learning. *See also* Child-directed play; Dramatic play; Sociodramatic play
early literacy development and, 239–241
engagement and motivation and, 173, 174
lessons from pivotal studies, 302–303
Morrow and Rand (1991): classroom environments, 245–253
Neuman and Roskos (1990): play environments and literacy development, 244–245, 245f
overview, 1–2, 238–239, 253, 254
Pellegrini (1985): relationship between symbolic play and literate behavior, 241–244, 242t
Policy, 249–251
Poverty
emergent bilingual (EB) students and, 30
home literacy experiences and, 263–264
Neuman and Celano (2001): access to print in low-income and middle-income communities, 280–282
parent–child read-alouds and, 291
preschool literacy education and, 304
quality of language input within, 13–16
vocabulary development and, 10–13
War on Poverty, 187–188
Prediction, 145

Prereaders, 101, 148–149. *See also* Emergent readers
Preschool classrooms
center time, 73–74
interest in print and, 67, 70–72
play environments and, 244–245, 245f
whole-group instruction and, 74–78, 76t–77t
Preschool literacy education. *See also* Instruction
Almy (1949): early experiences and success in reading, 182–186
history of, 186–195, 187f, 192f
home literacy experiences and, 273–274
lessons from pivotal studies, 298–303
1-year units of education and, 310–311
overview, 1–2, 181–182, 195–198, 304–305
play and, 239–241
storybook reading and, 202–211, 205t–206t, 208t, 210t
Teale and Sulzby (1986): emergent literacy, 189–195, 192f
Preschool PATHS Curriculum, 167, 171
Preschoolers
early reading and, 61–62
early writing and, 59–60
formal instruction and, 125–126
simple view of reading and, 45
teaching phonological awareness and, 130–134
writing centers and, 65–72
Print, attending to, 103–104
Print exposure, 119–120, 262–264. *See also* Access to print
Print referencing, 104
Print skills, 222
Professional development
formal instruction and, 123
overview, 213
preschool literacy education and, 197
responsivity to children and, 230
vocabulary development and, 229
Providence Talks, 20
Purcell-Gates (1996): relationships between home literacy and emergent literacy, 262–264
Push-down curriculum, 243–244

Q

Quality of language input, 13–16, 21–24, 302

R

Read (1975): categorization of speech sounds, 62–67
Read, Charles, 58
Read-alouds, 104, 265–267. *See also* Parent–child book reading; Storybook reading
Readiness. *See also* Engagement; Motivation; Reading readiness; Self-regulation
access to print and, 283
Blair (2002): neurobiological model of self-regulation, 166–168
emergent literacy and, 90–91
family involvement and, 259
Guthrie and Wigfield (2000): engagement in literacy, 164–166
implications for practice and, 171–172
lessons from pivotal studies, 299–300
overview, 161–163, 162f, 172–174
Spira, Bracken, and Fischel (2005): behavioral and social skills, 168–171
storybook reading and, 205t
Teale and Sulzby (1986): emergent literacy, 189–195, 192f
Reading comprehension. *See also* Comprehension
emergent bilingual (EB) students and, 29, 43–45
learning to read and write and, 118–119
simple view of reading and, 43–45
storybook reading and, 222, 226
vocabulary development and, 9–10
word recognition and, 154–155
Reading development. *See also* Developmental processes; Literacy development
instruction and, 154–156
phonological awareness and, 126, 128–130
role of parents in, 258–260
self-teaching hypothesis and, 151–154
Reading fluency, 146
Reading outcomes, 33–34
Reading readiness, 181–182, 259, 299. *See also* Readiness
Recess learning, 1–2
Recoding, 152, 156. *See also* Sounding out words
Referential transparency, 15
Replication, 309
Responsivity to children, 226–227, 230–231, 231f
Right-to-Read project, 61

S

Scaffolded Early Literacy Program, 168
Scarborough and Dobrich (1994): reading to preschoolers, 265–267
School accountability, 163
School readiness. *See* Readiness
Screen-based media, 289
Second language acquisition (SLA), 32–36, 45–47. *See also* English language learners (ELLs)
Segmentation, 113–117, 131
Self-efficacy beliefs, 173
Self-regulation
behavioral and social skills and, 168–171
Blair (2002): neurobiological model of self-regulation, 166–168
center time and, 73
implications for practice and, 171–172
lessons from pivotal studies, 302–303
overview, 160–163, 166, 172–174
struggling readers and, 120–121
Self-teaching hypothesis, 151–154, 155
Sénéchal, Lefevre, Thomas, and Daley (1998): home literacy experiences and oral and written language development, 268–270
Serial-stage model, 144
Share (1995): self-teaching hypothesis, 151–154
Shared reading, 216, 269–270, 274–275
Sign reading, 89, 90
Simple view of reading, 43–45
Skills-based instructional models, 240–241, 300–302
Social skills, 168–171, 173, 302–303
Sociocultural view, 188
Sociodramatic play. *See also* Dramatic play; Play-based learning
classroom environments and, 247
early literacy development and, 239–241
overview, 239, 254
Socioeconomic status
access to print and, 280–284, 282t, 284t
adult talk and, 212
bilingual education and, 42
emergent bilingual (EB) students and, 30
home literacy experiences and, 263–264
interventions and, 21
Neuman and Celano (2001): access to print in low-income and middle-income communities, 280–282

parent–child read-alouds and, 291
phonological awareness and, 116
quality of language input within, 13–16
vocabulary development and, 10–13
Sociopolitical events, 304
Sound categorization skills, 121
Sounding out words, 91–94, 152
Sound–symbol correspondence, 149. *See also*
    Letter names; Letter sounds
Speech sounds, 62–65
Spelling. *See also* Invented spellings
    alphabet learning and instruction and, 101
    formal instruction and, 121
    phonics instruction and, 149
    requests for, 68–69
Spira, Bracken, and Fischel (2005):
    behavioral and social skills, 168–171
Stage theory of development, 68
Stanovich (1980): top-down and bottom-up
    strategies, 143–146
Story production, 242–243, 242t
Storybook reading. *See also* Read-alouds
    Cochran-Smith (1984): storybook reading,
        202–211, 205t–206t, 208t, 210t
    Dickinson and Smith (1994): effect
        of teachers' talk on vocabulary and
        comprehension, 217–222
    home literacy experiences and, 271
    lessons from pivotal studies, 303
    overview, 201–202, 223–231, 223f, 231f
    preschool literacy education and, 304
    Sénéchal, Lefevre, Thomas, and Daley
        (1998): home literacy experiences and
        oral and written language development,
        268–270
    Whitehurst et al. (1988): language
        development through picture book
        reading, 211–217
Strategy Instruction, 165
Struggling readers, 119–121, 160
Summer slide, 283
Syllable segmentation, 113–117, 131
Symbolic play, 241–244, 242t. *See also* Play-
    based learning

T

Talking is Teaching, 20
Teacher–child ratios, 72–78, 76t–77t
Teacher-directed instruction, 74–78, 76t–77t.
    See also Instruction; Whole-group
    instruction
Teachers, role of, 252, 254

Teachers' language use, 22
Teale and Sulzby (1986): emergent literacy,
    189–195, 192f
Technology, 196, 289
Temperament, 166
Text-to-life interaction, 206t
Thematic play, 246–247. *See also* Play-based
    learning
Think alouds, 104, 228
Thinking skills, 225–226. *See also* Higher-
    level thinking
Thirty Million Words Initiative, 19–20
Threshold hypothesis (TH), 36–39
Tomasello and Farrar (1986): quality and
    quantity in context, 10, 16–19
Too Small to Fail Initiative, 20
Tools of the Mind curriculum, 168, 250–251
Top-down language processes
    overview, 143, 144–145
    simple view of reading and, 44–45
    Stanovich (1980): top-down and
        bottom-up strategies, 143–146
    word recognition and, 143–146
Training, 197. *See also* Professional
    development
Treiman and Broderick (1998): letter names
    versus letter sounds, 94–96

U

Uppercase letters, 98–99, 106, 106t
Utterance-level talk, 224–225

V

Vending machines for books, 284–292, 286f,
    287f, 290t
Veteran readers, 101
Video Interaction Project (VIP), 20
Visual confusability, 98–99
Visual recognition, 89, 90
Visual-phonetic recognition learning, 90
Vocabulary breadth, 227
Vocabulary depth, 227
Vocabulary development. *See also*
    Developmental processes; Literacy
    development
    access to print and, 279–280
    Dickinson and Smith (1994): effect
        of teachers' talk on vocabulary and
        comprehension, 217–222
    formal instruction and, 124
    Hart and Risley (1995): early input, 10–13
    home literacy experiences and, 271–272

Vocabulary development (*continued*)
  inferential thinking and, 229
  interventions and, 19–21
  lessons from pivotal studies, 301–302
  overview, 9–10, 21–24
  Pan, Rowe, Singer, and Snow (2005):
    parental language input, 10, 13–16
  phonological awareness and, 112, 126,
    128–130, 134
  preschool literacy education and, 197
  storybook reading and, 225–226, 227–228
  teaching phonological awareness and, 132
  Tomasello and Farrar (1986): quality and
    quantity in context, 10, 16–19
Vroom program, 20–21

W

War on Poverty, 187–188
Whitehurst et al. (1988): language
    development through picture book
    reading, 211–217
Whole-group instruction, 72–78, 76t–77t,
    173. *See also* Instruction
Willig (1985): effectiveness of bilingual
    education, 40–43
Word learning, 101

Word reading, 43–45
Word recognition
  Adams (1990): phonics instruction,
    146–151
  instruction and, 154–156
  overview, 142, 143
  Share (1995): self-teaching hypothesis,
    151–154
  Stanovich (1980): top-down and
    bottom-up strategies, 143–146
Writing centers, 65–72, 73–74
Writing practices
  Durkin (1966): early reading, 61–62
  emergent literacy and, 89, 90, 194
  Hildreth (1936): name-writing
    development, 59–60
  overview, 55, 78–79
  Read (1975): categorization of speech
    sounds, 62–65
  teaching phonological awareness and, 133
  whole-group instruction and, 74–78,
    76t–77t
Written language development, 268–270

Z

Zone of proximal development theory, 305